OXFORD ENGLISH MONOGRAPHS

General Editors

The Making of
Percy's *Reliques*

NICK GROOM

CLARENDON PRESS · OXFORD

OXFORD
UNIVERSITY PRESS

Great Clarendon Street, Oxford OX2 6DP
Oxford University Press is a department of the University of Oxford.
It furthers the University's objective of excellence in research, scholarship,
and education by publishing worldwide in

Oxford   New York

Athens Auckland Bangkok Bogotá Buenos Aires Calcutta
Cape Town Chennai Dar es Salaam Delhi Florence Hong Kong Istanbul
Karachi Kuala Lumpur Madrid Melbourne Mexico City Mumbai
Nairobi Paris São Paulo Singapore Taipei Tokyo Toronto Warsaw

and associated companies in Berlin Ibadan

Oxford is a registered trade mark of Oxford University Press
in the UK and certain other countries

Published in the United States
by Oxford University Press Inc., New York

© Nick Groom 1999

British Library Cataloguing in Publication Data
Data available

Library of Congress Cataloging in Publication Data
Data available
ISBN 0–19–818459–X

1 3 5 7 9 10 8 6 4 2

Typeset by J&L Composition Ltd, Filey, North Yorkshire
Printed in Great Britain
on acid-free paper by
Biddles Ltd, Guildford and King's Lynn

For Marina

Acknowledgements

Like Thomas Percy, my acknowledgements are raised 'as an amulet to guard [me] from every unfavourable censure, for having bestowed any attention on a parcel of OLD BALLADS'. But it is, of course, also a great pleasure to acknowledge the debts incurred in writing this book. First, institutions: I would like to thank the helpful, good-humoured, and forbearing staff and librarians of Balliol College Library, Oxford; Bedfordshire Public Record Office; the Bodleian Library, Oxford; Boston Public Library; the British Library; the Cathedral of Christ the Redeemer, Dromore; the Devon and Exeter Institution; the English Faculty Library, Oxford; Florida State University Library; Hertford College Library, Oxford; the Houghton Library, Harvard; the National Library of Ireland; Northamptonshire Public Record Office; The Queen's University Library, Belfast; Trinity College Library, Cambridge; Trinity College Library, Dublin; the University of Exeter Library; and the Widener Library. Postal queries were dealt with promptly by the Beinecke Library; the Folger Shakespeare Library; the Huntington Library; Pennsylvania Historical Society; and Armagh County Library. The British Academy funded me for three years' postgraduate research, and were generous with travel grants for visiting Ireland and America. I would also like to thank Hertford College, Oxford, for scholarships and grants, and the University of Exeter for research funding and a term's sabbatical leave which enabled me to complete this book.

Secondly, individuals: this study has also been possible only with the help, encouragement, and enthusiasm of many people. In particular, I owe much to Mark Allen, Paul Baines, Charlie Blake, Julia Briggs, Chris Brooks, Bert Davis, Gwyn Blakemore Evans, Howard Gaskill, Jonathon Green, Susan Halpert, Peter Jackson, Colin Kidd, Tim Morton, Michael Nath, Margaret Smith, Jane Spencer, Michael Suarez, SJ, Katherine Turner, Marina Warner, and 'Hewlett'. Early drafts of this book (as a D.Phil. thesis) were read by Inga Bryden, David Fairer, Sian Lewis, and Fiona Stafford, and I benefited a great deal from their attention and acumen. I was extremely fortunate to have Roger Lonsdale supervise my doctoral research, and I hope that the influence of his eloquent and rigorous scholarship is discernible in this study. Lastly, I would like to thank for their unerring moral support my colleagues in the School of English, University of Exeter; my friends at the Oxenham Arms, South Zeal; and my family.

N. M. G.

Contents

Notes on the Text

For the sake of convenience and brevity, the term 'ballad' is used to denote collective popular verse: metrical romances, narrative ballads, and old songs. This is how Percy himself used the word. Likewise, I favour Johnson's usage 'antiquarian' rather than 'antiquary'. The term 'bookseller' is also used in its eighteenth-century form, meaning a publisher as well as a retailer of books and publishing rights. All quotations retain original spelling and style, and titles of ballads remain in the forms preferred by individual writers.

References to the *Reliques* are integral to the text. In footnotes, the place of publication is London, unless otherwise indicated.

The following symbols have been used in transcribing from unpublished manuscripts:

<>	enclose words which have been deleted;
<???>	indicate an unreadable deletion;
⌈ ⌉	enclose words which have been interlined above the line, usually accompanied with a caret symbol '^' in manuscript;
[ ]	enclose a conjectural reading;
{}	indicate use of square brackets in MS;
bold	indicates when letters have been highlighted in manuscript without use of underlining;
/	indicates overwriting.

Some parts of this study have appeared in print elsewhere. Chapter 3 adapts an essay that was originally published in *Tradition in Transition*; a few sentences are taken from my introduction to *Johnson–Steevens–Malone*; finally, there is some inevitable overlap with the introduction to my facsimile edition of Percy's *Reliques*, though I have endeavoured to keep repetition to a minimum. Publication of manuscripts is by permission of the Houghton Library, Harvard University.

Abbreviations

Anecdotes	John Nichols, *Literary Anecdotes of the Eighteenth Century* (1812–15)
Ashe	A. H. Ashe, 'Miscellaneous Correspondence of Thomas Percy', B.Litt. thesis (Oxford, 1964)
Boswell's Life	James Boswell, *Boswell's Life of Johnson (Together with Boswell's Journal of a Tour to the Hebrides and Johnson's Diary of a Journey into North Wales)*, ed. George Birkbeck Hill, rev. L. F. Powell, 2nd edn. (Oxford, 1934–50)
Carver	Judith D. Carver, 'Thomas Percy and the Making of the *Reliques of Ancient English Poetry*: 1756–1765', B.Litt. thesis (Oxford, 1973)
Davis (1981)	Bertram H. Davis, *Thomas Percy* (Boston, 1981)
Davis (1989)	Bertram H. Davis, *Thomas Percy: A Scholar-Cleric in the Age of Johnson* (Philadelphia, 1989)
Fairer	David Fairer (ed.), *The Correspondence of Thomas Warton* (Athens, Ga., 1995)
Hales and Furnivall	John W. Hales and Frederick J. Furnivall (eds.), *Bishop Percy's Folio MS.* (1867–8)
Harlowe	'Letters from Dr. Percy to T. Astle, Esq., F.A.S., F.R.S.', ed. S. H. Harlowe, *NQ* 4th ser. 3 (1869)
Illustrations	John Nichols, *Illustrations of the Literary History of the Eighteenth Century* (1817–58)
Letters	*The Percy Letters*, ed. David Nichol Smith and Cleanth Brooks (Baton Rouge, La., 1944–57; New Haven, 1961–88), ed. Cleanth Brooks and A. F. Falconer (1977–88)
Letters, i	*The Correspondence of Thomas Percy and Edmond Malone*, ed. Arthur Tillotson (1944; 2nd edn. 1960)
Letters, ii	*The Correspondence of Thomas Percy and Richard Farmer*, ed. Cleanth Brooks (1946)
Letters, iii	*The Correspondence of Thomas Percy and Thomas Warton*, ed. M. G. Robinson and Leah Dennis (1951)
Letters, iv	*The Correspondence of Thomas Percy and David Dalrymple, Lord Hailes*, ed. A. F. Falconer (1954)

Letters, v	*The Correspondence of Thomas Percy and Evan Evans*, ed. Aneirin Lewis (1957)
Letters, vi	*The Correspondence of Thomas Percy and George Paton*, ed. A. F. Falconer (1961)
Letters, vii	*The Correspondence of Thomas Percy and William Shenstone*, ed. Cleanth Brooks (1977)
Letters, viii	*The Correspondence of Thomas Percy and John Pinkerton*, ed. Harriet Harvey Wood (1985)
Letters, ix	*The Correspondence of Thomas Percy and Robert Anderson*, ed. W. E. K. Anderson (1988)
Reliques	Thomas Percy, *Reliques of Ancient English Poetry: consisting of Old Heroic Ballads, Songs, and other Pieces of our earlier Poets, (Chiefly of the Lyric kind.) Together with some few of later Date*, 1st edn. (1765), 2nd edn. (1767), 3rd edn. (1775), 4th edn. (1794 [1795]), 5th edn. (1812); 1765 edn. unless otherwise indicated (in facsimile, ed. Nick Groom (1996))
Smith	Margaret M. Smith (ed.), *Index of English Literary Manuscripts*, iii. 2 (1989)
Tierney	James E. Tierney (ed.), *The Correspondence of Robert Dodsley* (Cambridge, 1988)
Vartin	Stephen Vartin, 'Thomas Percy's *Reliques*: Its Structure and Organization', Ph.D. thesis (New York, 1972)
Williams	Marjorie Williams (ed.), *The Letters of William Shenstone* (Oxford, 1939)

Libraries

BL	British Library
Bodl.	Bodleian Library, Oxford
Houghton	Houghton Library, Harvard
NRO	Northamptonshire Record Office
Queen's	The Queen's University Library, Belfast

Journals

BJECS	*British Journal for Eighteenth-Century Studies*
BJRL	*Bulletin of the John Rylands Library*
BLR	*Bodleian Library Record*
BNYPL	*Bulletin of the New York Public Library*
ECS	*Eighteenth-Century Studies*

ELH	*English Literary History*
ES	*English Studies*
HLB	*Harvard Library Bulletin*
JEGP	*Journal of English and Germanic Philology*
MLR	*Modern Language Review*
NC	*New Colophon*
NLWJ	*National Library of Wales Journal*
NQ	*Notes & Queries*
OED	*Oxford English Dictionary*
PBSA	*Papers of the Bibliographical Society of America*
PMLA	*Publications of the Modern Language Association of America*
PQ	*Philological Quarterly*
RES	*Review of English Studies*
SB	*Studies in Bibliography*
SGS	*Scottish Gaelic Studies*
SiR	*Studies in Romanticism*
TBS	*Transactions of the Bibliographical Society*
TGSI	*Transactions of the Gaelic Society of Inverness*
TLS	*Times Literary Supplement*
YULG	*Yale University Library Gazette*

We heard a ballad-singer singing songs of long ago . . .
(Anonymous singer, 'The Fair at Bampton-Ho!',
Oxenham Arms, Dartmoor Folk Festival, 1997)

Books and the Man I sing
(Alexander Pope, *Dunciad Variorum*)

I

Introduction

A Formal solemn Owl had many years made his habitation in a grove amongst the ruins of an old monastery, and had pored so often on some mouldy manuscripts, the stupid relicks of a monkish library, that he grew infected with the pride and pedantry of the place; and mistaking gravity for wisdom, would sit whole days with his eyes half shut, fancying himself profoundly learned. It happened as he sat one evening, half buried in meditation, and half in sleep, that a Nightingale, unluckily perching near him, began her melodious lays. He started from his *reverie*, and with a horrid screech interrupting her song—Be gone, cryed he, thou impertinent minstrel, nor distract with noisy dissonance my sublime contemplations; and know, vain songster, that harmony consists in truth alone, which is gained by laborious study; and not in languishing notes, fit only to sooth the ear of a love-sick maid. Conceited pedant! returned the Nightingale, whose wisdom lies only in the feathers that muffle up thy unmeaning face; music is a natural and rational entertainment, and though not adapted to the ears of an Owl, has ever been relished and admired by all who are possessed of taste and elegance.[1]

This extremely concise version of the thirteenth-century *disputatio* poem 'The Owl and the Nightingale' appeared in Robert Dodsley's *Select Fables of Esop and other Fabulists* (1761), with the moral ''Tis natural for a pedant to despise those arts, which polish our manners, and would extirpate pedantry'.[2] Dodsley's elegant little book, copiously illustrated and beautifully printed by John Baskerville, numbered among its contributors one Thomas Percy, an energetic young clergyman living in Northamptonshire. Percy had literary ambitions. He had written poetry, and now tried composing fables, providing Dodsley with 'The Toad and the Gold-fish' for this collection.[3] Four months after Dodsley's *Fables* was published, Percy borrowed a copy from his friend and

---

[1] Robert Dodsley (ed.), *Select Fables of Esop and other Fabulists* (1761), 110–11. According to Tierney, the reception of Dodsley's *Fables* was 'extraordinary' (15–16).
[2] *Fables*, Fable XXXVIII, n.p.
[3] *Letters*, vii. 234–8; see also Tierney, 449, 395.

neighbour Ambrose Isted and transcribed another four original fables into the copy, which he dedicated to Ambrose's wife Anne.[4] In one of these, 'The Nightengale [*sic*] and the Rose', Percy revealingly describes a thwarted love affair. The nightingale woos the rose by serenading her every evening, but meanwhile, during the day, the rose is being seduced by a foppish butterfly. The nightingale discovers this intrigue and his love fades. As with 'The Owl and the Nightingale', the moral of this Eastern tale identifies the nightingale with the man of sense, with taste, and with elegance.

For Percy as well as for Dodsley, the nightingale is considered a bird of genius. In the fable quoted above, the nightingale is specifically a 'minstrel', popular and melodious; whereas the owl is an antiquarian, unpopular and malodorous. In another of Dodsley's *Fables*, 'The Nightingale and the Bullfinch', the nightingale declares herself to be a '*native*' and '*original*' songster.[5] These nightingales are metaphors for poetry: they constitute an index of elegance and taste. They are sensible and rational, native and natural and original; absolutely characteristic of later eighteenth-century sentimental poetry. But despite this, they did not sufficiently inspire the young and ambitious Percy. Even as he transcribed his own fables, he was devoting most of his time to peering over and prying into mouldy manuscripts. Four years after the *Fables* appeared, James Dodsley published Thomas Percy's *Reliques of Ancient English Poetry* (1765).

Percy's *Reliques*, a three-volume anthology of ballads, songs, sonnets, and romances, is probably the finest example of the antiquarian tendency in later eighteenth-century poetry. It is also symptomatic of the anxieties of the emerging discipline of scholarly editing. It dramatizes the encounters between literate and oral media, between polite poetry and popular culture, and between scholarship and taste: in other words, the *Reliques* stages a debate between an owl and a nightingale. Moreover, the *Reliques* not only sketches the history of English literature; it offers a theory of textual transmission that defines precisely what 'English literature' is, and places this extraordinary cultural responsibility

---

[4] This copy is in private hands; there is a microfilm in the BL, RP 413. It was lent to Percy on 25 June 1761 and he returned it on 5 July (Bodl., MS Percy c 9, fo. 102^r).

[5] *Fables*, 199–200.

in the hands of the 'ancient English minstrels'. The *Reliques* provided definitive versions of popular and ephemeral poems, and was compendiously glossed with notes and reflections on native English customs, folklore, poetic traditions, and historical titbits. It established the ballad as a valid literary form, and influenced writers from Sir Walter Scott and Samuel Taylor Coleridge to Lewis Carroll and Oscar Wilde. A generation after it was first published, this popular and influential work was celebrated by William Wordsworth as belonging to 'the regions of true simplicity and genuine pathos'.[6] It is the seminal, epoch-making work of English Romanticism.[7]

This study of the *Reliques* is concerned with Percy's owlishness: his research among 'the stupid relicks of a monkish library'. It explains in detail Percy's working methods and the formation of the *Reliques*, to show that the methodological assumptions behind Percy's editing of the *Reliques* became part of the fabric of late eighteenth-century literary antiquarianism. The fable of 'The Owl and the Nightingale' is paradigmatic to the book's argument: Percy's *Reliques* is a marriage between the owl and the nightingale, a union of the antiquarian with the man of taste, of scholarship with poetry, of the pedant with the minstrel. Percy's aspiration to unite these conflicting positions is foreshadowed by Nicholas of Guildford, the mysterious authorial presence in the medieval source for 'The Owl and the Nightingale' who can only judge the birds silently after the poem itself has concluded.

As a tireless researcher of old English poetry, Percy himself mumbled over the secular relics of literary remains and bravely adopted this title for his book. The *Reliques* declares itself to be antiquarian; but it is perhaps ironically so. As an editor, Percy is

---

[6] *The Prose Works of William Wordsworth*, ed. W. J. B. Owen and Jane Worthington Smyser (Oxford, 1974), 'Essay Supplementary to the Preface' (*Lyrical Ballads*, 1815), iii. 75. See also preface to *Lyrical Ballads* (1800), ed. R. L. Brett and A. R. Jones, 2nd edn. (1991), 269–70.

[7] This point has been most recently endorsed by Landeg White in 'The Bishop's Move', a review of *Reliques* (1996), *TLS* (27 June 1997), 24. Perhaps surprisingly, Percy had several immediate (and unsuccessful) predecessors, most notably Edward Capell, *Prolusions: or, Select Pieces of Antient Poetry* (1760), and John '*Don*' Bowle, *Miscellaneous Pieces of Antient English Poesie* (1764). Thomas Warton too once had plans for a volume of 'Select Pieces of ancient English Poëtry: or such Poëms as thro' the Injuries of Time have been forgotten, but deserve to be reviv'd: Written in the Reigns of Q. Elizabeth; K. James & K. Charles the 1st' (*c*.1753: see David Fairer, 'The Origins of Warton's *History of English Poetry*', *RES* 32 (1981), 47–9).

not owlishly pompous. He does not stoop like Hogarth's connoisseur monkey, squinting over the supposedly rare beauty of the
twig-like 'Exoticks' he tends; neither is he a dunce, 'in closet close
y-pent, | Of sober face, with learned dust besprent'.[8] Thomas
Percy, in his strigrian fragments, attempts to catch the nightingale
voice of the minstrel, the echo of an oral tradition of native
English poetry and song.

The insistence on medium in the 'Owl and the Nightingale'
fable demonstrates the defining characteristic of Percy's brand of
literary antiquarianism: that the cultural value and significance of
a source is defined by its medium of transmission. Like Samuel
Johnson, who declared that 'composing a Dictionary requires
books and a desk: you can make a poem walking in the fields,
or lying in bed', Percy sought his songs in archives and libraries,
not in fields or streets, arguing that the oral tradition had left
visible literary traces.[9] Antiquarians demanded artefacts and
documents, manuscripts and texts, physical remains: they
demanded that the past be legible, if only as indecipherable
manuscrits trouvés.[10] It was in such places that Percy encoded,
inscribed, and canonized his version of the oral tradition, and in
doing so he spun together a poetic English heritage.

This analysis of Percy's *Reliques* combines historical chronology
with thematic threads. From the confusion of Percy's research, I
have untangled a series of specific narratives that each deal with an
episode in the story of the *Reliques*, providing a significantly new
version of the making, construction, and printing of Percy's major
work. The subjects of these narratives overlap—rather like heroes
and heroines of the ballads themselves, they often migrate from
one story to another—but the sections are arranged to avoid
repetition whilst maintaining a coherent account. The editorial
complexities of the *Reliques* are hair-raising, and its textual
problems are quite insoluble without lengthy exposition and
detailed analysis. One of the ambitions of this book, therefore,

---

[8] *Dunciad Variorum*, III. 181–2 (*The Twickenham Edition of the Poems of Alexander Pope*, v, ed. James R. Sutherland (1963), 170); Harlowe, 25.

[9] *Boswell's Life*, v. 47.

[10] Nicholas Hudson, 'Oral Tradition: The Evolution of an Eighteenth-Century Concept', in Alvaro Ribeiro, SJ, and James G. Basker (eds.), *Tradition in Transition: Women Writers, Marginal Texts, and the Eighteenth-Century Canon* (Oxford, 1996), 161–76.

is to clarify editorial rationale and enable the *Reliques* to be edited for a modern audience.

Simply put, the study focuses on what one man read, and how this affected his literary output. It provides a detailed analysis of Percy's reading, correspondence, and transcription habits to analyse the impact of a medium on the integrity of a text. But while the specific value of the following research remains in providing a detailed account of Percy's use of sources *c.*1756–65, it also sheds new light on the relationships of writers and publishers and the ensuing formation of the literary canon, and suggests how the book trade both influenced and came to terms with the style of scholarship adopted by Percy. It is my contention that the literary canon was formulated in the eighteenth century by a handful of antiquarians in their evaluation of the literary status of manuscript sources in a mass-print culture. Indeed, after Percy had read Dodsley's *Fables of Esop*, he penned a fable which revealed his critical sensitivity to the materiality of the literary medium. In 'The Pegasus and the Pack-horse', there is a glimpse of textual production in the packhorse's lament: 'tho' I cannot soar like you, but am doomed to plod on here below, still I am of use to the literary world: for see I bring Materials for the manufacture of that paper, without which the songs of the Muses would soon die and be forgotten.'[11]

Thomas Percy led a bibliographical life. He had almost 300 books by the time he went up to Oxford as a Christ Church Exhibitioner in 1746—an astonishing collection for a 17-year-old.[12] Ten years later he took some 455 volumes with him to the vicarage at Easton Maudit, writing to his cousin William Cleiveland, 'the Life I am going to be engag'd in ^ ⌈at Easton Maudit⌉ will be

---

[11] *Fables*, BL, RP 413.
[12] Bodl., MS Percy c 9, fos. 33–43. Percy's library was purchased by The Queen's University, Belfast, in 1969: see *The Library of Thomas Percy 1729–1811, Bishop of Dromore, Editor of the Reliques of Ancient English Poetry*, Sotheby & Co., 23 June 1969. A list of Percy's annotated books has been compiled by Smith, 319–39. Letters from Jacob Tonson and Lockyer Davis detailing Percy's avid book collecting are at NRO, Ecton (Sotheby) 1207, fos. 15–17 and E (S) 1211, fos. 2–3; Houghton (Pusey Library Theatre Collection), TS 934 5, ii. 298, 339; and Boston Public Library, MS Eng. 154 (1–2), respectively. For Percy's book catalogues, see Bodl., MS Percy c 9; for his account of borrowed and received books, see Bodl., MS Percy c 9, fos. 94–105; for his Shakespearean borrowings, see Bodl., MS Percy e 5, fos. 7–8; for his book bills, see Bodl., MS Percy b 3.

something of an Academical Nature: I shall be chiefly conversant with Books'.[13] And yet, strangely, Percy had no sense of scholarly destiny. In a fit of drastic pruning he reduced his beloved collection to a gentleman curate's library of less than two hundred volumes, and gave away such things as Gerard Langbaine's *Account of the English Dramatick Poets* (1698), Dodsley's *Collection* (1751), a 1617 edition of Spenser, and a 1595 Chaucer—works that he was soon to find indispensable (wisely, he did retain the 1623 Shakespeare folio he had bought for the princely sum of 1s. 6d.). So, having thoroughly weeded his books, Percy was almost immediately buying, begging, and borrowing them back. He had turned his attention to studying 'a curious old MS. ab^t. 1660', and within three years his library had almost doubled.[14]

In about 1753, Percy had paid a visit to Humphrey Pitt, an old Salopian friend. While there, he noticed that the maids in the parlour were lighting the fire with a bundle of paper that had been lying under a bureau. It was a poetry miscellany, transcribed by hand into a folio book, and Percy, enthralled, asked if he might have the curiosity before it was entirely consumed. He thereby acquired a seventeenth-century commonplace book containing transcripts of ballads, metrical romances, and popular songs, many of which he later learned were extant solely in this 'Folio MS'.[15] It was an amazing find. By 1757, Percy was copying pieces out of the 'old Folio M.S. Collection of Historical Ballads &c' for his friends, and as he spent evenings, months, and years editing and transcribing the unfamiliar characters, the historical significance of the tattered, torn, and dirty thing he had retrieved from the grate became increasingly clear.[16] It was a fairy-tale foundling, the last of its race, in which Percy perceived noble lineaments and a stately gravity: a last, remarkable example of the art of the ancient English minstrels.

With the help of writers as diverse as Samuel Johnson and William Shenstone (almost the only collaborators to see the artefact), Percy decided to edit and publish the Folio MS: in some of its earlier incarnations, *Reliques of Ancient English Poetry* would have been almost wholly and solely derived from

---

[13] Bodl., MS Percy c 9, fos. 1–19; BL, Add. MS 32333, fo. 2^v.
[14] Bodl., MS Percy c 9, fo. 24.   [15] Hales and Furnivall, i, p. lxxiv.
[16] BL, Add. MS 32333, fo. 17^v.

Percy's chance discovery of this *manuscrit trouvé*. It reveals therefore Percy's working methods and editorial assumptions, and
explains the genesis, development, and identity of the *Reliques*.
For Percy, the Folio MS was an owlish relic of the minstrel's
nightingale song.

The vicarage rooms filled with books, Percy's frequent forays to
ransack the Earl of Sussex's library at nearby Castle Ashby, the
boxes that regularly arrived from London booksellers and his
scholarly friends, create a crucial context for Percy's work. His
dedication to the printed word powered his research, but, by virtue
of the Folio MS, the *Reliques* would be characterized by a persistent fascination with the competition between oral, manuscript,
and print sources.

The *Reliques* was conceived and executed amid Percy's fabulous
bibliolatry, and published *in medias res*: in the middle of the
1760s, central to Percy's whole motivation and methodology in
conceptualizing the value of literary sources, and pivotal in his
work. And yet, as I will show, this seminal work got off the press
only slowly and laboriously, and its production was bedevilled
with difficulties, both practical and conceptual. When it was
finally published by James Dodsley on St Valentine's Day, 14
February 1765, it sold remarkably well, and until Walter Scott's
Minstrelsy of the Scottish Border (1802–3), no other collection
approached the popularity of the *Reliques*.[17]

The *Reliques* made Percy's name. He was elected to the Club in
1768, awarded a DD by Cambridge University in 1770, and by
Oxford in 1793. Yet despite frequent plans for a supplementary

[17] The 1765 *Reliques* was published in an edition of 1,500; by July, 1,100 copies
had been sold (*Letters*, iii. 119). Gaskell suggests that 1,500 was the most economical
press run (Philip Gaskell, *A New Introduction to Bibliography* (Oxford, 1985),
160–3), but it is clear from Tierney that Dodsley press runs were seldom generous and
that a run of 1,500 was exceptional for a first edition of a relatively unknown author:
the four-volume Pope's *Works* of 1755 was in an issue of 1,500 (29–30). John
Newbery published Johnson's *The Idler* in a run of 1,500 in 1761, and in 1770
Benjamin Collins and William Johnston published Smollett's *Humphry Clinker* in
2,000 copies (Marjorie Plant, *The English Book Trade*, 2nd edn. (1965), 235–6).
The 3rd edn. of the *Reliques* appeared in a run of 1,500, for which Percy was paid 40
guineas five years after printing; probably the 2nd edn. was in 1,500 as well. James
Dodsley relinquished the engraved copperplates to Percy in 1775, and bound Percy not
to print another edition until his edition was exhausted (*Willis's Current Notes*, 47
(Nov. 1854; 1855), 91). The 4th edn. was printed by John Nichols for J. & C.
Rivington, and, as they are absent from the Rivingtons' 5th edn., the copperplates
were presumably destroyed in Nichols's warehouse fire.

fourth volume comprising English and Scottish songs, within a decade Percy would all but disown the *Reliques*. He dismissed it as 'trash', merely 'the amusements of my youth', and was reluctant to acknowledge its impact.[18] It was a folly, a bastard offspring he could barely admit his own. Trumpeting the exploits of the Northumberland Percys had won him patronage; now it threatened to cast him as an upstart *arriviste* among his supposed kin. The popular success of the *Reliques*, which mimicked the rough popularity of its subject matter, was incompatible with the bearing of his adoptive family and the gravity of his mitre (he became Bishop of Dromore in 1782). This embarrassment perhaps explains his attributing the 1794 edition to his nephew (another Thomas Percy), his refusal to publish the Folio MS, and his attempts to efface himself from his work.[19] The foundling Folio MS was kept locked away like some dreadful family secret, a mad changeling, and Percy, effectively exiled to Ireland, occupied himself with researches into Fortean natural curiosities: a toad retrieved from a 400-foot bog, letters to the *Gentleman's Magazine* on the migration of birds and showers of stones, a receipt for curing rheumatism with brown paper.

This enforced retirement has been understood as Percy's retreat from the scathing attacks on the accuracy of his work by scholars such as Joseph Ritson, echoed by Hales and Furnivall and present-day commentators like G. Legman.[20] Percy has characteristically been criticized as a particularly bad and unreliable and overly imaginative editor: he compiled single texts of ballads from a variety of unacknowledged versions, and liberally rewrote these collages to suit the taste of a late eighteenth-century readership. Although noteworthy interpolations were often pinned within quotation marks (thus "), many minor revisions, and some major

---

[18] *Illustrations*, viii. 309, 341.

[19] Thomas Percy of St John's was paid £160 for the 4th edition (Bodl., MS Percy c 3, fo. 200ʳ), but 'his designation as editor of the fourth edition was almost certainly a polite fiction' (Davis (1981), 100). He unwisely revealed this to Steevens, who passed on the information to Joseph Ritson (*Ancient Engleish Metrical Romanceës* (1802), pp. cvii–cviii n.). Percy himself was paid for the Rivington editions (1794, 1811) through his accountant Crane Brush (Bodl., MS Percy c 4, fos. 32–3).

[20] Joseph Ritson, *Select Collection of English Songs* (1783 [1784]), i, p. x; *Ancient Engleish Metrical Romanceës*, i, pp. cviii–cix; Hales and Furnivall, i, pp. xvi–xxiii; G. Legman, *The Horn Book: Studies in Erotic Folklore and Bibliography* (1970), 500, 346; Dave Harker, *Fakesong: The Manufacture of British 'Folksong' 1700 to the Present Day* (Milton Keynes, 1985), 21–8.

rewritings, were rendered completely invisible. But Percy, an editor and an antiquarian, a rising poet and a man of taste, was faced with preparing for the press a fantastically diverse range of texts, mainly anonymous, existing in a profusion of editions, variations, and Grub Street abridgements, in which any signs of single author-ship had been effaced by generations of retellings, revisions, and rewritings. He could not reproduce a dozen different variations on the same narrative, as Ritson attempted in *Robin Hood* (1795), and Francis James Child carried through with such comprehensive pedantry in his *English and Scottish Popular Ballads* (1882–98). Percy, having to compromise from the outset, ultimately made his editorial problems a positive asset to his work.

Indeed, the problem of textual authority becomes intractable in the case of Percy's *Reliques*, and even contemporary theories of textual bibliography offer no solutions. Who authors the *Reliques*? Percy, or anonymous balladeers? Should we follow modern scholarship's increasing emphasis on absolute diplomatic fidelity and restore the texts to their earliest state, or their most popular or accurate versions, or should we allow that Percy is the author, and that authority lies in his revised and rewritten texts? It transpires that Percy was sensitive to this very problem. He was pulled in opposite directions: towards scholarly precision by his antiquarian associates, and towards polite, elegant revision (and marketability) by Shenstone and the Dodsleys. In other words, Percy himself was stuck between editing and authorship. If any-thing, Percy, an aspiring Sinologist who published six volumes of Chinoiserie, succeeded in producing a fashionable sharawaggi—a studied irregularity of intent. But his ultimate dissatisfaction with the *Reliques* suggests that the scholar (even the Chinese scholar) in him was seriously dismayed by the collection when it appeared, despite its runaway popularity and elevation of his social standing. The archaeology of the text displays this perpetual conflict of interests, and I suggest that his work is more significant today for articulating serious and insoluble anxieties about poetry, English literature, and the nature of the source in eighteenth-century letters, rather than as raw material for a single edition. But the problems of preparing a critical edition of Percy's *Reliques* today do demonstrate powerfully not only how profoundly differ-ent an activity it would be from preparing a critical edition of a book authored by a single person, or extant in a single text, but also that the Percy *œuvre* poses unanswerable questions for all author-text theories. Moreover, a brief recapitulation of bibliographical debates shows that Percy may be considered a victim of developing bibliographical orthodoxies.

Despite the clarity and pragmatism of Greg–Bowers, the rationale of copy-text immediately proves unworkable for Percy's *Reliques*.[21] Fredson Bowers's elaboration of W. W. Greg's work sought to recover an ideal text, based on original authorial intention, deduced from an examination of manuscript copies and authorially sanctioned editions, taking more notice of 'substantives' (changes in words) than 'accidentals' (changes in punctuation, often introduced by the compositor as house style). Such canons of textual bibliography follow the earliest attempts of Greek scholars to compile a written text of the oral Homer, and the work of biblical scholars who had to erase decades or centuries of scribal error in textual transmission and thus recover the intentional word of God. Clearly, the myth of origin is endemic in textual bibliography. Karl Lachmann, a nineteenth-century textual bibliographer who influenced Greg's endeavours to establish single, Adamic ancestors, was, like Charles Darwin and Karl Marx, a meta-narrator tracing *stemma codicum* (family trees of extant manuscripts) in which significant absences were filled by inferring lost texts. By recension (charting variants through *stemmata*, giving either 'true' readings or 'errors') and emendation (the rectification of error—often *divinatio*) Lachmann constructed (or reconstructed) the crucial lost witness or missing link: the archetype.[22]

The compilation of Homer, as D. C. Greetham comments, 'while itself subject to the dictates of personal judgment, was a conscious attack on the claim of the rhapsodes, or professional reciters of poetry, to have preserved the Homeric text perfectly, and marks the first acknowledgement that any act of transmission, oral or scribal, is inherently partial to corruption'.[23] Percy, while not engaged on the epics of a single author function, was coping with a comparably corrupt oral tradition, and had to deal with it

[21] See *Percy's Reliques of Ancient English Poetry nach der ersten Ausgabe von 1765 mit den Varianten der späteren Originalausgaben herausgegeben und mit Einleitung und Registeren Versehen*, ed. M. M. Arnold Schröer (Berlin, 1893).
[22] D. C. Greetham, *Textual Scholarship: An Introduction* (New York, 1994), 323.
[23] Ibid., 297.

in similar ways. Greetham shows that the rise of orthodox literary criticism is discernible in these classical debates on editing, in which 'Homeric' qualities are posited to allow the critic to perfect an author's work. 'Smoothness', 'consistency', and 'correctness' were valued over documentary 'authority', and there was even a legend that Aristotle had prepared an Aristotelian edition of Homer. Likewise, the literary values Percy proposed for minstrels suggested that ballads were part of an identifiable tradition, rather than anomalous utterances of local affect and immediate context.[24]

Philip Gaskell suggests that these editorial practices may not simply have encouraged but actually enabled the utopian work of Shakespeare's early editors, who perfected eclectic texts out of quartos and variant states of the first Folio, where, as Gary Taylor says, 'the English editorial tradition began'.[25] Interestingly, textual idealism is editorially most suited to analysing significant minor variation rather than providing a model for describing and explaining dramatic differences in manuscripts or editions, and for Shakespeare there were only printed sources, although his editors still found considerable difficulties in raising a single, sacred text.[26] Nevertheless, the leading eighteenth-century editions of Shakespeare exemplified the construction of a literary monument out of a shabby ruin, and so haunted Percy's ambition in the *Reliques*. Shakespeare was conceived as an individual author and a national genius, built from conjectural emendation (of which Alexander Pope was the most brilliant and inventive exponent), minute editorial collation, and historical explication. All these contributed to Percy's conception of the *Reliques*, and not least because Shakespeare had become the stamp of a characteristically English literary sensibility. If not the first, he was the origin of the definition of English literature: a national poet, a Gothic genius whose linguistic copiousness displayed both an instinctive love of liberty and a dismissive contempt (or a total ignorance) of the

---

[24] Ibid., 299–300.

[25] Gaskell, *New Introduction*, 336; see also Philip Gaskell, *From Writer to Reader: Studies in Editorial Method* (Oxford, 1978), 3; Gary Taylor, 'The Renaissance and the End of Editing', in George Bornstein and Ralph G. Williams (eds.), *Palimpsest: Editorial Theory in the Humanities* (Ann Arbor, 1993), 122.

[26] See Margreta De Grazia, *Shakespeare Verbatim: The Reproduction of Authenticity and the 1790 Apparatus* (Oxford, 1991), 31, for a brisk summary of the editorial problems facing 18th-century scholars.

tyrannical canons of neoclassical theatre and the Aristotelian unities. Furthermore, this formation of Shakespeare sanctioned textual revision on aesthetic and ideological grounds as much as on documentary or historical evidence.

Judged against this editorial tradition, however, the tradition in which he worked and to which he contributed, Percy's *Reliques* was an imminent disaster: texts existed in countless variations, flourishing rhizomically rather than arboreally, and authors were miscellaneous, minor, and often anonymous. Percy did not invent a new theory of textual criticism, but the *Reliques*, in its conception, execution, and publication, does exhibit serious anxieties about the culture of the book. It crystallizes fundamental problems of authorial and editorial intention, minor and major variation, aesthetic quality, historical corruption, and translation between media. My aim in this study is to show that the entire conception of the *Reliques* shifted frequently and dramatically in response to specific methodological difficulties.

This is evident when approaching Percy's *Reliques* from a different bibliographical perspective. In answer to the Greg–Bowers rationale has developed a more supple if less decisive school of sociological and materialist textual bibliography, led by D. F. McKenzie and Jerome McGann.[27] McGann found the constraints of Greg–Bowers simply inadequate for his seven-volume edition of Byron, for whom there exist a jumbled miscellany of manuscripts (often exhibiting his aristocratic disdain of pointing), amanuenses' copies (some copied by Mary Shelley, whom Byron encouraged to revise his texts), proofs (some diligently corrected, some carelessly returned unread), and various printed editions (some incorporating authorial changes, some annotated). McGann describes the impossibilities of Greg–Bowers for editing Byron in 'Theory, Literary Pragmatics, and the Editorial Horizon', and introduces a new emphasis in textual bibliography: 'texts are produced under specific social and institutional conditions, and hence . . . every text, including those that appear to be purely private, is a social text.'[28] McGann's interest

---

[27] D. F. McKenzie, *Bibliography and the Sociology of the Text* (1986); Jerome J. McGann, *Critique of Modern Textual Criticism* (Chicago, 1983).

[28] Jerome J. McGann, *The Textual Condition* (Princeton, 1991), 21. McGann's heroic frustration is evident in his long editorial introduction to *Lord Byron: The Complete Works* (Oxford, 1980), i, pp. xxvii–xlvii.

has necessarily shifted to the passage of texts through different historical and discursive contexts, and the transformations that such movements entail, which are discerned in the physique of the text. The text, McGann argues, is not an unrealized and ideal object, but a series of moments or situations. In his edition of the *Dead Sea Scrolls*, for example, Geza Vermes has established that Qumran scribes worked within a philosophy of cultural multiplicity and variegation, in opposition to any centralized orthodoxy, and consequently they enjoyed extensive 'creative freedom': 'Qumran manuscripts of Scripture . . . indicate that diversity, not uniformity, reigned there and then, and that redactor-copyists felt free to improve the composition which they were reproducing.'[29] These possibilities become acute in the interface between manuscript and print, perhaps nowhere more so than in Percy's *Reliques*.

The Byronic difficulties that McGann has faced (seemingly irreconcilable variations in manuscript, amanuenses' drafts, proof-sheets, first and subsequent printed editions, and annotated copies) are not too dissimilar to the situation facing an editor of Percy's *Reliques*. The production of the *Reliques* was slow and fitful, intentions changed radically several times, and we are left with a variety of conflicting potential texts. What this means is that an editor of the *Reliques* must make definite decisions regarding the competing authority of source, collations, transcripts, transcripts corrected by correspondents, proof, revise, trial issue, and first and succeeding editions, all with or without Percy's further thoughts. The internal dynamics of the work remain fabulously protean, and fundamentally resist comprehensive models like Lachmann's *stemmata*.

Although the current supporters of the Greg–Bowers rationale of copy-text, G. Thomas Tanselle and his ilk, have distanced themselves from edicts such as the distinctions of authorial intention between 'substantives' and 'accidentals', the notion of 'ideal copy' still governs eighteenth-century editing, which has generally not had to confront the relationship between manuscript copy and first printing. Hugh Amory's editorial innovations for Henry Fielding's *Miscellanies* do, however, deploy a manuscript draft of 'The Wedding Day' in an edition that reproduces Fielding's

---

[29] Geza Vermes (ed.), *The Complete Dead Sea Scrolls in English* (Harmondsworth, 1997), 23–4.

'intention to print' rather than his 'intention to write'.[30] Gaskell too has argued that authors' manuscripts are merely one stage in the production of a book: half-finished documents designed to be modified and completed in the printing house.[31] The act of publication presupposes the endorsement of changes from the manuscript to the printed text, unless there exists evidence to the contrary.[32] In contrast to printed works, modern editions of eighteenth-century manuscripts have been exactingly diplomatic in the reproduction of manuscripts (*'literatim'*, as David Fairer has it). It has become clear that apparently irrelevant or capricious features, such as capitalization and italicization, contraction and abbreviation, may add nuances of meaning, suggest tone of address, or simply indicate haste or leisure, and it is crucial to retain such elements. In the case of Percy, we have a rare chance to witness the genesis and evolution of a work, read his own commentary upon it in his correspondence, and witness his reaction to a succession of printed versions. The directions or interventions of an author in the printing process, and indeed the extent to which an author is able to influence subsequent printing practice, are explored in the brilliant study of David Foxon and James McLaverty, *Pope and the Early Eighteenth-Century Book Trade*, which concludes by stressing the need 'to study the practice of an author throughout his life before one can begin to formulate the principles on which any one of his works should be edited'.[33] The following account of the making of Percy's *Reliques* will, I hope, bear out this advice.

The problems of editing such complex material have been outlined by McGann in his hypothetical case of Dante Gabriel Rossetti's *The House of Life*.[34] McGann distinguishes three principal approaches for a critical edition: the Greg–Bowers eclectic text, diplomatic texts of each printed stage, or a genetic text that derives an evolving state from all extant versions, manuscript, printed, and miscellaneous (such as those described in

---

[30] *Miscellanies by Henry Fielding, Esq*, vol. ii, ed. Bertrand A. Goldgar and Hugh Amory (Oxford, 1993), 238–46.

[31] For examples of more radical editing opportunities, see Gaskell, *From Writer to Reader*, particularly 63–117.   [32] Gaskell, *New Introduction*, 339–40.

[33] David Foxon and James McLaverty, *Pope and the Early Eighteenth-Century Book Trade* (Oxford, 1991), 236.

[34] McGann, *The Textual Condition*, 23–33; Greetham, *Textual Scholarship*, 349–54.

letters or marginalia). In this last approach, the continuous state of variant texts would be indicated by a synoptic apparatus of codes, recording all variants equally. The record is spread and scattered over multiple documents, but, equipped with bespoke diacritical marks, the editor is theoretically able to preserve and indicate in the text 'false starts, *currente calamo* changes, in-document revision, or erasures . . . [and] revisions of the revision' (as Hans Walter Gabler described his controversial *Ulysses: A Critical and Synoptic Edition* (1984)).[35] In the case of Percy, the ambition is to describe both the continuous manuscript text and the continuous production text in order to create 'a continuous compositional text', embodying an authorial process rather than final decisions.[36] The following chapters will describe the preparation of a genetic text of Percy's *Reliques*. It is ironic, however, that the text is described most accurately in a monograph rather than an edition. A synoptic genetic edition of Percy's *Reliques* would probably look more like a monument to academic futility than a readable book. It would not serve anyone who wished to consult the work as an eighteenth-century text, and so a practical critical edition on Greg–Bowers lines should now be forthcoming.

It is apparent in the preceding survey of textual bibliography (and in most of the criticism cited on Percy's *Reliques* as well) that much of the most recent editorial debate has been concerned with the question of 'intention' and particularly 'final intention': 'how best to recognize it, represent it or reject it in favor of other competing ideologies.'[37] McGann has predictably attacked this editorial preoccupation, perhaps because having worked so energetically in the Romantic period he is ready to deconstruct the Romantic myth of the author as an original and creative (and intentionalist) genius, whose copy-texts are, for want of a better word, self-evidently 'auratic'.[38] McGann lays emphasis instead upon the historical materialism of the text, on its physical

---

[35] Hans Walter Gabler, 'On Textual Criticism and Editing: The Case of Joyce's *Ulysses*', in Bornstein and Williams, *Palimpsest*, 200.

[36] McGann, *The Textual Condition*, 30.

[37] Greetham, *Textual Scholarship*, 336.

[38] Walter Benjamin, 'The Work of Art in the Age of Mechanical Reproduction', in *Illuminations*, ed. Hannah Arendt, tr. Harry Zohn (New York, 1969), 220–2. See also Jacques Derrida, *The Truth in Painting*, tr. Geoff Bennington and Ian McLeod (Chicago, 1987), 175–6.

production, and on bibliographical codes (typography, layout, illustrations, paper) as much as linguistic ones. McGann therefore shifts the textual bibliographer's interest from intention to affect, and, crucially in examining a corpus of work, from the idea of a subject's intentions to the cultural discourse that is being constructed to support the notion of subject and intention. The text may be a representation of its author's intentions, but the most legible marks it carries are traces of its production, and it is upon these that I will focus in the case of Percy. With anonymous broadside ballads or chapbook garlands, it might be the printer who leaves the only trace of anything that could be called 'intention'.[39] In other words, traditional and ephemeral examples of literature do not conform to any recognizable concept of authorship. Most significantly, they elude the Foucauldian trajectory, in which the author arrives as an architect of the ideology of bourgeois capitalism, intimately and legally bound up with the Lockean 1710 Copyright Act. In any case, the distrust of authorship and intention has been aired in theoretical circles since at least the time of Oscar Wilde, and is most famously announced in Roland Barthes's 'The Death of the Author' and Michel Foucault's rejoinder, 'What is an Author?'[40] In all three essays, the intentions of the author, even if stated explicitly, do not command any more authority than the work: they simply enlarge the text under consideration.

Textual boundaries have now become notoriously fluid, and so the centralized author, who previously governed and determined the rationale of a critical edition, has also come under attack from all those apparently marginal elements of the publication process. Like a building, a book is a work of multiple authorship, and, as Ralph Williams remarks, 'textual boundaries and (hence) textual

---

[39] Mark Rose, *Authors and Owners: The Invention of Copyright* (Cambridge, Mass., 1993), 135.

[40] Oscar Wilde, 'The Critic as Artist', *Intentions*, in *The Artist as Critic: Critical Writings of Oscar Wilde*, ed. Richard Ellmann (New York, 1969), 340–408; Roland Barthes, 'The Death of the Author', in *Image-Music-Text*, tr. Stephen Heath (1977), 142–8; Michel Foucault, 'What is an Author?', in *The Foucault Reader*, ed. Paul Rabinow (Harmondsworth, 1984), 101–20; Roger Chartier, *The Order of Books*, tr. Lydia G. Cochrane (Cambridge, 1994). Marcus Walsh explores similar ground in 'Bentley our Contemporary; or, Editors Ancient and Modern', in Ian Small and Marcus Walsh (eds.), *The Theory and Practice of Text-Editing: Essays in Honour of James T. Boulton* (Cambridge, 1991), 157–85.

meaning' are indeterminate.[41] The ostensible text of an author's works, though it fills the upper-centre portion of the page, is positioned in opposition to extratextual material, which always threatens to usurp it. And in the case of Percy's *Reliques*, these incursions by the author-editor on the body of the ballad text may be invisible and insinuant, and critically unstable. The version of the *Reliques* eventually published in 1765 might therefore be called a '*tranche de texte*': 'the "slice" being arbitrary with reference to the various criteria that might be privileged as basic to an edition.'[42]

Tanselle's most recent comments return us to this question of authority. Surveying textual bibliography in the 1990s, he concludes that any editorial theory must have the flexibility to deal with particular problems and exceptional cases. The answers to questions of textual criticism will have to lie somewhere in the physical record, and so the comparative richness or poverty of the archive will determine which method seems most appropriate to tackle textual issues. Tanselle tentatively suggests that there are such things as 'mental texts' of successive versions, which leave various traces or impressions, but his goal is simply to 'build up a fuller sense of the past than is provided by artifacts alone'.[43]

Nevertheless, intentionalist editors must still decide which readings are more 'authorial', even if intention is dynamic rather than static. With Percy, there are pressures on the text other than simple authorial intention, intention to write, or intention to print. The sea of drifting textual variants, notebooks, letters, marginalia, and book borrowing, and in particular the calendar of these influences, constitute a rich enough archive. It is possible to locate precisely when Percy received certain books and when certain changes were made. Writers and researchers do not have perfect recall; therefore, to chart the progress of particular objects, books and documents, across the desk of an eighteenth-century man of letters allows a succession of potential drafts to be mapped. What follows is the beginning of what I would like to call a 'micro-bibliographical' analysis, using the whole of Percy's textual record

---

[41] Ralph Williams, 'I Shall Be Spoken: Textual Boundaries, Authors, and Intent', in Bornstein and Williams, *Palimpsest*, 45.   [42] Williams, 55.

[43] G. Thomas Tanselle, 'Textual Instability and Editorial Idealism', *SB* 46 (1996), 59. See also Ralph Williams's use of the Sumerian *Lamentation over the Destruction of Sumer and Ur* ('I shall be Spoken', 46–7).

to establish the tensions between scholarly method and literary media, and their impact on the making of the *Reliques*. It is the portrait of a process, in which a printed text is plotted on fragmentary manuscripts, in which incoherencies sing.

2

The Ballad and
Literary Antiquarianism

Stories of textual transmission are seldom straightforward. Manuscripts, documents, and books are rescued from fires, pie dishes, tailors, bookbinders, and urns in Dead Sea caves; they are plucked from chests in church muniment rooms, or, like Boswell's *Journal of a Tour to the Hebrides*, discovered lining a croquet box. Libraries burn and manuscripts rot, but somehow stories get by and are repeated to the next generation. Stories are framed by the stories of their own transmission, and these narratives act as guarantors of authenticity.

In Jeremiah, the prophet has been prophesying doom and is consequently barred from the temple. He is not permitted a public voice, so he is divinely instructed to write down all the words he has received from God. These he dictates to his amanuensis, Baruch, and news of this incendiary manuscript reaches King Jehoiakim, who orders it to be read to him. The King James version continues:

So the king sent Jehudi to fetch the roll: and he took it out of Elishama the scribe's chamber. And Jehudi read it in the ears of the king, and in the ears of all the princes which stood beside the king. Now the king sat in the winterhouse in the ninth month: and there was a fire on the hearth burning before him. And it came to pass, that when Jehudi had read three or four leaves, he cut it with the penknife, and cast it into the fire that was on the hearth, until all the roll was consumed in the fire that was on the hearth . . . Then took Jeremiah another roll, and gave it to Baruch the scribe, the son of Neriah: who wrote therein from the mouth of Jeremiah all the words of the book which Jehoiakim king of Judah had burned in the fire: and there were added besides unto them many like words.[1]

The manuscript has a magical life of its own: it communicates across distances (space and time), and across social divides, and

---

[1] Williams quotes Jeremiah 36: 21–32 (48–9).

yet it is reduced to ashes in a moment. Still, it is resurrected, or repeated, from the mouth of the prophet. Speech comes before writing in this little myth of origins, oratory precedes literature as the Word precedes the world—despite this story itself surviving through a text, a book. And yet the divine voice cannot last. It is incarnated in the physical word of writing, it is subject to material depredations, and in this episode is the shadow of a prophecy of doom. Moreover, this is also the tale of an adulterated text. Baruch is a creative editor: he adds his own words to those of Jeremiah, and the miraculous and the mundane become indistinguishable.

Percy's *Reliques* was published in 1765, after a long fermentation. There is something of the fiery roll in Thomas Percy's Folio MS, his seventeenth-century commonplace book of popular songs and ballads which he had retrieved from the grate in about 1753. He inscribed it thus:

This very curious Old Manuscript in its present mutilated state, but unbound and sadly torn &c., I rescued from destruction, and begged at the hands of my worthy friend Humphrey Pitt Esq., then living at Shiffnal in Shropshire. . . . I saw it lying dirty on the floor under a Bureau in y° Parlour: being used by the Maids to light the fire. It was afterwards sent, most unfortunately, to an ignorant Bookbinder, who pared the margin, when I put it into Boards in order to lend it to Dr. Johnson. . . .

N.B. When I first got possession of this MS. I was very young, and being in no Degree an Antiquary, I had not then learnt to reverence it; which must be my excuse for the scribble which I then spread over some parts of its Margin. and in one or two instances for even taking out the Leaves to save the trouble of transcribing. I have since been more careful.
T.P.[2]

There is also something of the solicitousness of Baruch in Percy's collaboration, especially with William Shenstone. Indeed, previous accounts of the relationship between Percy and Shenstone have argued that it was precisely Shenstone's meddlesome advice that encouraged Percy to fiddle with his Folio MS texts. In Chapter 4 the relationship with Shenstone is reassessed by examining the Folio MS texts that he and Percy edited and revised. The role traditionally ascribed to Shenstone, as a demon of temptation, is untenable: Percy played the role of Baruch himself, and his transcriptions from the Folio MS were only as scrupulous as he himself saw fit. But before we turn to Percy, Shenstone, and the Folio MS, the contextual background requires focusing. The following chapter will consider the nature of the source in terms of the ballad's relationship to literature and to antiquarianism, concluding with a reading of the *Reliques*, and the succeeding chapter will explain how Percy's theory of ancient English minstrelsy arose.

OLD BALLADS

The *Reliques* is a collection of old ballads, and although it is also a repository of sonnets, songs, and lyrics, old and new, Percy stressed the centrality of 'old ballads' to his collection in his correspondence and in his research notes. His working title was *A Collection of Old Ballads*; moreover, one of his principal printed sources was a three-volume edition of old ballads also called *A Collection of Old Ballads* (1st edn. 1723–5; 2nd edn. 1726–38; see below, Chapter 4).[3] 'Old ballads' meant King Arthur, Robin Hood, border wars, traditional pageantry, and forlorn love, madness, and death; 'old ballads' were doughty heroic narratives or popular historical broadsides, medieval ballades or simple songs to accompany dances. But 'old ballads' also featured in the debate about the nature of the antiquarian source, and Percy's treatment of the form was based upon antiquarian attitudes to ancient poetry and the interfaces between oral, manuscript, and printed evidence.

The ballad is difficult to define, but easy to recognize. It is characterized today as a verse-narrative recounted through dialogue and action, in a formulaic structure and simple style, usually accompanied by music. Much work has been done refining and particularizing the term, distinguishing medieval ballades (for example Chaucer's *Compleynt of Venus*), from oral folk traditions, popular broadsides, and literary ballads; but in the eighteenth century, the term 'ballad' simply signified any popular verse or song. Indeed the tunes to Francis James Child's great collection *English and Scottish Popular Ballads* have been collected

[3] *Letters*, vii. 181.

and edited by Bertrand Bronson, and many of Percy's *Reliques* are still sung today.[4]

In 1711, Joseph Addison famously devoted three *Spectator* papers to 'Chevy Chase', admiring the simplicity, heroic nationalism, and epic sentiments of the traditional ballad.[5] It was a popular vehicle for poets and indeed playwrights: Pope and Swift wrote ballads; John Gay and Robert Dodsley wrote successful ballad operas. But within a few years, the ballad had degenerated. A rump of historical tales, religious narratives, and hymns remained, as did the frequent employment of ballads for sharply focused political satire, but the form was now typified by perpetually recycled patterns of bloody or salacious plots, treacly sentimental trash, and popular songs stolen from parks, gardens, and playhouses. Still, it remained the staple literary product of many booksellers and printers trading around St Paul's Churchyard, and their presses churned out thousands of broadside ballads, garlands (which were booklets of songs and ballads), and chapbooks.

Although they might be printed, ballads were carried by the singing voice. Earlier ballad collections and drolleries, such the *Rump* of 1662, claimed, 'If thou *read* these Ballads (and not *sing* them) the poor Ballads are undone.'[6] Shenstone went through the popular collections of Allan Ramsay and the *Vocal Miscellany* in search of material for Percy, and admitted, 'I find myself liable to be prejudiced in favour of words by a remembrance of yᵉ tune annexed to 'em.'[7] Samuel 'Dictionary' Johnson, Percy's friend and adviser on the *Reliques*, declared a ballad was simply 'A song' (1755–6). As a literary term, the word was half-pejorative, signifying a verse that could not sing for itself but needed to be carried by a tune. Yet they were the most prominent constituent example of an oral literary tradition: a popular, living form, sung

---

[4] *Child Ballads Traditional in the United States*, ed. Bertrand H. Bronson (Library of Congress Music Division Recording Laboratory, n.d.). For contemporary recordings, see: *The Muckle Sangs: Classic Scots Ballads* (Greentrax Records, 1992); *Early Ballads in Ireland 1968–1985*, ed. Tom Munnely and Hugh Shields (CLCS, Trinity College, Dublin, 1985); and Nick Cave and the Bad Seeds, *Murder Ballads* (Mute Records, 1996).

[5] Joseph Addison, *Spectator*, 70 (21 May 1711), 74 (25 May 1711), 75 (7 June 1711).

[6] *Rump: or An Exact Collection of the Choycest Poems and Songs relating to the Late Times* (1662), i. 1.   [7] *Letters*, vii. 179.

on street corners—and it is precisely this literal profile that really defined the ballad in the eighteenth century. Despite its clear stylistic characteristics—iambic and anapaestic quatrains in a rising rhythm—Nathan Bailey's *Universal Etymological English Dictionary* defined a ballad as 'a Song commonly sung up and down the Streets', and Johnson's definition was illustrated with Isaac Watts's remark: '*Ballad*, once signified a solemn and sacred song, as well as trivial, when Solomon's Song was called the *ballad* of *ballads*; but now it is applied to nothing but trifling verse.'[8] Ballads were a popular, indigent, urban form of no fixed cultural abode: derelict and ephemeral.

After Johnson, Percy's guide on the *Reliques* was Shenstone, who was a much more positive, if rather fanciful, commentator on the subject of songs and ballads. He distinguished between the gullible opinions of the common people and the elegance of the man of taste. The populace believed that 'a Song becomes a ballad as it grows in years; as they think an old serpent becomes a Dragon': in other words, it was a creature of legend, fashioned by generations of storytellers and ballad-singers. But Shenstone himself, that delicate flower of Preromanticism and the most tasteful man in the kingdom, trilled, 'I . . . am apt to consider a Ballad as containing some little story'.[9] For him, the ballad was a domestic poetic narrative, rather than a descriptive lyric. The importance of story or narrative—indeed history itself—persisted in Percy's own ballad theories. Ballads remembered the momentous events of common history, and they did so in a way that made it possible for that history to be written. They had all the features of a realist narrative: the setting of scene, the grain of the voice, the claim to veracity.

Nevertheless, in 1765, the year the *Reliques* was published, the ballad was still living as rough as it ever had been: it was defined as 'a song, but now commonly applied to the meaner sort, that are sung in the streets by the vulgar'.[10] If the ballad was no longer

---

[8] Nathan Bailey, *An Universal Etymological English Dictionary*, 9th edn. (1740); Samuel Johnson, *A Dictionary of the English Language* (1755). Johnson also included the verb 'to ballad', and 'ballad-singer': 'one whose employment it is to sing ballads in the streets.'

[9] *Letters*, vii. 94. Shenstone, in an essay, 'On Writing and Books', added: 'THERE is a certain flimziness of poetry, which seems expedient in a song' (*The Works in Verse and Prose of William Shenstone, Esq; Most of which were never before Printed* (1764–9), ii. 155). See Bertrand H. Bronson, *The Ballad as Song* (Berkeley, 1969).

[10] Thomas Dyche, *A New General English Dictionary*, rev. William Pardon (1765).

displaying the simple nobility described by Addison, it was still alarmingly robust, and in its degraded form was coming up from the streets. By nature of their dissolute character and marginal status, ballads embodied and sounded a threat to polite society. They gave a voice to political unrest and the *mobile vulgus*. In 1756, the year in which Percy settled in Easton Maudit, a hundred ballad-singers paraded through the streets of Westminster singing, 'To the block with Newcastle and the Yard Arm with Byng' and 'Sing Tantarara Hang Byng'. Admiral Byng was indeed strung from the gallows.[11] In 1769, thirteen years after this popular demonstration and four years after the publication of the *Reliques*, the *London Magazine* proposed taming the ballad and developing it as an instrument of state propaganda:

I am sure money could not be better employed, and I am certain that no placemen, or pensioners, can be of so much service as a set of well-chosen balladsingers might be. We might have the discontented and turbulent populace sung into quietness and good humour, as froward children are by their nurses.[12]

This is a crucial reinvention in the aftermath of Percy's *Reliques*. The ballad-singer who could rally a lynch mob was reinvented. No longer a political agitator, but a minstrel who would sing soothing lullabies: a nightingale.

The deeply ambiguous status of the ballad meant, therefore, that the *Reliques* was animated by spirits of contrariety: of polite culture and street culture, of historical conservatism and political action; and so Percy's headnotes and footnotes offered a sustained apology for his interest in ballads. They might be anonymous ephemera, but they could also be epic in sentiments. He quoted lines from Rowe's prologue to *Jane Shore*, reminded the reader of Addison's celebration of 'Chevy Chase', recorded the interest shown by Dryden and Dorset, hoped that the current literati would excuse his researches, and employed Sidney, Selden, and Addison (again) for his epigraphs. Concurrently, Percy argued in his dedication that the ballads celebrated his patron, he devoted a book to Shakespearean ballads, and everywhere offered erudite reflections and learned disquisitions on textual cruces. Unfortunately at times

---

[11] John Brewer, *Party Ideology and Popular Politics at the Accession of George III* (Cambridge, 1976), 156.   [12] *London Magazine*, 38 (1769), 580.

he was reminiscent of the Grub Street hack William Wagstaffe, who parodied Richard Bentley by writing a commentary on *Tom Thumb*.[13]

But Percy's nationalist antiquarian approach to cultural heritage did help to defuse the explosive revolutionary politics of ballads. To an extent, Percy's *Reliques* was a conservative tactic to circulate 'ballads of a proper tendency'. Percy tended to avoid any direct confrontation with party politics and defended his ballads in terms of social history, reinforcing his position behind a thicket of antiquarian detail. Moreover, he neutralized the ballads by fixing them on the printed page. The ballads were an object of antiquarian scrutiny, and Percy's use of Selden was shrewd: 'More solid things do not shew the complexion of the times so well as BALLADS and Libels' (ii, p. A4^v). Local and national songs, ballads, and romances were fit objects for antiquarian and editorial scrutiny: exhibits in the cultural museum of Englishness and choice examples of the Gothic temperament. At their best, they were courtly documents that celebrated a Middle Ages of sophistication and culture, a rich feudal society that united the arts and the state in the figure of the minstrel.

Just seven years after the *Reliques*, the transformation of the ballad was complete. In 1772, John Aikin's *Essays on Song-Writing* clearly revealed the impact of the *Reliques* in 'An Essay on Ballads and Pastoral':

THE ballad may be considered as the native species of poetry of this country. It very exactly answers the idea formerly given of original poetry, being the rude uncultivated verse in which the popular tale of the times was recorded. As our ancestors partook of the fierce warlike character of the northern nations, the subjects of their poetry would chiefly consist of the martial exploits of their heroes, and the military events of national history, deeply tinctured with that passion for the marvellous, and that superstitious credulity, which always attend a state of ignorance and barbarism. Many of the antient ballads have been transmitted to the present times, and in them the character of the nation displays itself in striking colours. The boastful history of her victories, the prowess of her favourite kings and captains, and the wonderful adventures of the legendary saint and knight errant, are the topics of the rough rhyme and unadorned narration which was ever the delight of the vulgar, and is now an object of curiosity to the antiquarian and man of taste. As it is

[13] William Wagstaffe, *A Comment upon the History of Tom Thumb* (1711).

not my design to collect pieces of this sort, which is already done in a very elegant manner by Mr. Percy in his *Reliques of antient English poetry*, I shall proceed to consider the ballad more as an artificial than a natural species of composition.[14]

Aikin's selection of modern imitations opened with Percy's Shakespearean pastiche 'The Friar of Orders Gray'. In just a few years the ballad had been completely restored.

It is nevertheless surprising that the model of dangerous and incendiary popular verse of the eighteenth-century city should become the vehicle of an antiquarian rusticophilia and the favoured form of Romantic pastoral. The city was perceived as dangerous and corrupt because traditional hierarchies appeared to be in perpetual crisis, and so perhaps the fear of the older order could be allayed by recasting the ballad-singers' instruments of terror.[15] More interesting, though, is a comment by Michel de Certeau, who asks (in a different context), 'Where are we, outside of learned culture? Or, if you like: does popular culture exist outside the act that suppresses it?'[16] In the case of Percy's *Reliques*, the recognition of the popular tradition occurred simultaneously with his desire not to locate it on a map of present literary culture, but to treat it as a historical space to be filled in. Only once the ballad had been firmly resituated in the past could it be safely considered as a proper mode for the polite poet. This removal was a form of incarceration. The body of popular tradition that was being historically interred had first to be fabricated, and Percy fabricated this body from relics.

The circumscribing of supposedly ancient objects to create a past is of course the activity of the antiquarian, and in fact ballads had already been treated as historical records of past times. Just as literature provided a source for the antiquarian, so did popular broadside ballads. As Albert Friedman has shown, Elizabethan and Jacobean playwrights constantly quoted from popular ballads, and this frequency of allusion meant that post-Restoration editors of earlier literature began to trace these ephemeral sources, some of which were still current. Ballads were the fabric, the very stuff,

---

[14] [John Aikin], *Essays on Song-Writing: with a Collection of such English Songs as are most eminent for Poetical Merit* (n.d. [1772]), 26–8.

[15] Michel de Certeau, *Heterologies: Discourse on the Other*, tr. Brian Massumi (Manchester, 1986), 121.   [16] Ibid. 135.

of sixteenth- and seventeenth-century popular culture. Friedman goes so far as to state that 'From Munday to Nicholas Rowe, broadsides furnished playwrights with plots; broadsides were used to advertise plays; ballad farces rounded out dramatic performances; and the corpus of the pre-Restoration drama is studded with ballad allusions and quotations from ballads.'[17]

Thus, collectors such as John Selden and Samuel Pepys were attracted to the historical significance of ballads, and some of Pepys's most interesting broadsides are early records of oral ephemera in street calls.[18]

> Fine Oranges and Lemmons fair,
>   they are as good as e'er was cut . . .
> Here's Artichokes and Cucumbers
>   Colliflowers fresh and gay. . .
> Have you any old Brass to mend?
>   a Kettle? Skellet? Frying-pan? here . . .
> Will you have any Milk to day? . . .
> Here's honest Codpiece Points and Pins . . .
> Old Sutes and Cloaks, or Taffety? . . .
> I am a Chimney-sweeper Black . . .
> Here's knives to grind, here's knives to grind . . .
> Come buy a Steel, or a Tinder-Box . . .
>   *These are the Cries of* London *Town.*[19]

The voice textualizes the city. It captures the fragments of fleeting songs and turns them into a single experience. These ballads are highly self-reflexive: they are street songs that sing of streets and songs. But the streets they sing of are already in the process of being rusticated by fruits and vegetables from garden and empire, and domesticated by kitchen implements and hardware. The ballads are also oddly anti-oral: speech appears in the text as a ruin, as historical, as an echo of the dead or a shadow of a disappearance. And lastly, such ballads are also territorial: marking the districts and borders of a drift or a flight through the city

---

[17] Albert B. Friedman, *The Ballad Revival: Studies in the Influence of Popular on Sophisticated Poetry* (Chicago, 1961), 65; see also Gwendolyn A. Morgan, 'Percy, the Antiquarians, the Ballad, and the Middle Ages', in Leslie J. Workman and Kathleen Verduin (eds.), *Medievalism in England II*, Studies in Medievalism VII (Cambridge, 1996), 22–32.

[18] 'A Merry Nevv Catch of All Trades', *The Pepys Ballads*, ed. W. G. Day (Cambridge, 1987), i. 164.

[19] 'The City Rambler: or, The Merry Cries of London Town', *Pepys Ballads*, iv. 334.

and simultaneously colonizing them under a single, titled experience: 'These are the Cries of London Town.' The danger of the city is contained.

Interestingly, the popular ballad had already recognized its status as a maverick cultural source and was often marketed as ancient, traditional poetry at the popular as well as the sophisticated level. Even street ballads were sold as 'Ancient', and *A Collection of Old Ballads* (1723–5), the ballad history of Great Britain on which Percy relied heavily, provided balladmongers with excellent copy for broadsides, giving texts, illustrations, and even historical introductions.[20] There was a profitable market for antiquarian ballads.

Despite this, Flemming Andersen argues that most later eighteenth- and early nineteenth-century collections of ballads in the British Isles were Scottish—over half of the Child ballads are in Scottish versions only: 'Child's monumental collection, which has been the single most influential source for our concept of the ballad genre, reflects a primarily Scottish tradition.'[21] Examples of traditional English balladry in the eighteenth century, as opposed to the printed broadside tradition, are actually very scarce: the archive, substantially arising from Percy's *Reliques*, is predominantly of literate ballads. Unlike Walter Scott and James Hogg at the beginning of the nineteenth century, or Sabine Baring-Gould at the end, Percy did not gather ballads from the mouths or memories of ballad-singers: he relied on printed examples. Of the genuine oral tradition, with tunes, virtually nothing remains until the nineteenth-century collections of Baring-Gould and Cecil Sharp. And so inevitably, according to Andersen, the *Reliques* is 'among the many ballad collections not to be trusted as documents of the oral tradition'.[22]

Andersen does indicate that the success of the *Reliques* elicited oral ballads which were sent to Percy (Child reckons there to be thirty-three of these extant), and although again most of these came from Scotland, there were seven collected and transcribed

---

[20] Dianne Dugaw, 'The Popular Marketing of "Old Ballads": The Ballad Revival and Eighteenth-Century Antiquarianism Reconsidered', *ECS* 21 (1987), 71–90.

[21] Flemming G. Andersen, 'Oral Tradition in England in the Eighteenth Century: "Lord Lovel" (Child No. 75A)', in Flemming G. Andersen, Otto Holzapfel, and Thomas Pettitt (eds.), *The Ballad as Narrative: Studies in the Ballad Traditions of England, Scotland, Germany and Denmark* (Odense, 1982), 59.   [22] Ibid. 61.

from south of the Tyne, 'the sole reliable representatives of the southern English ballad tradition in the eighteenth century'.[23] Andersen may be right to suggest that it is fortunate Percy did not produce a fourth volume of the *Reliques*, in which case these transcriptions might have met the same fate as Shakespeare's foul papers, lost in the printing process, but it may be that the sudden discovery of this living oral tradition (confirming that he was actually right about his minstrels) contributed to Percy's continuing researches. On the other hand, Andersen concludes that the narrative technique in 'Lord Lovel', an oral ballad, is not qualitatively different from the technique of a printed broadside ballad like 'Lord Thomas and Fair Ellinor' (which ironically seems less sophisticated): 'As both kinds of balladry can be seen to employ the simple, popular style, the formal distinction between broadside ballads and traditional ballads is often extremely difficult to uphold.'[24] Suffice to say that in eighteenth-century England, the oral tradition of ballad-singing was alive and well, and is adequately represented by the broadsides that remain.

As I will argue below, Percy's lack of interest in collecting the living tradition may well have been influenced by his response to James Macpherson's Ossianic epics, which elided and segued oral performances into edited versions. Also, Percy did refer polemically to the oral tradition in developing his figure of the ancient English minstrel. But it is crucial to his work, and furthermore to the subsequent reception and development of the ballad tradition, that he positioned himself as a historian treating a historical phenomenon, most traceable in artefacts. Anonymous texts had enough confused boundaries without being allowed to drift and melt away along the stream of song.

For eighteenth-century antiquarians, then, ballads were perhaps more immediately significant for their material status as physical

---

[23] Ibid. 62. Percy's transcripts were from the Revd P. Parsons of Wye, in Kent, who in three packets (7 Apr. 1770, 22 May 1770, and 19 Apr. 1775) sent eighteen songs (mostly untitled): [Chorus], [Like Hermit poor in Pensive place obscure], [Oh when I was a Maid, a Maid], [There was a Lady fine and gay] (two versions), [The Unfortunate Love of a Lancashire Gentleman], 'Lord Randall' (two versions), 'Long Longkin', 'Ancient Madrigal', [The Maid freed from the Gallows], [A Newmarket Song], 'Lady Ouncibell' (two versions), [The Twa Sisters] (two versions), [Willie o Winsbury], 'Sweet William': see Houghton, bMS Eng. 893 (129A–I). Parsons claimed that some were 'taken down from the mouth of the Spinning Wheel'.

[24] Andersen, 'Oral Tradition', 70.

sources than for their contemporary popularity or subject matter. They were often unique artefacts in their own right; in any case, they were better than nothing. Even Johnson lamented the loss of ancient writings in *The Idler*, although he was considerably more aghast that so much time had been frittered away in antiquarian scholarship than he was in awe at the ancient knowledge that had been lost: 'Had all the writings of the ancients been faithfully delivered down from age to age, had the Alexandrian library been spared, and the Palatine repositories remained unimpaired, how much might we have known of which we are now doomed to be ignorant; how many laborious enquiries, and dark conjectures, how many collations of broken hints and mutilated passages might have been spared.'[25] The irony was that, no matter how much or how little survived, a great deal of ink would be spilt by antiquarians on these texts.

'DEFRAUDED PYES'[26]

Antiquarianism arose in the late Renaissance as an idea that the lost classical civilization could be recovered by a systematic retrieval of all the relics of the past. As is implied in Francis Bacon's *Dignity and Advancement of Learning*, it is a discipline of material objects, province and provenance, and collections and cabinets. Bacon distinguished 'Antiquities' from 'Memorials' and 'Perfect Histories' as 'history defaced or some remnants of history which have casually escaped the shipwreck of time'.[27] The antiquarian was motivated by nostalgia for the past and reverence for the embodiment of the past in artefacts: for origin and presence, for nation and narration. From the formation of the Society of Antiquaries in about 1570, antiquarians supplemented the work

---

[25] Samuel Johnson, *The Idler and The Adventurer*, ed. W. J. Bate, John M. Bullitt, and L. F. Powell (New Haven, 1963), *Idler* 66: 'Loss of ancient writings', ii. 205. He makes a similar comment on Shakespearean scholarship (*Johnson–Steevens–Malone*: Samuel Johnson, George Steevens, and Edmond Malone, *The Plays of William Shakespeare*, ed. Nick Groom (1995), i. 49).

[26] *Dunciad Variorum*, I. 136 (ed. Sutherland, 80).

[27] *The Works of Francis Bacon*, ed. James Spedding, Robert Lesley Ellis, and Douglas Denon Heath (1858), iv. 303. Percy alluded to Bacon's definition in *Northern Antiquities* (1770), describing the use to the antiquarian of 'those old *Reliques* of poetry, which have escaped the shipwreck of time' (i. 56).

of historians, stimulated political theorists, and inspired connoisseurs.[28] William Camden's *Britannia*, published in 1586, inaugurated the practice. Camden's work was profoundly nationalistic, and immensely learned. *Britannia* laid the foundations of a new patriotism. It ranged from topography to philology, developed a Saxon myth of origins in opposition to legendary history, and ultimately redefined the identity of Great Britain. Through the subsequent work of Henry Spelman, John Selden, Robert Cotton, and John Speed, a new post-Renaissance historical and constitutional identity was created for the country: the Gothic spirit of liberty and freedom, a new myth of national origins. Inevitably, James I suppressed the Society, and Charles I restricted access to the monumental resources of Cotton's library, where readers seemed able to challenge any decree in the land by citing historical precedent. The discipline was obliged to reassess itself.

It did so by rusticating its political agenda. During the English Civil War, antiquarianism wove itself more subtly and deeply into the fabric of national identity, gradually aestheticizing rural life and objectifying the peasant classes, and recording the survival of an elusive past, which remained most legible in the material evidence of monuments built against history and decay: funerary memorials. As Susan Stewart puts it, 'In order to awaken the dead, the antiquarian must first manage to kill them.'[29] Stewart goes on to suggest a Lacanian reading of this symbolic murder as the eternalization of desire. But, psychoanalysis aside, this comment is remarkably significant for Percy and his refusal of the living ballad tradition, and indeed the whole morbid atmosphere that pervades antiquarianism. William Dugdale's copiously illustrated works recording church memorials enabled a literal rebuilding of the country's monuments after the ravages of the Revolution: in one sense, the country became a vast necropolis. John Aubrey, on the other hand, led a revival in the archaeology of pre-Christian sites and collected local folklore in order to plot popular traditions and document the lives of the dead—in his case, history was incapable of remaining in the past and seemed to flourish everywhere. Unsurprisingly, Sir Thomas Browne, the last of these great

[28] Arnaldo Momigliano, 'Ancient History and the Antiquarian', *Studies in Historiography* (1966), 5.
[29] Susan Stewart, *On Longing: Narratives of the Miniature, the Gigantic, the Souvenir, the Collection* (Durham, NC, 1993), 143.

polymaths, wrote his famous *Hydriotaphia* (1658) on urn burial and funeral practices, and provided Neoplatonic meditations among the historical and spiritual ruins of the country. The first archaeological treatise in English literally digs up the dead.

Antiquarianism in the eighteenth century became a favourite pastime of the vernacular connoisseur with the revision and translation into English of Camden's epoch-making *Britannia* in 1695, and in 1718, the Society of Antiquaries was reconvened. Researchers like William Stukeley continued the tradition of scientific archaeology in his work on Stonehenge and Avebury, and also the enthusiasm for mysterious origins in his fascination with the Druids. Antiquarianism was still distinguished by its commitment to the Matter of Britain, its reworking and reinvention of myth in the guise of empirical historical enquiry. For example, the antiquarian Thomas Hearne suggested that *Tom Thumb* was based on 'King Edgar's dwarf': 'What makes me think *Tom Thumb* is founded upon history, is the method of those times of turning true history into little pretty stories, of which we have many instances, one of which is Guy of Warwick, which however corrupted and blended with fabulous accounts, is however in the main very true, as may appear from *Girardus Cornubiensis* that I printed at the end of the *Chronicle of Dunstaple*.'[30] It is almost as if Shenstone had read Hearne: for both, the ephemeral popular literature of ballads and chapbooks is characterized by the authenticating glimmer of some 'little pretty story', which, it is concluded, has a recoverable source and an origin. Moreover, like Percy, Hearne's cry is '*ad fontes*! [to the sources!]'. He does not recognize that he too is turning 'true history'—the survival of a chapbook—into 'little pretty stories' of antiquarian speculation.

Hearne had come across *Tom Thumb* in a collection of 'a great many of . . . little historical diverting Pamphletts, now grown wonderful scarce, . . . one of which is *The History of Tom Thumb*', bequeathed to the Bodleian Library by Robert Burton (author of *The Anatomy of Melancholy*) in 1640.[31] Alongside the nation's acceptance of the Cottonian and Harleian libraries, there was a growing interest in ephemeral collections. Hearne again:

[30] Thomas Hearne, *The Remains of Thomas Hearne: Reliquiæ Hearnianæ*, ed. John Buchanan-Brown (Carbondale, Ill., 1966), 424–5 (22 May 1734).
[31] Ibid. 410 (28 Jan. 1734).

'The late Earl of Dorset had a very large Collection of Old Ballads, which he used oftentimes to read, with very great Delight, much admiring the Simplicity and Nakedness of the Style; and yet he was a Man of admirable Sense and Understanding. I heard the late Dean of Xt Church, Dr. Aldrich say, the last time I was with him, that he would give a good Sum of Money for a Collection of such Ballads, whenever he could meet with one.'[32]

Good sums of money certainly did change hands and there was a market for such relics, but more nefarious dealings were not uncommon. Collectors like John Tradescant and Elias Ashmole in the seventeenth century were notorious for being extremely acquisitive and incessantly competitive, and even a comparatively mild collector like Samuel Pepys kept the archive of antique broadside ballads lent to him by John Selden, eventually absorbing it into his own collection. Augustan collectors were just as avid. They were connoisseurs like Francis Woodward and Horace Walpole, vying with each other to fill their cabinets with rarities and curiosities: antiquities, books, objets d'art, secular relics (clothing, effects, locks of hair), fossils, stones. John Tradescant's 'Ark' included preserved animals (a salamander, a goose hatched out of a tree, a squirrel that looked like a fish), petrifications (an ape's head, human flesh, a cheese), the hands of mermaids and mummies, a splinter from the Cross, precious stones, coins, perspective pictures; while Hans Sloane specialized in human oddities—horns, gallstones, and the like. They particularly coveted objects which had been bathed in the radiance of historical personages or great events, which were unique, or simply whose only quality might be that they were old—and these values of the antiquarian aesthetic crept into Percy's *Reliques*.

Antiquarians were, of course, mercilessly satirized—most famously in the *Memoirs of the Extraordinary Life, Works, and Discoveries of Martinus Scriblerus* (1741, written *c.*1713–14), but also in skits like 'Memoirs of a Sad Dog' (1770) by Thomas Chatterton. In *Martinus Scriblerus*, Dr Cornelius resolves to cradle the infant Martinus in a shield in imitation of Hercules, specifically in an antique buckler (on which he has written a dissertation), 'a most inestimable Relick'. When the baby is borne along, Dr Cornelius begins his peroration: 'Behold then my Child,

[32] Ibid. 13 (18 June 1711).

but first behold the Shield: Behold this Rust,—or rather let me call it this precious Ærugo,—behold this beautiful Varnish of Time,—this venerable Verdure of so many Ages—'. But in preparing Martinus' martial crib, the maid has, of course, polished away all the rust, revealing the antique shield to be nothing but a sconce with the nozzle broken off.[33] Interestingly, Percy, who adored the linguistic rust of the Folio MS, was involved in the Scriblerian gulling of a collector of antiquarian curios with a vernacular relic. He helped to trick John Scott Hylton into believing that a souvenir tobacco-stopper was carved from the wood of a mulberry tree planted by Shakespeare.[34] Hylton attempted to buy what wood remained of the tree before he discovered he had been duped. What is surprising is that Hylton reckoned he could obtain so much Shakespearean wood. The sacred mulberry tree had been chopped down in 1756 by the cantankerous owner of Shakespeare's house at New Place (he later demolished the building to discourage sightseers; they continued to visit in order to contemplate the hole in the ground), and there was in fact a lively market in bardolatrous relics carved from the timber—caskets, tea caddies, inkstands, toothpick cases, goblets, sugar tongs, snuffboxes, and tobacco-stoppers. This celebration of Shakespeare suggests the extent to which antiquarianism had shifted from the cultivation of ancient artefacts to a souvenir trade in indigenous curios.

As is demonstrated in these parodies, the antique object becomes merely a signifier of the past. It has no functional value, even when it purports to: it is exclusively mythological.[35] These objects receive their meaning in relationship to other collected objects. They are contained within a collection which, like all collections, articulates the taxonomic principle of resemblance

[33] Charles Kerby-Miller (ed.), *Memoirs of the Extraordinary Life, Works, and Discoveries of Martinus Scriblerus* (Oxford, 1988), 102–4. Shenstone again, 'Of Men and Manners': 'TO be entirely engrossed by antiquity, and as it were eaten up with rust, is a bad compliment to the present age' (*Works*, ii. 189).

[34] 'The Tobacco-stopper Plot': *Letters*, vii. 194–9, and Jean Marie O'Meara, 'Thomas Percy and the Making of the *Reliques of Ancient English Poetry*', Ph.D. thesis (Berkeley, 1990), 62–9. Shenstone, in an essay on 'Taste', remarked archly, 'THERE is a kind of counter-taste, founded on surprize and curiosity, which maintains a sort of rivalship with the true; and may be expressed by the name Concetto [thought, concept]. Such is the fondness of some persons for a knife-hast made from the royal-oak, or a tobacco-stopper from a mulberry tree of Shakespear's own planting. It gratifies an empty curiosity' (*Works*, ii. 275).

[35] Jean Baudrillard, *The System of Objects*, tr. James Benedict (1996), 74.

and difference, and equates knowledge with accumulation, and aesthetic value with monetary value: 'By analogy, correspondence and resemblance, the collection reconstituted the world, placing it within the publicly visible power of its owner.'[36] The objects in a collection form a series, or historical *œuvre*—in a sense a single work. And the author of this work, whose signature laces through the collection as an individual and discriminating taste, is the antiquarian connoisseur. The collection, as Stewart says, 'speaks to the possessor's capacity for otherness: it is the possessor, not the souvenir, which is ultimately the curiosity.'[37]

In this way, the curiosities in a connoisseur's cabinet are re-inscribed. They are taken from their historical context and function first as a sign of their own survival. The physical presence of an exotic object radiates an aura of authenticity, an authenticity which is founded on itself. 'The antique object thus presents itself as a myth of origins', and in doing so validates the creative genius of the collector who has authored its place within a collection.[38] Baudrillard and Stewart suggest that this imaginary context of origin is a projection of the possessor's childhood, though it may be ideological, restoring class relations.[39] Nevertheless, it is clear that the imaginary context of origin, like the collection itself, is a narrative trajectory. It tells a tale of history in order to disguise the nature of its acquisition. It is a way of containing, ordering, and thereby controlling the remains of the past, and ultimately the present. It enforces boundaries.[40]

The antiques that narrate the greatest story ever told are, of course, holy relics, and Percy, as a Protestant clergyman, was well aware of the sacred reverberations of his chosen title: *Reliques*. Relics are splinters of the absolute reality: they 'enshrine the identity of God'—in fact, the word shrine (Latin: *scrinium*) originally meant a reliquary chest, and the Roman Catholic altar is 'a tomb containing the relics of saints' (*sepulchrum continens reliquas sanctorum*).[41] Percy's *Reliques*, if they were not exactly

---

[36] John Brewer, *The Pleasures of the Imagination: English Culture in the Eighteenth Century* (1997), 254. The Society of Dilettanti was established in 1734, in which the study of virtu became associated with sexual licence and debauchery: 'promiscuity' of a different sort from that practised by Percy (see below).

[37] Stewart, *On Longing*, 148.   [38] Baudrillard, *The System of Objects*, 76.

[39] Stewart, *On Longing*, 150; Baudrillard, *The System of Objects*, 75 n.

[40] Stewart, *On Longing*, 159.

[41] Baudrillard, *The System of Objects*, 79 n.; David Sox, *Relics and Shrines* (1985), 28, 8.

fragments of the True Cross, at least unfolded the word of minstrels. His sources were embodied as material objects, with documented provenance, and were gathered in a collection (albeit a slightly chaotic one), which perhaps should have more properly been called 'Percy's *Reliquary* of Ancient English Poetry'. The pieces were literally arranged in 'series' articulating historical theories of the origin of poetry, ethnic English culture, and national borders. And, like sacred relics which removed the dead from the context of the grave, they suppressed the sepulchral concerns of the early antiquaries and revived the songs of old England. Most significantly, the antiquarian dynamic behind Percy's collection clarifies his new definition of authorship in the *Reliques*.

The authenticity of manuscript sources in general and the Folio MS in particular may be understood in terms of antiquarian collecting. They have survived and their narrative of survival is recounted by their provenance, they have a physical presence and an aura of authenticity in their trace of human gesture; they constitute a myth of origins. Like archaeological discoveries manuscripts were at the same time a 'symbol and proof of what happened'.[42] Moreover, when unique manuscripts are published they become fixed and contained within print, and are bound within an ideology of replication, uniformity, and reproducibility. Within the antiquarian tradition, the position of manuscripts is explained by their precarious quality of uniqueness: uniqueness defines the manuscript. Artefacts, whether buildings or relics, were the foundations of antiquarianism, and so, as Ian Haywood shows, manuscripts were considered good archaeological evidence. They became the empirical unit of historical knowledge.[43] Manuscripts had an aura and an authority, and were invested with noumen—James Boswell fell to his knees before what he believed to be genuine Shakespeare manuscripts.[44]

The antiquarian pressure brought to bear on ancient texts

---

[42] Momigliano, 'Ancient History', 14.

[43] Ian Haywood, *The Making of History: A Study of the Literary Forgeries of James Macpherson and Thomas Chatterton in Relation to Eighteenth-Century Ideas of History and Fiction* (1986), 19–24.

[44] *The Confessions of William Henry Ireland. Containing the Particulars of his Fabrication of the Shakspeare Manuscripts; together with Anecdotes and Opinions (hitherto unpublished) of many Distinguished Persons in the Literary, Political, and Theatrical World* (1805), 96.

horrified contemporaries, and as Arthur Johnston suggests, mid-century antiquarianism was directed against the style of Thomas Hearne's ponderous medieval editions.[45] Shenstone took fright at Walpole's *Anecdotes of Painting in England* (1762): 'I never knew so much Genius as Walpole's in such a Bigot to Antiquity—For, tho I call *you* an Antiquarian, yet you are not near so great a Bigot—He is extremely inaccurate in his Language, tho he says it was corrected by Gray.'[46] Percy accepted the backhanded compliment, and described the rhymes of Robert of Gloucester, edited by Hearne in 1724, to Shenstone as 'to the last degree mean and contemptible'; simply 'frightful'.[47] Should things that had no merit but their antiquity deserve to be published in exact versions that faithfully reproduced a crude or imperfect text?

Manuscripts also bore upon the seventeenth- and eighteenth-century controversy regarding the value of historical evidence, which led to a rise in the use of non-literary sources, such as coins:

> The Medal, faithful to its charge of fame,
> Thro' climes and ages bears each form and name:
> In one short view subjected to your eye
> Gods, Emp'rors, Heroes, Sages, Beauties, lie.
> With sharpen'd sight pale Antiquaries pore,
> Th' inscription value, but the rust adore;
> This the blue varnish, that the green endears,
> The sacred rust of twice ten hundred years![48]

Addison, in his third Dialogue 'Upon the Usefulness of Ancient Medals', drew specific attention to the physical characteristics of Greek and Latin medals: antiquaries did not merely discover the age of a coin by iconographic scholarship, but would engage all their senses in identifying its peculiarities. They would stroke the medals, strike the metal to hear it ring, even smell it, and 'I have seen an Antiquary lick an old Coin among other trials, to distinguish the age of it by its taste . . . when I laught at him for it, he told me with a great deal of vehemence, there was as much difference between the relish of ancient and modern brass,

---

[45] Arthur Johnston, *Enchanted Ground: The Study of Medieval Romance in the Eighteenth Century* (1964), 24; Charlotte Brewer, *Editing* Piers Plowman: *The Evolution of the Text* (Cambridge, 1996), 22.   [46] *Letters*, vii. 146.

[47] Ibid. 163.

[48] 'To Mr. Addison, Occasioned by his Dialogues on Medals', ll. 31–8, in *Poems of Pope*, vi: *Minor Poems*, ed. Norman Ault and John Butt (1964), 203.

as between an apple and a turnep.'[49] Indeed, Bailey mentions currency three times in defining an antiquary: 'one that is well skill'd in, or applies himself to the Study of Antiquity, or ancient Medals and Coins, in order to the Explanation of the Motto's upon Medals, the Inscriptions upon Statues, &c.' Incidentally, the excitement provoked in the eighteenth century by antique coinage marks a shift in antiquarian sensibility from the previous century's necrography, from the gruesome horrors of civil war to a new economic society.

The antiquarian interest in manuscripts was also, as we will see, a challenge to the mainstream ideological supremacy of print. Every manuscript was a unique artefact, laboriously transcribed in a certain place in a certain style, clearly encoding moments of production within its physical state. The distinctive features of print—mass-produced multiplication and uniformity—were not the concerns of scribes. For this reason, the antiquarian interest in manuscripts emphasized a deliberate obscurity of sources, and by accrediting such manuscripts, scholarship was made exclusive to those who owned or had access to or simply could decipher such exotic evidence. Private ownership of a manuscript meant monopoly scholarship. There was also a class dimension to this exclusivity. John Warburton famously lost a pile of manuscripts which his cook used up lining pie dishes, James Macpherson claimed to have saved Ossian's manuscripts from the scissors of tailors, and Percy's own Folio MS was of course a firelighter before it was a literary find.[50] One class's rubbish was another class's wealth.

The *Reliques* exhibits all these (sometimes contradictory) characteristics of ballads and of literary antiquarianism, and these elements are clearly articulated in Percy's description of his archetype, the Folio MS, quoted at the beginning of this chapter. The Folio MS, almost abject in its physical state, is clearly an antiquarian relic. Its broken leaves dramatize the rescue of ancient English poetry from the ashes, from women, from the lower classes, from the domestic space, and from the young parson Thomas Percy himself. It is moreover a decomposing original

---

[49] *The Works of the Right Honourable Joseph Addison, Esq.* (1721), i. 527.

[50] See Percy's remark to John Pinkerton modestly dismissing his work: 'Whatever slight attempts in the "Belles Lettres," &c. have escaped the fire and pastry-cook, are peacably slumbering in my closet in Northamptonshire' (*Letters*, viii. 41).

from which one can make only phantasmal copies. As the original rots, transcripts or printed copies become copies without an exemplar, like stepchildren. In other words, the Folio MS is a fallen text. The accuracy of its transcripts seemed increasingly to be emphasized in difference and deviation from the original rather than in fidelity.[51] But a national literature was about to rise from the dust of history and the furnace of revolution. The Folio MS was in many ways the most significant source used for the *Reliques*: it provided the impetus to publish, gave Percy sole access to many unique verses, and whetted the appetites of Shenstone and Johnson, and even the Dodsleys. Indeed a whole network of scholars witnessed Percy flourishing this rarity, this relic, although precious few were allowed to see it, let alone read it. He claimed in his preface to the *Reliques* that it was his primary source for the collection: 'This manuscript was shown to several learned and ingenious friends, who thought the contents too curious to be consigned to oblivion, and importuned the possessor to select some of them, and give them to the press' (i, p. xi). It was a miraculous relic, enumerating magic and wonder, with alchemical powers to transform Percy's life and work, and he fearfully admitted his reverence of it.

With the exception of its dramatic rescue, the history of the Folio MS is brief and unprepossessing. Percy suggested that it was compiled about the middle of the seventeenth century and once owned by Thomas Blount, author of *Jocular Tenures* (1679), who had 'a remarkable Fondness for these old things'. Blount's library was sold by a descendant to Humphrey Pitt, who gave it to his nephew Robert Binnel: 'Mr. Binnel accordingly had all the printed Books; but this MS., which was among them, was neglected and left behind at Mr. Pitt's House, where it lay for many years.' It has possibly spurious associations with an earlier reader, who apparently perused the manuscript a few years before Percy came to it, and with another manuscript, again a seventeenth-century commonplace book 'found in the same basket'.[52] The Folio MS

---

[51] Derrida, 'Cartouches', in *The Truth in Painting*, 216–20.

[52] See Leslie Shepard, 'The Finding of the Percy Folio MS: A Claim of Prior Discovery', *NQ* 212 (1967), 415–16. Armagh Public Library has a 17th-century commonplace book (MS G V 21) which might once have belonged to Percy. An unidentified owner has noted on the cover, 'This book was found in the same basket with the celebrated MSS from which the principal writing of the *Reliques* of ancient English Poetry was extracted.'

(now in the British Library, Additional MS 27879) is a long, lean folio of some 500 pages, containing seventeen romances, twenty-four metrical histories, about a hundred miscellaneous songs, some broadside ballads, and forty-five of what Child described as 'popular ballads'.[53]

What Percy did with this unparalleled source will be described in detail in Chapter 4. In order to edit the Folio MS, he had to assign an author, or rather an authorship. How he managed this will be explained in the next chapter, which considers the context of Ossianic poetry and its relevance to Percy's *Reliques*. But before we examine the making of the *Reliques*, we should explore its remarkable contents.

'A STRANGE COLLECTION OF TRASH'[54]

Percy worked for five years on the ballads that were to fill the three volumes of the *Reliques*—and yet he barely mentions the content of the pieces in his correspondence, research notes, or even in his printed introductions and headnotes. He is almost entirely distracted by authors and literary context, by names (of legendary and historical personages), verifiable dates, identifiable places, substantiable events, and circumstantial details: whatever internal and external evidence there might be to authenticate and date the texts—and he succeeds in distracting the reader also. But Percy's *Reliques* is haunted by the contents of its ballads, which act as an imaginary or phantasmic force animating the body of his scholarship. And though these contents are barely acknowledged (Percy usually dismisses the ballads defensively as mere 'trash'), they do occasionally flash into view as brash bodies, not as spectres. In a letter to his close friend Richard Farmer, Percy wrote: 'Dear Farmer, I haunt you upon Paper like your Evil Genius; and break in upon your Philosophical and Tutorial persuits with my old ballads; as Punch interrupts the most solemn scenes of the puppet-show with his impertinent ribaldry.'[55] The ballads were carnivalesque and bawdy, grotesque and violent; rude challenges to the traditional pomp of culture.

[53] Davis (1981), 76.
[54] Letter to Birch describing the *Reliques*, 2 Feb. 1765 (*Illustrations*, vii. 577).
[55] *Letters*, ii. 66.

Percy declares in his preface, 'such specimens of ancient poetry have been selected as either shew the gradation of our language, exhibit the progress of popular opinions, display the peculiar manners and customs of former ages, or throw light on our earliest classical poets' (i, p. ix). As is demonstrated in the following chapters, Percy focused his energies on irrefutably establishing popular (printed) ballads as a crucial ratification of English cultural identity. In doing so, he drew attention away from the material of the ballad-singers and towards the treatment of ballads as historical corroboration and documentary evidence; traces and exemplars of an authenticating medium of transmission. But what strikes the modern reader is the sensational content of the *Reliques*. The pieces are excessively violent and brutal. It seems today that whatever textual changes Percy introduced and however many antiquarian protestations he made, his literary-historical argument was in danger of being completely obliterated by the obsessive and insistent themes of sex and death. Yet the literary-antiquarian method was secure enough for Percy to make his readers (and himself) oblivious to the disturbing nature of his material. In fact, as the following reading shows, the lewd themes of the ballads—rape, pillage, and carnage—served to support the sobriety of textual criticism and antiquarian research of Percy's method.

The structure of the *Reliques* is deceptively straightforward—three volumes of three books or series each—and the order of pieces is fairly coherent, if lively and often eccentric.[56] Volume i contains antique martial and magical ballads, a book of Shakespeare ballads, Percy–Douglas border conflicts, and love songs from the seventeenth century to the present (indeed each volume concludes with 'a few modern attempts in the same kind of writing', imitations of traditional ballads and popular songs) (i, p. x). Volume ii shows '*the gradual changes of the* ENGLISH *Language thro' a succession of* FIVE HUNDRED *years*', in three chronological sequences: 1265–1550, 1550–1603, 1603–86 (ii, p. 5). The volume concludes with six mad songs and again

---

[56] Vartin overstates the case when he claims that 'A tight chronological sequence development, combined with skilfully contrived connecting prefaces, demands that the reader [of the *Reliques*] proceed in order and not skip ballads at random' (Vartin, 18).

some modern examples. The third volume is headed 'Ballads on King Arthur, &c.' and introduced as *'chiefly devoted to Romantic Subjects'*: Arthurian ballads, adulterous tales, gruesome accounts of thwarted and fatal love affairs in counterpoint with short merry love songs, four songs on fairies and witches, and finally modern love songs (iii, p. i).[57] Within this overall structure lyrics are 'intermingled' among the weightier pieces, there are frequently short runs of related ballads on subjects such as the Reformation, or heroes such as Fair Rosamond, and Scottish pieces are 'interspersed' throughout each volume (i, p. x).

RELIQUES OF ANCIENT ENGLISH POETRY: CONSISTING OF *Old Heroic* BALLADS, SONGS, *and other* PIECES *of our earlier* POETS, *(Chiefly of the* LYRIC *kind.) Together with some few of later Date* commences with a dedication to the Countess of Northumberland that reassures the reader of the nobility of the project:

By such Bards, MADAM, as I am now introducing to your presence, was the infancy of genius nurtured and advanced, by such were the minds of unlettered warriors softened and enlarged, by such was the memory of illustrious actions preserved and propagated, by such were the heroic deeds of the Earls of NORTHUMBERLAND sung at festivals in the hall of ALNWICK: and those songs, which the bounty of your ancestors rewarded, now return to your LADYSHIP by a kind of hereditary right. (i, p. vii)

To support this pedigree, Percy cited critics such as Addison, Dryden, Dorset, and Selden, listed his major sources, and thanked Shenstone, Johnson, Farmer, and many others: 'The NAMES of so many men of learning and character the Editor hopes will serve as an amulet to guard him from every unfavourable censure, for having bestowed any attention on a parcel of OLD BALLADS' (i, p. xiii–xiv).

As Stephen Vartin has shown, Percy's headnotes cite an impressive range of sources: not only the Folio MS, but a dozen or so printed books: Thomas Deloney's *Garden of Goodwill* (1586), Richard Johnson's *The Crown Garland of Golden Roses* (1612) and *The Golden Garland of Princely Delights* (1620), Richard Edwards's *The Paradice of Dainty Deuises* (1576), Nicholas Ling's *England's Helicon* (1600 and 1614), Thomas D'Urfey's *Wit and Mirth, or Pills to Purge Melancholy* (1698–1714, reprinted 1719–20), and

---

[57] Plan based on Vartin, 96–7.

Allan Ramsay's *Tea-Table Miscellany* (1723) and *The Ever Green* (1724).[58] He also used William Warner's *Albion's England* (1602), Thomas Deloney's *Strange Histories* (1607), *Davidson's Poems* (1621), *Wit Restor'd* (1658; reprinted as *Wit and Drollery*, 1682), Dryden's *Miscellany Poems* (1684–1708), *The Hive* (1721), *A Collection of Old Ballads* (1723–5), *The Vocal Miscellany* (1734), Elizabeth Cooper's *The Muses Library* (1737), and Edward Capell's *Prolusions* (1760).[59] In addition to these sources, Percy examined Anthony à Wood's collection of ballads in the Ashmolean Library, the holdings of the Antiquarian Society, the Harleian Collection, and 'one large folio volume which was lent by a lady' (Ballard's Collection); he read poets from the fifteenth to the seventeenth centuries, Elizabethan, Jacobean, Caroline, and Restoration playwrights, and hunted through miscellanies; and he received verses collected by correspondents (especially Scottish pieces sent by David Dalrymple, Lord Hailes), and bought bales of street broadsides (i, p. xii).

Percy followed his prefatory remarks in the *Reliques* with 'An Essay on the Ancient English Minstrels', confirming the noble pedigree of the minstrels. They were held in such respect and reverence by the Saxons that King Alfred could disguise himself as a minstrel in order to infiltrate the invading Danish camp. Their status had gradually decayed, however: 'the Minstrels continued down to the reign of Elizabeth; in whose time they had lost much of their dignity, and were sinking into contempt and neglect. Yet still they sustained a character far superior to any thing we can conceive at present of the singers of old ballads' (i, p. xix). By comparing the old minstrel ballads with printed broadsides, Percy argued that the North was the last region of the country to be civilized: the former 'are in the northern dialect, abound with antique words and phrases, are extremely incorrect, and run into the utmost licence of metre; they have also a romantic wildness, and are in the true spirit of chivalry', whereas the latter are more regular and southern in dialect (i, p. xxii).

So to the ballads themselves. The first encountered is 'The Ancient Ballad of Chevy-Chase'. Percy quotes Sidney's praise— 'I never heard the old song of Percie and Douglas, that I found not my heart moved more than with a trumpet'—and claims that he

[58] Ibid. 55.   [59] Ibid. 45–57; Davis (1981), 73.

has discovered the original version, '*so evil-aparelled in the rugged garb of antiquity*' (i, [p. xxviii]; i. 2). The ballad describes a hunting incident in which a bellicose dispute swiftly escalates into a bloody battle. Limbs are hacked off, the dead and dying are mercilessly trampled, and both the lords Douglas and Percy are slain. 'Chevy-Chase' is followed by 'The Battle of Otterbourne'. After some initial verbal baiting and bullying threats (reminiscent of flyting), a Percy (Hotspur) and a Douglas are fighting again. They meet on the battlefield, encased in armour:

> The Percye and the Douglas mette,
>   That ether of other was faine,
> The swapped together, whille that they swatte,
>   With swoards of ffyne Collayne;
>
> Tyll the bloode from the bassonets ranne,
>   As the rocke doth in the rayne.
> Yeld thee to me, said the Dowglàs,
>   Or else thowe shalte be slayne. (i. 28, ll. 145–52)

They batter away at each other, their helmets cave in, and another Douglas is slain by another Percy.

The third ballad in the *Reliques* is a Scottish interlude, 'The Jew's Daughter': a 'blood libel' on Jewish infanticide based on the martyrdom of Little St Hugh of Lincoln. The nameless Jew's daughter entices the young Hew into her lair with the erotic promise of an apple, then stabs him and vampirically drains his blood. She 'drest him like a swine' (i. 33, l. 22), rolls him 'in a cake of lead' (i. 34, l. 25), and throws his corpse down a well. The little boy calls out to his mother:

> The lead is wondrous heavy, mither,
>   The well is wondrous deip,
> A keen pen-knife sticks in my hert,
>   A word I dounae speik. (i. 34, ll. 45–8)

Finally among this opening quartet is a legendary tale, 'Sir Cauline'. The lovesick Sir Cauline fights a 'A furyous wight and fell', for the princess Christabelle (i. 40, l. 87). Cauline chops off the hand of the 'Eldridge knighte', but spares him after taking the rings from his dead fingers. The king's response is to throw Cauline 'in dungeon deepe' for daring to kiss his daughter, yet

Cauline reappears in disguise to compete at a tournament (i. 45, l. 18). Unfortunately, he has a rival:

> A hugye giaunt stiffe and starke,
>   All foule of limbe and lere;
> Two goggling eyen like fire farden,
>   A mouthe from eare to eare. (i. 47, ll. 74–7)

This revolting creature is accompanied by a dwarf bearing five decapitated heads of kings slain by the giant. The giant is seeking to avenge his cousin, the Eldridge knighte. Cauline defeats the giant, but is mortally wounded and lies 'all walteringe in his gore' (i. 52, l. 173). He reveals his true identity, dies, and Christabelle's heart breaks also.

The *Reliques* itself welters in gore: the bloodiness of death and dismemberment incarnadines the entire three volumes, and if occasionally watered by humour or levity, it is more often deepened by a colossal amorality. These four opening ballads catalogue the hacking and slaying of battle, fairy-tale infanticide and implicit cannibalism, and the fatality of love. There is no aesthetic of suffering because there is no redemption, no humanity: merely butchers and meat. The aesthetic models of sentimentality and sensibility that structure Burke's theory of the sublime and the emergent Gothic novel are simply absent. The ballads in Percy's *Reliques* have all the rude vigour of the anecdote—they are outside discursive history; they have the cataclysmic fatalism of Greek tragedy, and the lawless challenge of rebellion, and they offer no catharsis. And it is precisely because they are innocent of such controlling narrative structures that they appear primitive.

Characters, moreover, are barely characters at all; they exhibit no psychological development. In 'Edward, Edward', the fifth ballad in the *Reliques*, a mother learns that her son's sword drips with his father's blood. Edward exiles himself, his castles fall down, his family is beggared, and his mother curses him. We never learn the reason for Edward killing his father—he is simply a figure animated by patricide and is consequently spectacularly damned. Many of the stories are compellingly senseless. 'Sir Patrick Spence, A Scottish Ballad' begins with the vulpine threat of a king:

> THE king sits in Dumferling toune,
>   Drinking the blude-reid wine. (i. 72, ll. 1–2)

This capricious monarch demands that the great sailor Spence sail his boat. Spence has a terrible foreboding, 'I feir a deadlie storme', but he blindly obeys his king and takes out the boat (i. 73, l. 24). A storm rises and he drowns. There is no consolation offered, no catharsis.

Things are no better in England. The only Robin Hood ballad in the *Reliques* is 'Robin Hood and Guy of Gisborne', probably the most feral outlaw ballad in the canon. Percy's headnote reminds the polite eighteenth-century reader of the chilling penalty for killing the king's deer: loss of eyes and castration. The ballad describes the lawless existence of Robin and his merry men, all exiled to the greenwood, all unruly vandals (or Goths . . .). There is even an unsettling shadow of pagan ritual slaughter hanging over Robin himself. Robin kills Guy in the greenwood, decapitates him, and then literally defaces the head by slashing its face:

> Robin pulled forth an Irish knife,
>   And nicked sir Guy in the face,
> That he was never on woman born,
>   Cold know whose head it was. (i. 84, ll. 169–72)

Guy's mangled head is left stuck on the end of his bow.

The Robin Hood ballads do of course have an ostensible, levelling morality, but the Scottish traitor Edom o' Gordon is simply an evil thug. Gordon and his gang harass a fortified house while the lord is away, brutally threatening and callously wooing the lady who stands on the ramparts, awaiting the return of her husband. Gordon sets fire to the house. Amid the rising smoke and crying children, the lord's daughter jumps from a window to save her life, but is peremptorily killed by Gordon. The lord returns to find only embers; Gordon is long gone. Again, there is no moment of release; rather a sense of entrapment.

There are examples of the triumph of good over evil, such as 'King Estmere' and 'The Child of Elle' (both, it transpires, re-written by Percy). 'King Estmere' is based on the king disguising himself as a harper, and contains much circumstantial detail about minstrelsy:

> Itt shal be written in our forheads
>   All and in gramaryè,

>   That we towe are the boldest men,
>   That are in all Christentyè. (i. 65, ll. 163–6)[60]

Percy also offers the sumptuous moral allegory of 'The Tower of Doctrine', which describes a remarkably rich, exotic, and sensuous shining coppery tower to entice the reader into spiritual beauty:

>   Gargeyld with grayhounds, and with many lyons,
>   Made of fyne golde, with divers sundry dragons. (i. 88, ll. 20–1)

But there is little respite in the landscape of indiscriminate killing, mutilated corpses, and ruin. The first series of ballads in the *Reliques* ends, fittingly, with an elegy.

There follows a collection of 'Ballads that illustrate Shakespeare'. 'Adam Bell, Clym of the Clough, and William of Cloudesly' is another outlaw ballad. Although these three fellows are more like Robin Hood than the diabolical Edom o' Gordon, they nevertheless massacre 300 men in the course of the ballad, and threaten to bring down the law of the land:

>   Fyrst the justice, and the sheryfe,
>   And the mayre of Carleile towne;
>   Of all the constables and catchipolles
>   Alyve were scant left one:
>
>   The baylyes, and the bedyls both,
>   And the sergeaunte of the law,
>   And forty fosters of the fe,
>   These outlawes had yslaw:
>
>   And broke his parks, and slayne his dere;
>   Of all they chose the best;
>   So perelous out-lawes, as they were,
>   Walked not by easte or west. (i. 155, fitt III, ll. 165–76)

To win their pardon Cloudesly shoots an apple from his son's head, and the stupefied king employs the trio of terrorists to dissuade them from further outrages.

Although many of the other Shakespearean ballads are less dramatic and include some merrie England love songs (such as 'The Passionate Shepherd to his Love'), most are steeped in cruelty and blood, and even Percy's collage of Shakespearean fragments,

---

[60] See also ll. 221–2. Two other ballads contain notable ballad-singing scenes: 'The Beggar's Daughter of Bednall Green' and 'The Lady Turned Serving-Man' both include disguises, ballads-within-the-ballad, and fortunate disclosure.

'The Friar of Orders Gray', is a mournful song. 'Sir Launcelot du Lake', for example, describes Lancelot beheading the giant Tarquin, and 'Gernutus the Jew of Venice' is the anti-Semitic tale of mutilation that inspired *The Merchant of Venice*. 'Titus Andronicus's Complaint' is as recklessly bloodthirsty as the play, and achieves an extremely eerie effect by being written in the first person. After all twenty-five of Titus' sons have been slain, Lavinia has been raped and mutilated, and Tamara's sons are murdered, baked, and devoured, 'then myself: even soe did Titus die' (i. 209, l. 116). This first-person immediacy is deployed elsewhere. 'Jane Shore', for instance, is wed against her will, becomes lewd and wanton, and eventually concubine to the king. The first-person account is lascivious, almost pornographic, as is her degradation: forced into public penance wrapped in a sheet, wandering as a beggar, and dying in a sewer (Shoreditch): 'Within a ditch of loathsome scent, | Where carrion dogs did much frequent' (ii. 257, ll. 131–2). 'George Barnwell', on the other hand, begins in the first person, but shifts in horror to the third person as if the ballad is distancing itself from Barnwell's accelerating corruption. This urban ballad describes a torrid affair with a harlot. Barnwell's thieving to satisfy Sarah, his whore, culminates in the robbery and murder of his uncle, where he 'beat his brains out of his head' (iii. [239], part II, l. 135). Sarah betrays Barnwell and they are both hanged.

The first volume concludes with more martial art: the military history of 'The More Modern Ballad of Chevy Chace', 'The Rising in the North' (describing the Northern Insurrection of 1569 and the fateful death of one Thomas Percy, seventh Earl of Northumberland), and 'Northumberland Betrayed by Douglas'. 'Death's Final Contest', a seventeenth-century funeral song by James Shirley, is inserted as a 'Dirge' to reiterate the implacable power of death (as if it needed to be stressed), but this dark political brew is lightened by some merry songs ('My Mind to Me a Kingdom Is' and 'You Meaner Beauties') and some ballads of sexual intrigue. In 'The Patient Countess', an earl bargains with the parents of a young girl—enjoying the juxtaposition of estate, the commoditization of the female body, and taking her to bed. Eventually his wife the countess visits his extramarital love-nest and redecorates the bedroom there, re-creating the space of her relationship. The earl slinks home and apologizes;

the young daughter prostituted by her parents is literally forgotten.

Michael Drayton's 'Dowsabell' is a more straightforward love song, in which Dowsabell is described in luscious detail:

> Her features all as fresh above,
> As is the grasse that growes by Dove;
>   And lyth as lasse of Kent.
> Her skin as soft as Lemster wooll,
> As white as snow on Peakish Hull,
>   Or swanne that swims in Trent. (i. 284, ll. 25)

As the martial ballads yoke barons to their estates and evoke the impression that the very matter of Britain goes to war, so the topographical descriptions in 'Dowsabell' politicize love-making as an expression of national identity. A few English love songs follow 'Dowsabell', including 'Winifreda'—a celebration of conjugal love (Percy tartly notes that this is unusual, '*a subject too much neglected by the libertine muses*', i. 304). But this sequence is interrupted by 'Gilderoy', the tale of a handsome lad whose deserted lover is left to retrieve his corpse from the gallows and bury him. Shenstone's ballad 'Jemmy Dawson' describes a similar affair, in which Dawson joins the Pretender's army. The next time his lover sees him he too is hanging on the gallows, his corpse is mangled and cremated before her eyes, and she dies herself. 'Bryan and Pereene, A West-Indian Ballad' describes a horrific episode in which Bryan is swimming ashore to his Indian love Pereene, until a shark bites him in half. Pereene dies of shock. 'Gentle River, Gentle River', translated from the Spanish by Percy (and also Johnson), is no less bloody: the ballad describes the aftermath of battle and a river stained with gore.[61]

The obsessive anatomizing of bodies in the ballads is striking. It is first a claim for the authenticity of the archive at large. Bodies in ballads are seldom allowed to remain whole: they are fragmented by plot or eventual death. These decapitations, mutilations, and manglings create broken bodily remains, which might be considered as shards of the shattered ballad corpus itself. Antiquarian ballads are simply not permitted to be found perfectly preserved: their broken, ruined, fragmentary condition is a prerequisite of

---

[61] *Samuel Johnson: The Complete English Poems*, ed. J. D. Fleeman (New Haven, 1971), 130.

their antiquarian status as evidence, as relics. In other words, the ballads reproduce as manifest content the latent conditions of Percy's editorial collecting and collating. Stewart phrases this point in the context of historical quotation, which can only verify by being detached from its origin and thereby becoming an incoherent symbol:

> The quotation appears as a severed head, a voice whose authority is grounded in itself, and therein lies its power and its limit. For although the quotation now speaks with the voice of history and tradition, a voice 'for all times and places,' it has been severed from its context of origin and of original interpretation, a context which gave it authenticity.[62]

What we effectively find in the *Reliques*, then, are severed heads singing the songs of their beheadings, from which the editor Percy has regenerated animate bodies. That these fragments might necessarily be fragments is disallowed, and so they become the constituents of national history. It is a sacrifice in reverse.[63] Whereas sacrifice destroys victims to accord the sacrificers some escape from the world, Percy's reanimation projects not only bodies, but an entire society, from broken remains. The world made thus is emphatically material: flesh and bone. There is no transcendent escape from this world—which is why the *Reliques* is so disturbing, and why a poet like Coleridge, who took so much from Percy's *Reliques*, made his 'Ancient Mariner' and 'Christabel' profoundly less bloody and brutal than their sources—and consequently produced cathartic and redemptive poems. In the *Reliques*, it is the economy of sacrifice which has really been slaughtered to usher in the present.

This present is defined by literary production. By implicitly dwelling on narratives of dismemberment, Percy creates an ideological contrast between the savage, savaged body of the other and his noble Gothic minstrels, forerunners of the present social order. The Goths, whether barbarians or medievals (as argued below, Chapter 3), are not cannibals or polygamists (or rapists) like their

---

[62] Stewart, *On Longing*, 19.
[63] This passage is based on the work of Georges Bataille, especially 'Sacrifice, the Festival and the Principles of the Sacred World' (in *The Bataille Reader*, ed. Fred Botting and Scott Wilson (Oxford, 1997), 210–19) and 'Sacrificial Mutilation and the Severed Ear of Vincent Van Gogh' (in *Visions of Excess: Selected Writings, 1927–1939*, ed. Allan Stoekl (Minneapolis, 1985), 61–72).

enemies: they are principally poets.[64] They do not physically consume the bodies of others, but turn them into song. Ballads, especially love songs and war songs, ensure that beauty does not come from the body, but from refrains that anatomize and sacrifice the body to poetry: whether one's own body or one's enemy's. Indeed, Percy's *Reliques* emphasizes this textualization of the body by almost completely silencing the music of the minstrels and leaving only the voice—the text, the body—of the ballad. As Certeau puts it,

The undone body was a precondition of the speech it sustained up to the moment of death; in the same way, this undone speech, split apart by forgetting and interpretation, 'altered' in dialogic combat, is the precondition of the writing it in turn supports. That speech makes writing possible by sinking into it. It induces it.[65]

Hence the insistence of the 'death song' in eighteenth-century accounts of primitive literary cultures. The singing bodies that fall apart necessarily leave only the *disjecta membra* of poetic traces, the hallmarks of heroic epic, which makes possible the work of the literary antiquarian who rebuilds the corpus. And of course the most famous and enigmatic song of rape, mutilation, murder, and cannibalism is that of the nightingale. Percy did originally print John Lyly's 'The Song-Birds' for the *Reliques*, but it was cancelled before publication (see Appendix IX):

> WHAT bird so sings, yet does so wayle?
> O tis the ravish'd nightingale.
> Jug, jug, jug, jug, tereu, she cries,
> And still her woes at midnight rise.
> Brave prick-song![66]

The second volume of the *Reliques* presents a chronology of mainly historical ballads: an early elegy on Edward I, a rondeau by Chaucer, and 'For the Victory at Agincourt' (the only piece given with music in the entire collection). A series of English military campaigns are described. 'Mary Ambree' is an early transvestite who fights for England disguised as a man. 'Brave

---

[64] Certeau argues that these two taboos represent society's relation to its exteriority (war) and interiority (marriage) (*Heterologies*, 70).   [65] Ibid. 78.

[66] *Reliques* (1996), iii. 369, ll. 1–5.

Lord Willoughby' recounts the engagement with the Spanish at
Flanders, and remembers the privations of the campaign: after a
bloody seven-hour fight the English soldiers had to dine on their
horses and quaff from puddles—but still they fought on to victory.
The lads singe the Spaniards' beards again in 'The Winning of
Cales', which marvels at the precipitate flight of the enemy: 'In
sòme places wè did find, pyès baking left behind, | Meate at fire
rosting and folk run away' (ii. 226, ll. 54–5). What is not looted
by the English is left in flames.

'K. Edward IV. and Tanner of Tamworth', a burlesque ballad in
which the king banters with an oblivious peasant, is rather more
jolly. There is a similar (and better) version in the third volume:
'The King and the Miller of Mansfield'. In this ballad the divine
body of the king lodges with the miller and has to sleep with his
son, who asks whether he has louse or scabs (the son later
complains 'Thou with thy farting didst make the bed hot', iii.
187, l. 70). The king eventually knights the miller, ostensibly
because he is amused by his pranks, but conceivably to maintain
social order as well: only knights could remain in such close
proximity to the monarch.

'Sir Aldingar' returns the *Reliques* to the omnipresent themes of
sex and violence. A false steward, having failed to seduce his queen,
resolves to have her burnt at the stake. He places a lazar ('blinde
and lame') in her bed and betrays her to the king (ii. 48, l. 14). She
asks for trial by combat, and is defended by a 'tinye boye' who
fights with a dazzling sword against the incredulous Aldingar: 'The
first stroke stricken at Sir Aldingar | Smote off his leggs by the
knee' (ii. 55, ll. 179–80). This is the first, mysterious, appearance
of the 'tinye boye' or page, a stock character. A series of demented
lover verses follow: in 'Harpalus', the first English pastoral, Harpalus dies lovelorn, his body pale, lean, grey, unkempt, weeping,
and dirty; in 'Gentle Herdsman, Tell To Me', a woman disguised
as a pilgrim asks the way to Walsingham: 'verry crooked are those
pathes' (ii. 73, l. 7). She scorned her lover, who died lovelorn, and
is now searching for 'some secrett place' in which to die herself.[67]

The disguised women in 'Mary Ambree' and 'Gentle Herdsman'
anticipate another form of disguise: confinement, characterized by
'Q. Elizabeth's Verses, while Prisoner at Woodstock, Writ with

---

[67] Ralegh's 'As Ye Came from the Holy Land' tells a similar tale.

Charcoal on a Shutter', and 'Fair Rosamond'. In the introduction to the latter, renowned ballad, Percy describes how Henry II built the house Labyrinthus, '*which was wrought like unto a knot in a garden, called a Maze*', as a lodging for his concubine Rosamond (ii. 133). Unfortunately, Queen Ellinor ravels up the guard's silk guide through the maze, and forces Rosamond to drink poison. In the next ballad, 'Queen Eleanor's Confession', the king and his earl disguise themselves as friars to hear the queen's confession: she admits losing her virginity to the same earl, trying to poison the king, poisoning Rosamond, and loving the earl. The body, particularly the female body in these cases, is hidden or opaque, but so powerful are its secrets that their revelation causes sudden change, even catastrophe.

Even the shadow of a feared revelation is catastrophic. 'Young Waters', a Scottish piece, is characteristic of the capricious love ballad in which a noble lady flirts (by winking) with a younger man, who is then murdered by a jealous husband. The queen's gaze is like that of the basilisk. She simply admires Waters; that is a death sentence:

> They hae taen zoung Waters, and
> Put fetters to his feet;
> They hae taen zoung Waters, and
> Thrown him in dungeon deep. (ii. 174, ll. 37–40)

Young Waters, his wife, son, and effects are taken to 'the heiding hill' (beheading hill), 'And for the words the queen had spoke, | Zoung Waters he did dee' (ii. 174, ll. 54–5). Gill Morice, mistaken for an errant lover, suffers a similar fate. He sends his page boy Willie to Lady Barnard, thereby provoking the jealous Lord Barnard to hunt him down. The baron discovers Gill Morice combing his yellow hair, and stabs him:

> And he has tain Gill Morice' head
> And set it on a speir:
> The meanest man in a' his train
> Has gotten that head to bear. (iii. 99, ll. 141–4)

Lady Barnard responds by kissing this grisly relic. It transpires that Gill Morice was her secret son.

Although there are Arcadian love songs like 'Fancy and Desire: by the Earl of Oxford' intermixed with these grim stories, the collection remains inescapably bloody. In 'Sir Andrew Barton', the Scottish pirate is harried by young Lord Howard, whose hand-picked crew exterminate the Scots with deadly accurate arrows: 'Eighteen Scots alive they found, | The rest were either maimd or slain' (ii. 191, part II, ll. 135–6). Howard decapitates Barton's corpse, throws away the body, and sails back to London with the pirate's head as a trophy. In 'The Murder of the King of Scots', a dozen treacherous lords plot against their king, Henry Stewart (the husband of Mary Queen of Scots and *'a vain capricious worthless young man'* to boot): 'With gun-powder they strewed his roome, | And layd greene rushes in his waye' (ii. 199, ll. 33–4). They ignite his chamber, and Henry leaps 30 feet out of the window into the arms of the rebels:

> Through halls and towers the king they ledd,
>   Through towers and castles that were nye,
> Through an arbor into an orchàrd,
>   There on a peare-tree hangd him hye. (ii. 200, ll. 57–60)

Again, despite the theological leanings of 'The Complaint of Conscience' and the essay 'On the Metre of Pierce Plowman's Visions' ('Plain Truth and Blind Ignorance' and 'The Wandering Jew'), the main interest in the final series of volume ii is with cruel laments. In 'Lord Thomas and Fair Annet, a Scottish Ballad', Thomas weighs up the charms of Annet against the wealth of 'the nut-browne bride', to whom he is engaged. When he spurns his bride at the wedding, she stabs Annet, and Thomas, enraged, stabs her and then himself. A more brutal version is given in the third volume: 'Lord Thomas and Fair Ellinor'. When the 'browne girl' stabs Ellinor, Thomas watches her blood drain away before 'He cut off his brides head from her shouldèrs, | And threw it against the walle' (iii. 85, ll. 71–2). 'Corydon's Doleful Knell' is a simpler variation of this theme, in which a bride dies in anticipation of her marriage and her funeral replaces her wedding. A further sequence of tragic love songs in volume iii is more sensational. In 'Fair Margaret and Sweet William', Margaret dies and her ghost haunts William before his wedding: 'I dreamt my bower was full of red swine, | And my bride-bed full of blood' (iii. 123, ll. 31–2). He visits Margaret's corpse, kisses her, and dies. In 'Barbara Allen's Cruelty', Jemmy dies for love of Barbara, but her first inclination is to laugh horridly at his corpse, before dying herself. There are many other lovers dying for love: 'Sweet William's Ghost' and 'Margaret's Ghost', 'Lucy and Colin' and 'Sir John Grehme and Barbara Allan'. These are domestic death songs, in which the body is betrayed (or undone) as it aspires to a new social identity—marriage. The clearest examples of this occur in the third volume. 'The Lady's Fall' and 'Waly, Waly, Love Be Bonny' are the songs of abandoned pregnant women who willingly embrace death as their only consolation.

The last poems in the volume centre on the Civil War, the Interregnum, the Restoration, the Glorious Revolution, and the '45: 'Verses by K. Charles I.', 'The Sale of Rebellious Houshold Stuff' (which catalogues domestic effects as political evidence), 'Lilli Burlero', and 'The Braes of Yarrow'. There are also six mad songs, the most notable being 'The Distracted Puritan' on the Ranter Abeizer Coppe, and 'The Lady Distracted with Love', which gives a physical taxonomy of madness: *'In the several stanzas, the author represents his pretty mad woman as 1. sullenly mad: 2. mirthfully mad: 3. melancholy mad: 4. fantastically mad: and 5. stark mad'* (ii. 353).

The third volume is introduced by Percy as *'being chiefly devoted to Romantic Subjects'*, and the essay 'On the Ancient Metrical Romances, &c.' includes a romantic genealogy, bibliography, and plot summaries (iii, p. i). The volume opens with 'Ballads on King Arthur', the cuckold king, and these include ballads on sexual politics and adultery, sexual misdeeds (lewdly described), and cat fights, such as 'The Boy and the Mantle' and 'The Marriage of Sir Gawaine'. When Guenever insults Cradock's lady in 'The Boy and the Mantle', the ubiquitous little boy declares:

> She is a bitch and a witch,
> And whore bold:
> King, in thine owne hall,
> Thou art a cuckold. (iii. 9, ll. 147–50)

'King Ryence's Challenge' describes the arrival of a dwarf sent to collect Arthur's beard 'Or else from thy jaws he will it off rend' (iii. 26, l. [14]). The body is already being undone, and Ryence already has the beards of eleven knights. 'King Arthur's Death' details the butchery of the last battle with Mordred. Arthur and Mordred duel, until Arthur impales Mordred—and yet still he comes like a dreadful and implacable fate to kill his father: 'He thruste himselfe upon the speare, | And strucke a deadlye blowe' (iii. 33, ll. 111–12).

A series of gruesome love ballads follow. In 'Glasgerion' a lovelorn harper is tricked by his page who seduces the king's daughter in the guise of his master. She, realizing his caresses are churlish, commits suicide, and Glasgerion beheads the page before killing himself. 'Old Sir Robin of Portingale' describes an old man married to a young wife, who is plotting with her lover to kill him. They are overheard by another page (another boy), and when the murderous crew arrive to kill the old husband, he beheads their leader and the others flee. The young wife arrives to find her lover dead, and her husband turns to torturing her:

> Hee cutt the pappes beside her brest,
>   And did her body spille;
> He cutt the eares beside her heade,
>   And bade her love her fille. (ii. 53, ll. 109–12)

Lady Barnard is dismembered in a similar way in 'Little Musgrave and Lady Barnard'. A 'tiney foot-page' overhears them planning a liaison (iii. 69, l. 30). Lord Barnard catches them naked in bed, kills Musgrave, and savagely mutilates his wife: 'He cut her pappes from off her brest' (iii. 72, l. 101). Certeau argues that 'Through the death of the warrior or the service of the wife, the body becomes a poem', but there is a darker side to this insight.[68] The opaque body is made starkly visible, and the mutilation or death of the wife or lover is a final, indisputable intimacy. Again, this is not sacrifice, but the cold assertion of the dark confines of the world.

The body becomes identity and destiny most spectacularly in legendary ballads. In 'The Legend of Sir Guy', Guy of Warwick is defined by the extent of his killing sprees: he has slaughtered knights, armies, kings, dragons, a lion, giants, a giant boar, and the dun cow, before he forgoes arms and dies (in the eternal present of the material champion: that is, in the first person). St George matches Guy for slaughtering: Saracens, giants, and an Egyptian dragon, and he also wrecks Persian idols, dispatches a treacherous Moroccan king, and slays a pride of lions, before

---

[68] Certeau, *Heterologies*, 76.

retiring to England. 'The Dragon of Wantley' tips such feats into satire. More of More-Hall, a glutton who once ate a whole horse (except the head), is hired to kill a dragon which has gorged on children, cattle, trees, forests, houses, and churches. More, who receives advance payment in sexual favours, dresses himself in a spiked suit of armour (like 'Some Egyptian porcupig'), fights the farting dragon, kicks its arse, and kills it (iii. 283, l. 84). There are other satirical ballads, such as John Grubb's 'St. George for England, the second Part', a facetious catalogue of heroes with a refrain to St George. Included is Achilles, whose bodily fate is compared to that of a lobster:

> And, as from lobster's broken claw,
>   Pick out the fish you might:
> So might you from one unshell'd heel
>   Dig pieces of the knight. (iii. 304, ll. 323–6)

Percy's most striking ballad here is 'Guy and Amarant', in which Guy fights the evil giant Amarant, and after much hectoring cuts off his head. Guy releases Amarant's prisoners to find famished men strung up by their thumbs (described as 'like deathes picture, which the painters draw' (iii. 119, l. 178)), and cannibal lovers:

> There tender ladyes in darke dungeon lay,
>   That were surprised in the desart wood,
> And had noe other dyett everye day,
>   Than flesh of humane creatures for their food:
> Some with their lovers bodyes had been fed,
> And in their wombs their husbands buryed. (iii. 118, ll. 163–8)

Cannibalism is a particularly acute ballad theme, because it threatens to consume the cultural archive: leaving no bodies, no heads, no trace. 'Lady Isabella's Tragedy' describes a wicked step-mother who plots to kill Isabella. Like many of Percy's ballads, this is a reworking of fairy-tale motifs; ballads, however, are seldom so happily resolved, and Lady Isabella does not fare as well as Snow White. When she asks after dinner, the cook replies, 'Thou art the doe, that I must dresse; | See here, behold my knife' (iii. 157, ll. 49–50), and although the scullion boy gallantly cries out, 'O save her life, good master-cook, | And make your pyes of mee!' (iii. 157, ll. 55–6), Isabella is slaughtered, gutted, and cooked. Her father, however, refuses to eat until his missing daughter returns:

> O then bespake the scullion-boye;
>   With a loud voice so hye:
> If now you will your daughter see;
>   My lord, cut up that pye:
>
> Wherein her fleshe is minced small,
>   And parched with the fire;
> All caused by her step-mothèr,
>   Who did her death desire. (iii. 158, ll. 77–84)

The stepmother is burnt at the stake, the cook boiled in lead, and the scullion boy made the father's heir.[69] Although not directly concerned with cannibalism, 'The Children in the Wood' expresses similar fears: every character dies, and the ballad is only held together by the power of narrative. Parents sicken unto death, their orphaned children are brought up by a wicked uncle who hires two ruffians to murder them, the ruffians fight among themselves and the milder thug kills the other and leads the children away to safety—but presently he is arrested and the two babes wander and die. The uncle dies in gaol, the good ruffian is executed for robbery. 'The Wandering Prince of Troye' is also a ballad of loss, which ends not in oblivion but in a medieval hell. Although it is based on Aeneas and Dido, Percy's version is remarkable for its conclusion. He notes: '*The reader will smile to observe with what natural and affecting simplicity, our ancient ballad-maker has engrafted a Gothic conclusion on the classic story of Virgil*' (iii. 192). Aeneas is visited by Dido's ghost:

> And thus, as one being in a trance,
>   A multitude of uglye fiends
> About this woefull prince did dance;
>   He had no helpe of any friends:
> His body then they tooke away,
>   And no man knew his dying day. (iii. 197, ll. 134–8)

These Gothic demons summoned, Percy introduces a series on '*witches, hobgoblins, fairies, and ghosts*'. In 'The Witches' Song', a dozen witches gather together the fantastical ingredients

---

[69] For a burlesque on cannibalism, see the cancelled ballad 'Cock Lorrel's Treat' (*Reliques* (1996), iii. 381 ff.).

for their orgy (including victims of infanticide and cannibalism, brain of cat, and so forth), whereas the tiny fairies in 'The Fairy Queen' feast on the brains of nightingales (iii. 198).

The final series of ballads is characterized by birth and resurrection in which the body remains the determining force. In 'The Birth of St. George', a pregnant woman dreams of 'a dragon fierce and fell | Conceiv'd within her womb' (iii. 217, ll. 21–2). Her husband is sent to consult the 'weïrd lady of the woods', who predicts his wife will have a fierce son but will die in childbirth. The husband arrives home to find his wife dead, and his son (who bears various curious birthmarks) is soon spirited away to be raised by the weïrd lady. 'Valentine and Ursine' also explores the mysteries of birth and the recovery of identity. Valentine is an abandoned child discovered by the King of France, whose first adventure as a knight is to tame a savage boy:

> 'Mong ruthless beares he sure was bred;
>   He lurks within their den:
> With beares he lives; with beares he feeds,
>   And drinks the blood of men. (iii. 263, ll. 73–6)

They meet and fight, Valentine subdues Ursine, who becomes his servant. In a later adventure, they defeat a giant together, and explore his brass castle. They discover a lady who turns out to be a princess, and who recognizes them by their birthmarks as her children. The body is articulated, and may confirm as well as condemn. Indeed, this quality of destiny was not lost on Percy's friend James Grainger, who wrote of his body of ballads, 'I hope you will sing yourself at least into a stall, if not into a throne.'[70]

Percy's *Reliques* is about eating, drinking, fornicating, singing, and killing. The ballads are obsessed with the body: how it is dressed, how it might be disguised; what it consumes and excretes; how it is inscribed and articulated and eviscerated. The body that is anatomized in this way is solely a physical remain, as is the ballad archive, as is the social projection of the world that Percy extrapolates. Textual authority is the stuff of reality. This is why so many of the stories hinge on the words or deeds of little boys. The primary *OED* meaning of the word 'boy' is of a servant, not a

---

[70] Letter from Grainger, 25 Mar. 1765 (*Illustrations*, vii. 290).

male child. Whether serving or betraying their lords and ladies in the ballads, servants, like kings and queens, are corporeal embodiments of world order.

Essentially, the ballads in Percy's *Reliques* present us with miniature epic narratives pared down to the bone. This is not epic on the drawing-room scale of Pope's *Iliad*, but what Simone Weil defines as epic poetry: 'It may be that the only theme great enough for an epic poem is an entire civilization in its prime, dealt a sudden death-blow by force of arms, fated to disappear for ever, and shown in the last struggles of its death agony.'[71] Weil's corporeal images are well chosen. In her essay on the *Song of the Crusade against the Albigensians*, Weil suggests that reading epic poetry re-enacts the annihilation it describes, but at the same time may function as a melancholy celebration of the dead, as a memorial. But Percy's ambitions were Promethean. By validating the authenticating mechanisms of literary antiquarianism, his ambition was nothing less than to animate the corpses he had meticulously reconstructed, breathing the fire of life into a fabricated body.

[71] Simone Weil, 'A Medieval Epic Poem', in *Selected Essays: 1934–1943*, ed. Richard Rees (1962), 35.

3

Macpherson and Percy

On a rock, whose haughty brow
Frowns o'er old Conway's foaming flood,
Robed in the sable garb of woe,
With haggard eyes the poet stood;
(Loose his beard and hoary hair
Streamed, like a meteor, to the troubled air)
And, with a master's hand and prophet's fire,
Struck the deep sorrows of his lyre.[1]

By 1757, Thomas Gray had raised the popular conception of the mysterious figure of 'The Bard' to that of a prophetic ancient poet.[2] The idea was immediately taken up by literary antiquarians, and indeed used by Percy to help bind his work together conceptually. Percy invented a tradition of ancient English poetry, and in doing so he redefined the nature of the Gothic, suggesting that it was a crucial influence on the emergence of the national canon. Percy's creation of English minstrelsy was part of the cultural ideology of the English national myth. He argued that medieval minstrels were the descendants of Gothic scalds and Celtic bards, but that their status and genius had gradually been eroded until they became the maggoty balladmongers of the eighteenth century. Ballads had a significance which had been hitherto overlooked: they embodied a native tradition that reached far back into the past.

In defining 'this strange institution called literature', Jacques Derrida suggests:

The question of its [literature's] origin was immediately the question of its end. Its history is *constructed* like the ruin of a monument which basically never existed. It is the history of a ruin, the narrative of a

---

[1] 'The Bard' ll. 15–22 (*The Poems of Thomas Gray, William Collins, Oliver Goldsmith*, ed. Roger Lonsdale (1969), 185–6).
[2] Edward D. Snyder, *The Celtic Revival in English Literature 1760–1800* (Cambridge, Mass., 1923), 63–7.

memory which produces the event to be told and which will never have been present.[3]

But the archive is not so easily assembled or recognized. The history of literature is perhaps more the hallucination of a ruin that never existed, a dream of a ruin that on waking discovers itself in the landscape of the present. With the Folio MS, Percy had his ruin; he now dreamt up its ghosts—the minstrels.

Percy's inspiration, or rather his foil, was the debut of James Macpherson's third-century Celtic bard Ossian, who was launched as literature's most eligible and venerable debutant in 1760. Macpherson's *Fragments of Ancient Poetry* was published within a context of Scottish and Gaelic poetry, during a critical reassessment of literary originality, and as part of a continuing historiographical antiquarian debate regarding oral tradition and racial theory. Macpherson had a significant impact upon these issues, particularly on the antiquarian researches into ancient history, and consequently Percy's work elaborated on these theories as well. Fundamentally, accounts of ancient cultures were determined by problems caused by the nature of the literary source, whether oral or literate. The rival claims of Percy and Macpherson on the literary establishment reveal that the handling of the source was crucial to the antiquarian reception of literature and its incorporation into the canon. The two writers derived exclusive methodologies from opposed theories of British history to validate their respective ancient poetry. The effects of Percy's critical debate with Macpherson are therefore full of significance for eighteenth-century poetic history, and the effects of his critical debate with Macpherson are clearly perceptible in how the literary canon henceforth evolved as a hierarchy of physical texts, distinct from the popular oral traditions which the next century codified as 'folklore'.

The story begins with the English cultivation of Scottish ethnicity, as a way of policing the other; it ends rancorously amid uncanny Celtic mysticism and accusations of forgery. Percy's account of the ancient English minstrels appears here, in order to place the editorial work on his sources in context.

---

[3] Jacques Derrida, *Acts of Literature*, ed. Derek Attridge (1992), 42.

OLD RUNIC BARDS

The eighteenth-century taste for ancient vernacular Scottish songs
is clear from the popularity of editions of such verse. In 1718
Allan Ramsay caused a minor stir with his antiquarian pastiche
Christ's Kirk on the Green, derived from the Bannatyne manuscript, and this was directly followed by Elizabeth Wardlaw's (née
Halket) celebrated storm in a fashionable teacup, *Hardyknute: A
Fragment of an Ancient Scots Poem* (1719), a 'fine morsel' supposedly rescued from 'shreds of paper, employed for what is called
the bottoms of clues [tailors' patterns]' (ii. 87–8 (italics
reversed)). Indeed, the archaic pastiche *Hardyknute* was believed
genuine until Percy, suspicious of its authenticity, established the
identity of its eighteenth-century author in the *Reliques*.[4]
Ramsay's popular anthology *The Ever Green, being A Collection
of Scots Poems, Wrote by the Ingenious before 1600*, again freely
edited from the Bannatyne manuscript, was published in 1724,
and in the same year the first volume of his *Tea-Table Miscellany
or A Collection of Scots Songs* appeared. Each volume of the
anonymous *A Collection of Old Ballads* (1723–5) also was concluded with fashionable Scottish verses. The next few years saw a
proliferation of Scottish poetic antiquities, both genuine and
fraudulent: further volumes and reprints of Ramsay and
Hardyknute, William Thomson's *Orpheus Caledonius* (1725),
Robert Forbes's Scottish rendering of *Ajax his Speech to the
Grecian Knabbs* (1742), *Poems in the Scottish Dialect by Several
Celebrated Poets* (1748), popular works such as *The Charmer: A
Choice Collection of Songs, Scots and English* (1749), *Three Scots
Poems* (1751), Thomas Warton's *The Union* (1753) (which
included 'The Thistle and the Rose' and, inevitably, *Hardyknute*),
David Dalrymple's anonymous publications for Foulis (*Gill
Morice, Young Waters*, and *Edom of Gordon*, subtitled 'An
Ancient Scottish Poem. Never Before Printed') in 1755, and
William Hamilton's 'The Braes of Yarrow' (1760). All these
were known and used by Percy. He included a number of familiar
Scottish songs in the *Reliques* and planned a future edition of

---

[4] First mooted to Warton, June 1761 (*Letters*, iii. 17–18; Fairer, 95; see also
Letters, iv. 42–5 for Dalrymple's additional remarks); it was later completed with
more mischief than sense by John Pinkerton. In *Reliques* (1794), ii. 111, *Hardyknute*
is attributed to Sir John Bruce (*Letters*, i. 173–4).

Ancient English and Scotish Poems [*sic*]. Indeed, Percy's most
enduring original composition, 'The Fairest of the Fair', was
most popular in its Scottish version, 'O Nancy'.[5] In spite of the
stock vocabulary and strained dialect of much of this poetry, the
form was enjoyed for its lyrical historicism and displays of spirited
nationalism. This is perhaps remarkable in the face of the Union
of 1707 and the aftermath of the '45, but the conventions of
depiction and indeed national closure were narratives that sought
to realize a certain formulation of a world in which Scotland was a
recognizable, and a limited, component. Scottish poets as early as
Ramsay focused on the medium as an authentically national
guarantee. In the preface to *The Ever Green*, he championed the
traditional indigenous verse of 'these good old *Bards*' over the
Classical urbanity of Augustanism: 'Their *Images* are native, and
their *Landskips* domestick; copied from those Fields and Meadows
we every Day behold.'[6] Thus was Scotland pastoralized.

Although lost until 1788, William Collins's 'An Ode on the
Popular Superstitions of the Highlands of Scotland, Considered as
the Subject of Poetry' was presented to John Home in 1749 or
1750, and presents a startling image of the bards of bonny
Scotland. The 'Ode' has a prophetic feel to it, not dissimilar to
Coleridge's 'Kubla Khan', and remarkably anticipates many of the
central images of Macpherson's *Ossian*. The reflexive verse traces
the mytheme of poetic paternity:

> Even yet preserved, how often may'st thou hear,
>   Where to the pole the Boreal mountains run,
>   Taught by the father to his listening son
> Strange lays, whose power had charmed a Spenser's ear.

It mystifies the Highlands, animates the dead, casts its spell, and
clatters with the din of war:

> At every pause, before thy mind possessed,
>   Old Runic bards shall seem to rise around
> With uncouth lyres, in many-coloured vest,
>   Their matted hair with boughs fantastic crowned:
> Whether thou bidd'st the well-taught hind repeat

---

[5] 'O Nancy' was Scotticized as 'O Annie' by Percy, Shenstone, and John Macgowan
('A Song in imitation of the Scotch Manner', National Library of Scotland, MS 3135).
[6] Allan Ramsay, *The Ever Green, being A Collection of Scots Poems, wrote by the
Ingenious before 1600* (Edinburgh, 1724), i, pp. vii–viii (italics reversed).

The choral dirge that mourns some chieftain brave,
When every shrieking maid her bosom beat,
    And strewed with choicest herbs his scented grave;
Or whether, sitting in the shepherd's shiel,
    Thou hear'st some sounding tale of war's alarms;
When at the bugle's call, with fire and steel,
    The sturdy clans poured forth their bonny swarms,
And hostile brothers met to prove each other's arms.[7]

Synonymous with this vernacular popularity was a revival of interest in Gaelic poetry. In 1751, Alexander MacDonald published his *Ais-Eiridh na Sean Chánoin Albannaich* ('The Resurrection of the Ancient Scottish Language'). A staunch Jacobite, MacDonald hoped to bridge the recent chasms in Scottish history that had deprived the Scots of national pride and political homogeneity. He invoked traditional Gaelic forms of poetry, con-juring a new spirit of nationalism.[8] The poem 'In Praise of the Ancient Gaelic Language' knitted together the discourses of faith, text, and identity with a self-awareness that Macpherson would later employ to evoke the orality of Ossian. The poem's admitted ethnicity was superseded by its apparent antiquity, and claim of divinity. Gaelic had prelapsarian pretensions, and MacDonald proudly boasted that the Scottish tongue was Edenic. It is not surprising that the demand for liberal English translations became increasingly insistent.

In response, the *Scots Magazine* ran a piece by Jerome Stone, who in 1755 promptly discussed the neglect of Celtic etymologies in Johnson's *Dictionary*. Stone claimed that Celtic was an original European language: the 'parent' of Saxon.[9] The following year the magazine published his '*ALBIN* and the *DAUGHTER* of *Mey*: An old tale, translated from the *Irish*'. This was an English rendering of the Gaelic 'Bas Fhraoch' ('The Death of Fraoch'), which Stone compared to the story of Bellerophon in the *Iliad*.[10] Stone's poem was a frothy affair, but it nevertheless caught the imagination of

---

[7] Gray, *Poems*, 492–3, 504–5.
[8] Derick S. Thomson, *An Introduction to Gaelic Poetry* (1974), 157–80; *The Poems of Alexander MacDonald*, ed. A. and A. MacDonald (Inverness, 1924).
[9] *Scots Magazine*, 17 (1755), 91–2; *Scots Magazine*, 18 (1756), 341.
[10] *Scots Magazine*, 18 (1756), 15. The poem was later republished by Thomas Blacklock, in *A Collection of Original Poems, by the Rev. Mr Blacklock and Other Scotch Gentlemen* (Edinburgh, 1760–2), ii. 127–34 (Shenstone annotated Percy's copy of this work: see below, Chapter 6).

readers of the journal, and was doubtless read by Macpherson. Stone drew attention to the 'uncommon turn of several expressions, and the seeming extravagance'. Yet despite this apology, 'Albin and the Daughter of Mey' was revised to conform to the conventions of eighteenth-century poetry: rewritten in pentameters, employing extended metaphors, Latin phrasing, and abstract personification, and interjecting frequent apostrophes. It was an imitation, considered as 'the production of simple and unassisted genius, in which energy is always more sought after than neatness'.

The Aberdeen school of primitivism produced two writers who helped to redirect the presentation of old, and ultimately Ossianic, literature: Thomas Blackwell and Alexander Gerard. Fiona Stafford has carefully detailed the impact that Blackwell's reassessment of Homer had upon the Scottish Enlightenment, interpreting his work as a thesis on the humanism of savage societies.[11] In *An Enquiry into the Life and Writings of Homer* (1735), Blackwell emphasized the importance of the Archaic Greek background in the creation of Homeric verse. The concept of universal genius was not entirely dismissed, but it was subordinated to the immediate effects of primitive language, religion, and society. Blackwell's peripatetic *Letters Concerning Mythology* (1748) provided further material for the imminent Gaelic revival. In this, he considered the necessary pliability of the mythological subject matter: 'Mythology confines you to no Creed, nor pins you down to a Set of Principles.'[12] In both these works Blackwell stressed historical specificity and imaginative recreation: both were mandates for the inventive translations of Stone, and later Macpherson.[13]

Alexander Gerard's prize-winning *Essay on Taste*, written in 1756 and published in 1759, also stated that 'The first and leading quality of genius is *invention*.' Invention was defined as perceiving the artist's presence in any production, whether in the ordering of the imagination or the conscious design of imitation. For Gerard, genius was an 'associating power', a magnet that sifted and synthesized the fancy (a term synonymous with

---

[11] Fiona J. Stafford, *The Sublime Savage: A Study of James Macpherson and the Poems of Ossian* (Edinburgh, 1988), 28–34.

[12] Thomas Blackwell, *Letters Concerning Mythology* (1748), 120.

[13] Blackwell also directly inspired the blind poet Blacklock: see 'Advice to a young Poet' in *Poems*, i. 221.

'imagination' at this time): 'Thus from a confused heap of materials, collected by fancy, genius, after repeated reviews and transpositions, designs a regular and well proportioned whole.'[14] Finally, Edward Young's *Conjectures on Original Composition*, published in 1759, was a highly influential tract and a sensitive register of these ideas. It appeared in extracts in the *Scots Magazine* in 1759. Shenstone urged Percy to read Young's *Conjectures* in light of the latter's Chinese miscellanies: 'even tho' it shou'd dissuade you . . . from undertaking any more *translations*. I should not *murmur* at the *effect*; provided it stimulate you to write *Originals*.'[15]

Young roundly condemned imitations because, unlike colonizing originals, they sprang from over-considered words, books, and texts:

> *Imitators* only give us a sort of Duplicates of what we had, possibly much better, before; increasing the mere Drug of books, while all that makes them valuable, *Knowledge* and *Genius*, are at a stand. The pen of an *Original* Writer, like *Armida*'s wand, out of a barren waste calls a blooming spring: Out of that blooming spring an *Imitator* is a transplanter of Laurels, which sometimes die on removal, always languish in a foreign soil.

Young offered the advice: 'Let us build our Compositions with the Spirit, and in the Taste, of the Antients; but not with their Materials': precisely what Stone had already done.[16] Mark Rose, in a materialist interpretation, argues that in Young the commercial is 'the unconscious of the text'.[17] Young dwells on the author's originality just as copyright is founded on the concept of the unique individual, and a mystification of the creative process becomes the compensation for this degradation.[18] The artist as a transcendent genius appears, it is argued, precisely when the artist is being debased as a producer of commodities.

Both MacDonald and Stone were careful to position their work within a historical and linguistic framework. But poetic originality was also part of a much more basic question of origins: the

---

[14] Alexander Gerard, *An Essay on Taste* (1759), 173, 49, 174.
[15] *Letters*, vii. 26.
[16] Edward Young, *Conjectures on Original Composition: In a Letter to the Author of Sir Charles Grandison* (1759), 10, 22. Percy alluded to Young in his 'Advertisement' to 'Fragments of Chinese Poetry' (*Hau Kiou Choaan* (1761), iv. 199).
[17] Rose, *Authors and Owners*, 118.   [18] Ibid. 2.

origins of race and language.[19] The literary-antiquarian debates
of the eighteenth century were all to a degree concerned with the
ethnographical origins of culture and society: the invention of
language, letters, and poetry. In Britain, these issues focused in
two particular areas: ascertaining the original inhabitants of
Great Britain, and tracing their descendants. Macpherson and
Percy were both concerned to establish the pure racial origins of
their material, but the ways in which they went about it were
radically different. Each argument developed in a way that
legitimized one poetic lineage and excluded the other.

The question concentrated on the Goths and the Celts. The
word 'Gothic' is a semantic minefield in the eighteenth century.[20]
The historical Goths were a particular tribe who crossed the
Danube in AD 376 on their way to sack Rome. Following the
sixth-century historian Jordanes, however, the term was used to
describe the Germanic tribes in general, including the Angles,
Saxons, and Jutes, who had landed with Hengist and Horsa in
Kent and invaded England in AD 449. The Goths were reinvented
and glorified in the sixteenth century as the aboriginal race of the
vagina gentium ('womb of nations'), and therefore displaying in its
purest form the instinctive love of liberty that had enabled them to
overcome the tyranny of the Roman Empire, and later assert the
rights of Magna Carta over the Norman Yoke. Consequently the
word was used extensively by seventeenth-century Parliamentar-
ians against the absolutist aspirations of the monarch, and subsequently by eighteenth-century Whigs to defend the peculiar
advantages of the English constitution.

But the word also retained a strong pejorative sense which dated
from the Renaissance. This usage deplored the fall of Rome to the
Goths, which was interpreted as the displacement of classical
genius by a barbarism that had heralded the onset of the Dark
Ages. Hence the Goths became gradually confused with the
medieval period, a time despised for its 'Gothic' taste. Yet at the
same time the medieval pageantry of romantic Gothic was itself

---

[19] Eisenstein notes the semantic shift of 'original' at this time, which she attributes
to print (Elizabeth L. Eisenstein, *The Printing Press as an Agent of Change: Commu-
nications and Cultural Transformations in Early-Modern Europe* (Cambridge, 1979),
i. 192).

[20] Samuel Kliger, *The Goths in England: A Study in Seventeenth and Eighteenth
Century Thought* (Cambridge, Mass., 1952), *passim*.

being revived: in architecture by Horace Walpole, who bought the Strawberry Hill pile in 1748, and in literature by Thomas Warton, whose *Observations on the Faerie Queene of Spenser* was first published in 1754. Lawrence Lipking suggests that the Walpole set 'enjoyed the iconoclastic feeling of daring that accompanied their praise of a word so weighted with derogatory connotations'.[21]

There still remained a lingering popular distrust of the Gothic. In a 1765 dictionary, 'Classick' was derived from Johnson: a '*classick* author' being 'one that is placed in the first rank of credit among scholars'. 'Gothick', absent from Johnson, was defined 'rude, inartificial, rustick, after the manner, or like to the *Goths*, whose architecture was very heavy and rude, like most of our old churches'.[22] The pejorative meaning of the word, already becoming glamorous, remained a barrier. John Newbery's *Art of Poetry on a New Plan*, possibly revised by Oliver Goldsmith in 1762, gave a typical popular description of the Gothic culture that had superseded the Roman Empire: 'absurd and unmeaning tales of giants, champions, inchanted knights, witches, goblins, and such other monstrous fictions and reveries, as could only proceed from the grossest ignorance, or a distempered brain.'[23] There was a fundamental confusion, both historical and semantic, between ancient Scandinavian marauders and the romances of chivalry. Even Thomas Percy retained a pejorative understanding of the English Gothic. Viewing the ruins of Melrose Abbey on the Tweed, he drafted a letter to Henry Revely on 9 August 1766 in which he gave his opinion of Gothic architecture: 'what I have ⌈generally⌉ <ever> observed as faulty in our old Gothic Churches, has been for the most part a heavy clumsiness in the principal parts; and in the more minute, an injudicious load of fantastic and unnatural <load>ornaments, crowded too thick together.'[24]

Percy's description is half in love with the Gothic. He perceives that the monstrous quality of the Gothic lies in its mix of crude and the fantastic, the colossal and the minute, and the monolith and the multitude. In other words, the Gothic combines opposites, escapes categories, and refers its definition to another world. It

---

[21] Lawrence Lipking, *The Ordering of the Arts in Eighteenth-Century England* (Princeton, 1970), 149.   [22] Dyche, *Dictionary,* K7^{r-v}, Z2^r.
[23] John Newbery, *The Art of Poetry on a New Plan* (1762), ii. 154; see also Johnson, *Idler,* 211–14.   [24] BL, Add. MS 32335, fo. 12^v.

exists between the visible and the invisible—or between the
present and the past. The old Gothic churches are like arks or
juggernauts, gliding through the present, hopelessly in search of
their distant historical homelands.

The definition of Celtic is as complicated as Gothic, but in a
different way. As Michael Hechter suggests, the Celts (the Irish,
Scots, and Welsh) were imagined as a collection of peripheral
peoples, excluded from the central core of power and resources
by an English policy of internal colonialism. The Celts had
resisted the Roman Invasion and enjoyed an indigenous geo-
graphical concentration; they had nurtured their own language,
culture, and society and had ambitions of political self-
determination. They therefore had a profound sense of identity
and locality which denied them the full integration afforded to the
Picts, Frisians, Angles, Saxons, Danes, and Normans.[25]

The rhetoric of the Celtic Fringe was also obscured by a rift
between the Irish and the Scottish, who both claimed to be the
original Celts. The Irish pedigree was the more respectable,
originating with John of Fordun of the fourteenth century, and
in the 1760s the argument was receiving most of its impact
through the seventeenth-century historians Geoffry Keating and
Roderic O'Flaherty. Central to the Irish claim was the evidence—
indeed the existence—of manuscript archives. Fordun's *Scotichronicon*, reprinted in Edinburgh in 1759, relied on written records
for its account: 'E Codicibus MSS. editum, cum notis et varianti-
bus lectionibus.'[26] O'Flaherty, whose title-page likewise boasted
evidence 'Ex Pervetustis Monumentis fideliter inter se collatis
eruta', claimed that Ireland was nothing less than Homer's fabled
island Ogygia, and entirely dismissed Scottish history as 'no more
than a fabulous modern production, founded on oral tradition,
and fiction'.[27]

In response, the Scottish Celtic was remodelled along the
primitive lines of Archaic Greek: a symbolic classical stand against

[25] Michael Hechter, *Internal Colonialism: The Celtic Fringe in British National
Development, 1536–1966* (1975), 9–11, 53–9, 73–123.
[26] Johannis De Fordun, *Scotichronicon* (Edinburgh, 1759), title-page (edited from
manuscripts with notes and variant readings), 43.
[27] Roderico O'Flaherty, *Ogygia* (1685), title-page (collected from antiquarian
records faithfully compared with one another); Roderic O'Flaherty, *Ogygia, or, A
Chronological Account of Irish Events*, tr. James Hely (Dublin, 1793), i. 226.

the new eruption of the Gothic, derived from the Homeric criticism of Blackwell.[28] Blackwell postulated the poetic status of Αοιδος, stressing that '*Homer's* being born poor, and living a stroling indigent Bard, was in relation to his Poetry, the greatest Happiness that cou'd befall him' because it exposed him to all the local influences of climate, manners, and religion. Savage societies bred poets: primitive language was constructed by metaphor and those metaphors were natural images. The very ground validated culture, and across it swept poets, like nomadic prophets. They were possessed, haunted by the muse, falling into frenzied extemporizations.

Naturally, under these conditions, original poetic genius did not need to be confined to the Greek world, and Blackwell's description provided an important basis for the development of a comparable Gaelic (not to mention English) poet. And although Blackwell was 'unwilling to admit the *Irish* or *Highland Rüners* the honour of Homeric dignity, there were undeniable resemblances. Blackwell was not precise in distinguishing the Celts from the Goths, who merged in the term '*Highland Rüners*', but Homer's alleged education had also included induction into the 'oral Mysteries' of the Druids. Blackwell found the versifiers of medieval romance had more right to inherit the Homeric legacy.

The *Trovadores* or *Troubadours* of *Provence*, the earliest of the Moderns that shewed any Vein for Poetry, have a better Claim. They sung their Verses to the Harp, or other Instrument they cou'd use, and attained to a just *Cadence* and *Return* of Verse in their Stanza's [*sic*]; but had neither Manners nor Language for great Attempts.[29]

Jerome Stone, then, like Macpherson after him, was invoking the figure of Homer described by Blackwell in a Scottish Celtic context. Ironically, Blackwell's sympathy for the troubadours also provided a useful model for Percy's ancient English minstrel.

Wales occupied a less prominent and less antagonistic position in the definition of the Celtic. The country's Celtic roots were obscured first by the establishment in 1751 of the Honourable Society of Cymmrodorin, which occupied itself with the medieval

---

[28] Gerard, for example, championed Greek simplicity over the barbaric novelty of 'the *Gothic* taste' (Gerard, *An Essay on Taste*, 7–8).

[29] Thomas Blackwell, *An Enquiry into the Life and Writings of Homer* (1735), 103, 112, 163 (italics reversed).

manuscripts of the Morrisian Circle, and secondly by Thomas
Gray's unproductive researches and disingenuous translations.
Gray intended to examine the early Welsh in his 'History of
English Poetry', periodically abandoned and revived—at one point
he was inspired to return to it in 1760 after receiving
Macpherson's *Fragments* and reading a manuscript of Evan
Evans's 'Dissertatio'.

But, curiously, Wales had a Blackwellian living poetic tradition
that had wandered as far as Gray in the Fens. When he finished
'The Bard' in May 1757, he wrote to Mason with an account of
John Parry, a blind Welsh harper who had recently visited
Cambridge '& scratch'd out such ravishing blind Harmony, such
tunes of a thousand year old with names enough to choak you'.[30]
Gray's interest in mythography, however, did not allow him to keep
this fragmentary living tradition pure, and he permitted the
Gothic to intrude into his Celtic Odes.[31] He filled his Welsh
translations with Scaldic fragments because he ultimately attributed alliteration ('pseudo-rhythmus') to the ancient Germans, and
complained to Mason of 'that scarcity of Celtic Ideas' which
necessitated his use of other 'foreign whimsies' to supplement
them.[32] Wales remained a footnote to Celtic researches in the
1760s.

These speculations and researches into racial origins were
keenly contested because a great deal of pride rested on their
conclusions: which northern race had carried letters, and by
implication poetry, from the fabulous heats of the East to the
moody epic wastes of the North? There was nothing less at stake
than a proof of cultural supremacy. A taste of the intricacy of this
work, contemporary with Macpherson's *Ossian* and Percy's
Reliques, may be found in Francis Wise's *Some Inquiries concerning the First Inhabitants Language Religion Learning and Letters
of Europe* (1758). Wise, a Fellow of Trinity College, Oxford, and
the first Radcliffe Librarian, argued that the Flood had dispersed

[30] *The Correspondence of Thomas Gray*, ed. Paget Toynbee and Leonard Whibley
(Oxford, 1935), ii. 502.
[31] For example, Gray took 'The Fatal Sisters' from his list of 'Gothic' poems (*Poems*,
213).
[32] 'The Bard', ll. 47–8 (Gray, *Poems*, 189); Gray, *Correspondence*, ii. 550–1.
'Observations on the Pseudo-Rhythmus' is reprinted in *The Works of Thomas Gray*,
ed. Edmund Gosse (1902), i. 361–75.

the One Speech into many dialects and languages, and he described the ethnological migrations of these different races by etymological research. The Titans remained in possession of the North after the Deluge, and their language remained uncorrupted in the Highlands and Islands and in Ireland:

Antiquaries are sufficiently justified in calling these dialects Celtic, because they are the first known language in Europe or Celtica. Perhaps they may deserve a much higher title, namely that of the Universal Language of the postdiluvian world.

It is an extraordinary example of the return of the repressed. The ethnic charm of Scottish verse could not be contained as sweet examples of alterity. The Celtic fringe harboured Titans, and they threatened to storm merrie England.

The Titanic language (also known as Cimmerian, Celtic, and Pelasgic) gave rise to such great languages as ancient Greek, but the Gothic was a mysterious exception to the Titanic 'Great Hive' of nations in the north. Gothic was not Celtic, but Asiatic Scythian, and the Goths were moreover 'in truth the most civilized of all the Northern nations of their time'. Indeed, 'Odin brought with him many useful arts; and amongst the rest, that of letters'. Moreover, the Goths kept their identity among the Celtic progeny by maintaining their characteristic Runic alphabet.[33] It was to prove a crucial footnote.

'THE SUBLIME SAVAGE'[34]

Thomas Percy could never have achieved what he did in the *Reliques* without the cautionary tale of James Macpherson. Percy tracked his career closely and learned from his mistakes. Macpherson was Percy's predecessor in the mythic construction of a national past, the testimony of authentic voices, and the textual medium of transmission. But he was exposed.

James Macpherson had begun collecting old Gaelic poetry from 1756, while working as a teacher in his native Ruthven, Speyside, forming a collection that included both transcriptions of local

[33] Francis Wise, *Some Inquiries Concerning the First Inhabitants['] Language Religion Learning and Letters of Europe* (Oxford, 1758), 31, 3, 84–5, 125–6.
[34] *Boswell's London Journal 1762–1763*, ed. Frederick A. Pottle (1950), 265–6.

ballad-singers and manuscripts. His nationalist aspirations were already evident in his own poetry, published in the *Scots Magazine* in 1755 ('To a Friend, mourning the death of Miss —') and later in 1758 ('On the Death of Marshal Keith'). Two years after Stone's publication Macpherson published another original strongly partisan poem, the six-canto *Highlander* (1758), before turning his full attention to translating his old Gaelic poetry.[35]

Macpherson was put to the task of translating by John Home, a Scottish playwright whom he had met in Moffat in 1759. Home had a keen interest in Highland culture, but could not speak Gaelic himself, so he persuaded Macpherson to translate some pieces for him. Macpherson reluctantly did so, and Home excitedly carried them to Edinburgh, showing them to the Scottish literati: Alexander Carlyle, Hugh Blair (who was about to be appointed Professor of Rhetoric and Belles Lettres at Edinburgh University), William Robertson, Adam Ferguson, and Lord Elibank.[36] Having spent a decade searching for ancient Highland verse, these Scottish intellectuals had their own cultural agenda, and Macpherson was rather overtaken by events. Blair managed to persuade him to produce a few more translations, sent copies to Gray, Walpole, and Shenstone, and began making preparations for publication.

Macpherson attributed the poems to a third-century bard Ossian, the son of Fingal, the last of the Celts. Ossian was Homerically blind, and so even in singing his pre-literate songs articulated the end of writing. The Blackwellian conception of the bard had already re-emerged in Thomas Gray's poem 'The Bard' (quoted above), but bards were also part of Macpherson's Highland background. Stafford indicates that the bardic tradition had in some places survived the suppression following the '45, and

---

[35] Bailey Saunders, *The Life and Letters of James Macpherson* (1894), 59–60. Jerome Stone (d. 1756) was also a collector of Gaelic poetry: D. Mackinnon, 'A Collection of Ossianic Ballads by Jerome Stone', *TGSI* 14 (1887–8), 314–69; *Scots Magazine*, 17 (1755), 249; *Scots Magazine*, 20 (1758), 550–1 (Stafford, *The Sublime Savage*, 43–51). James Macpherson, *The Highlander; A Poem: In Six Cantos* (Edinburgh, 1758) (Stafford, *The Sublime Savage*, 61–75). Another of Macpherson's early poems was reprinted in Blacklock's *Poems*, ii. 134–7.

[36] Richard B. Sher, *Church and University in the Scottish Enlightenment: The Moderate Literati of Edinburgh* (Edinburgh, 1985), 243–5; Rober Hay Carnie, 'Macpherson's *Fragments of Ancient Poetry* and Lord Hailes', *Essays and Studies*, 41 (1960), 17–26; *Fingal*, p. A2[r].

clan chiefs were still sometimes attended by a bard 'who was responsible not only for the composition of poetry, but also for preserving the history of the Clan'.[37] In *Ossian*, Macpherson blended an idealized product of antiquarian poetry with the living poets who recited Gaelic verse.

Macpherson's first Ossianic poems were published on 14 June 1760 in the anonymous anthology *Fragments of Ancient Poetry, collected in the Highlands of Scotland, and translated from the Galic or Erse Language*. This was a deceptively slim pamphlet containing fourteen prose pieces (fifteen in the second edition) which purported to be translated from Ossian. They were a spectacular success. The *Fragments* appeared, and the *Gentleman's Magazine* immediately printed two complete 'Fragments' which by the next month a reader, 'F.M.', had put into heroic couplets, in spite of believing them to be 'modern Compositions'. These were republished later in the same year in Thomas Blacklock's *Collection of Original Poems*. September saw 'Fragments VI' and 'VII' printed, and a letter from one 'Caledonius' arguing that the Fragments were authentic. This letter was transcribed by Percy into his copy of the work.[38]

Ossian was presented as an oral phenomenon. Macpherson made a crucial contribution to the antiquarian debates of racial origins and historiography by postulating that Celtic society was entirely illiterate: it was an oral culture. Macpherson's point was that this did not diminish the historical significance of the culture: on the contrary, it was an absolute proof of its antiquity. There was already a sense of the primal orality of language in mid-eighteenth-century thinkers as diverse as Johnson and Hume, and Macpherson capitalized on this feeling to stress the staggering age of his Celtic fragments and to scotch the arguments of Irish antiquarians who relied on the documentary evidence of a later age. Furthermore, the preface of Macpherson's *Fragments*,

[37] Stafford, *The Sublime Savage*, 13. Stafford also considers Ossian's status as the last bard in *The Last of the Race: The Growth of a Myth from Milton to Darwin* (Oxford, 1997), 83–108, and remarks of Gray's Bard that he is 'the image of a primitive poet, uninhibited by libraries and burgeoning lists of new books' (101).

[38] *Gentleman's Magazine*, 30 (1760), 287–8, 335–6, 407–9, 421; Ludwig Stern, 'Ossianic Heroic Poetry' (*Die Ossianischen Heldenleider*), tr. J. L. Robertson, *TGSI* 22 (1897–8; Inverness, 1900), 274 n. (both fragments later appeared in the *Fingal* volume: one in 'Carric-Thura', the other, 'Fragment XII', was absorbed in the 'Songs of Selma'); Blacklock, *Poems*, i. 171–4. Percy's copy is at Queen's, Percy pamph. 61 (5).

ghost-written by Hugh Blair, not only invoked the oral tradition of
the Highlands; it actually resisted any indigenous literacy supposedly contemporary with the composition of the poems:

In a fragment . . . which the translator has seen, a Culdee or Monk is
represented as desirous to take down in writing from the mouth of
Oscian [*sic*], who is the principal personage in several of the following
fragments, his warlike atchievements and those of his family. But Oscian
treats the monk and his religion with disdain, telling him, that the deeds
of such great men were subjects too high to be recorded by him, or by any
of his religion.[39]

It was claimed the poems had only survived through bardic tradition, a specifically oral tradition. Even the name 'Oscian' declared
this: amazingly, it means 'mouthy' (from the Latin *os*, mouth),
which suggests that Oscian was either a traditional role rather
than a particular figure, or a Macphersonic joke. As Blair
explained, by the succession of clan bards 'such poems were
handed down from race to race'.[40] Gray, witnessing what
appeared to be the incarnation of his 'Bard', was '*extasié*' with
the 'infinite beauty' of the *Fragments*, believing Macpherson was
'the very Demon of Poetry, or he has lighted on a treasure hid for
ages'.[41]

This bardic oral tradition defined the poems on every level, and
the poems themselves constantly stressed their oracy. They were
full of sound, several were dialogues, and 'voices' served as a
metaphor for poetry, memory, the past, and the present. A sense
of evanescent orality was also present in the structure of the
Fragments: the collection was the shadow of something larger, a
broken fragment of something complete. The whole work was
finely structured through subtle allusion and shifting perspective,
which gave the sense of another, archetypal work struggling to find
form, of a lost northern oral epic articulated as a printed
pamphlet. The resonances and repetitions of character, scene,
memories, mourning, and most frequently of death accumulated
in a vertiginous sense of the past. Conflicts were tragic, inter-
necine, futile, and irrevocable. Orality also contributed to the

---

[39] *Fragments*, p. vi. Johnson, *Dictionary*, i, p. A2^r; David Hume, *Enquiries concerning Human Understanding and concerning the Principles of Morals*, ed. L. A. Selby-
Bigge, rev. P. H. Nidditch (Oxford, 1975), 224, 241; *Fragments*, pp. iv–v.
[40] *Fragments*, p. vi.   [41] Gray, *Correspondence*, ii. 680.

distinctive style of *Ossian* in a more subtle way. The stylistic features of *Ossian* have been analysed by several critics since Walther Drechsler, and can be summarized as alliteration, concatenation, parallelism, amplification, accumulation, internal rhymes and half-rhymes, parataxis, anastrophe, parenthetical phrases, genitives of description, hypotyposis, anamnesis, and prosopopoeia.[42] These features were already an established characteristic of ancient poetry—Robert Lowth's *De Sacra Poesi Hebræorum* (1753) devoted an entire lecture to the use of parallelism in ancient Hebrew poetry—but they also have affinities with actual oral tradition.[43]

Oral tradition as it is at present understood does not mean the verbatim transmission of texts, but the employment of a formulaic poetic language in extemporizing songs, especially in the creation of epic poetry. As Milman Parry demonstrates in his work on Homer, the poetry is orally composed by using words (especially names and epithets) and phrases (such as fixed metaphors) chosen 'for their metrical convenience, rather than for their appropriateness to the particular context in which they appear'.[44] This definition stresses the particularity of the tradition and the subordination of the poet to the tradition. Post-literate, post-typographic concepts such as composition and recitation are irrelevant to oral literature. *Ossian* does show marked similarities to the techniques of oral composition (a small, repetitive vocabulary; formulaic phrases and metaphors; awkward sentence structures) and, bearing in mind that eighteenth-century understanding of the oral tradition falls considerably short of our own, such internal evidence is the clearest indication that *Ossian* was not entirely spurious.[45]

As predicted at the end of the *Fragments*, Macpherson published his first Ossianic epic, *Fingal, An Ancient Epic Poem, in Six*

---

[42] Walther Drechsler, 'Der Stil des Macphersonschen Ossian', Ph.D. thesis (Berlin, 1904); Robert P. Fitzgerald, 'The Style of Ossian', *SiR* 6 (1966), 23, 29–31; Stafford, *The Sublime Savage*, 103–11.

[43] Robert Lowth, *De Sacra Poesi Hebræorum* (Oxford, 1753), 24–59.

[44] Milman Parry, *The Making of Homeric Verse: The Collected Papers of Milman Parry*, ed. Adam Parry (Oxford, 1971), pp. xxv, 195; Albert B. Lord, *The Singer of Tales* (Cambridge, Mass., 1964), 30–67; H. Munroe Chadwick and N. Kershaw Chadwick, *The Growth of Literature* (Cambridge, 1932–40), iii. 682–93.

[45] Nicholas Hudson, '"Oral Tradition": The Evolution of an Eighteenth-Century Concept', in Ribeiro and Basker, *Tradition in Transition*, 175.

Books, on 1 December 1761. *Fingal* was introduced with an account of Macpherson's manuscript-collecting expedition in the Highlands, undertaken in 1760 and sponsored by the Scottish literati, but it still renewed the *Fragments'* commitment to orality and Macpherson's own account of the trip did not mention tangible manuscripts. Instead he claimed that it was 'in order to recover what remained of the works of the old bards'.[46] This was in spite of his haul of 'two Ponies laden with old Manuscripts'.[47] Indeed Macpherson persisted in marginalizing manuscripts from *Ossian*, to the extent of protecting the publications even from contamination by contemporary manuscript culture.[48] He described the Gaelic oral tradition by analogy with Tacitus' references to song in *Germania*, and disputed the emphasis on written records in eighteenth-century accounts of ancient history, in which he claimed the Celts had been misrepresented: 'They trusted their fame to tradition and the songs of their bards, which, by the vicissitude of human affairs, are long since lost. Their ancient language is the only monument that remains of them.'[49] Macpherson also elaborated the role of the bards, appointing them to the Druidic theocracy. They played a symbolic part in battle, chanting 'the *death-song*' or 'the *song of victory*', and more or less performed the duties of a medieval herald.[50] The poem itself was full of episodes from the *Fragments*, though there was more emphasis on the singing of the bards as a universal metaphor than on the disembodied voices of the *Fragments*.

Indeed, the orality of *Fingal* was most clearly demonstrated in Macpherson's use of episodes derived from the *Fragments*, episodes that were substantially changed.[51] Macpherson indicated this in his profligate footnotes—virtually every page of *Fingal* was annotated. This annotation was ideologically significant. The

[46] *Fingal*, p. a1ʳ.
[47] Robert Lingel, 'The Ossianic Manuscripts: A Note by Gordon Gallie MacDonald', *BNYPL* 34 (1930), 80.
[48] *Fingal*, p. a1ʳ. For examples, see Margaret M. Smith, 'Prepublication Circulation of Literary Texts: The Case of James Macpherson's Ossianic Verses', *YULG* 44 (1990), 132–57. [49] *Fingal*, p. ii.
[50] Ibid., pp. x, 179 n., 193 n., 253. For example, 'Carric-Thura' included the command, 'Send a bard to demand the combat' (202).
[51] Derick S. Thomson, The *Gaelic Sources of Macpherson's 'Ossian'* (Edinburgh, 1952), 59. Macpherson's sources were probably medieval (1200–1600) oral ballads: see Donald E. Meek, 'The Gaelic Ballads of Scotland', in Howard Gaskill (ed.), *Ossian Revisited* (Edinburgh, 1991), 19–48.

fluctuation of each version demonstrated the inherent orality of the verses. Footnotes literally underwrote Macpherson's editing methods, not by positioning the text in the canon of antiquarian scholarship as Percy's would, but by exposing the evolution of the text and preventing closure. Macpherson was demonstrating by the constant fluctuation of each version the inadequacy of letters in communicating ancient Celtic poetry. In contrast, Percy would devise single texts out of many versions.

A storm of protest greeted *Fingal*, in which Irish nationalists, Wilkesites, and textual pedants forged an unlikely alliance against the Scottish literati, poets, and antiquarian cranks. The two camps were so fundamentally different that there was no hope of any dialogue. Many of these publications appeared hard on the heels of *Fingal*. Ferdinando Warner, *Remarks on the History of Fingal, and other Poems of Ossian* (1762), argued that *Fingal* was of Irish antiquity, proven by the existence of manuscript copies in Ireland (one of which was supposedly under the press in Dublin). It was an Irish appropriation of *Ossian* on the strength of manuscript archives, and therefore bound to appeal to Percy, who recommended the work to Evans. Charles O'Conor attacked on this point too.[52] His *Dissertations on the History of Ireland* (1766) highlighted the incompatibilities between lettered and unlettered poets, and the attack was consolidated in his entertaining *Dissertation on the First Migration* (1766), which was heavily scornful of oral literary tradition.[53] Like O'Flaherty, O'Conor worked solely with written records, dismissing all others. Macpherson's methods were ridiculed and the oral tradition was judged by manuscript standards of minuscule precision. O'Conor mocked '*Ossian's Erse*, a Dialect kept from Corruption *by the Salt* of *oral Tradition* only, and luckily preserved *from* the Infidelity of Books, or Errors of Transcribers'.[54]

Irish critics were accompanied by the satirists. John Hall-Stevenson published *Three Beautiful and Important Passages omitted by the Translator of Fingal* (1762) under the pseudonym

---

[52] Charles O'Conor, *Dissertations on the History of Ireland* (Dublin, 1766), 23 n.
[53] Charles O'Conor, *A Dissertation on the First Migrations, and Final Settlement of the Scots in North-Britain* (Dublin, 1766), 27–8.
[54] Ibid. 42–3. O'Conor concluded with an appropriately spoken dialogue between Ossian and Macpherson, in which Macpherson's nationalist ambitions were ridiculed (50).

Donald Macdonald, which featured three salacious sexual
parodies in Ossianic prose, detailing a southern distemper
(masturbation), a northern malady (the pox), and a Highland
coronation which precipitated a deluge (urination). This was an
attack on that hated Scot, Prime Minister Bute, as was *Gisbal, An
Hyperborean Tale* (1762). The bawdy punning on Gisbal's
'*upright staff*' was carried over into popular broadsides such as
The Staff of Gisbal and *Gisbal's Preferment*.

'What say you to Fingal—?' asked Shenstone, who had sub-
scribed to the Scottish edition, 'What a treasure *these* for a
modern Poet, before they were published!'[55] Percy's opinion was
divided, noting 'too little simplicity of narration . . . affected and
stiff . . . turgid and harsh . . . not what it is made to pass for', yet
richly 'sublime and pathetic: and shews a Genius in the Composer
equal to any Epic production'.[56] His opinion remained divided: he
dismissed the productions in the 1765 *Reliques*, but, after hearing
an Ossianic recital during a visit to Edinburgh, admitted, 'I am
forced to believe them, as to the main, genuine in spite of my
teeth'; he even defended *Ossian* in the second edition of the
Reliques in 1767.[57] But aesthetic defences of *Ossian*, along
the lines suggested by Shenstone, were common. Versifications
of *The Battle of Lora* (1762) and *The Songs of Selma* (1762)
were at the booksellers, and the plays of David Erskine Baker (*The
Muse of Ossian*, 1763) and John Home (*The Fatal Discovery*,
published 1769) were at the playhouses. There was a sudden
demand for literary antiquarianism, and an explosion of books,
pamphlets, essays, and letters.

Critical defences were, however, fairly scarce. John Gordon's
comparison between Homer and *Ossian* in his *Occasional
Thoughts on the Study and Character of Classical Authors*
(1762) argued that language had fallen and images become
arbitrary and lost their ancient simplicity. Words had become 'a
specious kind of skreen between us and nature', but *Ossian* could

---

[55] *Letters*, vii. 138, 125. Percy wrote to Evans on 15 Oct. 1761 that 'hardly one
reader in ten believes the specimens already produced to be genuine' (ibid., v. 19).

[56] Ibid., vii. 141–2.

[57] Ibid., v. 117. The sentence in the 1767 *Reliques* reads: 'Several fragments of
which the editor of this book has heard sung in the original language, and translated
vivâ voce, by a native of the Highlands, who had, at the time, no opportunity of
consulting Mr. Macpherson's book' (i, p. xlv). Percy subsequently retracted this
statement.

resanctify language (in ways in which Coleridge would have approved): 'Who then can look at the following description, and not forget almost, that he is reading words?—so naturally do the real objects themselves rise to our view!'[58] Macpherson also received support from the aged antiquary William Stukeley, who defended *Ossian* archaeologically—by the incontrovertible evidence of coins. Stukeley envisaged the Celts, under the guidance of the Druids, as literally carrying letters on their ancient migration from the East. Poetry was supposed to have had its origins in the East, and different antiquarians proposed different racial migrations to explain how verses (and purses of money) had been brought to the West. Language, for the English antiquarian, was an artefact.

The most extreme of these theories were proposed by Rowland Jones. Jones's thesis was that the Celts comprised the lost tribes of Israel, and that Celtic was the Edenic language. The prelapsarian status of Gaelic had been proposed in Alexander MacDonald's verse and Jerome Stone's criticism, and even Francis Wise had argued a similar position. Jones claimed in *Hieroglyfic* (1763) that the Titanic Celtic language had inspired classical tongues in its westward migrations, and that the Druids' secret alphabet, which so intrigued eighteenth-century antiquarians, comprised the 'hieroglyphic, universal representation and meaning, which the first universal language must be supposed to express'.[59] Celtic letters comprised a symbolic representation of reality, and Jones provided a table explaining their relevance. *The Origin of Language and Nations*, published the following year (1764), included a lexicon in which the meanings of words were derived from these mystic alphabetical resonances. This absurd cryptogrammar was also pursued by an unlikely Celtic philologist, the reformed pornographer John Cleland. Cleland followed Jones in *The Way to Things by Words, and to Words by Things* (1766), an occult Celtic etymology which attempted to restore the Titanic language, and he twice

---

[58] John Gordon, *Occasional Thoughts on the Study and Character of Classical Authors, on the Course of Litterature, and the Present Plan of a Learned Education* (1762), 39–40, 97.

[59] Rowland Jones, *Hieroglyfic: or, A Grammatical Introduction to an Universal Hieroglyfic Language; consisting of English Signs and Voices* (1763), pp. A3ᵛ–A4ʳ, 12.

published proposals for *The Celtic Retrieved* (1768 and 1769).[60]

The compelling arcane nonsense of writers like Jones explains one of Macpherson's wilder schemes: of printing his Gaelic originals in the Greek alphabet 'to avoid the disputes about Gaelic orthography'.[61] Macpherson had romantic intentions in hinting at the classical splendour of the Celtic Highlands and apocalyptic aspirations in reminding his readers of the passing of *Ossian*, as he told Adam Ferguson: 'I have resolved to follow the example of the old Druids, in writing the Celtic language in Greek characters.'[62] He also meant to dissociate Celtic from English. When he printed part of the Gaelic text of *Temora*, Macpherson compared the power of the Celtic alphabet to the bastardized strain of English letters: 'the power of one of them requires, sometimes, a combination of two or three Roman letters to express it.'[63]

The most influential work of 1762, however, was Richard Hurd's *Letters on Chivalry and Romance*. This publication defined the place of ancient poetry in the popular imagination, marking the 'enchanted ground' on which Percy's Goths would battle against Macpherson's Celts. In a letter to David Dalrymple in September 1763, written while Percy was working on his essay 'On the Ancient Metrical Romances', Percy deliberately placed his edition of metrical romances (later abandoned) within Hurd's conceptual framework: 'M[r] Hurd's Letters of Chivalry (which you must have seen) may perhaps dispose the public to give a favourable reception to a few of the best of these ancient Romances.'[64]

---

[60] John Cleland, *Specimen of an Etimological Vocabulary, or, Essay, by means of the Analitic Method, to Retrieve the Antient Celtic* (1768), 228–32; John Cleland, *Additional Articles to the Specimen of an Etimological Vocabulary, or, Essay, by means of the Analitic Method, to Retrieve the Antient Celtic* (1769), 42–7. See also Umberto Eco, *The Search for the Perfect Language*, tr. James Fentress (Oxford, 1995), 102.

[61] Henry Mackenzie, *Report of the Committee of the Highland Society of Scotland, Appointed to Inquire into the Nature and Authenticity of the Poems of Ossian* (Edinburgh, 1805), appendix IV, 61–2.   [62] Saunders, *Life and Letters*, 295.

[63] *Temora*, 226.

[64] Richard Hurd, *Letters on Chivalry and Romance* (1762), 54. *Letters*, iv. 56; *Reliques*, iii, p. ix. Percy borrowed a copy of Hurd's *Letters* from Farmer (*Letters*, ii. 5). He had read it twice by 5 June 1762 and was encouraged that Hurd placed 'the Old Romances . . . in a very respectable light' (*Letters*, ii. 7). Twelve days later he wrote to Shenstone, 'Have you seen Hurd's new Letters on Chivalry? he is clever, but he is a Coxcomb' (*Letters*, vii. 157). For Percy's proposed edition of English metrical romances, see five volumes of transcripts made *c.*1761 (Houghton, fMS Eng. 748) and letters to Samuel Pegge (Bodl., MS Eng. lett. d 46, fos. 649–[58]: in Ashe, ii. 22–3).

Like Thomas Warton, who published the second edition of his *Observations on the Fairy Queen of Spenser* in 1762, Hurd was interested in the pervasive influence of the apparently low literature of Gothic Romance (which he had not read) on the great English poets: Spenser, Shakespeare, and Milton (whom he had). Hurd redefined the Gothic by paralleling the cultural and artistic fecundity of ancient Greece with medieval Europe, re-evaluating the medieval by redefining the Hellenic. The petty tyrannies, incessant warring, and feudal values of the Middle Ages were not unlike the martial politics of ancient Greece that had created the institutions of chivalry and bardism:

when we see a sort of chivalry springing up among the Greeks, who were confessedly in a state resembling that of the feudal barons, and attended by the like symptoms and effects, is it not fair to conclude that the chivalry of the Gothic times was owing to that common corresponding *state*, and received it's character from it?[65]

Hurd's strategy, however, was not simply to impose an anachronistic social and linguistic model on the classical canons of literature and taste, and he was not so naïve as to find classical beauties in Gothic art. Instead, he tried to demonstrate that, if the conditions and therefore execution of Gothic and classical art differed, their theories of composition coincided.

When an architect examines a Gothic structure by Grecian rules, he finds nothing but deformity. But the Gothic architecture has it's own rules, by which when it comes to be examined, it is seen to have it's merit, as well as the Grecian. The question is not, which of the two is conducted in the simplest or truest taste: but, whether there be not sense and design in both, when scrutinized by the laws on which each is projected.[66]

Although he did not support Ossianic revivalism ('I would advise no modern poet to revive these faery tales in an epic poem') Hurd did propose an indigenous autonomy for Gothic art, rather than simply condemning it as mongrel degeneration.[67] In this way, Hurd's *Letters* helped to develop an English aesthetic by placing original genius in the Middle Ages, distinguishing it from the Franco-Scottish Celts.

[65] Hurd, *Letters*, 37–8.   [66] Ibid. 61.   [67] Ibid. 101.

For a literary antiquarian like Percy, the work was a godsend. The Goths were simultaneously being reinvented in two different ways: as both ancients and medievals. Hurd was effectively legitimizing the medieval ballads Percy was editing in his Folio MS for the *Reliques* as examples of native Gothic genius. Moreover, the publication of the *Fragments* directly inspired two of Percy's works: *Five Pieces of Runic Poetry translated from the Islandic Language* (1763) and *Northern Antiquities* (1770). An advance copy of Macpherson's *Fragments* was sent to the Leasowes, Shenstone's country retreat. Percy, who had as yet done virtually nothing with the *Reliques*, immediately proposed a comparable anthology of the Gothic; Shenstone responded that a selection of these Gothic 'Fragments' could be included in a four-volume *Reliques*.

Percy's *Runic Poetry* and the putative *Reliques* had therefore an identical Gothic pedigree. As indicated elsewhere, however, Percy's sudden and absorbing enthusiasm in the *Fragments*, which he read while staying with Shenstone in August 1760, is not surprising. The Anglo-Saxon scholar Edward Lye was parson of Yardley Hastings, Bedfordshire, just a mile and a half away from Percy at Easton Maudit. He was a close and obliging neighbour—on 24 April 1759 he gave away Anne Gutteridge, Percy's bride.

As is apparent from Percy's surviving papers on Runic poetry (including notes on Wise's *Some Enquiries*) and his correspondence with Lye, Percy's Runic researches were conducted within a context which sharply distinguished the Gothic from the Celtic, and moreover an immediate literary context that thirsted for ancient poetry. James Dodsley signed the contract for '*five* pieces of *Runic Poetry translated from the Islandic Language*' (with *The Song of Solomon*) on 21 May 1761, the day before the *Reliques* deal was struck, and within a month 'The Incantation of Hervor' was published in the *Lady's Magazine*.[68] The Runic collection itself took another two years to leave the press, however, by which time Percy's prefatory apology seemed unnecessary: 'It would be as vain to deny, as it is perhaps impolitic to mention, that this attempt is owing to the success of the ERSE fragments'.[69] But *Five*

[68] Bodl., MS Eng. lett. d 59, fo. 8ʳ; *Lady's Magazine* (1761), 487–9.

[69] Thomas Percy, *Five Pieces of Runic Poetry translated from the Islandic Language* (1763), p. A4ᵛ (italics reversed). Earlier (1761) Percy had placed his 'Fragments of Chinese Poetry' (*Hau Kiou Choaan*, iv. 197–254) in the context of Macpherson's *Fragments*, which he called '*striking and poetical*' (iv. 200). This whole section of *Hau*

Pieces of Runic Poetry was clearly a direct, if delayed, response to Macpherson. Like the *Fragments* it was a slim octavo containing short pieces of apparently ancient foreign verse translated into distinctive English prose. Percy, however, legitimized his sources in a very different way.

The entire structure of Percy's *Runic Poetry* served as an authenticating mechanism. Its title-page was more elaborate than that of the *Fragments*, and displayed an engraving of a number of untranslated runes, serving to underline the palpability of Percy's sources. Like the Chinese characters which adorned the *Miscellaneous Pieces* and the representation of the incomplete Folio MS introducing the *Reliques* (and even the Reynolds portrait of Percy showing him clutching a bundle of 'MSS'), this was an opportunity to authenticate the work. This was true of Macpherson's *Fingal* too, which portrayed a blind Ossian extemporizing his verses in the Celtic wilderness, with no manuscript in sight.[70]

Both the *Fragments* and *Runic Poetry* quoted Lucan as an epigraph—the *Fragments* a remark on bards and *Runic Poetry* a battle scene—but there the immediate similarities ended. *Runic Poetry* was printed on quality paper, was set more accurately, and the text was enlivened with frequent ornaments. It was not designed to be bound sympathetically with the *Fragments*, but to replace it. Percy's poems were not translated in the Ossianic style, and were prefaced with notes, clarified with footnotes, and concluded with endnotes. 'The Incantation of Hervor', for example, had a lengthy preface 'To prevent as much as possible the interruption of notes', but there were still footnotes throughout the entire piece.[71] Macpherson's collection was lean by comparison: it simply had a brisk preface contributed by Blair, and occasional, usually brief, explanatory footnotes. Shenstone approved far more of the latter style, because it presented the pieces as poetry, and he disliked the antiquarian lumber that burdened Percy's poems. Percy in fact apologized for this in a letter to Shenstone: 'You will probably be disgusted to see it so incumbered with Notes; Yet some are unavoidable, as the Piece

---

Kiou Choaan was modelled on the layout of the Ossianic pamphlet and possibly was intended to be marketed separately.

[70] In fact the runes were not transcribed accurately, as the above copy shows (Queen's, Percy 598).   [71] *Runic Poetry*, 6 (italics reversed).

would be unintelligible without them.'[72] Percy would not relinquish any verifying apparatus and did not appreciate that it was the very unintelligibility of the pieces that had so appealed to Shenstone.[73]

In *Runic Poetry*, Percy outlined scholarly precedent, pleaded editorial integrity and verifiable sources, and listed appropriate references. In other words, he placed the work in a diagrammatic scholarly context: the literary establishment of books and writing, rather than the oral bardic tradition claimed by Macpherson. This is demonstrated most clearly in the Runic originals that were appended to the translations, of which he wrote: 'The Editor was in some doubt whether he should subjoin or suppress the originals. But as they lie within little compass, and as the books whence they are extracted are very scarce, he was tempted to add them as vouchers for the authenticity of his version.'[74] In fact, these originals were printed in roman, rather than Runic, characters, because they were themselves Swedish and Latin translations. They were included for the sake of form rather than to encourage scholarly precision, as part of a grand textual conspiracy. Without authentic originals, Percy had no way of knowing whether his Gothic translations were more or less accurate than Macpherson's Celtic translations. But what is important about Percy's operation of his textual machine is that it fixed the notion of extant manuscripts onto his work.

Percy emphasized this in his account of the Goths. The remnants of Gothic culture were a rich resource for the national historian, and Percy argued that in his translation of Mallet (begun in 1763, later published as *Northern Antiquities* in 1770) 'the English reader' would 'see the seeds of our excellent Gothic constitution . . . many superstitions, opinions and prejudices . . . that the ideas of Chivalry were strongly rivetted in the minds of all the northern nations from the remotest ages . . . and . . . an ancient Islandic Romance that shews the original of that kind of writing which so long captivated all the nations of Europe'.[75]

Percy's Goths were the ancient ancestors of the English, and had laid the foundations of national character, culture, and politics: 'It

---

[72] *Letters*, vii. 70.   [73] Ibid. 74.
[74] *Runic Poetry*, p. A7^r (italics reversed).   [75] *Letters*, v. 84–5.

will be thought a paradox, that the same people, whose furious ravages destroyed the last poor remains of expiring genius among the Romans, should cherish it with all possible care among their own countrymen: yet so it was.'[76] They also invented rhyming verse, a claim Percy could 'prove' because they were inveterate scribblers, or rather carvers, of runes. Just as the verbal clamour of Macpherson's Ossianic fragments underlined the oral culture of the Celts, so the prodigious textuality of *Five Pieces of Runic Poetry* underlined the rampant literacy of the Goths. Percy demonstrated that his Goths differed from Macpherson's Celts in the crucial area of extant records, records which were keys to unlock 'the treasures of native genius', meaning, of course, English genius.[77] The confrontational preface challenged Macpherson to publish his Ossianic originals: 'till the Translator of those poems thinks proper to produce his originals, it is impossible to say whether they do not owe their superiority, if not their whole existence entirely to himself. The Editor of these pieces had no such boundless field for licence.'[78]

Blair had in part already responded to this argument in his *Critical Dissertation* published early in 1763 and designed to be bound into *Fingal*. Macpherson's publications found their defenders among the Scottish intelligentsia, for whom they formed the focus of a whole poetic and critical school. Blair argued against Hurd that there was an archetypal genius common to all nations at a certain primitive stage of their development, and that this original genius was the modernity of sentiment displayed by *Ossian*. He therefore attacked Percy's Gothic fragments for their barbaric and bloodthirsty images, which revealed them to be worthless trash.

Blair further postulated that in early societies (for example, in Old Testament times) language was purely figurative. From this childlike state, 'Language advances from sterility to copiousness, and at the same time, from fervour and enthusiasm, to correctness and precision. Style becomes more chaste; but less animated.'[79]

---

[76] *Runic Poetry*, p. A2ᵛ (italics reversed).   [77] Ibid., p. A8ʳ (italics reversed).
[78] Ibid., p. A4ᵛ (italics reversed).
[79] Hugh Blair, *A Critical Dissertation on the Poems of Ossian, the Son of Fingal* (1763), 3. A letter to Davies of Cadell and Davies (21 May 1782) reveals that the *Dissertation* was based on a lecture Blair sold to Becket for 50 guineas (Historical Society of Pennsylvania, Gratz Collection, Case 10, Box 27). For Macpherson's hand in the published *Dissertation* see R. W. Chapman, 'Blair on Ossian', *RES* 7 (1931), 80–3: Macpherson effectively wrote the final paragraph.

Society progressed in a similar way: the four stages of hunters, gatherers, farmers, and traders. Although *Ossian* was nominally set in the primary moment of this Aristotelian social theory, it displayed all the artistry and enlightenment of later stages. Blair emphasized this social modernity in the language he used to compare Celtic with Gothic verse: 'When we turn from the poetry of Lodbrog to that of Ossian, it is like passing from a savage desart, into a fertile and cultivated country.'[80] The image was used advisedly. By demonstrating the Augustan sophistication of *Ossian* he could both prove the authenticity of this Celtic epic, and show its superiority to the Goths. 'In one remarkable passage, Ossian describes himself as living in a sort of classical age, enlightened by the memorials of former times, conveyed in the songs of bards; and points at a period of darkness and ignorance which lay beyond the reach of tradition.'[81] The pejorative shades of Gothic were reinscribed, once again merging the shadow of barbarism into the dark night of medieval ignorance. *Ossian* trod a fine, Homeric line between primitivism and enlightenment; a chiaroscuro of antiquity and modernity that was likely to disorientate the reader:

It is necessary here to observe, that the beauties of Ossian's writings cannot be felt by those who have given them only a single or a hasty perusal. His manner is so different from that of the poets, to whom we are most accustomed; his style is so concise, and so much crowded with imagery; the mind is kept at such a stretch in accompanying the author; that an ordinary reader is at first apt to be dazzled and fatigued, rather than pleased. His poems require to be taken up at intervals, and to be frequently reviewed.[82]

As with the *Fragments*, the aesthetic of the Celtic past disorientated the Enlightenment reader. It was part of Percy's project to embed his Gothic aesthetic in the taste of the present.

To defend the Scots from the incursions of Percy's Goths, Blair again stressed the primacy of Celtic heritage: 'The Celtæ, a great and mighty people, altogether distinct from the Goths and Teutones, once extended their dominion over all the west of Europe.' He imagined that the bards studied arts, contributed 'not a little to exalt the publick manners', and lived with the Druids in Pythagorean colleges. Even after the demise of the

---

[80] Blair, *Critical Dissertation*, 11.   [81] Ibid. 15.   [82] Ibid. 21.

Druids, the bards retained respect 'almost down to our own times'.[83] Although the *Dissertation* did not necessarily claim the genesis of poetry for the Highlands, it extolled the originality of a unique northern epic. The similarities of diction and metaphor among all ancient epics (or rather, between *Ossian* and Homer) were not the result of the translator's studied imitation but of archetypal original genius.

More importantly, Blair made a lengthy case against the Gothic fragments, retranslating the ubiquitous Nordic poem 'Regner Lodbrog'. The response of the Celtic *Ossian* supporters to 'Regner Lodbrog' was profoundly different from that of the Gothic revivalists, and clarifies how ancient poetry was being employed in new nationalist discourses. William Temple had translated this poem from Latin into English in 1690, but it had of course appeared most recently in Percy's versions in the *Lady's Magazine* and *Runic Poetry*. Blair's version in his *Critical Dissertation* was certainly less florid than Percy's, but he emphasized the bloodthirsty images and formlessness of 'Regner Lodbrog'. *Ossian* was, of course, completely different, combining 'the fire and the enthusiasm of the most early times . . . with an amazing degree of regularity and art'. Blair discounted claims that the Goths invented rhyme and characterized the style of *Ossian* as a 'measured prose' which exhibited all the native, ancient, and original genius of the works: 'His imagery is, without exception, copied from that face of nature, which he saw before his eyes; and by consequence may be expected to be lively. We meet with no Grecian or Italian scenery; but with the mists, and clouds, and storms of a northern mountainous region.'[84] The description recalled Ramsay's *Ever Green*, Gerard's *Essay on Taste*, and Edmund Burke's definition of the sublime.

Macpherson's second epic, *Temora, An Ancient Epic Poem, in Eight Books*, published in 1763, attempted to divide and rule the clamour of opposition that had risen against *Ossian*. As he wryly remarked, 'WHILE some doubt the authenticity of the poems of Ossian, others strenuously endeavour to appropriate them to the

---

[83] Ibid. 11–15. Blair also annexed Welsh history: 'The Welch bards were of the same Celtic race with the Scottish and Irish' (15 n.).

[84] Frank Edgar Farley, *Scandinavian Influences in the English Romantic Movement* (Cambridge, Mass., 1903), 59–69; Blair, *Critical Dissertation*, 11, 4 n.–6 n., 53.

Irish nation.'[85] Macpherson introduced *Temora* with an emphatic attack on the Irish claim to be the original Celts and the composers of *Ossian*. He refuted the Irish and delivered an Ossianic account of the racial composition of ancient Britain. The Irish were denied pure Celtic origins, in support of which *Temora* was presented as proof. *Ossian* was more than a cultural product: it was national identity.

    Temora also placed the bards in a more contemporary light. Macpherson concentrated on their decline in status: they were expelled from clans for 'dull and trivial' compositions, took to 'satire and lampoon', and were accommodated by 'the vulgar'.[86] They began to invent incredible stories, interpolated the remains of Ossian with their 'futile performances', and subsequently created the romance. Macpherson extended his Ossianic theory of the origin of poetry in the wake of Hurd's *Letters*: 'I firmly believe, there are more stories of giants, enchanted castles, dwarfs, and palfreys, in the Highlands, than in any country in Europe' in which, of course, 'the very language of the bards is still preserved'.[87] Macpherson was retheorizing his material and belatedly considering *Ossian* manuscripts.

    In *Temora* Macpherson's use of oral imagery was more symbolic than the earlier works, and the dominant impression was of colours. The poems became visual and therefore literate rather than vocal and illiterate. The oral tradition was now defined by manuscripts, a new fidelity of the source:

The reader will find some alterations in the style of this book. These are drawn from more correct copies of the original which came to my hands, since the former publication. As the most part of the poem is delivered down by tradition, the style is sometimes various and interpolated. After comparing the different readings, I always made choice of that which agreed best with the spirit of the context.[88]

The context in fact overwhelmed the poetry. *Temora* was more fictional than earlier works, so Macpherson verified it historically. Fragments and poems that would have graced an earlier collection

---

    [85] *Temora*, p. xx.   [86] Ibid. 126 n.
    [87] Ibid. 184 n.; see also John Macpherson's *Critical Dissertations on the Origin, Antiquities, Language, Government, Manners, and Religion of the Ancient Caledonians, their Posterity the Picts, and the British and Irish Scots* (1768), 204–6, 213–25, in which James had a hand (Stafford, *The Sublime Savage*, 152–3).
    [88] *Temora*, 4 n.

in their own right were literally reduced to footnotes in a larger argument, to prove the Gaelic language was purely and divinely harmonious. The integrity of Gaelic was its oracy. In other words, the language and style of the poem was not merely a source to settle the Celtic ancestry of the Scots over the Irish; it was the very object of their national quest, their true heritage.

Blair's preface to the *Fragments* had, on Macpherson's advice, completely rejected the possibility that the poems were really songs. The 'Dissertation' prefaced to *Fingal*, however, stated that this linguistic harmony was easily adapted to music and formed a memorable—and uniquely Celtic—concatenation. It is worth noting that modern editors still examine mnemonic patterns and chain alliteration in restoring corrupt Celtic texts.[89] Macpherson even claimed that the whole of *Fingal* was originally composed to be sung to the harp.[90] For 'Berrathon', 'Ossian's last hymn' which concluded the volume, Macpherson was forthright: 'It is set to music, and still sung in the north, with a great deal of wild simplicity, but little variety of sound.' By the time Macpherson was writing his final notes to *Temora*, he considered that bards performed 'the double capacity of poet and harper'. Blair consequently revised his opinions in his own *Dissertation*.[91]

These ideas were developed in *Temora* by advocating the inherent musical nature of the ancient Celtic language, which had produced an oral tradition carried along by song. *Ossian* preserved 'the very language of the bards', and enabled Macpherson to reconstruct imaginatively the original Celtic: 'The first part of the speech is rapid and irregular, and is peculiarly calculated to animate the soul to war . . . like torrents rushing over broken rocks; the second like the course of a full-flowing river, calm but majestic.'[92] The Gaelic language was universal and sentimental like music, rather than pictorial and abstract like hieroglyphs or runes: 'So well adapted are the sounds of the words to the sentiments, that, even without any knowledge of the

---

[89] David Greene and Frank O'Connor (eds. and trs.), *A Golden Treasury of Irish Poetry: A.D. 600 to 1200* (1967), 2–3.

[90] *Fingal*, 61 n., 87 n. When Milman Parry asked the Yugoslavian bard Avdo Meðedović to 'sing as long a song as he could', he sang for two weeks (Parry, *Making of Homeric Verse*, 476).

[91] *Fingal*, 267 n.; *Temora*, 132 n., 126 n.; Blair, *Critical Dissertation*, 3–4.

[92] *Temora*, 50 n., paraphrasing ll. 7–12 of Gray's 'The Progress of Poetry'.

language, they pierce and dissolve the heart.'[93] By arguing that the language was inherently musical, Macpherson was able to print part of an original. Whether it was an original manuscript or dictated by oral tradition was irrelevant: the harmony of antique sounds was sufficient evidence for its authenticity. The text comprised twenty pages of what purported to be the ancient Gaelic text: 'A SPECIMEN OF THE ORIGINAL OF TEMORA BOOK SEVENTH.' *Ossian*, for at least three years an oral phenomenon, in 1763 sought the sanction of literacy.[94]

The effect was disastrous. The introduction of manuscripts was not simply incongruous. It was lethal to the culture Macpherson and Blair had laboured to realize—the bardic oral tradition of the primigenial Highland Celts—because it dramatically increased the demand to see manuscript sources. The demand could not be met and, after an extended public controversy, *Ossian* was dismissed as a forgery.[95]

'A MERE ANTIQUARIAN IS A RUGGED BEING'[96]

This belated literation and its attendant ruinous effect on Macpherson confirmed Percy's formulation of Gothic poetics, which he was now rewriting for the *Reliques*. *Ossian* trespassed upon the written records of literate ancients like Percy's Goths, and paid the price. The source had become the deciding factor in the antiquarian canonization of literature. Percy's counter-attack against Macpherson appeared in the *Reliques* in 1765 as the 'Essay on the Ancient English Minstrels', written during the summer of 1764—one of the last things he wrote before publication. Percy

---

[93] *Temora*, p. xvii. William Warburton outlined the history of writing from pictorial Egyptian and Mexican hieroglyphics to 'characteristic Marks to Images' (*The Divine Legation of Moses demonstrated on the Principles of a Religious Deist* (1738–41), quoted by Percy in *Miscellaneous Pieces relating to the Chinese* (1762), i, p. A5^r).

[94] See the appendix to the dissertation, also presumably written by Hugh Blair, in *Works of Ossian* (1765), ii. 451 (this had in fact been Macpherson's technique since the beginning: see Andrew Gallie's evidence in Mackenzie, *Report*, 44). Although the dissertation continued to be printed with the *Poems*, this appendix was dropped from subsequent editions (see Steve Rizza, 'A Bulky and Foolish Treatise? Hugh Blair's *Critical Dissertation* Reconsidered', in Gaskill, *Ossian Revisited*, 131).

[95] Howard Gaskill, 'What Did James Macpherson Really Leave on Display at his Publisher's Shop in 1762?', *SGS* 16 (1990), 67–89.

[96] Johnson's testimonial to Percy, 23 Apr. 1778: see *Boswell's Life*, iii. 278.

considered the medium of literate poetry in a new way. His essay outlined a theory of oral composition as the direct progenitor of written verse, and so attempted to synthesize the conflicting and contradictory discourses of racial myth and medieval Gothic. Percy emphasized the written, indeed the physical, antiquarian status of ancient English poetry—embodied by his Folio MS and later the *Reliques*, but his thesis hinged on the representation and reputation of the ancient poets themselves. Although indebted to French works on romance and chivalry by Claude Fauchet, Sainte-Palaye, Abbé Lenglet du Fresnoy, and Paul-Henri Mallet, Percy's immediate source was John 'Estimate' Brown's *Dissertation on the Rise, Union, and Power, the Progressions, Separations, and Corruptions, of Poetry and Music* (1763).[97]

Brown asserted that poetry and music were naturally united, but that civilized refinement had gradually separated them. Uncultivated societies, such as the American Iroquois and Hurons, relied on bards for their history and ultimately for their cultural identity: 'The Profession of *Bard* or *Musician* would be held as very honourable, and of high Esteem. For he would be vested with a kind of *public Character*: and if not an original Legislator, yet still he would be regarded as a *subordinate* and *useful Servant* of the *State*.'[98] Emphasis was placed on the civic duties of the bard. At the cusp of literacy they remodelled their traditional ancient songs as written verse, severed the connection with music, and broke with the past. The new literacy legitimized itself by rewriting history.

Brown did not commit himself to either side in the Goths and Celts debate. He agreed that 'the *Scythian* or *Runic* Songs' were the oldest in the North, and quoted Odin, who boasted that 'his Runic Poems were given him by the Gods'; at the same time *Ossian* had been composed 'during the second Period of Music . . . when the Bard's Profession had separated from that of the Legislator, yet still retained its Power and Dignity in full Union'.[99] His conclusion, 'Of the possible Re-Union of Poetry and Music', was strangely expectant:

---

[97] 'Estimate' Brown accompanied Thomas Percy and his charge Algernon Percy on their 1765 tour of Scotland (Davis (1989), 144–6).

[98] John Brown, *A Dissertation on the Rise, Union, and Power, the Progressions, Separations, and Corruptions, of Poetry and Music* (1763), 44.

[99] Ibid. 51, 158–9.

The *Legislator's* and *Bard's* Character cannot again be *generally* and *fully* *united*. We have seen, they naturally separate in an early Period of Civilization: And the Departments become so distinct, as to create a general Incompatibility and Repugnance too clear to need an Illustration. But although the Legislator cannot generally maintain the poetic and musical Character, he may still continue to *protect*, and sometimes even to *possess* it: And when Poetry and Music are united in their proper Ends, there are few *secondary Accomplishments* which do truer Honour even to the highest Stations.[100]

Percy's minstrel evolved from Brown's anticipation of cultural and national renewal. He devised a state role for the poet, and defined the relationship of the arts to the court by reviving patronage.[101] For his models, Percy returned to *Runic Poetry* and the scalds.

Percy derived most of his information about ancient Scandinavia from Paul-Henri Mallet's *Introduction à l'histoire de Dannemarc* (1755–6). He had read Mallet by 1761 and, with the help of Lye, began translating it on 21 November 1763, devoting a whole week to the business.[102] Scalds were central to Scandinavian society. Their spiritual father was Odin, inventor of poetry and runes, and their Runic poetry was both a divine gift and a social asset: 'Those that excelled in it, were distinguished by the first honours of the state: were constant attendants on their kings, and were often employed on the most important commissions.'[103] To understand the scalds he had to re-examine the bards—not the fictions of *Ossian* but the remote antiquities of Wales.

In Percy's first letter to the Welsh antiquarian Evan Evans (21 July 1761) he asked whether there was any truth in Gray's proposition that Edward I massacred all the Welsh bards. Evans replied that it was true; sent a bardic commentary by Goronwy Owen, one of the Morrisian Circle; and informed Percy of his unpublished 'De Bardis Dissertatio', written in 1759. Percy had

---

[100] Brown, *A Dissertation on the Rise, Union, and Power, the Progressions, Separations, and Corruptions, of Poetry and Music*, 222.

[101] Samuel Johnson's famous letter to Lord Chesterfield (7 Feb. 1755: *Boswell's Life*, i. 261–3) is often seen as the symbolic end of 18th-century literary patronage (for example, Alvin Kernan, *Samuel Johnson and the Impact of Print* (Princeton, 1987), 200–1). It is therefore unsurprising that, in view of his attempts to revive aristocratic patronage, Percy's relationship with the Duke of Northumberland was ridiculed by Johnson (see below, Chapter 5).

[102] *Letters*, v. 16–17; BL, Add. MS 32330, fos. 41ᵛ–2ᵛ.

[103] *Runic Poetry*, p. A3ʳ (italics reversed).

some criticisms of Owen's remarks but requested a copy of Evans's dissertation.[104] An infirm Evans responded on 6 December with a brief description of the Welsh bards: 'Our Bards were cotemporary with the persons, whose actions they celebrate, and acted the part of historians as well as poets . . . And such were all the antient Bards of Britain whose compositions are extant.'[105]

But Percy had to wait for publication of Evans's *Specimens of the Poetry of the Antient Welsh Bards* (1764) before he could read the dissertation, and, while he published *Runic Poetry*, the bards were absent from their letters. In February 1764, Percy raised the subject again. He had been working on his essay 'On the Alliterative Metre of Pierce Plowman's Visions', and wrote to Evans that he believed the bards had modelled their alliteration on the scalds, because at the time Runic was socially elevated: 'Islandic was a kind of court language, as French is now.'[106] Evans disagreed. There were traces of alliteration and rhyme in pre-Roman Druidic literature, written long before contact with the Goths: 'most probably the Scalds borrowed this poetic ornament from their Bards, and even the very word Bard itself, as you acknowledg [*sic*] in your Runic Poetry. This word is certainly of Celtic origin and signifies an inspired person.'[107] Their duel continued. Evans argued that the medieval romance writers took alliterative rhyming verse from the Gothic scalds who had received it from the Celtic bards, among whom the Welsh were the finest exponents.

Percy's response was to send a draft of his proposal to translate Mallet, describing the genesis of 'our excellent Gothic constitution'.[108] Both Percy and Evans were writing national myths: Evans instinctively spoke of 'our' bards and celebrated the Cymmrodorin Society, Percy was perfecting the word 'Gothic'. Percy warned Evans that Mallet's biggest mistake was to compound the Goths with the Celts, 'a mistake which I shall endeavour to rectify in my translation'.[109] Percy worked hard to expunge all references to the Celts from Mallet's book. He produced a list of page references headed 'Notes concerning the Author's Confounding of Celtic &

---

[104] Lonsdale notes that, early in 1760, Thomas Gray was shown Evans's *De Bardis Dissertatio* (Gray, *Poems*, 212).   [105] *Letters*, v. 25–6.
[106] Ibid. 61–2.
[107] Ibid. 66–7. Percy quoted these objections in *Northern Antiquities*, ii. 198–9.
[108] *Letters*, v. 84–5.   [109] Ibid. 88.

Gothic Antiquities' and methodically changed every Celt into a Goth.[110]

Evan Evans's *Some Specimens of the Poetry of the Antient Welsh Bards* was published by James Dodsley on 5 June 1764, and Percy read it while Johnson was staying with him at Easton Maudit. Although Evans had conceived the work much earlier, he placed it in the context of Macpherson, which was noticeable even in printing the work as a large quarto. This was a fatal mistake: reviewers pounced on Evans's dull translations and even Percy, repeating Johnson's irascible criticisms, attacked Evans's use of the disgraced *Ossian*. The Welsh bards were, rather unfairly, guilty by association with oral tradition. Percy found nothing in Evans's long-awaited dissertation. It simply outlined the by-now predictable duties of the bard: they were Celtic poets who wrote songs in praise of the great, and historians and genealogists who recorded the deeds and pedigree of their people. Evans's style was self-effacing and pedagogic and his translations were insipid, even if he did stress his use of written records. It was an unthreatening performance.

Nevertheless, Percy was decidedly influenced by the *Specimens*. Evans began with a dedication to Sir Roger Mostyn, whose ancestry legitimized both the verses themselves (not least because he owned manuscripts) and their transmission, which was analogous to lineal descent. Evans then outlined his bardic theory, drawn from Brown's *Dissertation*, of which he reprinted a passage. Evans, like Percy, described a single manuscript source from which his *Specimens* were selected, translated, and edited. This manuscript lingered on a precarious threshold, not simply in 'great risque of mouldering away', but in its relation to Edward I's massacre of the Welsh bards.[111]

---

[110] Bodl., MS Percy c 7, fo. 42[r]. See Prys Morgan, 'From a Death to a View: The Hunt for the Welsh Past in the Romantic Period', in Eric Hobsbawm and Terence Ranger (eds.), *The Invention of Tradition* (Cambridge, 1983), 68. For Percy's calendar of translation, see Margaret Clunies Ross, 'Percy and Mallet: The Genesis of *Northern Antiquities*', in *Sagnaþing helgað Jónasi Kristjássyni* (Reykjavík, 1994), 107–17; and Andrew N. Deacon, 'The Use of Norse Mythology and Literature by Some 18th and 19th Century Writers, with Special Reference to the Work of Bishop Thomas Percy, Thomas Gray, Matthew Arnold and William Morris', B.Litt. thesis (Oxford, 1964), 46–91, 198–9.

[111] Evan Evans, *Some Specimens of the Poetry of the Antient Welsh Bards* (1764), preface, p. iii.

Like Percy's Folio MS, Evans's source was a copy of an original which was not itself a contemporary record. But although Evans committed himself neither to Percy's theory of literate Goths, nor to Macpherson's mysterious oral tradition, his work was ultimately an attempt to usurp *Ossian* with a new claimant for the British Homer: the ancient Welsh bard Taliesin. Evans's source was literate: 'It has been my luck to meet with a manuscript of all his genuine pieces now extant,' an astonishing artefact which was verified by appeal to the Welsh literati. Evans's most interesting comment, however, was that the manuscript was only half comprehensible because of the antiquity of the language:

This should be a caveat to the English reader concerning the great antiquity of the poems that go under the name of Ossian, the son of Fingal, lately published by Mr. Mackpherson. It is a great pity Taliesin is so obscure, for there are many particulars in his poems that would throw great light upon the history, notions, and manners of the ancient Britons, especially of the Druids, a great part of whose learning it is certain he had imbibed.[112]

Evans saw the retrieval of this language in terms of manuscript rescue, as a physical (literate) artefact, rather than an oral evolution: 'I wish learned men would think of this ere it be too late; for one century makes a great havock of old MSS. especially such as are in the hands of private persons, who understand not their true value, or are suffered to rot in such libraries, where nobody is permitted to have access to them.'[113] Essentially, then, *Specimens* was a shaky compromise between the two camps of Goths and Celts. In a sense, Evans got everything wrong: he attributed the works to a single bard who had left an unreadable manuscript. But this showed Percy that he had to place his Folio MS in the broad context of transmission, explaining the position of the poet within the mechanisms of literacy and the state. In other words, Percy had to construct a cultural provenance.

So, with Evans harmlessly in print, the stage was set, as Percy sat down in 1764, for a dramatic remodelling of the transmission of national literature. Percy was ready to draw together the threads of many arguments as he sought to reinvent the English poetic tradition, and it cannot be a coincidence that such an

[112] Ibid. 54.   [113] Ibid. 158.

ambitious essay was begun under the eye of Johnson, who was
staying at Easton Maudit with Percy at that time. Percy began his
essay on 16 August 1764, when it originally formed part of the
preface.[114] He combined all his sources (the Folio MS, transcripts,
broadside ballads, and printed poems) with his antiquarian
researches on scalds and bards. The scalds became the Gothic
forefathers of the ancient English minstrels and were disingenu-
ously merged with the bards.[115] He united the different senses of
Gothic, attributing the invention of writing and poetry to the
scalds, who became almost divine; dehistoricizing the bards by
applying the term indiscriminately to scalds and minstrels; and
making the medieval minstrels the inheritors of the Runic tradition. In contrast to Evans, Percy invented a contemporary role,
both cultural and ideological, for his English minstrels: they were
the embodiment of the Gothic aesthetic.

The 'Essay on the Ancient English Minstrels' began by picking
up the thread of Brown's *Dissertation* and ignoring the recent
discussions with Evans:

THE MINSTRELS seem to have been the genuine successors of the ancient
Bards, who united the arts of Poetry and Music, and sung verses to the
harp, of their own composing. It is well known what respect was shown
to their BARDS by the Britons: and no less was paid to the northern SCALDS
by most of the nations of Gothic race. (i, p. xv)

Percy argued by analogy, claiming, in Hurd's style, that the bloody
ferocity of scaldic society would have produced the codes of
chivalry. In his essay on metrical romances, the last to be finished,
on 1 November 1764, Percy concluded, 'That our old Romances
of Chivalry are derived in a lineal descent from the ancient historical songs of the SCALDS, is incontestible, because there are many of
them still preserved in the North, which exhibit all the seeds of
Chivalry, before it became a solemn institution' (iii, p. iii (italics
reversed)).

Like the scald, Percy's minstrel was originally a 'privileged
character' among the Anglo-Saxons and Danes: a historian,
genealogist, poet, and harpist. Alfred and later Anlaff adopted
minstrel disguises and were able to infiltrate their enemy's camps

---

[114] Davis (1989), 118 n.; BL, Add. MS 32330, fo. 54ᵛ.
[115] This poetic genealogy was deservedly ridiculed by Ritson (*Ancient Engleish
Metrical Romanceës*, i, p. xxx).

unchallenged. By obscuring the role of the Welsh bards he was able to annex their court status, yet retain the marginal and indigent nature of the minstrels. The minstrels, moreover, were oral poets. Percy therefore argued that the Gothic literacy of the scalds generated an oral tradition, which was in turn absorbed into the ephemeral publishing of popular balladry and chapbook romance, and ultimately the inaccuracies of the Folio MS. It is no surprise considering Percy's absolute emphasis on written sources that he imagined writing somehow came before speech. To distinguish his noble minstrels from the (usually female) hack ballad-singers who regaled passing Londoners with their wares in the 1760s, he once more adapted Brown and combined the oral ballads of the minstrels with the press-work of the ballad-singers:

so long as the Minstrels subsisted, they seem never to have designed their rhymes for publication, and probably never committed them to writing themselves: what copies are preserved of them were doubtless taken down from their mouths. But as the old Minstrels gradually wore out, a new race of ballad-writers succeeded, an inferior sort of minor poets, who wrote narrative songs merely for the press. (i, p. xxii)

Percy's account of the decline of the minstrels exactly mirrored Macpherson's bards. They 'gave more and more into embellishment, and set off their recitals with such marvelous fictions, as were calculated to captivate gross and ignorant minds' and predictably created the romance (iii, p. iii (italics reversed)).

Percy rescued the minstrel tradition even as he reinvented it. His minstrels were in peril on the literary sea, abandoned by Thomas Bodley's ark, their 'precious relicks swallowed up and lost in the gulph of time', as he put it to Evans in 1763.[116] Their ballads were victims of the treacherous vagaries of oral tradition: 'From the amazing variations, which occur in different copies of these old pieces, it is evident they made no scruple to alter each other's productions, and the reciter added or omitted whole stanzas, according to his own fancy or convenience' (i, p. xvi).

So at one level oral tradition did legitimize Percy's project and, more importantly, permitted his editorial revisions. He positioned his minstrels at the moment of national literacy. In one neat move the minstrel corpus was translated from the vocal to the literate

[116] *Letters*, v. 51.

and crystallized cultural identity in physical texts. Percy was fascinated by this textual shift. His interest in oral traditions ranged from the Mandarin tongue of the Chinese to the secret language of the Druids, and he recognized the precariousness of such linguistic and social structures. The Druidic language had disappeared without a trace, taking with it all details of their history, theology, and manners. Losses on a somewhat smaller scale were still occurring in the 1760s: 'Jephthah Judge of Israel' was incorporated in the second edition of the *Reliques*, having been 'retrieved from utter oblivion by a lady, who wrote it down from memory as she had formerly heard it sung by her father'. It was the only piece of pure oral transmission in the *Reliques*.[117] Revealingly, Percy knew nothing of music, and only included one melody in the whole book, and so he handled his ballads in different ways. As Lennard Davis points out, ballads are as much a part of the ideology of print, analogous to newspapers: 'the printed ballad was not conceived of as an oral form . . . its layout, woodcuts, and typeface are consciously assembled to add to its graphic and typographic presence.'[118] It will be seen that this typographic presence, or physical status of printed ballads, helped to define and clarify Percy's position with regard to his sources. The conversion of speech into writing, of songs into texts, produced a hybrid, an imagined world of authenticity and presence generated by the dream of origin. Indeed, as Stewart notes, 'the notion that writing endows the oral with materiality is another facet of the collector's interest in establishing the ephemerality of the oral, an interest that puts the oral in urgent need of rescue', which is Flemming Andersen's point about the extermination of the oral tradition in the printing house.[119] James Hogg's grandmother objected to Walter Scott's transcription of her songs: 'there war never ane o' my sangs prentit till ye prentit them yoursel', an' ye hae spoilt them awthegither. They were made for singing an' no for reading; but ye hae broken the charm now,

---

[117] *Reliques* (1767), i. 176 (italics reversed). Percy also had a copy of 'Jephthah's Rash Vow', transcribed from Ballard's white-letter ballad collection (Houghton, bMS Eng. 893 (19D)).
[118] Lennard J. Davis, *Factual Fictions: The Origins of the English Novel* (New York, 1983), 46–7.
[119] Susan Stewart, *Crimes of Writing: Problems in the Containment of Representation* (Durham, NC, 1994), 104.

an' they'll never be sung mair. An' the worst thing of a', they're nouther right spell'd nor right setten down.'[120] It seems that folklore scholarship might be a way of liquidating oral genres.

Perhaps most provoking to the Ossianists, Percy's minstrels were frequently northerners and thrived on the Gothic border and the Celtic fringe, and Stewart sees in their liminal situation an 'eroticization of boundary'.[121] This is another example of containment of the other, of internal colonialism. Minstrels also developed at the margins of orality and literacy. By plotting the borders, Percy melded together a national tradition, and clarified Englishness.

Ironically, Percy's beloved spiritual home of Northumberland was, as Linda Colley has pointed out, much more like Scotland than England: there were many more Scottish newspapers and books available than those printed in London, and levels of literacy were comparable with the Lowlands. Oats provided subsistence food, and Northumbrians and Scots even looked alike, 'with the same raw high-boned faces and the same thin, angular physiques'.[122] This may explain the crucial role played in Percy's *Reliques* of a resolutely *English* poetry. It was precisely at the border that Percy discerned the most defining characteristics of national literature. Indeed, Colley herself argues that the British nation was forged by internal colonialism in the wake of the Jacobite Rebellion of 1745: 'The two decades that followed the Battle of Culloden were an intensely creative period in terms of patriotic initiatives and discussion of national identities both in Great Britain and in other parts of Europe.'[123] The British Museum was founded in 1753 and opened in 1759; the *Encyclopaedia Britannica* was first issued (by a 'Society of Gentlemen in Scotland') from 1768 to 1771; whereas closer to Percy the literary culture was being formed by works such as Robert Dodsley's *Collection of Poems by Several Hands* (1st edn. 1748), Thomas Warton's *History of English Poetry* (1774–81), and the Shakespeare industry.

As has already been indicated, the very title *Reliques* suggested

---

[120] James Hogg, *The Domestic Manners and Private Life of Sir Walter Scott* (Glasgow, 1834), 61.   [121] Stewart, *Crimes of Writing*, 109–10.
[122] Linda Colley, *Britons: Forging the Nation 1707–1837* (1992), 16. See also Lane Cooper, 'Dr. Johnson on Oats and Other Grains', *PMLA* 52 (1937), 785–802.
[123] Colley, *Britons*, 85.

something archaic, something tangible and solid, and something incomplete yet fortuitous: an antiquarian artefact—certainly not a vocal performance. Percy's treatment of the Folio MS, explained in the next chapter, demonstrates that he was treating ballads as antiquarian relics. A literary text could be a document of social history, full of details of paintings, sculptures, tapestries, geography, and ancient manners, not to mention etymology and dialect. Percy's project was to salvage these evanescent records, in the course of which he frequently compared himself to Virgil reading Ennius (a poet who believed himself to be Homer *redivivus*, now singing in Latin), discovering the occasional jewel among piles of dung.[124]

The Folio MS was also an antiquarian relic itself, a pearl among the historical detritus. Not only the content, but the form—the medium—of ballads and literature was further proof of its antiquarian status. Percy kept tight hold over his unique source: it was a metaphor for his work and a symbol of his unique access to the medieval past. In his portrait by Joshua Reynolds, Percy grips a large bundle of 'MSS' underneath his arm. This was about as close as anyone outside the inner circle ever got to the source. The Folio MS was never lent, never exhibited, and never placed on public view. Percy's ambiguous editorial technique hindered other ballad scholars, but he refused access to editors like John Pinkerton even when his own plans to publish further items were evaporating. It was an invention: 'there is no "natural" form here, but a set of documents shaped by the expectations that led to their artifactualization in the first place.'[125] The Folio MS was not really an artefact, but an artefiction.

As I will show, Percy used printed sources very heavily and his acid test for dating was antique typefaces, rather than an appeal to a higher form of authenticity. In correspondence with John Wilson over 'The Dragon of Wantley', he noted:

in all Pepys's Collection of Ballads, consisting of many thousands, carefully preserved and arranged, (which I very minutely examined some years ago,) I did not find any copy of this ballad that had ever been printed in black letter.

---

[124] For example, Harlowe, 25.   [125] Stewart, *Crimes of Writing*, 106.

There were one or two editions of it, in the most modern Roman type, in which spelling was quite modern.[126]

He introduced himself to Thomas Astle in 1763, who was 'curious in collecting original Manuscripts', with the words, 'I am somewhat inquisitive after the old black-letter remains of our first English printers.'[127]

It is a revealing comment. Typography was a national determinant: the black-letter was rescued from its earlier eighteenth-century associations of illiteracy and puerility (children traditionally learnt to read from this old-fashioned fount). In 1754, when Percy was already poring over the Folio MS, Bonnel Thornton and George Colman had emphasized the nationalist implications in the use of particular typefaces: 'I could assure any patriot the most certain success, who should manifest his regard for *Old England* by printing his addresses in the *Old English Character*.'[128] This, then, finally locates Percy's ballads in the context of national culture and literary history: his ancient English minstrels were all, to a man, 'Old English Characters'. For the new generation of Romantic, Gothic Revival, and Pre-Raphaelite writers, the stamp of Englishness was the black-letter fount.

Percy's response to Macpherson's *Ossian* was to invent a Gothic tradition, and in the end he reinvented himself. He performed all the duties of a minstrel for his patrons the Northumberland Percys: acting as chaplain to the family and tutor to Algernon Percy, cataloguing the books at Syon House and writing visitors' guides to the Alnwick estate, compiling a genealogy and a history of the dynasty, and ultimately composing a lengthy pastiche of a Northumbrian ballad, *The Hermit of Warkworth* (1771). It could even be argued that this social toadying lay behind Percy's entire elaborate construction of state Gothicism. But in doing so he fundamentally shifted the attention of scholars to the medium of literary remains, and all that that entailed: reading the interfaces of oral, manuscript, and print cultures, and the coefficient of transmission, in terms of national myths—or the spatialization of culture. The effect of this endeavour was to confirm the limitations of the evolving canon and to confine it to physical rather than evanescent texts. This effect is also seen in other literature of the period as diverse as *Tristram Shandy*, Boswell's *Life of Johnson*,

---

[126] *Illustrations*, viii. 176.   [127] Harlowe, 53.
[128] *Connoisseur*, 21 Mar. 1754 (use of black-letter italicized).

and the Gothic novel, where the validity of different literary media (speech, manuscripts, and the press) is explored. Percy's *Reliques* stands as an example of the literary-antiquarian taste, an early attempt to assemble the nation's literary inheritance, and an influential anthology of popular verse; but it is also a resounding response to Macpherson's *Ossian*, a reinvention of the Gothic, and ultimately a manifesto for a new poetics of the source.

The last two chapters have shown that Percy restored the ballad its dignity by placing it in the evolving canon of English literature. He gave minstrels a voice, ballads a pedigree, and English literature a heritage. In 1782, Vicesimus Knox summarized the changes wrought by Percy's *Reliques*:

The popular ballad composed by some illiterate minstrel, and which has been handed down by tradition for several centuries, is rescued from the hands of the vulgar, to obtain a place in the collection of the man of taste. Verses, which, a few years past, were thought worthy the attention of children only, or of the lowest and rudest orders, are now admired for that artless simplicity, which once obtained the name of coarseness and vulgarity.[129]

Despite the ravings of Ritson, Percy's theory of ancient English minstrels continued to inspire both poets and antiquarians. Rose argues that the predominant images of authorship shifted from the singing shepherds, tillers of soil, magicians, and monarchs of the sixteenth and seventeenth centuries to the idea of paternity and parenting in the eighteenth.[130] The image of the bard, however, was already established by the middle of the century, and the image of the poet as a minstrel, inspired by Percy's *Reliques*, was predominant in the latter half of the century.[131] Thomas Chatterton's *Rowley* creation was directly inspired by Percy's minstrelsy, and James Beattie's derivative poem *The Minstrel* (1771–4) was a palpable influence on Wordsworth. George Ellis, writing in his collection *Specimens of Early English Poets* (first published in 1803), gently revised Percy's conception for the new century, and in 1821–2 the *London Magazine* ran an essay series on 'Traditional Literature' and 'On the Songs of the People of

---

[129] Vicesimus Knox, 'On the Prevailing Taste for the Old Poets', in *Essays Moral and Literary* (1782), ii. 214.   [130] Rose, *Authors and Owners*, 38.
[131] Kathryn Sutherland, 'The Native Poet: The Influence of Percy's Minstrel from Beattie to Wordsworth', *RES* 33 (1982), 414–33.

Gothic, or Teutonic Race'. By the end of the nineteenth century, Sabine Baring-Gould could publish eight volumes of *English Minstrelsie*, subtitled *A National Monument of English Song*. Within such a tradition, the minstrel may indeed be considered as a paternal figure: a mentor, certainly; but perhaps also, like Percy, an archetype of the poet as scholar. The minstrel had restored some of the ruins of literary origin; the word functioned as a single name appended to an enormous and anonymous body of work, and it had the power to determine the editorial treatment of that work. Having unravelled this context of production, we can now examine the more particular features of Percy's editing.

4

The Genesis of the *Reliques*

One day in September 1760, three men met to discuss James Macpherson's *Fragments of Ancient Poetry*. Their host was the poet William Shenstone, their rendezvous the Leasowes, his fashionable garden. The publisher Robert Dodsley had been staying with Shenstone during the summer preparing his edition of Aesop's fables, and these two writers were joined by Thomas Percy, who had already visited the Leasowes and had been corresponding with Shenstone regarding what was to become the *Reliques*. Percy had yet to find a publisher for his work.

Shenstone had been sent an early copy of the *Fragments* by John Macgowan on 21 June 1760, who accompanied the book with an evangelizing letter.[1] Shenstone informed Graves on 7 July, and told Percy on 11 August, and Percy visited Shenstone and Dodsley shortly thereafter.[2] Percy consulted the new work, later transcribing 'The Six Bards', another Ossianic piece, into Shenstone's copy. Eventually published as a footnote to 'Croma' in 1762, this somehow originated from James Bruce, whose letter to Shenstone was forwarded via James Turton and Macgowan.[3]

The heady presence of both Dodsley and the *Fragments* at Shenstone's Leasowes, and Percy's arrival with the Folio MS tucked underneath his arm, is the precise point at which serious work began on the *Reliques*. The momentous episode inspired Percy and Shenstone to produce two books within five years: *Five Pieces of Runic Poetry* appeared in 1763 (although it was apparently ready for the press in 1761), and *Reliques of Ancient English Poetry* in 1765. Both were published by the Dodsley firm.

By the time the fruits of their labours appeared, Shenstone was,

[1] Smith, 'Prepublication Circulation', 153–4.
[2] Williams, 556; *Letters*, vii. 68; Tierney, 19.
[3] Smith, 'Prepublication Circulation', 140–6. Percy's diary entry for 30 Oct. 1761, while staying with Shenstone, reads, 'Wrote out an Erse Fragmᵗ.' (BL, Add. MS 32336, fo. 34ᵛ). If this was 'The Six Bards', it is significantly later than Smith suggests.

unfortunately, dead, as was Robert Dodsley. They had proved, however, of considerable help to Percy—if more in encouragement than application. This chapter considers the genesis of the *Reliques*: Percy's relationship with Shenstone, the use of the Folio MS, and the source book *A Collection of Old Ballads*. The chronology of the Percy–Shenstone correspondence is outlined and then the undated transcripts from the Folio MS are described. These transcripts have not appeared in any edition of Shenstone's or Percy's letters, and are published here for the first time; their evidence shows that Shenstone was as much an irritant to Percy as an aide, and that the apparently close collaboration between Percy and Shenstone was in fact brief and inconclusive. Following the lapse in relations with Shenstone, Percy turned his researches to previously published collections, which are examined in the last section of the chapter.

'AN ANTIQUARIAN OR A MAN OF TASTE'[4]

'POETRY and consumptions are the most flattering of diseases,' wrote William Shenstone—and as if to prove this *aperçu*, he spent his life mildly indulging in both of these elegant and enervating conditions.[5] Shenstone was considered a poet of great taste and sensibility; he was also fashionably negligent and chronically indolent, frequently wintering in his bed, the victim of seasonal disorders. As the recipient of a small fortune, and enjoying a compelling charm, Shenstone never needed to become a prolific writer, and he exercised his pen only rarely and in the most desultory fashion.

Robert Dodsley, shortly after Shenstone's death, wrote: 'he chose rather to amuse himself in culling flowers at the foot of the mount, than to take the trouble of climbing the more arduous steps of PARNASSUS.'[6] It is an apt image. Shenstone (1714–63) was born and died at the Leasowes, his little estate, or *ferme ornée* (as the elderly Lady Luxborough called it), in Hales-Owen.[7] He spent his later years cultivating and improving these gardens and

---

[4] *Letters*, vii. 156.
[5] Shenstone, 'On Writing and Books', in *Works*, ii. 164. In a sudden fit of liveliness a few pages later (169), Shenstone compares a poet to a racehorse!
[6] Shenstone, *Works*, i. 9–10.   [7] Ibid., *Works*, ii. 321.

prospects, and by the 1750s was attracting a succession of fashionable visitors. Society became his main occupation, and Shenstone clearly enjoyed entertaining his set at his house and gardens. He acquired for himself the reputation of a mediator of taste, and advocated gentle pastoral simplicity in the verses and inscriptions he scattered about the Leasowes. His own compositions were most frequently ballads or songs, treated for the most part with the utmost diffidence, and he had plans to publish at least one anonymously, 'on ye same Paper & in ye same Form wth common Ballads'.[8] (This piece, 'Jemmy Dawson', was later included in the *Reliques* (i. 306).[9]) He wrote his letters (billets) on tiny rectangles of paper, and encouraged the deliberately slight literary productions of his circle of friends by transcribing their verses into 'vastly pretty, because . . . vastly little' books.[10]

Shenstone's modesty, cultivation, and homosocial charisma were evidently captivating. Robert Dodsley, a frequent guest at the Leasowes, was inspired to pen uncharacteristically gassy exclamations of gratitude whenever he wrote to thank Shenstone after a stay there. He declared in his posthumous edition of Shenstone's *Works* (1764–9) that the Leasowes 'is now considered as amongst the principal of those delightful scenes which persons of taste, in the present age, are desirous to see'.[11]

Taste was the professed keynote of Shenstone's arboreal endeavours. The Leasowes was a cultivated wilderness inspired by Chinese sharawaggi: a mixture of Gothick wilds and idealized scenes of Augustan cultivation.[12] There were no flowers, only views and prospects—of leafy bowers, noble landscapes, cosy cottages, and mossy ruins—and the whole park was laced around with streams and lakes and miniature waterfalls. In the 'Description of the Leasowes' prepared by Dodsley, Percy, and Richard

---

[8] Williams, 141.

[9] Shenstone's most anthologized piece today is a pseudo-archaic Spenserian pastoral, 'The School-Mistress' (*Works*, i. 320–32).

[10] Williams, 294; Chesterfield's tart comment on 'vastly' is from his article in the *World* (28 Nov. 1754).

[11] 'A Description of the Leasowes, the Seat of the late William Shenstone, Esq; by R. Dodsley', in *Works*, ii. 331–71 (written by Percy and Richard Jago: Bodl., Percy 82, p. 331). Dodsley had worked with Shenstone since *The Judgment of Hercules* (1741) and *The School-Mistress* (1742); they were closest 1754–8, collaborating on the last three volumes of Dodsley's *Collection*. During this period, Dodsley was a regular visitor at the Leasowes (Tierney, 115 n.).   [12] Shenstone, *Works*, ii. 311.

Jago (which included an engraved coordinated map for the virtual traveller), the gardens were persistently and approvingly described as 'irregular': Shenstone was considered a master at combining and extemporizing.[13] He appeared to follow no strict rules of composition—which is of course why Percy was eager for him to collaborate on the *Reliques*. And yet the description of the Leasowes does reveal Shenstone's technique of 'cultivation'. Cultivation here is not simply the art of tending oak trees, but is the acculturation of nature: Shenstone literally planted culture in his garden. The Leasowes was full of seats (as if Shenstone could not go anywhere without having first to sit down), placed so that the visitor could read a succession of poetic inscriptions— archaized ballads or sentimental memorials—each of which aestheticized an immediate view or landscape. (He even positioned a fake Venus de' Medici in his shrubbery and eulogized *her* with a set of verses.) Of course other scenic features, like birdsong, already had a history of aestheticization, and Shenstone treated them in the same way. In the elegy 'To a Lady on the Language of Birds', Shenstone identifies himself with Philomela who, unusually, is male. The warning notes of the nightingale's 'mellifluent strain', recalling Tereus' 'lawless love', are like a morality clause inscribed in a Leasowes grotto, and make a virtue of Shenstone's suspiciously unmarried state. He is Philomela, a man-nightingale, an exemplum of chastity (or, more probably, prudence).[14] The Leasowes, where Shenstone queened about, petting fairies, resting, gazing upon a ruined wall, lingering over a fey inscription, and resting again, framed the real as if it were a modest work of art— or at least appeared to. Percy's attraction to Shenstonian taste was drawn to precisely this illusionism: presenting an invisibly doctored scene as authentic because it was modest and because it was framed by self-evident fictions. It was a way in which Percy could take possession of his ballads.

In the last half-dozen years of his life, Shenstone was engaged in a number of literary projects: editing his own works, compiling for Dodsley's *Collection of Poems* and *Esop*, and of course assisting Percy with the *Reliques*. They were fellow Salopians: although Hales-Owen was bordered by Warwickshire and Worcestershire, it

---

[13] Ibid. 287–318.
[14] Elegy VI: 'To a Lady on the Language of Birds' (ibid., i. 39–41).

was part of Percy's home county of Shropshire. They also shared many Shropshire friends, most significantly Humphrey Pitt.[15] Percy had obtained the Folio MS from Pitt in about 1753, and Shenstone had known him from before 1741.[16] The earliest surviving letter in the Percy–Shenstone correspondence is dated 24 November 1757, but evidently the two already knew each other by this time.[17]

Initially, Percy craved Shenstone's endorsement of his ballads and sought the sanctuary of the older man's garden society. Percy elicited Shenstone's opinion of several pieces in the Folio MS by sending his friend transcripts, which were annotated and returned. Only six such manuscripts survive, and none appears in editions of Shenstone's or Percy's correspondence. At least one was rescued from the printer.[18] The verso of 'A Lover of late was I' contained Shenstone's annotations to 'When first I sawe thee', marked by Percy, 'This song is not to be printed: but carefully return'd.'[19] With such care taken of the surviving manuscripts, it is unlikely that many have been lost, and read alongside the published letters and 'Shenstone's Billets' (a long list of popular songs graded by Shenstone on a sheaf of little slips of paper), they add a further dimension to the genesis of the *Reliques*. Percy, however, soon tired of Shenstone's mincing objections. He heavily deleted many of Shenstone's comments from these manuscripts, suggesting that the two writers were confused regarding the precise nature of their relationship and their venture.

Percy's earliest extant letter to Shenstone (24 November 1757) thanked him for correcting his song 'O Nancy', and so immediately established a hierarchy of taste and a precedent for revision: writing was as much a collaborative industry as printing.[20] Percy described his initial plans to publish the Folio MS in his second letter (9 January 1758), and demonstrated his belief that in order to be printed, the Folio MS required not only the revision, but the contribution of accomplices:

---

[15] Williams, 32, 215, 218; *Letters*, vii. 19.   [16] Davis (1989), 24.

[17] *Letters*, vii, pp. v–vi; Williams, 390–1.

[18] The six manuscripts are Houghton, bMS Eng. 893: 'The Enquiry'/'Now the Springe is come' (14), 'The Shepherd's Resolution'/'See the building' (155), and 'A Lover of late was I'/'When first I sawe thee' (157).

[19] Houghton, bMS Eng. 893 (157ᵛ).   [20] *Letters*, vii. 1.

If I regarded only my own private satisfaction I should by no means be eager to render my Collection cheap by publication. It was the importunity of my friend M[r] Johnson, that exhorted a promise of this kind from me.—Indeed he made me very tempting offers: for he promised to assist me in selecting the most valuable pieces and in revising the Text of those he selected: Nay further, if I would leave a blank Page between every two that I transcribed, he would furnish it out with proper Notes, etc. etc.—a work for which he is peculiarly fitted by his great acquaintance with all our old English Romances etc of which kind of reading he is uncommonly fond.[21]

So, Percy never intended or claimed to be printing the entire Folio MS as it stood. He imagined each of the pieces he had selected and corrected being judged and revised, a process that would refine mere manuscript copies until they were fit to be printed. A manuscript had to be translated into print: the transition was not automatic. And it was Samuel Johnson who suggested Percy edit what was to become the *Reliques*, not Shenstone (who nevertheless crowed to Richard Graves, 'I proposed the scheme for him *myself*').[22] But Johnson was occupied with his edition of Shakespeare and his help never materialized.[23] Instead, Shenstone found himself in the role.[24] Johnson's failure to keep his promise to Percy delayed the *Reliques* and allowed Shenstone to intervene, but the Johnsonian imprimatur seems to have affected Percy profoundly.

Percy was first introduced to Johnson by James Grainger on 2 May 1757, and they met frequently thereafter in London.[25] Percy was familiar enough with Johnson by 31 May 1761 to take him to dinner at Oliver Goldsmith's and formally introduce the two.[26] By November, Percy had showed Johnson the Folio MS, 'and he never ceased urging me to print the Selection in the Reliques'.[27] Percy's desire to find collaborators may have arisen from Johnson's collaborative working methods on the *Dictionary* and later on his edition of Shakespeare. Certainly Johnson's plan for annotating the *Reliques*—preparing copy by interleaving

---

[21] Ibid. 9–10.   [22] Williams, 573.

[23] Percy later added the following note to the letter: 'This promise he never executed: nor except a few slight hints delivered *vivâ voce*, did he furnish any contributions, &c.' (*Letters*, vii. 10 n.). See below, Chapter 6.

[24] Irving L. Churchill, 'William Shenstone's Share in the Preparation of Percy's *Reliques*', *PMLA* 51 (1936), 965.   [25] *Letters*, ix. 83.

[26] Davis (1981), 19.   [27] *Letters*, ix. 84.

Percy's transcription—could have been suggested to him from his experience on the *Dictionary*. As Allen Reddick has shown, Johnson made several attempts at developing a method for compiling the *Dictionary*, and his advice to Percy suggests the need for a short explanatory essay on each piece rather than a host of minute notes.[28] Indeed, he had remarked in the *Rambler*,

It is very difficult to write on the minuter parts of literature without failing either to please or to instruct. Too much nicety of detail disgusts the greatest part of readers, and to throw a multitude of particulars under general heads, and to lay down rules of extensive comprehension, is to common understandings of little use. They who undertake these subjects are therefore always in danger, as one or other inconvenience arises to their imagination, of frighting us with rugged science, or amusing us with empty sound.[29]

Percy stresses that Johnson's knowledge of romances, rather than his lexicographical achievement, should fit him as a collaborator, which also implies that the work was being envisaged freighted with short essays. But in the event, Percy generally ignored this advice, turning his texts into palimpsests of accumulated wisdom.

Shenstone was a very different writer from Johnson. He was a gentleman poet, diffident about publication, he had the leisure to assist Percy—but he too warned against excessive annotation. It seems a preoccupation of the antiquarian poets: Gray wrote to Walpole in July 1757 regarding 'The Progress of Poetry': 'I do not love notes. . . . They are signs of weakness and obscurity. If a thing cannot be understood without them, it had better not be understood at all.'[30] Shenstone, in an essay 'On Books and Writers', complained that notes jarred the harmony of a text: 'how much more agreeable would be the effect, than to interrupt the reader by such frequent avocations? How much more graceful to play a tune upon one sett of keys, with varied stops, than to seek the same variety, by an awkward motion from one sett to another?'[31]

Percy's first letter to Shenstone had also requested a transcript of Shenstone's copy of 'Child Maurice', to be collated with the

---

[28] Allen Reddick, *The Making of Johnson's Dictionary* (Cambridge, 1990).
[29] Samuel Johnson, *The Rambler*, ed. W. J. Bate and Albrecht B. Strauss (New Haven, 1969), *Rambler*, 90: 'The pauses in English poetry adjusted', iv. 109–10; note use of 'rugged'. [30] Gray, *Correspondence*, ii. 508.
[31] Shenstone, *Works*, ii. 235.

Folio MS. Shenstone sent his version ('Gill Morice'), and asked Percy to improve a line or two. Percy's next, containing the news of Johnson's collaboration (quoted above), requested Shenstone's revision of some of his poetic translations of Ovid and Tibullus intended for James Grainger's forthcoming edition, 'And that I may if possible bribe you to undergo this Drudgery, I here inclose at the same time a Fragment of an old Song, extracted from my Ancient Folio MS.'[32] This was a copy, now lost, of 'As she came from the Holy Land' (based on the verse by Sir Walter Ralegh), and it marks the beginning of Percy's solicitation of Shenstone's aid in editing the Folio MS. Significantly, it also marks the beginning of a thread of economic imagery in their discussions of the Folio MS. The old ballads were described as if they were ancient currency, fit antiquities for middle-class connoisseurs.

In his third letter (October 1758), Percy asked for 'a finishing Hand' to his 'Ode, on the Death of Augustus Earl of Sussex'.[33] He admitted he could not improve Shenstone's 'Gill Morice', but did tentatively suggest an image for a line. Throughout their early correspondence Percy shrank from correcting Shenstone's verses— he was not prepared to share in the creative process of his mentor.

On 4 February 1759, Percy sent another 'bribe', this time 'very large Transcripts from my MS Collection of Ballads', for correcting his translations from Ovid.[34] He recorded the transcripts sent in his *Journal* (11 February): 'List of old Ballads communicated to M[r]. Shenstone. The 2 Pilgrimages to Walsingham. The Boy and the Mantle. The Marriage of S[r] Gawain Fragment of turning the Lady &c. Col. Lovelace's Song. Chloris. &c.'[35]

By the time Shenstone replied on 6 June 1759, Percy had evidently also sent 'Edom o' Gordon'. Shenstone informed him that he had 'retouch'd' that ballad, and 'Gentle Herdsman' as well, but despite his eager requests, Percy did not see these texts until 1763.[36] Shenstone did, however, include them both in his *Miscellany*,

---

[32] James Grainger, *A Poetical Translation of the Elegies of Tibullus; and of the Poems of Sulpicia* (1759), see Bodl., Percy 19–20; *Letters*, vii. 12.

[33] *Letters*, vii. 14. Shenstone included this ode in his 'Miscellany' (*Shenstone's Miscellany 1759–1763*, ed. Ian A. Gordon (Oxford, 1952), 57–60).

[34] *Letters*, vii. 22.

[35] Printed by Brooks, ibid. 22 n.; BL, Add. MS 32336, fo. 18[v]. These ballads were (in the Folio MS) 'Gentle Heardsman', 'As yee came from the Holye', 'Boy and Mantle', 'The marriage of Sr Gawaine', 'Cloris'.

[36] *Letters*, vii. 25; *Miscellany*, pp. xiv–xv.

together with the next two pieces that Percy sent, two translations from the Chinese.

Shenstone's *Miscellany* was a manuscript book compiled as a poetic anthology of the works of his friends, and includes pieces by Richard Jago, Robert Binnel, and Richard Graves, as well as by Percy, and Shenstone himself. It was not printed in the lifetimes of either Percy or Shenstone.[37] There is in Shenstone's *Miscellany* unfortunately no indication of when transcripts were received, and furthermore Shenstone spent time rewriting all the submissions to some extent. Altogether, he included six pieces derived from the Folio MS. The first was his version of 'Gentle Herdsman', titled 'From the old M.S.S. Collection of Ballads', and this was followed by 'As ye [*sic*] came from the holy Lande', 'The Boy and the Mantle', 'Edom of Gordon', 'Old Sir Simon the King', and lastly 'Captain Carre' (the original Folio MS text of the heavily revised 'Edom of Gordon').[38] By 15 February 1760, Shenstone had lost confidence in his versions of 'Edom of Gordon' and 'Gentle Herdsman', and continued to parry Percy's requests for copies. He did however send notes to 'John de Reeve', which Percy had doubtless sent him.

For over two years, therefore, Percy and Shenstone corresponded, transcribed, and revised merely a handful of texts. Although Percy had declared his intention to publish a selection from the Folio MS, and Shenstone had leisurely collected some ballads from other parts of the country, the two simply diverted themselves with poetry. The completion of the *Miscellany* appeared to be their main aim, although Shenstone's refusal to lend his friend his improved ballads suggests that even this was foundering. All this changed when James Macpherson's *Fragments of Ancient Poetry* (1760) exploded like a thunderclap over the Leasowes.

As explained in the last chapter, *Fragments of Ancient Poetry* was the first appearance of the third-century Celtic bard Ossian in

---

[37] It was edited by Ian Gordon in 1952.

[38] Percy's original contributions to the *Miscellany* were 'Verses on leaving **** in a tempestuous night; March 22, 1758', 'At the Squire's long board', 'A celebrated sonnet, from the Spanish of Cervantes', 'The Disappointment', 'Ode on the Death of Augustus, Earl of Sussex', 'A Romance, Gentle River', 'From the Chinese, The Willow', 'Spanish Romance, Saddle me my milk-white stallion', and 'Disappointment, as written in 1752'.

the eighteenth-century world of letters. The pamphlet consisted of a handful of short, dark, mysterious prose poems supposedly carried by the oral tradition of the Highlands of Scotland. The sudden appearance of the *Fragments*, Percy's arrival at the Leasowes with the Folio MS, and the presence of Dodsley, seems to have galvanized the collaborators. Up until this point there had been no solid conception of the *Reliques*—Percy had presumably been waiting for Johnson. Now, however, their correspondence hummed with publishing projects. Percy wrote to thank Shenstone for his hospitality and for the inspiration that the visit had afforded: his letter of September 1760 (as he later dated it) contained a proposal for what ultimately became *Five Pieces of Runic Poetry* (eventually published by Dodsley), included a number of Runic fragments and printed ballads, and mentioned 'our Collection' for the first time.[39] Macgowan's letter sent with the *Fragments* had dated the pieces with reference to 'the ancient Bards of Iceland and other Northern countries'.[40]

There is a further important (if minor) point to be made with regard to Shenstone and the genesis of the *Reliques*. The postscript to Percy's letter of September 1760 was not printed by Brooks in the Yale edition of the *Percy Letters* because it was separated from the main letter and lost among Percy's *Runic Poetry* notes. Margaret Smith discovered and published it in 1988, and also retrieved the Runic enclosures of this letter. Smith, however, assumes that Percy first refers to *Runic Poetry* in this letter—'I am making up a small Collection of Pieces of this kind for the Press, which will about the Size of the Erse Fragments'—and then in the restored postscript refers to the *Reliques*—'Will it be worth while to select some of the best of these . . . in order to *fill up* our Collection?'[41] Smith's interpretation assumes that the *Reliques* was under way by this time, which has been shown not to be the case: sending ten transcripts to Shenstone was all that had so far been accomplished. The sentence 'I am making up a small

[39] Margaret M. Smith, 'Thomas Percy, William Shenstone, *Five Pieces of Runic Poetry*, and the *Reliques*', *BLR* 12 (1988), 473; omitted from *Letters*, vii. 71. On 3 Mar. 1758, Percy had seen Shenstone 'for about 5 or 6 minutes' at John Scott Hylton's house, but although 'he had his M: S: collection of Old=Ballads in his portmanteau', he would not stay (Tierney, 348).   [40] Smith, 'Prepublication Circulation', 153.
[41] *Letters*, vii. 70; Smith, 'Thomas Percy', (1988), 473.

Collection of Pieces of this kind' should be read as affirmative rather than informative.

Shenstone's response, dated 1 October 1760, has consequently been regarded as an editorial mandate for the *Reliques*, rather than as an articulation of one printing project in response to another.[42] He began his letter with considerable relish, 'There will indeed be no *end* of writing all we have to say on the present occasion: A week's Conference on the Subject, when things are in somewhat greater Forwardness, will be more effectual than fifty Packets, as much distended as your last,' which Percy had crammed with Runic fragments and printed ballads.[43] Evidently Shenstone and Percy had agreed something during the latter's stay at the Leasowes, but Percy's immediate interest was taken up by ancient fragments, perhaps hoping to court Dodsley (though Percy seems never to have got on with the senior partner, Robert, and instead dealt with his brother James).[44] This letter of Shenstone's gives, at least in retrospect, a competent abstract of the *Reliques*: a three-volume anthology of ballads, loosely edited.

There is nothing to suggest that Shenstone envisaged an independent collection of Runic poetry, and he mentioned the 'Celtic Poem' towards the end of his letter, after considering the inclusion of '*Scotch* Ballads'. The implication is, therefore, that the two had sought a means of combining the burgeoning vogue for ancient poetry with their own ballad interests and resources. Such broad ambition for the *Reliques* would explain why Shenstone was advocating three volumes (or even four, the last consisting solely of the generically and ideologically problematic Scottish pieces), whereas he later urged Percy to produce only two. Percy's own plans for the collection at times shrank to two volumes, sometimes swelled to four.

Furthermore, the amount of detail and advice in this letter shows just how little could have been agreed at the Leasowes. Shenstone said he would promptly return Percy's 'Parcells . . . together with my Judgment of *acceptance* or *reprobation*'. Brooks glosses this remark as 'Shenstone's Billets', but the 'Billets', as Percy christened them, were neither in Percy's hand nor sent by

[42] Churchill, 'William Shenstone's Share', 966–8; *Letters*, vii, pp. xv–xxiii; Vincent H. Ogburn, 'Further Notes on Percy', *PMLA* 51 (1936), 451.
[43] *Letters*, vii. 71–2.   [44] Tierney, 293 n.

him, so Shenstone could hardly 'return' them.[45] Shenstone can only have been referring to more transcripts Percy was sending, now to be considered for their anthology rather than the *Miscellany.*

In addition, Shenstone made a Johnsonian demand for a 'Large Paper-book' of the transcripts as they would be arranged for the press, 'and let me reconsider them *all together,* before they are sent away to Press'.[46] In fact, as the next chapters show, Percy was nowhere near completing his text in manuscript before printing.

Shenstone also offered Percy advice regarding arranging, improving, printing, and selecting the material, and indicated his own 'three marks of approbation, + for the least, ++ for the next, and # for the highest'.[47] It can be assumed therefore that Shenstone included the first 'Billet', now lost, in this letter. Its subject can reasonably be guessed at: Shenstone mentioned two anthologies in this letter: *A Collection of Old Ballads* (1723–5), which was the subject of the second 'Billet'; and Dryden's *Poetical Miscellanies* (1684–1709), presumably the subject of the first.

So the *Reliques* was taking shape in the following way: Percy was to send transcripts from the Folio MS and elsewhere. He would also send any printed ballads he thought fit. Shenstone would decide which to include, and would revise these. At the same time he would search printed anthologies, and send Percy accounts of his reading.

There is a note in Shenstone's letter that clarifies these roles further: 'I believe I shall *never* make any objection to such *Improvements* as you bestow upon them; unless you were plainly to *contradict* Antiquity, which I am pretty sure will never be the Case.'[48] If Shenstone had been sought by Percy as an arbiter of poetic taste, Percy was to reciprocate with antiquarian scholarship by recovering lost literature and restoring the pedigree of a debased popular tradition.

Unfortunately, Percy's reply to this letter has been lost, and his next surviving one (27 November 1760) makes cryptic reference to the queries it must have contained. But it is evident from Percy's correspondence with Johnson that he was almost immediately in negotiation with the Dodsleys, who were clearly interested in, if

---

[45] *Letters*, vii. 72.   [46] Ibid.   [47] Ibid. 73.
[48] Ibid. 72.

not completely smitten by, the project. A contract had been drafted in a matter of days, offering Percy up to £108 (£3 a sheet, at twelve sheets a volume); Percy, however, wanted 100 guineas for a three-volume *Reliques*, and part-payment in advance. Johnson calculated the profits that would accrue and wrote to Percy on 4 October with his opinion of the Dodsleys' offer, 'which I think moderately good, that is, not so good as might be hoped, nor so bad as might be feared'. He advised, 'upon the whole, I would not have you reject the offer as it is, for I know not who will make a better'.[49] But Percy spent the next eight weeks haggling with Robert Dodsley.

Meanwhile, the correspondence with Shenstone trundled on. Shenstone's letter for 10 November is extant. He had not yet received Percy's copy of *A Collection of Old Ballads*, but seems already to have had some suggestions from Percy concerning that early anthology. Percy owned at least two copies, and the collection proved to be an important influence on the *Reliques*. Shenstone also offered Dodsley's advice regarding annotation, Shenstone's chief objection to the inclusion of Runic pieces. Percy had apparently sent him one more transcript.

Percy's letter of 27 November 1760 marked, however, the beginning of the end of this cosy collaboration between 'the judicious Antiquary and the Reader of Taste'.[50] 'You will perhaps be surprised', he informed Shenstone cagily, 'when I tell you that Mr Dodsley and I have broke off all treaty on the Subject of the Old Ballads: James Dodsley is generous enough and offered me terms that would have repaid my Labour: but his brother (who if you remember had never much opinion of the work) has I suppose persuaded him to desist: for the other has receded from his own offers.—And we are now quite off, as the trading term is.'[51] Johnson, on 29 November, went rather gallantly to the bookseller Andrew Millar, who agreed in principle to Percy's terms—but still the deal was not struck, and as we shall see, when Percy visited London in May 1761 to barter his ballads to each house, they were eventually bought up by the Dodsleys after all.

But none of this uncertainty appeared to trouble Percy in writing to Shenstone. Rather, the work was gaining momentum and his web of correspondents was beginning to thicken. Percy had received a letter from Edward Blakeway of Magdalene College, Cambridge, who had obtained permission for him to consult the Pepysian Library there. He was also endeavouring to borrow two folio volumes of ballads from the Society of Antiquaries, and had been working in Lord Sussex's library at nearby Castle Ashby. He suggested including 'half a Score' of Spanish ballads he was translating, and sent Shenstone 'The Moor's Revenge' to correct, and also a copy of Swift's 'Behold those Monarch-Oaks' that he had discovered in Lord Sussex's library.[52]

Their correspondence was then abruptly suspended for about four months during Shenstone's seasonal ill-health—he preferred to winter in his bed. This gap allows an examination of Percy's treatment of the Folio MS, to quote the transcripts Percy made for Shenstone, and the opinions that his friend scribbled on them.

'A VERY CURIOUS OLD MS'[53]

The earliest transcriptions were taken from the Folio MS by Percy and an unknown copyist, and Percy collated these transcripts with other copies, or sent them to Shenstone. These are published for the first time below. At least two ('A Lover of late was I'/'When first I sawe thee', and a later transcription of 'Cock Lorrel's Treat') have survived as rejected printer's copy, and many of these neglected manuscripts are still to be found among the Percy Papers at Harvard.[54] Not only do they reveal quite literally the hand of Shenstone in the editing of the *Reliques*, but they show Percy's selectivity in the first stages. As it stood, the Folio MS was never destined for the printing house, and was never intended as a sole source.

These earliest transcripts are recognizable by paper and layout (in particular Percy's use of ruled red lines under titles is characteristic of his earliest transcripts). Although it is impossible to restore many lost transcriptions, those which do survive provide a valuable source (see Appendix I). Seventeen pieces were

---

[52] Ibid. 81.   [53] Ibid. 3.

[54] Smith declines to catalogue them (Smith, 255). Some of Shenstone's annotations are quoted by Albert B. Friedman, 'The First Draft of Percy's Reliques', *PMLA* 69 (1954), 1237.

transcribed from the Folio MS in this format. Percy also transcribed pieces from *The Golden Garland* (13), Dodsley's *Old Plays* (5), the Cottonian Library (3), the Pepysian Library (2), and Carew (13), Lyly (7), Cockain [*sic*] (2), and Prestwich (2) in the same early format.[55] With eight other transcriptions, these total seventy-two. It is possible to date these transcriptions from Percy's access to two of the sources: he visited the Pepysian Library in August 1761, and on 29 November 1762 Ballard's Collection was offered for sale.[56] Percy borrowed it on 15 February 1763.[57] If there is a genesis for the *Reliques*, it is in a motley collection of songs taken from the Folio MS and a miscellany of seventeenth-century poetry books. From these suggestions, only a handful of variations on love lyrics, from lament to burlesque, were included in the 1765 *Reliques*: from the Folio MS 'A Lover of late was I' and 'The Shepherd's Resolution', and from the *Golden Garland* 'The lover's lamentation for the death of fair Phillis' ('Corydon's Farewell to Phillis'), 'Corydon's doleful Knell', and 'The shepherd's dialogue' ('The Willow Tree').[58]

Nevertheless, what we see of Percy's working methods in his first eighteen months is a heavy use of the Folio MS to find ballads thematically linked. He titled two folders containing these transcriptions 'Hunting' and 'Sportive', and these tend to disprove the theory that ballads in the Folio MS (and consequently the *Reliques*) were organized in 'clusters', as these folders collect material from across the Folio MS.[59] Criticism of the Folio MS has concentrated mainly on the considerable discrepancies between it and the text of the *Reliques*. The famous commentary that runs through the edition of John Hales and Frederick Furnivall (*Bishop Percy's Folio MS.*, 1867–8) cantankerously demonstrates the shortcomings of the *Reliques* insofar as it was an edition of the Folio MS.[60] Critics since then have been more

---

[55] See Appendix I.

[56] Davis (1989), 87; Percy–Darby *Reliques* (Houghton, *EC75 P4128 765[ra]), i, pasted to p. xxiv; noted by G. L. Kittredge, Houghton, bMS Eng. 893 (25). Ballard's collection was of 300 'scarce Old English Ballads', advertised in his catalogue, 29 Nov. 1762. James Dodsley obtained the collection, following Percy's desperate pleas (see an undated draft for a letter, *c*.7 Jan.–12 Feb. 1763: Bodl., MS Percy c 2, fo. 233[v]).

[57] Bodl., Percy MS c 9, fo. 103. See the triumphant (and undated) letter to Farmer (*Letters*, ii. 34).   [58] *Reliques*, iii. 178, iii. 120, i. 187, ii. 298, iii. 136.

[59] Houghton, bMS Eng. 893 (162), (166).

[60] Hales and Furnivall, especially i, pp. xvii–xx.

forgiving, if no more understanding, and have been alarmed instead at the surprisingly few pieces derived solely from that particular source.[61] Walter Jackson Bate and particularly Albert Friedman have written convincing, but ultimately speculative, accounts of Percy's editorial treatment of his find.[62] More recently, Stephen Vartin has found thematic 'clusters' in the Folio MS which, he claims, influenced the organization of the *Reliques*.[63] Friedman had already excused the relatively poor representation of the Folio MS in the *Reliques* by arguing that the Folio MS pieces occur at key points in the *Reliques* and focus a 'cluster' of related songs and ballads, effectively making the *Reliques* a selective poetic commentary on the Folio MS.[64]

The readings of Friedman and Vartin are ingenious, but like all these accounts do not analyse sufficiently Percy's use of the Folio MS from the moment he commenced editing it for the press. The *Reliques* evolved so dramatically that any similarities between the seventeenth-century *manuscrit trouvé* and what emerged from Dodsley's shop under the sign of Tully's Head in 1765 are more likely to be coincidental than symptomatic of any consistent editorial theory. Percy never considered the Folio MS—which he described as 'an infinite farrago'—to be an authoritative foundation for the *Reliques*, and commentators have so far failed to appreciate the ebb and flow of Percy's different versions of the *Reliques*.[65]

The key text here is Percy's handwritten index to the Folio MS.[66] On 20 December 1757, a little more than a year after he had rashly pruned his library of works of old English literature, Percy prepared his index. This now exceptionally faded document, copied onto the Folio MS itself, seems to have gone through several stages of revision. Percy listed the texts, and, perhaps later, perhaps in the company of Shenstone and Dodsley, marked them with a variety of different symbols. He also starred the most promising titles on the folio pages themselves. These two lists coincide only in about two-thirds of cases, and the pieces are

---

[61] Vartin counts 47 (76). The Folio MS contained 194 pieces, and the first edition of the *Reliques*, 176.

[62] Walter Jackson Bate, 'Percy's Use of his Folio-Manuscript', *JEGP* 43 (1944), 337–48; Albert B. Friedman, 'Percy's Folio MS Revalued', *JEGP* 53 (1954), 524–31.

[63] Vartin, 74–5.   [64] Friedman, 'Percy's Folio MS Revalued', 527.

[65] *Letters*, iv. 54.   [66] BL, Add. MS 27879, fos. 266–8.

rated very differently in each list. In other words, Percy assessed the entire Folio MS, pen in hand, at least twice. But the index actually discloses a more complex pattern of decision-making. Pieces were in fact rated three times: with a superscript '+', with asterisks, and then with a red pencil to denote quality ('+' or '++'). Usefully, Percy also highlighted those published in *A Collection of Old Ballads*: 'NB I have used a Red Line under such Ballads I have seen in print. The Vols refer to the printed Collection of old Ballads in 3 vols.' He later added, '—a black Line under such as I printed in my Reliques of Anc^t. Poetry 3^v.' Altogether, sixty-eight titles were annotated in these different ways, and most found their way into the *Reliques*, but even then another eight with no notes of interest were included in the final collection. On the pages of the Folio MS he marked sixty-one pieces in total: he starred thirty-five noteworthy pieces, and thirteen more with various patterns of crosses or asterisks, and thirteen presumably second-rate pieces were given the mark 'O' (this included all the Robin Hood ballads). Eighteen obscene pieces had their titles crossed out in the text, twenty in the index (this is half what Hales and Furnivall censored from the Folio MS and issued in a separate, connoisseurs' volume of *Loose and Humorous Songs*). Finally, Percy used further indexing marks to indicate metrical romances and martial ballads.

The achievement of this crabbed and complicated index was to create several different shortlists. But why would Percy go to the trouble of marking the texts on the pages, and then producing three different, if overlapping, sets of ballads on the pages of the index? It seems likely that he was not the sole reader to peruse the manuscript in this way. One set of suggestions were probably Shenstone's, and if these were made during Percy's visit to the Leasowes of 1760, it is possible that Robert Dodsley made the other. Who decided what is now impossible to discern, but the fortuitous collaboration of these three gentlemen on the Folio MS, having lately examined Macpherson's *Fragments*, is an enticing prospect. More usefully, it explains the accretion of annotation and shows Percy characteristically capitalizing on any help at hand.

Of course, being a private anthology, the Folio MS was already a transcription of debatable quality and authority, and so Percy had no qualms about altering its conventions of spelling and punctuation—indeed, the pedants Hales and Furnivall added punctuation marks to their own edition. A transcript of 'Peblis to the Play', later sent to the Scottish antiquarian George Paton, gives the most cogent account of Percy's method. The following note to Paton is absent from the published volume of Percy–Paton correspondence:

If I sh^d. be thought to have taken too great Liberty in altering &c the above: it was owing to the <badly> Experience I have had of great Incorrectness & <???> Negligence of the Copyist in other Pieces, [without y^e.] opportunity of comparing them with <other> ⌈better⌉ Editions.—NB. The Copyist lived about 1650, and seems to have studied to reduce (always) the Orthography, & (as often as he could) the Expression ∧ ⌈nearly⌉ to the standard of his own time.—This appears from every Page of the MS:—But is especially apparent in Scotch Pieces, which he has ∧ ⌈always⌉ labour'd to divest of all the Scotticisms.^{67}

Percy's own transcription was characterized by an attention to metre and language only, although he did frequently admit the archaism of a final 'e'.

In his transcriptions from the Folio MS, Percy modernized spelling and punctuation as a matter of course, and such revisions were silently accepted in the *Reliques*. The extent of his changes can be seen by juxtaposing individual lines from the Hales and Furnivall transcription of the Herrick poem 'Mrs. Eliz. Wheeler, under the name of the lost Shepardesse' ('Amongst the mirtles') with Percy's own version, '<Among the Myrtles> The Enquiry':

> Amongst the Mirtles as I walket,
> Among the myrtles, as I walked
>
> loue & my thoughts sights this inter-talket:
> Love and my thoughtes thus intertalked
>
> "tell me," said I in deepe distresse,
> Tell me, say'd I in deepe distresse,
>
> "Where may I find [MS cut away]
> Where may I finde my shepherdesse?^{68}

The Folio MS was annotated by Percy: 'this' revised to 'thus' and 'sights' deleted (line 4); and the transcription was collated with the

---

^{67} Houghton, bMS Eng. 893 (7), fo. 13^v. Percy had copied it from the Maitland MS in 1761; Paton returned the transcript *c*.21 Nov. 1772. A. F. Falconer (*Letters*, vi. 46 n., 48–51) does not mention this manuscript, which also includes Paton's comments.

^{68} Hales and Furnivall, ii. 35 (corrected); Houghton, bMS Eng. 893 (14)^r.

third edition of Carew's *Poems* (1651), giving 'Amongst' and 'walk't' (line 1), and exposing Percy's erroneous revision, 'sighes intertalkt' (line 2).[69]

A more revealing revision occurred in the fourth stanza. Hales and Furnivall render this:

> "In brightest Lyllyes y^t heere stand,
> the emblemes of her whiter hands;
> in yonder rising hill, their smells
> such sweet as in her bosome dwells."

Percy's transcription showed intrusive and confusing conjecture:

> In ⌈<Thus>⌉ <In> brightest Lill<y>⌈i⌉es that there stands
> The ⌈<Are>⌉ <The> Emblems of her whiter hands.
> In yonder ⌈rising⌉ <rising> ⌈<violet>⌉ hill there smel<l>s
> Such sweets, as in her bosom dwel<l>s.

A note was added to the margin appealing to Shenstone (the following notes between Percy and Shenstone are all unpublished): 'NB. Help me to fill up this blank in the 3^d. Line with a good Word.—In the Orig^l. MS. it was **rising hill**. but this c^d. never have been the Original Word.' Shenstone idly suggested, 'Suppose, "*Violet*" instead of *rising Hill*', which Percy jotted down and then deleted, but not even by sympathetically recasting the song in contemporary diction could Percy tempt his friend. Shenstone, in his role as poetic adviser, wrote a lengthy note at the end of the transcription:

For aught I see at present, <???> I do not think this has y^e. Least claim to be inserted. The best use you can make of it, so exceptionable *upon y^e. whole*, is to draw *hints* from them for any little *Original* of your *own*. The reigning thought here, is better expressed in a stanza of Gay's black-eyd Susan. WS.[70]

Percy was nettled at his friend's opinion: it belittled his own taste. He heavily deleted the whole note, and it is now barely legible. But such harsh judgements from Shenstone were by no means unusual. On the verso of 'The Enquiry', Percy transcribed 'Now the Springe is come' from the Folio MS. His marginal query to stanza three was addressed to Shenstone and shows that he was

[69] Thomas Carew, *Poems* (1640), 170; *The Poetical Works of Robert Herrick*, ed. L. C. Martin (Oxford, 1956), 106.   [70] *Letters*, vii. 26, 118.

already considering how to present the material in print: '{And here is a change in the versification, this & the following staz^a shall be printed in seven lines, like the song "**What care I how faire she be.**}'

Shenstone again dismissed the piece, and Percy again struck out his scornful comment: 'I can see no possible Reason why this should be inserted, as the stanzas, in themselves irregular, contain nothing more y^n. the common Cast of Love-songs, and this awkwardly enough conceived.' Particularly revealing was Shenstone's rejection of 'When first I sawe thee': 'I do not think this proper for your Collection, by any means. There is indeed something like a thought in ye four first lines of y^e. last stanza. W.S.' It is clear that Shenstone was distancing himself from Percy's ('your') collection. But Percy still saw Shenstone as deeply implicated in the project, especially in its publication. Another note, also judiciously deleted by Percy, this time written by him to Shenstone, described his friend's approval as an effective licence to print:

M^r. Shenstone is desired to peruse the $\wedge \lceil$ se $\rceil$ Ballads within written, & give me his opinion whether he thinks $\wedge \lceil$ them $\rceil$ worthy to appear in my 2d. Vol. of *ancient Ballads*. In either case he is desired to return $\lceil$ the Copies $\rceil$ <it> with all <speed $\wedge$. If it has> $\lceil$ care: yet if they have $\rceil$ not he is imprimatur <???> $\lceil$ these $\rceil$ shall be suppressed.[71]

Yet curiously, and in spite of such a mandate, any positive suggestions Shenstone did make were certainly not accepted uncritically by Percy. One of Shenstone's desultory revisions to 'A Lover of late was I' was incorporated in the printed text of the *Reliques* ('*fond* I think preferable here, & let it be so corrected if you please', line 17); one was not ('*never will* reads better', line 20) (iii. 178). Shenstone's influence is more noticeable in the printed version of 'The Shepherd's Resolution', in which he proposed omitting the second stanza but transposing its catch to the third. This was a significant change because the second stanza was, as indicated by Percy, unique to the Folio MS: 'NB. This 2^d. stanza is in no printed Copy that I ever saw', unrecorded by *The Golden Garland*, the *Tea-Table Miscellany*,

---

[71] Houghton, bMS Eng. 893 (20A), fo. 140^v. Percy had first written to him on 24 Nov. 1757, declaring, 'I am possess'd of a very curious old MS Collection of ancient Ballads many of which I believe were never printed . . .—Mr Johnson has seen my MS. and has a desire to have it printed' (*Letters*, vii. 3–4).

and Dryden's *Miscellany.* Shenstone remained unimpressed: '* I do not think y^e. addition of this whole stanza any improvem^t. to y^e. song; as it contains y^e. *same* thought (*worse expressed*) with y^e. stanza following: yet I would substitute y^e. 5th & 6th. Lines of *this* instead of y^e. 5 & 6th. *Lines of* y^t., as being much more poetical.'[72] Having made such a concession, Percy ignored Shenstone's other suggestions, '"*wooe*" I would read here to avoid ambiguity' (line 29), adding 'born' (line 31), and the insertion extending the final line: 'form'd for' (line 32) (iii. 253). In the second edition, however, Percy dismissed the provenance of the Folio MS, having found a printed copy from 1614 which incidentally restored a version of the second stanza.

Shenstone's notes also survive on a further transcript which became the printer's copy for 'Cock Lorrel's Treat', but he showed no enthusiasm for printing this piece either: 'I don't take the Humour here . . . nor here . . . some little gleam of Humour . . . more dirty y^n. witty. . . Tolerable.'[73] He recanted a little at the end: 'I *may* have been too severe on this Ballad, in what I've said—At least it may please A good ma[n]y People, better y^n. *me.* I have therefore scrawled some of my Sensations, on y^e. margin wth. a black Lead Pencil—venture to insert it, if he pleases. WS.' Percy's response was encoded in a note to the printer, 'The printer is to take no notice of the marginal notes &c writ with a black lead pencil', and although this piece got no further than proofs, it demonstrates Percy's eventual acceptance of his editorial responsibilities.

The first stage of collecting materials for the *Reliques* was therefore hardly a success, because Percy and Shenstone had quite different ideas regarding the composition of the work. After the excited activity at the Leasowes, Percy was now searching for sixteenth- and seventeenth-century songs and poems, using principally his Folio MS and the *Golden Garland*; whereas Shenstone began an exhaustive analysis of eighteenth-century miscellanies of popular verse and sent Percy his opinion of hundreds of songs ('Shenstone's Billets'). The work of the two only coincided again when Shenstone finally received the 1723–5 anthology *A Collection of Old Ballads*, but before discussing that source it will be useful to complete this account of the Folio MS.

[72] Houghton, bMS Eng. 893 (155).   [73] Houghton, bMS Eng. 893 (165).

Percy's handling of the Folio MS source changed neither when the *Reliques* was in proof nor in print. A version of 'Northumberlande betrayed by Douglas' was compiled from the Folio MS and an untraced manuscript copy. Most of the text was lifted straight from the Folio MS, in the main transcribed with more accuracy than 'The Enquiry'. The first two stanzas of the Folio MS read:

> now list and lithe you gentlemen,
>   & Ist tell you the veretye,
> how they hane delt wth a banished man,
>   driuen out of his countrye.
>
> when as hee came on Scottish ground,
>   na woe & wonder be them amonge,
> ffull much was there traitorye
>   thé wrought the Erle of Northumberland.[74]

Which Percy transcribed as follows:

> Now<e> list and lithe you, gentlemen,
>   And <1st> ⌈Ile⌉ tell you the veritye
> How they have delt with a banished man
>   Driven out of his countrye
>
> When as hee came on Scottish ground
>   As woe & wonder be them <amonge> ⌈amang⌉
> Full muche was their traitorye
>   The wrought the Erle of Northumberland[75]

These stanzas show Percy's characteristic changes. Conventions were modernized: words commencing lines capitalized, contractions and initial ampersands expanded, obsolete forms such as 'ff' and u/v were revised; and most interest in punctuation was abandoned after the first line. Spelling, however, was only semi-modernized (for example, 'veritye' for 'veretye'), the terminal 'e' being a favourite retention. Indeed, the first word was initially copied as 'Nowe'—a quite spurious archaism. This brings us to an interesting feature of this transcription: that it shows evidence of later correction unsupported by the Folio MS text. While initially there was effectively only one change, 'As' for 'na', two further changes were subsequently made: 'Ile' for 'Ist', and the Scotticism 'amang' for 'amonge'. This feature is repeated through all

---

[74] Hales and Furnivall, ii. 218 (corrected).
[75] Houghton, bMS Eng. 893 (20A), fo. 147^r.

fifty-four stanzas, giving a total of thirteen divergent revisions. These may be attributed to Percy's second manuscript copy, which perhaps also contributed to some of the more significant re-writings, but he did practise the gentle art of archaization.

Eighteenth-century literary archaism is apparent in criticism and poetry, from the 'monstrously eccentric' title of John Holt's (?) *An Attempte to Rescue that Aunciente, English Poet, and Play-Wrighte, Maister Williaume Shakespere, from the Maney Errours, faulsely charged on him, by Certaine New-fangled Wittes; and to let him Speak for Himself, as right well he wotteth, when Freede from the many Careless Mistakeings, of the Heedless first Imprinters, of his Workes* (1749), to George Darley's 1821 poem 'To Helene, On a gifte-ringe carelesslie loste. A. D. 1672', beginning:

> I sente a ringe, a little bande
> Of Emerauld and rubie stone.

The most renowned example is of course the first published version of 'The Rime of the Ancyent Marinere'.[76] Johnson had warned of the dangers of this brand of Spenserian imitation in the *Rambler*: 'His stile was in his own time allowed to be vicious, so darkened with peculiarities and of phrase, and so remote from common use, that Johnson [Ben Jonson] boldly pronounces him "to have written in no language". . . . The imitators of Spenser . . . seem to conclude, that when they have disfigured their lines with a few obsolete syllables, they have accomplished their design, without considering that they ought not only to admit old words, but to avoid new. . . . It would indeed be difficult to exclude from a long poem all modern phrases, though it is easy to sprinkle it with gleanings of antiquity.'[77] Perhaps Percy felt that the ancient subject matter of his ballads would prevent him tumbling into such grotesque anachronism.

Percy employed inverted commas to indicate significant deviation in his transcription of 'Northumberlande betrayed by

---

[76] Arthur Freeman, *Eighteenth Century Shakespeare*, 6 (New York, 1971), preface. Darley's poem (signed 'GUILLIAME') is printed in *London Magazine*, 3 (Mar. 1821), 267, and is reproduced in Jerome J. McGann (ed.), *The New Oxford Book of Romantic Period Verse* (Oxford, 1994), 590, which also reprints 'The Rime of the Ancyent Marinere', 143–61.

[77] Johnson, *Rambler*, 121: 'The dangers of imitation. The impropriety of imitating Spenser', iv. 285–6.

Douglas', and this synoptic editorial tactic was deployed in the
Reliques as well. He was more consistent in his use of the device in
manuscript than he was in print. Inverted commas feature seven
times, and the transcript also contains two marginal notes giving
the original manuscript reading, although minor deviations are far
more numerous, and in some instances these marks in fact indicate
interpolation rather than revision. Lines 143–52 of the Folio MS
read:

> "now hold thy tounge, Ladye," hee sayde,
>   "& make not all this dole for mee,
> for I may well drinke, but Ist neu[er] eate,
>   till againe in Lough Leuen I bee."
>
> he tooke his boate att the Lough Leuen
>   for to sayle now ou[er] the sea,
> & he hath cast vpp a siluer wand,
>   saies "fare thou well, my good Ladye!"
> the Ladye looked ouer her left sholder;
>   in a dead swoone there fell shee.[78]

Percy rendered this:

> Nowe hold thy tongue, Ladye, he sayde
>   And make not all this dole for mee
> For I may well drinke but Ive never eate
>   Till againe in Loughe Leven I bee
>
> <Has took his boat at the Lo>
> 'The winde was fayre, the boatman called,
>   'And william Douglas was readye'
> Hee tooke his boat at the Lough Leven
>   For to sayle now over the sea
>
> And he hath cast up a silver wand
>   Sayse fare thee well my good Ladye
> The Ladye look'd over her left shoulder
>   In a dead swoon there fell shee[79]

It is worth showing how these stanzas ultimately appeared in
the printed *Reliques* of 1765, especially considering Percy did
indicate nine changes in his transcription. The printed version
contains no such editorial marks, and the introduction, 'The

---

[78] Hales and Furnivall, ii. 223 (corrected).
[79] Houghton, bMS Eng. 893 (20A), fo. 149ᵛ.

following is printed . . . from two copies: one of them in the Editor's folio MS', seemed to permit any textual infidelity (i. 258 (italics reversed)).

> [stanza 37 is omitted]
>
> The wind was faire, the boatman call'd,
>   And all the saylors were on borde;
> Then William Douglas took to his boat,
>   And with him went that noble lord.
>
> Then he cast up a silver wand,
>   Says, Gentle lady, fare thee well!
> The lady sett a sigh soe deepe,
>   And in a dead swoone down shee fell.[80]

It may be no surprise to learn that Percy accepted the deficiencies of the Folio MS version, since he prefaced his printed version with the note, 'To correct this by my other copy which seems more modern. The other copy in many parts preferable to this.'[81] It should be stressed, however, that Percy's Folio MS transcriptions were sound, at least initially.

This fidelity is further borne out by a transcript made very much later, possibly the last Percy ever made. It occurs in a letter to Robert Jamieson, dated 4 April 1801. Jamieson was editing his own anthology, *Popular Ballads and Songs*, subtitled '*Reliques* of Ancient Scotish Poetry'. He sent Percy a selection of '⌈curious⌉ specimens' he had collected and transposed, and requested some transcriptions from the Folio MS, probably the Robin Hood ballads. With great reluctance, Percy returned only one, 'Fragment of the Old Song of Robin Hood and the <Beggar> Old Man' (Percy's title), and in his letter he again justified his treatment of the Folio MS, much as he had done to George Paton in the 1770s:

I have copied for you here that ∧ ⌈one⌉ which you particularly pointed out as I was unwilling to disappoint your expectations & wishes altogether. By it you will see the defective and incorrect state of the old Text in the ancient folio MS, & the irresistable Demand on the Editor of the *Reliques* to attempt by some ⌈of those⌉ ∧ Conjectural Emendations, wch. have been blamed by <some> ⌈one or two⌉ rigid Critics, but without which the Collection w^d. not have deserved a moment's attention.[82]

---

[80] i. 265–6.   [81] *Reliques* (1889), i. 280.

[82] Florida State University Special Collections, MSS RARE 78–6 (*Illustrations*, viii. 341).

Those 'rigid Critics', however many, would have had little cause to criticize this transcript, which was extremely precise.

Because the copy is so exact, one stanza will be sufficient, followed by Hales and Furnivall's version.

> But Robin did on the old Man's hose
> this were torne in the wrist [a]
> when I look on my leggs said Robin
> then for to laugh I list

> But Robin did on this old mans hose,
>   thé were torne in the wrist;
> "when I look on my leggs," said Robin,
>   "then for to laugh I list."[83]

Percy characteristically abandoned punctuation, aligned the lines, modernized 'mans' to 'Man's', and misread 'the' as 'this' (the accented 'thé' is, like their punctuation, a convention of Hales and Furnivall). It was otherwise accurate. In addition, he offered a marginal gloss for 'wrist': '(a) sic MS forté *twist* (the *hose* I conceive at that time to have been both breeches and stockings see the Engravings of M[r]. Struth[r].).' Jamieson gladly (and accurately) made use of the transcript in his collection.[84]

The conjectural emendation that Percy defends here involved using the editorial marks '' to enclose his own revisions and interpolations. He made use of inverted commas in precisely the opposite way to quoting: to quote a text that did not exist. The quotation marks do not represent actual absent texts, but hint at the absent archetypal source or ur-text. In acting thus, Percy laced through the corrupt documentary evidence that did exist a version of the original—his historical speculation—that did not, and the whole fabric of the text was made to appear original by the occasional evidence of stitching and mending. The earliest eighteenth-century editions of Chaucer had used square brackets to distinguish conjectural emendations, and Edward Capell had used a black-letter fount for the same purpose in his Shakespeare of 1768. But in Elizabethan texts inverted commas were used to

---

[83] Hales and Furnivall, i. 15 (corrected).

[84] Robert Jamieson, *Popular Ballads and Songs* [subtitled 'RELIQUES OF ANCIENT SCOTISH POETRY'] (Edinburgh, 1806), ii. 49. Jamieson noted, '* This fragment is given *verbatim et literatim*, from the folio MS. so often referred to in the Reliques of Ancient English Poetry.'

highlight *sententiae*. Proverbial sayings received 'gnomic pointing': as Margreta De Grazia puts it, 'What had formerly marked the universal and true (and therefore public) had come to designate the unique and exclusive (and therefore private). The sign once distinguishing the commonplace sets the bounds for private enclosure.'[85] Interestingly, to highlight the work of the editor in this way is to celebrate the whole discipline of textual criticism. The editor moves within a closer proximity to the mystical (and true) source than the text itself.

The quotation marks do, then, act as quotation marks, gesturing to an original context and pegging out a fragment of an earlier text. But it is the editor who achieves the primacy of original utterance, who appears within the text as a particular presence, leaving the traces of genius. Percy's very marks " had also appeared previously as marginal notes in Pope's edition of Shakespeare to indicate 'the most shining passages'.[86] Johnson wrote in the preface to his own Shakespeare that he had retained all of Pope's notes, 'that no fragment of so great a writer may be lost'.[87] The quotation mark textualizes the utterance. In the case of Percy, the ambition to 'textualize the utterance', to make the evanescent voice into a physical document—in contrast to the orality of *Ossian*—is of course paramount.[88]

'I NEVER PRETENDED TO GIVE HIM ANYTHING MORE THAN AN *OLD SONG*'[89]

It is quite possible that Percy sent Shenstone these various transcripts in the first half of 1761, and certainly they would offer an account of his reading from the beginning of that year. Although Percy's letters from 27 November 1760 to 22 May 1761 have been lost, Shenstone's do survive, and they show that he was gradually compiling his 'Billets'. Shenstone, however, delayed sending these, because he admitted that his grasp of Percy's plan was still shaky: 'The Adjustment of This, will be a matter of Importance, and pretty intricate determination.'[90] Shenstone

---

[85] De Grazia, *Shakespeare Verbatim*, 217.
[86] *Johnson–Steevens–Malone*, i. 122.   [87] Ibid. 44.
[88] Stewart, *On Longing*, 19.
[89] *A Collection of Old Ballads* (1723–5), i, p. iii.   [90] *Letters*, vii. 94.

was anxious to learn how Percy distinguished a song from a ballad (unfortunately we do not have Percy's answer), and what dates the collection would span. Neither had the question of the Scottish pieces been settled: should they be included and, if so, where?

Interestingly, Percy was now biding his time until he could consult Johnson for advice. In spite of his September visit to the Leasowes and Shenstone's apparent commitment to the project, Percy tried to return to his original partner. He met Johnson for 'a council of war' on 20 May while he was in London to negotiate contracts with Millar and the Dodsleys.[91]

Percy wrote to Shenstone from a London coffee-house on the same day, and informed his friend, 'To oblige *you* I have stipulated with the Bookseller only to print *two Volumes*.'[92] A third was negotiable, but 'no inducement whatever is to give birth to a fourth'. But the contract signed with James Dodsley (and not Shenstone's crony Robert—nor indeed with Andrew Millar) tells a rather different tale. It is transcribed by James Tierney from Isaac Reed's notes, edited by Alexander Chalmers:

Signed articles of agreement whereby P. assigns JD the copy of his Collection of Ancient English Ballads, proposed to be printed in three volumes, 12mo, for 100 guineas. Should only two volumes be printed, payment to be £70; an additional £35 for a third volume, for which P. hereby engages JD. If any accident prevents P.'s completeing the work after he had received any part of the payment, the Folio MS of ballads shall become JD's property.[93]

Three volumes, and Percy was soon planning a fourth.

The contract, perhaps under the renewed interest of Johnson, resorted to the apparent authority of the Folio MS. The source was now valued as much as a capital investment as an aesthetic commodity. Shenstone had consistently described it as 'gold', in the sort of rapacious terms favoured by Edward Young in *Conjectures on Original Composition*.[94] Paul Baines has argued that this sort of gloating by Shenstone helped to precipitate the Ritsonian charge that Percy's *Reliques* was counterfeit. Ritson's attack used legalistic rather than scholarly terminology, and 'This language is constitutive of the claim for absolute truth, not a

[91] Ibid. 96; Davis (1989), 76–7. Percy had signed contracts for *The Song of Solomon* and *Five Pieces of Runic Poetry* on 21 May, and the *Reliques* on 22 May.
[92] *Letters*, vii. 97.   [93] Tierney, 522.   [94] *Letters*, vii. 6, 136.

reflection of it; if it is an appropriate language for scholarship, that is only because antiquarians are economic.'[95]

Johnson, whose businesslike treatment of the Folio MS is discernible in the contract, gave Percy deceptively clear guidelines on planning the *Reliques*, and Percy now called it '*My* Collection'. Shenstone was informed of some of the decisions taken:

Imprimis, My Collection will be promisc[u]ous, yet so distributed that the pieces shall if possible illustrate each other, I don't mean by throwing those of the same subject together . . . but only when any little stroke in one serves to explain an obscurity in another. Where nothing of this kind offers, I shall distribute them so, as to prevent the reader from being tired: I shall not easily suffer two long ditties to come together: nor permit a long series of Love Songs to remain undivided.[96]

Like Dodsley's own *Select Collection of Old Plays*, Percy would only include pieces up to the Restoration, but allowed exception for some modern imitations. Percy's reference to this particular work was revealing, because it supports my contention that his first transcripts were being made at about this time. It also puts the *Reliques* into a specific publishing context. Percy had struck his bargain with James Dodsley earlier that day, and was now implying that his work was part of that publisher's popular series: Robert Dodsley's *Old Plays* and *A Collection of Poems by Several Hands*, the later volumes of which Shenstone had been partly responsible for compiling. As far as the arrangement went, the definition of 'promiscuous' in Johnson's *Dictionary* was taken from Bailey: 'Mingled; confused; undistinguished'. It suggests that the architecture of the book was to be irregular, free from Augustan restraints, Gothic: a counterpoint to Percy's developing theories of ancient English minstrels.[97]

Shenstone's reply, I believe, was to finally send his second 'Billet', recommending *Old Ballads*. The elegance of this work, in three compact octavos, seems to have belatedly impressed Shenstone, who noted with unwitting irony, 'I like 3 vols as well, or better than two, provided they can be furnished with *good* Materials.'[98] Each volume of *Old Ballads* concluded with

---

[95] Paul Baines, '"Our Annius": Antiquaries and Fraud in the Eighteenth Century', *BJECS* 20 (1997), 50.   [96] *Letters*, vii. 96.
[97] Vartin, 88–92.   [98] *Letters*, vii. 177.

Scottish songs, which would require a glossary if they were to be included in the *Reliques*.

A *Collection of Old Ballads* (1723–5) was a popular three-volume anthology of historical ballads and miscellaneous songs derived from broadsides. Its editor, once thought to be Ambrose Philips, has not been established.⁹⁹ It is regarded as an influential collection in eighteenth-century literary antiquarianism, and Friedman calls it 'something of a landmark in the ballad revival because it sets us on the road to the *Reliques*'.¹⁰⁰ In fact, the work had an even more crucial role than Friedman suggests in the genesis of the *Reliques* because it provided an early model for Percy's work, more specific than Dodsley's *Old Plays* or *Collection*, and much more accessible than the Folio MS. The working title of Percy's anthology was 'a Collection of Old Ballads', and even the full title of *Old Ballads* could almost have stood for the *Reliques*: 'A COLLECTION OF OLD BALLADS. *Corrected from the best and most Ancient* COPIES *Extant.* WITH INTRODUCTIONS HISTORICAL, CRITICAL, OR HUMOROUS. *Illustrated with* COPPER PLATES.' Shenstone expected the *Reliques* to go into print as '*A Collection of Old Ballads*'.¹⁰¹

The striking similarities of the two works are outlined by Vartin: both arranged their material chronologically and introduced pieces with long introductions. The two collections also shared epigraphs, illustrations, and twenty-five ballads. *Old Ballads*, however, was arranged entirely chronologically and by subject. The anonymous editor of *Old Ballads* had pedagogic pretensions, but the headnotes displayed a light and ironic touch in introducing each piece, and ignored the scholarly problems of which Percy was so fond. Vartin lists twenty-five pieces Percy derived from *Old Ballads* and a further twenty-one were included in what Friedman calls 'The First Draft of Percy's *Reliques*', dated by him October–November 1761 (Appendix II). This total of forty-six is however misleading when one examines Percy's own copy of *Old Ballads*.

---

⁹⁹ Mary Segar, 'A Collection of Ballads', *TLS* (2 Mar. 1932), 154; Lillian de la Torre Bueno, 'Was Ambrose Philips a Ballad Editor?', *Anglia*, 59 (1935), 252–70.
¹⁰⁰ Friedman, *The Ballad Revival*, 146.
¹⁰¹ *Letters*, vii. 79, 181; *Reliques* (1765), i, p. xiv.

This heavily annotated book is in the British Library and has been entirely neglected by scholars.[102] The initial impression on leafing through it is of an early draft of the *Reliques*, which at one time may have been conceived as merely an updated edition of *Old Ballads*. Percy's notes commence on the endpapers and fill the margins with corrections, references, and anecdotes, many of which were to feature in the *Reliques*. For example, Percy's first note on the frontispiece recto, volume i, extracted three paragraphs regarding ballads from *Spectators* 70 and 85, later referred to in the preface to the *Reliques*, and quoted in part as the epigraph to the third volume.[103]

In the winter of 1760 Percy lent this copy to Shenstone, who marked the same ballads he later listed in his second 'Billet'. Shenstone had probably received *A Collection of Old Ballads* in December 1760, but did not write to Percy again until 2 March 1761 due to his 'Nervous Fever'.[104] A day earlier he had explained their scheme to Richard Graves, which reminded him of his responsibilities to Percy: 'I was also to have assisted him in selecting and rejecting; and in fixing upon the best readings—But my illness broke off our correspondence, the beginning of winter— and I know not what he has done since.'[105] Shenstone consequently apologized to Percy for any delay his illness had caused, but gave no more thought to the project other than acknowledging that he had received *Old Ballads*.

The copy was sent by Percy to Shenstone via Dodsley. Percy himself had at least two copies of the work: the heavily annotated copy in the British Library, and a dismembered second now scattered through the Percy Papers at Harvard. The first he picked up for 9s. in 1759; the other arrived from James Dodsley on 15 February 1762, bought on Percy's behalf from Curtis's book sale for 2s.[106] It was the British Library copy that was sent to Shenstone, who 'read them over and marked several, according

[102] Percy's copy comprised 1st vol., 3rd edn. (1727); 2nd vol., 2nd edn. (1726); and 3rd vol., 2nd edn. (1738). Percy's *Old Ballads* is shelved in the BL, C 60 e 15.
[103] *Reliques* (1765), i, p. x n., iii, p. iv.   [104] *Letters*, vii. 88–9, 20 n.
[105] Williams, 573.
[106] Bodl., MS Percy c 9, fo. 24; Bodl., MS Percy c 2, fo. 233^r (Tierney, 556), Bodl., MS Percy c 9, fo. 103^r. The copy from Curtis was erroneously dated by Percy '1716' and arrived with Ballard's Collection of ballads. He was also lent a copy of 'Old Songs' in three volumes by Dodsley on 29 Mar. 1762 (Bodl., MS Percy c 9, fo. 96^v).

to different degrees of Approbation'.[107] It still displays these marks, which exactly correspond with Shenstone's second 'Billet'. This 'Billet' was eventually sent to Percy between May and June 1761, and answers Percy's letter of 22 May: it would therefore appear to be the missing letter xxxvi of Brooks's edition. Shenstone awarded twenty-five pieces '#', and thirty-seven '++' (one subsequently downgraded to '+'), using the same system as the 'Billets'.

From a total of 159 pieces in *Old Ballads*, Percy annotated 112, noting the occurrence of other examples (principally in the Folio MS, Pepysian Library, and *The Golden Garland*) and adding historical detail to the often slight printed introductions. Sixty of these annotated pieces were collated, again primarily recording variation with the Folio MS, Pepys ballads, and *Golden Garland*. Percy's attention did not, however, slavishly follow Shenstone's 'Billet'. Of the twenty-five Shenstone marked with highest approbation, only fourteen found their way into the 1765 *Reliques*, while only another one was in the 'First Draft'.[108] Of the remaining thirty-eight suggested, only six reached print, with a further nine in the 'First Draft'.[109] Percy printed five other pieces himself, and eight in the 'First Draft' were also unnoticed by Shenstone.[110]

Shenstone's influence was further diminished when one realizes that several ballads suggested by Shenstone and apparently accepted by Percy were in fact derived from other versions. Vartin's collation of *Old Ballads* with the *Reliques*, although

---

[107] *Letters*, vii. 89.

[108] 'King Leir', 'Chevy-chase' ('The more modern ballad'), 'Gilderoy', 'Queen Eleanor', 'Blind Beggar' ('The Beggar's Daughter of Bednal Green'), 'Spanish Lady', 'King John & the Abbot', 'Lord Thomas & fair Eleanor', 'Wife of Bath', 'Children in the Wood', 'First Part of ye King & ye Miller', 'The baffled Knight', 'Moore of Moorehall' ('The Dragon of Wantley'), 'William and Margarett' ('Margaret's Ghost'), Shenstone's titles. Shenstone also recommended 'Time's Alteration', and Percy included it in the 'First Draft'.

[109] 'Launcelot', 'Andrew Barton', 'Jane Shore', 'Lady's Fall', 'Second part of King & Miller', 'St. George & the Dragon' (also subsequently 'Bride's Burial'); and 'Seven Champions', 'King Alfred', 'Alphonso', 'Godina', 'The unfortunate Concubine' ('Rosamond'), 'Sir Richard Whittington', 'Patient Grissel', 'The Black-moore', 'Crafty Lawyer' ('The Crafty Lover'), Shenstone's titles.

[110] 'King Cophetua and the Beggar-maid' ('Cupid's Revenge'), 'Fair Rosamond', 'The Gaberlunzie Man', 'The Lady turned Servingman', 'The King of France's Daughter'; and 'The Scotsman outwitted' ('The Northern Ditty'), 'The Roman Charity', 'Buckingham betrayed', 'The beggar wench of Hull', 'Maudlin', 'The Hunting of the Gods', 'Ballad on Tobacco', 'Suffolk miracle', Percy's titles.

very useful, is unfortunately naïve. Two ballads ostensibly drawn from *Old Ballads* are entirely unmarked in Percy's copy, four more only note other versions and are themselves uncollated.[111] These figures are much higher for the 'First Draft': seven are unmarked and another five uncollated.[112]

Consequently, we can see that Shenstone's 'Billet' was not used uncritically by Percy. When his copy of *A Collection of Old Ballads* was returned to him, he set to work on its songs and ballads, and his note-taking continued at least until 1765. Out of sixty collations, less than half (twenty-seven) followed Shenstone's 'Billet'. In addition, most of these occur in the first volume and only one in the third. If Percy was working through the volumes following Shenstone, it may indicate that he was losing faith in his friend's judgement.

The different ambition that each had for the *Reliques* is well illustrated by the Robin Hood ballads. In spite of several such pieces in the Folio MS, Percy had early decided to exclude them from his collection. There were none included in the 'First Draft' although ultimately he did admit 'Robin Hood and Guy of Gisborne' (i. 79). He collated just one from *Old Ballads*, and that simply with a version from Dryden's *Miscellany* ('The Pedigree, Education, and Marriage of Robin Hood, with Clorinda, Queen of Titbury Feast').[113] Shenstone had recommended seven.

There is, however, a Robin Hood collection that has been over-looked in the Percy–Shenstone collaborations, among thirty of Percy's chapbooks acquired by the Houghton Library in 1884.[114] One of these is *Robin Hood's Garland* (1749: see Appendix III). This is a substantial chapbook garland, of more than a hundred pages, and contains twenty-four songs and ballads. It is annotated by Percy much as he annotated *Old Ballads*, with notes on sources, some collation and revision, and seven of the pieces are numbered to enable them to be cross-

---

[111] 'Launcelot' and 'Queen Eleanor's Confession'; and 'The Gaberlunzie Man', 'St. George and the Dragon', 'The baffled Knight', 'Margaret's Ghost' ('William and Margaret'), Percy's titles.

[112] 'The seven Champions', 'The Scotsman outwitted' ('The Northern Ditty'), 'The Roman Charity', 'The beggar wench of Hull', 'Ballad on Tobacco', 'The revengeful Moor', 'The Lawyer outwitted' ('The Crafty Lover'); and 'Buckingham betrayed', 'When this old Cap was new' ('Time's Alteration'), 'Sir Rich[d] Whittington', 'The London Prentice', 'Suffolk miracle', Percy's titles.   [113] Percy's *Old Ballads*, i. 64.

[114] Harvard 25276 44* (1–30), lot 302 of the 1884 sale.

referred to the Robin Hood ballads in the Folio MS. Two ballads ('Robin Hood and the jolly Pinner of Wakefield' and 'Robin Hood and Allen-a-Dale') are revised by Shenstone. He was either collating with an unrecorded source, or making his own changes to improve the metre of the lines. Shenstone made only ten textual changes (and several minor deletions) to 'Robin Hood and the jolly Pinner of Wakefield', but three times as many for 'Robin Hood and Allen-a-Dale', for which he also proposed a new title. At one stage, Percy too was bent on 'Robin Hood and Allen-a-Dale', spurred on by the hope that it would confirm his theory of ancient English minstrelsy.[115] On the Robin Hood ballads, Shenstone seems to have been prepared to work uncharacteristically hard on textual collation. By this stage, however, his industry failed to move Percy.

The contents of *Old Ballads* overlap with the *Reliques* less than one might imagine. Although it did influence the material in Percy's work, *Old Ballads* was not the chief source—in fact the Folio MS was, with forty-seven derived titles compared with at most twenty-four. *Old Ballads* did feature far more in the earliest surviving draft of the *Reliques*, contributing at most thirty-seven intended pieces, and some of these, like 'Alphonso and Gonsalez', lasted to the proof stage of the first edition before they were suppressed.

What Percy's annotations to *Old Ballads* do reveal, however, is his work on dozens of ballads that he never published. Typically, he noted the whereabouts of other copies and variant texts at the head of each piece, then indicated any changes in diction or spelling in the margins, and added lengthier notes or further stanzas as footnotes that occasionally spilt onto the endpapers. He ignored variation in punctuation (except for six notes to 'King Leir'), a lack of interest paralleled by his barely punctuated transcriptions from the Folio MS.

His collations were otherwise scrupulous. For example, 'King Alfred and the Shepherd' was annotated in three different inks over the title, noting the occurrences of the ballad in the Pepysian Library, *Pills to Purge Melancholy*, and Ballard's Collection.[116] Copious collation notes with a Pepys copy follow: ninety-six terminal 'e's and 'es' for 's' were added, such as 'Crown/e',

---

[115] See *Reliques* (1996), iii. 364.   [116] Percy's *Old Ballads*, i. 43–52.

'Hour/es', 'sat/e', and 'been/e'; and a further seventy-three minor spelling alterations, including 'a' frequently (but not consistently) added to 'shepherd', 'i' occasionally changed to 'y' ('lie', 'blithe'), and such emendations as 'smoaky Roof' to 'smoakie roofe'. No variations in diction were recorded.

The precision exhibited in his notes suggests a degree of care which was later belied by the printed versions of Folio MS pieces. It is also worth noting Percy's indication of the founts of his collating copies, a constant thread in these notes, showing his particularity over the niceties of typography and layout.

Percy wrote a lengthy footnote into his copy of *Old Ballads*, concerning 'Cupid's Revenge' and *Romeo and Juliet*. He donated this note to Johnson for his edition of Shakespeare, published in the same year as the *Reliques*, and in a revised version later printed it himself in the *Reliques*.[117] The collation that followed Percy's note in *Old Ballads* is also interesting because it contains a number of emendations signed 'conject.', others assigned 'so in Shakespear' or 'so Shakesp', and some whole stanzas are rejected. The fact that the footnote was inscribed in his copy of *Old Ballads* shows the extent to which this was a working copy for Percy.

'The Battel of Agincourt between the French and English' perhaps best demonstrates the complexity of Percy's annotations, and his attitudes towards his collations. He emended the title to 'The Battel of Agincourt betweene English-men and French Men', and recorded three collating copies—*Pills*, Pepys's 'Merriments', and the Folio MS.[118] The name of the tune was revised, 'Flying Fame' to 'When Flying Fame', and Percy added a source for the music (from *Pills*).

The text of the ballad was collated with Pepys and the Folio MS, and variations signed either 'P' or 'MS'. There were also interpolations in red ink referring to further manuscript notes added at the end of the volume, consisting of four numbered groups of stanzas absent from the *Old Ballads* text but present in the Folio MS (and one also present in Pepys). These totalled twenty-one stanzas, and were headed in red, 'The stanzas wanting in page 87. from the MS Copy corrected'. Note that this was a 'corrected'

---

[117] *The Plays of William Shakespeare*, ed. Samuel Johnson (1765), viii, pp. Kk8ᵛ–Ll1ʳ; Percy's *Old Ballads*, i. 138–44; *Reliques*, i. 166.
[118] Percy's *Old Ballads*, ii. 79–89.

copy of the Folio MS. The extent to which these stanzas differ from those in the Folio MS demonstrates the extent to which Percy actually honoured no textual authorities—neither Pepys, the Folio MS, nor *Old Ballads*. This does not bring the motives of his collations into question, but emphasizes that his editorial role was to synthesize.

For example, the nine stanzas comprising group IV of 'The Battel of Agincourt' in the *Old Ballads* additions Percy marked in the Folio MS: 'The Nine Stanz^s. following not in print', and emended them by conjecture.[119] These changes were copied wholesale into *Old Ballads*, whilst purporting to be the Folio MS text. The marginal corrections were therefore recorded not as revisions of a corrupted original, but as Percy's alternative readings for his own version of the ballad.

Hales and Furnivall give lines 157–60:

> 200000 ffrenchmen our Englishmen had,
> some 2, & some had one;
> eu[er]ye one was commanded by sound of trumpett
> to slay his prisoner then.[120]

Percy emended the Folio MS:

> 10,000 ffrenche our English had,
> Some one and some had two.
> And each was bid by Trumpets sound
> To slay his prisoner tho,
> (or)
> His Prisoner to slo.

This was transcribed in *Old Ballads* as:

> ^{x}Ten ^{x}*Twenty* thousand French the English had
> Some one and some had two
> And each was bid by Trumpets sound
> <To slay his prisoner ^{x}tho>   <^{x}ie then>
> His Prisoner to slo^x ^{x}ie slay

This version, typical of the stanzas in this group, shows Percy's rending and rendering of his sources. To improve the jerky rhythm of the original, he deliberately resorted to the contrived archaism, 'slo'. The metrical emphasis on this word drives the reader away

---

[119] Hales and Furnivall, ii. 172.   [120] Ibid. 173 (corrected).

from the text to the explanatory note, and demonstrates how the experience of reading the text relies on editorial explication (and a complete lack of sympathy for the French casualties).[121]

Shenstone continued to send 'Billets' throughout the Summer, although he was gradually becoming aware that he and Percy held divergent opinions on the work. Shenstone intimated this in a note to the third 'Billet', which covered Ramsay's *Tea-Table Miscellany* and was probably sent in May or June 1761—'I do not imagine M[r] P. will admit a tenth part of what are marked here.'[122] It would appear that *A Collection of Old Ballads* was returned to Percy at the end of June 1761, and, now able to consult the work with the second 'Billet', he must have dashed off a set of queries which elicited a reply from Shenstone on 5 July.[123] In this letter, Shenstone boasted that he had read six volumes of poetry since receiving Percy's last letter, and his instructions were eventually written up as 'Billets' 4, 5, and 6, which covered *The Hive* (1732–3) and *The Vocal Miscellany* (1733). This work was to prove futile: out of an astonishing 833 poems marked by Shenstone, Percy chose only ten, and even this paltry total was taken independent of Shenstone's advice.[124]

There are two reasons why Percy declined Shenstone's help and interest. First, he was by now corresponding with other members of the literati, professional scholars like Thomas Warton and Thomas Astle, and needed to rely less on the unreliable amateur Shenstone.[125] His letters to the Leasowes consequently became generalized in their enthusiasms and vacuous in their ambitions. The second reason was Percy's increasing commitment to the project as he conceived it, in both his time and his money. During his visit to London at the end of March he had worked with Edward Lye at the Society of Antiquaries for two days, and in the British Library for three. He was also planning a fortnight's research in Cambridge. His library at Easton Maudit was filling with books purchased from Lockyer Davis, and broadsides from

---

[121] Friedman, 'First Draft', confuses 'The Battel of Agincourt' with 'For the Victory at Agincourt', but does recognize that a transcript in the Houghton (bMS Eng. 893 (12A)) is annotated by Farmer rather than Warton. *Letters*, ii. 68 n.; *Letters*, iii. 91 n.; Fairer, 156 n.   [122] *Letters*, vii. 181.
[123] Ibid. 103–4. Brooks's chronology is awry here.   [124] Vartin, 54.
[125] Percy's first letter to Warton was dated 28 May. He met Astle in May/June 1761, and Edward Capell on 5 June, exchanging letters shortly after. He began corresponding with Evan Evans on 21 July.

Cluer Dicey, and he was borrowing dozens of volumes from his friends.[126] Shenstone's sporadic activity could not compare with this industry. Percy's growing confidence was displayed in his letter of 28 July, which contained revisions of some verses by Dodsley to be printed in Shenstone's *Works*. The revisions were incorporated.

Percy's new correspondence surprisingly offers little overall insight into the genesis of the *Reliques*. He was no longer developing editorial principles, but wanted answers to specific queries. His introductory letter to Warton is, however, of great significance because it was written during his pivotal stay in London, and proposed a plan of the *Reliques* highly coloured by concert with Johnson: 'to shew that many passages in our ancient English Poets may be illustrated from these Old Ballads.'[127] The *Reliques* was to be a determining force in the formation of the canon of English literature and the historical principles of literary criticism. He continued to outline his intellectual agenda and marketing strategy: 'My design is to give not only the best in my own Manuscript Collection, but also of those preserved in the Libraries of our Universities, as well printed, as otherwise, in 3 very neat Vol^s 12mo.'[128] It had not taken him long to guarantee materials for a third volume.

Clearly in one sense Percy was simply trying to justify the scholarship of his work to the Oxford Professor of Poetry, and indeed his letters bristle with an erudition noticeably absent from the Shenstone correspondence. But it is important that Percy's appeal to Warton should have come right in the middle of his London trip. Shenstone had never had much sympathy for Percy's antiquarianism, but that feature was now redefining the work, presumably under the palpable influence of Johnson. Moreover Percy sent two prized transcripts from the Folio MS to Warton, 'The Marriage of Sir Gawaine' and 'The Boy and the Mantle', and tried to persuade him to complete the *Squire's Tale*. Shenstone's influence was waning, and Percy was keen for fresh advice and new directions.

---

[126] Boston Public Library, MS Eng. 154; *Letters*, vii. 109.

[127] *Letters*, iii. 3; Fairer, 87.

[128] *Letters*, iii. 7; Fairer, 89. Warton too had been a guest at the Leasowes as early as 1758 (Tierney, 371), and contributed an inscription for a Hermitage. Percy's contract with James Dodsley was for three volumes, 'to contain all that I will ever print of this work' (*Willis's Current Notes*, 91).

We can now see that Shenstone's status as a collaborator was remarkably brief, just nine months, and for much of that time he and Percy seemed to be at cross-purposes. The letters to Warton mark the beginning of a new chapter in the genesis of the *Reliques*.

5
1761: The Making of the *Reliques*

On Sunday, 12 April 1778, Samuel Johnson, Anna Williams, and James Boswell dined with Percy, his children, and some Northumbrian guests, at Piccadilly. Johnson was in a brittle mood. On arrival, he immediately called for a drink, and then drained the bottle; but dinner went off well, despite Percy reading fifty lines of his nephew's poetry to the company. They retired for dessert and Johnson fell asleep. Percy, meanwhile, spying the Duke of Northumberland outside, excused himself for a moment's toadying. Johnson awoke, found his host fawning over the Duke, and resolved to have his sport. On Percy's return, the conversation turned to travel writing, and Johnson spoke deliberately highly of Thomas Pennant. Percy disagreed: Pennant had written disrespectfully of Alnwick Castle, Pennant was a mean writer, Pennant was wrong. 'Pennant', responded Johnson provokingly, 'in what he said of Alnwick, has done what he intended; he has made you very angry.' Percy objected to Pennant calling the garden 'trim', and eagerly described it; Johnson replied, 'According to your own account, Sir, Pennant is right. It *is* trim.' Johnson was enjoying baiting Percy, and they bickered for a while until Percy lost all patience.

'Pennant does not describe well.'
'I think he describes very well.'
'I travelled after him.'
'And *I* travelled after him.'
'But, my good friend, you are short-sighted, and do not see as well as I do.'

There was an almost audible gasp from Boswell, Johnson fell into an icy silence, but Percy prattled on, still disparaging Pennant until Johnson remarked scathingly, 'This is the resentment of a narrow mind.' Both hurt, they rowed furiously until Percy came to his senses, recovered himself, and took Johnson by the hand. The storm blown over, the guests were exhilarated and remained for supper. Percy, however, fretted. He had hoped to impress one of the Northumbrian guests, who was in competition for patronage, and feared he might lose favour should word get to the Duke of the unruly behaviour of his chaplain. He asked Boswell to intercede on his behalf, and Boswell wrote a formal letter to Johnson, who replied with a testimonial of Percy's character to be read at table to the Duke. Boswell reported the good news to Percy, who had the letter copied—to Johnson's renewed chagrin. Percy declared he 'would rather have this than all the degrees from all the Universities in Europe': it would become a family heirloom. Johnson disagreed. Percy would 'run about with it', he reflected bitterly. It might be published: 'That is the mischief of writing a letter.' 'I did this to help Percy. But I would not degrade myself. I have no high opinion of Percy.' Percy, however, was Dean of Carlisle by the end of October; the two old friends saw less and less of each other.[1]

The episode is paradigmatic for a discussion of Percy's correspondence. Percy obtained a physical, written reference rather than a private apology. This concern to cancel an oral moment by means of the authority of a written text is made clear in a later attack by Percy on Boswell himself, who, it seems, would often lay down his knife and fork in order to jot down any good anecdote about Johnson. Percy complained in Anderson's *Johnson* that, 'It is surely an exception more than venial to violate one of the first and most sacred laws of society by publishing private and unguarded conversation of unsuspecting company into which he was accidentally admitted' and censored his own unguarded correspondence with Evan Evans.[2] 'That is the mischief of writing a letter.' The following chapter should indicate why Percy was so extremely sensitive to the mischief of certain letters being published.

---

[1] *Boswell's Life*, iii. 271–8; James Boswell, *Boswell in Extremes 1776–1778*, ed. Charles McC. Weis and Frederick A. Pottle (1971), 274–319; Davis (1989), 223–9. Percy had already told tales to Boswell that, as a child, Johnson was so shortsighted he needed to crawl on all fours (Mar. 1776, in James Boswell, *Boswell's Notebook 1776–1777*, ed. R. W. Chapman (1925), 12).

[2] *Letters*, ix. 175; v, p. xxxiv. On 22 May 1798, Percy wrote to Thomas Stedman regarding the publication of the late Sir James Stonhouse's correspondence to forbid the publication of any of his letters among Stonhouse's papers, warning that by such indiscretions James Boswell had excluded himself from polite society and, aghast at his fall from social grace, drank himself to death (Bodl., MS Percy c 1, fos. 180–1).

The previous chapter argued that in the context of his developing theory of the profound literacy of ancient English minstrelsy, Percy's commitment to the *Reliques* became a careful task of collection and collation. It was an activity that could only be conducted—indeed only had meaning—in dealing with written records. Through the precision of his textual criticism, whether fancifully archaizing or being impeccably precise, Percy was ensuring that the *Reliques* would be a collection of literary texts rather than the oral invention spouted by Macpherson. But still the legendary history that empowers ballads, romances, fairy tales, and folklore spoke from outside the annals of history and outside written literature. And he now faced another threshold: that of manuscript and print. In order to publish, he had to negotiate these media as successfully as he had done the oral. As the next two chapters show, he was only partially successful, and there would be a considerable residue of the chirographic medium left in the finished book.

Perhaps the fragmentary, unfinished, manuscript state of the first edition of the *Reliques* acted like a Gothic charm. The printed pages were slightly awry, there were small but persistent confusions, strings of Shandean notes, and vertiginous Borgesian addenda.[3] The effect was uncanny. The familiar ballad, appearing in Percy's strangely academic garb, emphatically substantiated the alterity of others: dragons and giants, heroes and outlaws, minstrels and Goths— and in his weird gestures Percy incorporated them into the canon of English literature.

This chapter, then, introduces more original material to the early history of the *Reliques*, examining two crucial influences upon Percy's putative anthology: Pepys's collection of seventeenth-century broadsides and Percy's own collection of eighteenth-century broadsides. On 17 August 1761, Percy arrived in Cambridge. The very next day he was in the library, and for two six-day weeks toiled 'At Magd. transcribing old Ballads', where Samuel Pepys's broadside ballads remain to this day.[4] They consist of about 1,800 mainly black-letter broadsides pasted into five folio volumes, plus a few other relevant volumes of

---

[3] Borges had a taste for such things: he mentions the *Reliques* in 'The Congress' (Jorge Luis Borges, *The Book of Sand*, tr. Norman Thomas di Giovanni (Harmondsworth, 1979), 27).   [4] BL, Add. MS 32336, fos. 29–31.

ephemera collected by Pepys, such as the 'Pepys Merriments' (chapbooks), which Percy also used. Percy's own collection was largely the reward of his dealings with Cluer Dicey, who sent him his first bundle in June 1761. Over 300 of these ballads have survived, almost all white-letter. (Percy's black-letter collection was destroyed in the Northumberland House fire of 1780.)

When Percy returned home to Easton Maudit on 5 September from his Pepysian Library visit, he began to plan the publication of the *Reliques*. Percy was confronted with a conflict of media as he moved to printing his manuscripts alongside printed sources. As has been shown, his editorial method was derived from the relationships between oral and literate sources (privileging the written source), and manuscript and printed sources (privileging the printed source), but this chapter will demonstrate the inescapably chirographic nature of Percy's project, and establishes the problems he was to be confronted with when the printing of the *Reliques* really did start.

As with the last chapter, the impact of these two sources will be assessed by explaining Percy's own working methods, and, again, such a methodological approach has not been hitherto undertaken. The chapter concludes with the two earliest drafts of the *Reliques*—outlines which pre-date any previously published drafts—and I compare these with Percy's subsequent arrangements. It is a microbibliographical account, but does demonstrate that there was a profound shift in Percy's organization of his material when he began to arrange for the press. This chapter charts that movement. The first part will discuss the implications of Percy's visit to the Pepysian Library, the second will explain how Percy related the Pepys ballads to his own 'Alphabet Collection' of printed broadsides. Finally, the third part will assess Percy's method of arranging the *Reliques* in manuscript. This last section serves as both a conclusion to the making of the *Reliques* and an introduction to the printing of the *Reliques*, examined in the next chapter.

'A LITTLE CLUSTER OF INGENIOUS MEN'[5]

The visit to the Pepysian Library was undertaken in the context of Percy's expanding correspondence and book borrowing, and these

---

[5] Percy's marginalia in Shenstone, *Works*, iii, p. $\pi 1^r$: Bodl., Percy 83.

conditions surrounding the trip need to be set forth. Two things will come to light during this survey of his mid-1761 literary intercourse: Percy's deliberate manipulation of acquaintances, and his frequent precautions to conceal his own motives or projects. Percy cultivated a different voice for each of his correspondents, and the self-portrait that is adumbrated from reading his letters is in perpetual flux—doubtless one reason why Yale chose to edit his exchanges of correspondence rather than the complete or selected letters. This mutating persona operated solely within the chirographic environment of correspondence, and was therefore an expression of the relationship between the written manuscript (private letter) and the anticipated printed text (*Reliques*). Percy's letter-writing provides a commentary on his editorial practices in the *Reliques*, and these letters can be read as a domestic version of later eighteenth-century antiquarian theories of bibliography and the treatment of literary sources. Percy carefully revised his style for publication, and feared that untouched manuscript letters might be published. Again this demonstrates an acute awareness of the nature of the written source, the medium of the message, and the total transformation of the content that the form entails.[6]

Bruce Redford's deeply humanistic critique of the eighteenth-century 'familiar letter', *The Converse of the Pen*, emphasizes the importance of the speaking subject—the 'speaking *tone* of voice'—in eighteenth-century epistolary writing, and the semiotics of speech acts (such as raised eyebrows) implied in manuscript texts.[7] A little is known of Percy's conversation—too little and too contradictory to be of much help: Cradock called it 'lofty', and Boswell said that he flowed with anecdotes; Fanny Burney described him as 'perfectly easy & unassuming, very communicative, & though not very entertaining, because too prolix, . . . intelligent & of good commerce', while Hannah More called Percy 'quite a sprightly modern, instead of a rusty antique, as I expected'.[8] Johnson had

---

[6] There is no complete edition, or even checklist, of Percy's letters, but see Ashe, ii. appendix 2, 1–24.

[7] Bruce Redford, *The Converse of the Pen: Acts of Intimacy in the Eighteenth-Century Familiar Letter* (Chicago, 1986), 5–6.

[8] Joseph Cradock, *Literary and Miscellaneous Memoirs*, 4 vols. (1828), i. 243; *Boswell's Life*, v. 255; Fanny Burney, *The Journals and Letters of Fanny Burney (Madame D'Arblay)*, ed. Joyce Hemlow, with Curtis D. Settle and Althea Douglas (Oxford, 1972), i. 52; *Johnsonian Miscellanies*, ed. George Birkbeck Hill, 2 vols. (1897), ii. 179–80.

of course warned against the difference between an author's writings and his conversation: 'A transition from an author's books to
his conversation, is too often like an entrance into a large city, after
a distant prospect. Remotely, we see nothing but spires of temples,
and turrets of palaces, and imagine it the residence of splendor,
grandeur, and magnificence; but, when we have passed the gates, we
find it perplexed with narrow passages, disgraced with despicable
cottages, embarrassed with obstructions, and clouded with
smoke.'[9] But what is significant in the following account is the
interface between speaking and writing. It is a part of the same
argument that differentiates between Macpherson's Celts and
Percy's Goths: the difference between orality and literacy, between
textuality as a performance and textuality as an artefact—or
indeed the difference between harsh words before supper and a
written character reference from the great Cham.

Percy first told Shenstone of his plans to consult Pepys's broadside
ballads on 27 November 1760, having received permission from
'my Correspondent in Cambridge', probably Edward Blakeway,
another Shropshire man. At this early stage, Percy promised to
send Shenstone further details from Cambridge, although in the
event he never did.[10] By the time Percy wrote to Warton from
London on 28 May 1761, he was already in correspondence with
other scholars, although very few of these early letters have
survived.[11] According to Bertram Davis, he had exchanged letters
at least with Blakeway and Richard Farmer, and probably Thomas
Astle.[12] He had met Astle in the British Library during his
watershed trip to London, but their incomplete correspondence
survives only from 19 July.[13] Astle was compiling a catalogue of
the Harleian manuscripts in the British Library, and was therefore
a useful contact to cultivate.[14]

He probably met Edward Capell in the British Library too.[15]
Capell was, like Percy, a collector and literary-antiquarian. He was
the erstwhile Deputy Inspector of Plays, had catalogued David
Garrick's library, and was a precise, if eccentric, editor of
Elizabethan poetry. Capell was working on his textually influential

[9] Johnson, *Rambler*, 14: iii. 79–80.   [10] *Letters*, vii. 81.
[11] Ibid., iii. 1; Fairer, 87.   [12] Davis (1989), 82.
[13] Harlowe, 25. The original is now in the Folger Shakespeare Library, Y c 1452.
[14] Ashe, ii, appendix 1, 1.   [15] Davis (1989), 77–8.

edition of Shakespeare (published in 1768), having already produced *Prolusions* in 1760. The loss of the Percy–Capell letters is
unfortunate, but understandable in light of the pair's competitive
and tempestuous relationship, which reached its argumentative
climax with a '*final rupture*' in 1766.[16] Lists of books lent by
Capell to Percy do, however, survive, and as is suggested below
cast significant light on the material formation of the *Reliques* and
Percy's ultra-bibliographical working methods.

Although Percy borrowed only ten books from Capell, they
numbered crucial copies of *The Golden Garland* (1690) and
The Paradice of Dainty Deuises (1596), and Capell twice lent
The Palace of Pleasure (1569–80). Percy certainly knew Capell
by 5 June 1761 when he spent the day with him, and was
conceivably lent the books there and then, as they were returned
a month later (17 July 1761).[17] Through Capell, Percy was
conveniently introduced to Farmer, who accommodated him in
Cambridge.[18] Capell possibly recommended Percy to his friend
and colleague David Garrick as well—in which case Percy and
Capell could have been corresponding in 1760.

Unfortunately, Percy's correspondence with David Garrick from
this period does not survive either, but, as with Capell, comprehensive details of Percy's borrowings from Garrick are extant.[19]
Garrick allowed Percy to borrow dozens of volumes from his
collection of old English plays—almost 400 plays (a privilege he
never extended to Johnson for the *Dictionary*)—which he sent via
the bookseller Jacob Tonson.[20] Indeed Tonson may have
negotiated the loan: he had contracted Percy for the edition of
Buckingham. Halfway through this play-reading marathon

---

[16] *Letters*, ii. 106. Their relationship had been stormy since 1762 (ibid. 31); it
became tempestuous with the publication of the *Reliques* (ibid. 87).

[17] Bodl., MS Percy c 9, fos. 97ʳ, 101ᵛ, 102ᵛ. See, however, a remark to Farmer on 18
Oct. 1762, in which Percy determines to borrow Richard Edwards's *Paradice of Dainty
Deuises*, and a note on 30 Jan. 1763 confirming that Capell had lent this and William
Painter's *Palace of Pleasure*; presumably they too were lent twice (*Letters*, ii. 16). Percy
left a few notes in *Dainty Deuises* (Trinity College Library, Capell S 8 1) and, perhaps
after the publication of the *Reliques*, in Nicholas Breton's *Arbor of Amorous Deuices*
(1597) (Capell S 8 3).

[18] Davis (1989), 78; *Letters*, ii. 106–7. Percy lent Farmer Capell's copy of *Dainty
Deuises* in Feb. 1763 (*Letters*, ii. 35–6; Bodl., MS Percy c 9, fo. 98ᵛ).

[19] See *The Letters of David Garrick*, ed. David M. Little and George M. Kahrl
(1963), i. 913.   [20] Reddick, *The Making of Johnson's Dictionary*, 35–6.

(10 November 1762), Percy wrote to David Dalrymple declaring that he had gone over almost 200 plays for Buckingham.[21]

Tonson sent the first batch of Garrick's plays before January 1761, and during that year Percy borrowed thirty-nine volumes.[22] Percy generally returned the batches within six months.[23] He probably borrowed consistently throughout 1762 as well, as in March 1763 he was still returning twenty-volume boxes and borrowing five volumes at a time.[24] Most significant among the Garrick volumes borrowed were not plays at all, but two volumes of sixteenth-century romances.[25] Percy borrowed these collections twice, in both 1761 and 1763. Tonson sent piles of other material too. Between 1761 and 1763 more than a dozen boxes arrived, containing in addition to the Garrick plays almost a hundred more books. These were mainly works of or about the Restoration theatre: Dryden and Rochester, Winstanley and Gildon, Anthony à Wood, *Spectators*, *Guardians*, *Tatlers*.

Books also arrived by the crate from Tully's Head, and it is possible that Percy ran an account with the Dodsleys.[26] The earliest records of Dodsley sending books to Percy are for April 1761: fifteen books were sent (including a copy of Mallet, a romance of King Arthur, *Orpheus Caledonius*, *The Musical Miscellany*, and several books on China).[27] On 14 July 1761, Dodsley sent another seven: again, ancient manners, popular songs (*The Hive*, *Loyal Songs*, *Comic Miscellany*), and histories of China. By 10 August, Percy was returning books 'by Rogers's Olney Waggon', though some were retained until March of the following year. Another fourteen were received in November, several of which Percy kept (including *The Hive*, *Pills to Purge*

---

[21] *Letters*, iv. 1.   [22] Bodl., MS Percy c 9, fos. 103^v–105^r.

[23] Bodl., MS Percy c 9, fos. 97^r, 97^v.

[24] Bodl., MS Percy c 9, fos. 102^v, 97^v. Percy favoured 'Silby's Waggon' for returning the plays to Tonson, whereas he used 'Rogers's Olney Waggon' for returning books to Dodsley.

[25] *The Garrick Collection of Old English Plays*, ed. George M. Kahrl (1982), 36–7: vol. K.IX: *Guy of Warwick* (1560?), *Sir Bevis of Hampton* (1565?), *Sir Degore* (1565?), *The Squire of Low Degree* (1560?) (Percy does not list *Sir Isumbras* (1565?) in his notes on this volume); and vol. K.X: *Sir Eglamour of Artois* (1570?), *Sir Tryamour* (1561?), *Robin Hood* (1560?), *Adambel Clym of the Clough* (1550?), *Howleglas* (1528?), *The Knight of the Swan* (1565?), *Virgilius* (1562?); see Bodl., MS Percy e 5, fos. 7–11.

[26] Tierney remarks, 'Another form of payment [from Dodsley] came in the way of books' (31).   [27] Bodl., MS Percy c 9, fo. 96^r.

Melancholy, and *The Muses Library*). Shenstone bought an edition of Surrey's poems sent in this parcel.

Just four books arrived on 26 January 1762 (three Spanish books and an intriguing 'Old English Poetry MSS. 4to.'), Percy bought the black-letter *Seven Champions of Christendom* on 25 February (1s. 6d.) and parcels were sent almost every month of the following year, totalling about seventy books.[28] All bore witness to Percy's wide-ranging interests, his publishing commitments, and his profound reliance on the authority of the printed word. Percy paid for and kept about a third of those sent— mainly rare books he had instructed James Dodsley to obtain from auction catalogues.[29] In 1763, Dodsley sent books most months, totalling some fifty volumes. Percy kept only a few, but these parcels included Ballard's Collection of 300 ballads (15 February 1762), and Astle's volume of black-letter romances (3 March 1763)—the latter of which Percy desperately tried to keep.[30] This bibliopegic traffic dried up in 1765, and the only remaining records are of a half-dozen which arrived from Dodsley on 9 April. They were all returned, save *Poems: Written by Will. Shake-speare. Gent.* (1640), which Percy bought for a shilling.

Dodsley provided more than books, however: he provided a mechanism for Percy's research. Percy was quick to employ Dodsley as a sorting house for his scholarly network. He used Dodsley's wagons to ferry books to and from other scholars— Farmer, Warton, Lye, Apperley, Capell, even the bookseller Tonson.[31] And alongside these regular deliveries from Pall Mall, other packets arrived from other booksellers: from Lockyer Davis, who provided Percy with *Felixmarte de Yrcania* (famously read by Johnson whilst staying at Easton Maudit) and various

---

[28] Percy boasted to Warton that Dodsley 'transmits me books every week' (*Letters*, iii. 59; Fairer, 136).

[29] See, for example, a letter to Dodsley, Bodl., MS Percy c 2, fos. 233–4. Farmer also purchased books for Percy at auction (*Letters*, ii. 25–6: see Bodl., MS Percy c 9, fos. 140–5).

[30] Bodl., MS Percy c 9, in chronological order: fos. 96^r, 101^v, 96^v, 102^v, 103^r, 94^v; Bodl., MS Percy c 1, fo. 11^v, Bodl., MS Percy c 9, fo. 96^r. See also a letter from James Dodsley to Percy, 10 May 1764, requesting return of books; Percy complied promptly (Bodl., MS Percy c 1, fo. 9^r). On the Astle volume, see Ashe, ii, appendix I, 15, and *Garrick Collection*, 19. Percy once kept a MS book of William Cole's for fourteen years (BL, Add. MS 5825, fo. 7^v). [31] Bodl., MS Percy c 9, fos. 101^v, 102^v.

romances, and from John Newbery, who provided another copy of Mallet.[32]

Percy also borrowed from nearer to home, for example from his first patron, Lord Sussex. By the beginning of 1761, he had taken possession of twenty-two volumes (including an 'Old Chronicle black Lett^r.' and Olaus Wormius' *Literature Runica*), and over the next three years took more than forty others (including Camden's *Britannia* thrice, more Wormius, and several bibles and dictionaries: ordering the sacred, the secular, and the historical).[33] Percy also carried away a large part of Edward Lye's library (almost a hundred books: many works of Runic and medieval literature and history, including three editions of *Piers Plowman*, dictionaries and thesauri, dozens of plays and pamphlets), and Lye procured more than a dozen books of mainly seventeenth-century poetry from Lord Northampton's library.[34] When one adds this to the other dozen or so lenders from whom Percy borrowed while working on the *Reliques* (and Buckingham), it appears that in the first five years of the 1760s he borrowed at least 1,000 works.

Armed with this formidable library, Percy fired off dozens of queries to correspondents, and it is no accident that Dodsley supplied Percy with his literary comestibles: quires of paper and sealing wax by the pound. For example, on 30 June 1763, Percy bought enough paper to write 1,000 letters and 6,000 pages of notes.[35]

Many of Percy's letters have survived; evidence of his 'literary drudgery', as he described it at the time.[36] Although the correspondence with Shenstone faltered over the summer of 1761, Percy anticipated this, and his most excited letter (dated 19 July) described a new circle of correspondents:

I have had another Letter from Mr Warton, who has promised to ransack all their hoards at Oxon for me . . . I thankfully accept your offer of applying to your *virtuoso* friend in Scotland in my favour [John Macgowan] . . . I have settled a correspondence in the very heart of Wales [Evan Evans], and another in the Wilds of Staffordshire and

---

[32] Bodl., MS Percy c 9, fo. 98^r, see also fo. 101^r for later borrowings; *Boswell's Life*, i. 49.   [33] Bodl., MS Percy c 9, fo. 95.
[34] Bodl., MS Percy c 9, fos. 99^r–100^r.
[35] Bodl., MS Percy c 9, fo. 102^v: a quire is twenty-four or twenty-five sheets.
[36] Letter to William Cleiveland, 19 Nov. 1761, BL, Add. MS 32333, fo. 29^v.

Derbyshire [Thomas Astle, to whom he wrote on the same day] . . . I
intend also to write to a friend in Ireland [unidentified] . . . nor will I fail
to mention our scheme to Grainger in the West Indies.[37]

Shenstone's influence was undoubtedly waning. He had been
reluctant to mediate between Percy and Warton, and once Percy
had made the move himself he began to realize the benefits of
corresponding with antiquarians rather than men of taste. To
demonstrate this change, each of the correspondents here alluded
to will be discussed. It is also worth bearing in mind that this
diversification of *Reliques* research correspondence was in direct
contrast to the agonistic relationship with Shenstone, and enabled
Percy to spatialize his methodology before focusing it for the press.

The correspondence with Warton ran in phases, instigated by
Percy. In the first phase (28 May–11 July 1761), Percy made all
the running. Evidently he was trying to impress Warton with the
range of his library, the depth of his scholarship, and the influence
of his friends: recurring themes of these letters. He sent transcripts
from the Folio MS, including two Arthurian pieces (which were no
more accurate than those he sent to Shenstone), and flaunted his
scholarly credentials.[38] The Folio MS was not permitted to remain
a seventeenth-century commonplace book, but was mythologized:
'I must inform you that my *MS* appears to have been transcribed
(about 100 years ago) from another Copy much older.'[39] It was
simply a single stage in the chain of literate transmission that
might go back centuries. But Percy now politely denied access to
it. He had taken the precious source to the Leasowes the previous
summer and had generously lent it to Johnson, but it never again
left his possession (the Folio MS had suffered at the hands of a
binder when it was lent to Johnson).[40] Percy was again giving
himself the opportunity and justification to revise in transcription,
telling Warton that 'the Writer has every where accommodated the
Orthography, and even (where he could) the Style to that of his
own time'.[41] The manuscript source was not inviolable: it was like

---

[37] *Letters*, vii. 108–10.
[38] The transcripts of 'The Boy & the Mantle', 'The Marriage of Sir Gawaine', and
'Gentle Heardsman' are in the BL, Add. MS 42560, fos. 71–6.
[39] *Letters*, iii. 5: Fairer, 88.
[40] Hales and Furnivall, i, p. lxxiv. Despite Percy's protestations (*Reliques* (1794), i,
p. x), it is doubtful that the Folio MS was ever exhibited.
[41] *Letters*, iii. 5; Fairer, 88.

a palimpsest, recording layers of deviations for an editor to recover. Access to the Folio MS was therefore only available through the medium of Percy's transcriptions, and ultimately the *Reliques* itself, which eventually would be puffed as 'a select Collection of the best and most poetical of them'.[42] Many years later, Warton did reprint a piece derived directly from the printed *Reliques* in his *History of English Poetry*.[43] This immediately provoked an enraged response from the eccentric textual critic Joseph Ritson, who recognized the tampering hand of Percy in the 'transcription'.[44]

Nevertheless, at this stage Percy's strategy implied a fidelity to the Folio MS because he stressed the shortcomings of its provenance. This demanded a reciprocal rigour from Warton. In addition, Percy continued to pepper his letters with references gleaned from his researches in Icelandic saga, Arthurian romance, and medieval philology, and this flood of learning quickly secured him a place in the second edition of Warton's *Observations on the Fairy Queen of Spenser* (1762): significantly, a Percy letter to Warton was reproduced fairly accurately as a footnote to Warton's work.[45] In his correspondence with Warton, Percy was writing for the press. Warton, however, was unable to reciprocate: amazingly, he claimed there was nothing in the Bodleian that could help Percy in any way regarding the *Reliques*.

John Macgowan was the Scottish solicitor and antiquary who had been instrumental in winning Shenstone's approval of Macpherson's *Fragments*, although Shenstone did not reply to his enthusiasm for *Ossian* for over a year, eventually writing on 24 September 1761. Shenstone's belated reply was even then probably the result of a letter from Percy now lost. It is possible to reconstruct Percy's missing letter (xlv) by inference from Shenstone's letter to Macgowan. Presumably Percy had reminded Shenstone of his promise to apply to his '*virtuoso* friend in Scotland'. From what Shenstone told Macgowan of Percy's recent movements, it would appear that in this lost letter Percy described

---

[42] *Letters*, iii. 7; Fairer, 89.

[43] Thomas Warton, *The History of English Poetry* (1774–81), i. 43–6. The poem was 'Richard of Almaigne' (*Reliques*, ii. 3–5).

[44] Joseph Ritson, *Observations on the Three First Volumes of the History of English Poetry* (1782), 5.

[45] Thomas Warton, *Observations on the Fairy Queen of Spenser* (1762), i. 139–42.

his trip to the Pepysian Library and congratulated himself on cementing his new correspondences. The urgency of the undertaking was beginning to impress Percy.

Shenstone's letter to Macgowan is quite astonishing for the idiosyncratic account he gives of the *Reliques*. Shenstone takes on the airs of a patron:

I come to ask, whether you have any old Scotch ballads, which you would wish preserved in a neat edition. I have occasioned a friend of mine to publish a fair collection of the best old English and Scotch ballads; a work I have long had much at heart. Mr. Percy, the collector and publisher, is a man of learning, taste, and indefatigable industry; is chaplain to the Earl of Sussex. It so happens that he has himself a folio collection of this kind of MSS; which has many things truly curious, and from which he selects the best. I am only afraid that his fondness for antiquity should tempt him to admit pieces that have no other sort of merit. However, he has offered me a rejecting power, of which I mean to make considerable use.[46]

Shenstone here patronizingly presented Percy as his scribe and amanuensis—which would have been news to Percy—but Shenstone was perhaps still harbouring ambitions for a joint project of popular songs, tastefully modernized. Shenstone went on to boast to Macgowan that Johnson, Garrick, and Warton were all contributing to the publication, before copying out Percy's own remarks on his new circle of correspondents.[47]

Percy himself wrote to Thomas Astle on 19 July, in thanks for two collations from him and a copy of Surrey's *Songes and Sonnettes* (1559). Grainger, meanwhile, eventually replied miserably from the West Indies: 'I am sorry to tell you that I can be of no service to you in either of your schemes as to the illustrating Don Quixote, or getting you Indian poetry.'[48] The Irish correspondent has nowhere been traced, and may evince Percy's poetic licence in order to suggest the imperial sweep of his resources.

Percy's most interesting correspondence at this time was in Wales. He made contact with Evan Evans through Rice Williams, but when he wrote to Shenstone in July had not yet made independent contact with Evans. He was out to poach a Welsh scholar by using the unwitting Williams as bait. Rice Williams, described by Shenstone as 'a Little good-natur'd, welch-man', was

[46] Williams, 597.   [47] Ibid. 597–8.   [48] *Illustrations*, vii. 277.

Rector of Weston-under-Lizard, Staffordshire, coincidentally close
to Shifnal in Shropshire, where Percy had discovered the Folio
MS.[49] Just as Percy's introductions to the Leasowes and
Cambridge were the result of his Shropshire connections
(Shenstone and Blakeway, respectively), so Percy took advantage
of Williams to colonize Wales. Percy's literary circle was a
Salopian claim to regional hegemony.

Macpherson's *Fragments* had inspired not only Irish claims on
ancient poetry; it stirred Rice Williams to become a patriotic
champion of ancient Welsh poetry. Although unfamiliar with any
actual pieces, he nevertheless had absolute faith in its merits. In
fact, Williams spoke no Welsh at all, but eagerly wrote to Percy on
12 March 1761 with the news, 'I make no doubt but the welsh
poetic genius, if properly ushered on the stage, would make a much
better appearance than any of the pigmy race of the Caledonian
muses.'[50] Williams, however, was unable to find any Welsh scholar
who could provide Macphersonic translations of ancient poetry, so
the two settled upon editing a collection of Welsh proverbs instead,
which would be providentially garnered from Thomas Richards's
Welsh–English Dictionary (1752).[51] This project was undoubtedly
Williams's own hobby-horse: there is no evidence to suggest that
Percy shared Williams's enthusiasm for such an undertaking. Elsewhere, he did not even acknowledge the scheme.

Williams began to search for a translator and collector of
unpublished proverbs, and encountered Evan Evans, who was at
that time (1761) a curate in north Wales. Evans was an itinerant
scholar who had already translated Welsh poetry and had also
transcribed ancient pieces from several libraries. Williams trium-
phantly wrote to Percy, 'Evans is the right man for us', meaning
that he now expected the three of them to collaborate on his
beloved proverbs.[52] But Percy had other plans, and manipulated
Williams to gain the trust of Evans, recognizing that he was
potentially a far more serious scholar, and one who could provide
some Welsh material for his own researches. In the Gothic
panorama of the ancient English minstrels, Wales was literally
and figuratively a mere background.

---

[49] *Letters*, vii. 115.   [50] Ibid., v. 149.
[51] Percy did possess a small (32–page) booklet of 'Welsh Proverbs' (Bodl., MS Percy
b 2, fos. 10–26).   [52] *Letters*, v. 153.

On 26 July, Williams forwarded Percy's letter of 21 July to Evans with a eulogy of praise for his friend:

He has considerable abilities, he is inquisitive and indefatigable, with a good share of taste, Judgement and poetic Genius, alias, *Awen Prydyd-diaeth* in your own style; and holds correspondence with some of the most ingenious men of the age; if not better engaged I dare recommend him as a very fit person to dress out your welsh odes agreeable to the taste of the English reader.[53]

Evans was then conspiratorially invited to take the office of 'PRINCIPAL in this affair', the lamentable affair of the proverbs.[54] It is significant that Williams dismissed Percy's interest in Welsh odes, 'if not better engaged . . . '. There is a game being played here: Percy looking to ghost-write ancient poetry, Evans needing a publisher, Williams letting slip that Percy is too busy for Evans, but magnanimously proposing the three collaborate on his project as the fairest alternative. From Williams's letter to Percy (14 March) it is apparent that Williams had merely suggested a translation of ancient Welsh poetry as an incentive for Evans's help with the Williams–Percy proverbs. But Percy had not told Williams of the *Reliques*. One gets the impression that Percy and Williams did not trust each other. Evans was anyway at this time seeking to solicit Thomas Gray with his Welsh odes, and was searching for intermediaries to introduce his work to the Cambridge don. Williams suggested his own friend Richard Hurd, but Evans had meanwhile won the support of the renowned judge and antiquary Daines Barrington.

Percy's first letter to Evans was in great contrast to the method of the meddling Williams. He called not for Welsh proverbs, but flattered Evans for a 'satisfactory account of the literary productions' of Wales: 'You have translated, I am informed, some of the Odes of your ancient bards. I wish you would proceed and make a select collection of the best of them.'[55] Such a collection would provide yet another nationalistic response to Macpherson's *Fragments*. In this way, Percy presented himself as an ethnic literary agent rather than an editor or writer, as Williams had implied. He boasted of his 'credit with the Booksellers, and with Mr Dodsley in particular', to whom he had only just sold his 'Old

[53] Ibid. 156.   [54] Ibid. 157.   [55] Ibid. 2.

Ballads', and rashly promised the favour of Samuel Johnson. Percy painted his own literary ambitions in a fanciful way. He again made no mention of the *Reliques*, presumably to prevent the wily Williams detecting the project, but outlined instead a little series of ancient poetry pamphlets, inviting Evans to join his stable:

I have prevailed on a friend to attempt a Translation of some ancient Runic Odes composed among the snows of Norway, which will make their appearance at Mr Dodsley's shop next winter: My very learned Friend and Neighbour the Revd Mr Lye . . . is now rescuing some valuable remains of Saxon poetry from oblivion . . . I have not been altogether idle myself but my attention has been chiefly bestowed on the Languages spoke in the southern Parts of Europe: I have collected some curious pieces of Spanish Poetry, and when I have translated a select collection of them, may perhaps give them to the public.—Amidst this general attention to ancient and foreign Poetry, it would be a pity to have that of the ancient Britons forgot.[56]

The absence of the *Reliques* from this catalogue of forthcoming publications is just excusable, but *Runic Poetry* has been relegated to anonymity and Percy now styles himself as a Spanish expert, delivering his plans for *Ancient Songs chiefly on Moorish Subjects*.[57]

Percy received Evans's reply before he left for Cambridge. Evans sent his translation of an ancient Welsh ode, 'Arwyrain Owain Gwynedd', which Barrington had earlier communicated to Gray, Evans telling Percy, 'I have not the happiness to be acquainted with Mr Gray.'[58] Percy, ever the opportunist, was then able to favour Evans himself. In his next communication, he told the Welshman how he had taken the letter to Cambridge and used it in introducing himself to Gray, who had promptly transcribed a passage quoting the account of Edward I's massacre of the bards. Percy thus secured Gray's interest in his own work while ostensibly promoting Evans.

But Percy's blatant deviousness in his letters to Evans did not

---

[56] *Letters*, v. 3–4.

[57] Percy's correspondence with John Bowle is not extant before 1767 (*Thomas Percy and John Bowle: Cervantine Correspondence*, ed. Daniel Eisenberg (Exeter, 1987), 3), and his *Ancient Songs chiefly on Moorish Subjects translated from the Spanish* was not published until 1932. See Gisela Beutler, 'Thomas Percy's Spanische Studien: Ein Beitrag zum Bild Spaniens in England in der Zweiten Hälfte des 18. Jahrhunderts', Ph.D. thesis (Bonn, 1957).   [58] *Letters*, v. 11.

stop there. It was not until his third letter (23 November) that he tactfully admitted any interest in 'good old popular ballads'.[59] Having seduced Evans with a show of interest in Welsh, and chat about publishing and patronage, he wrote a letter remarkably similar to his first to Warton. It was an introduction to the *Reliques*, predictably enclosing the transcripts of 'The Boy and the Mantle' and 'The Marriage of Sir Gawaine', and making the standard disclaimer regarding the transcriber of the Folio MS. But although Percy may be forgiven for his tactical deployment of resources, his postscript remains troubling:

As my friend Mr Williams knows nothing of my design, relating to the publication of the *Old Ballads* within mentioned: please not to drop the least hint of it to him. I intend to keep it a profound secret from him, 'till I surprize him with a present of the [boo]ks, which I shall also beg your acceptance of, wh[en p]rinted.[60]

The pretence of the proverbs was entirely forgotten. By September, however, Williams had visited Shenstone, taking him a copy of one of Evans's translations (Shenstone later admitted he thought little of the performance), where he presumably learnt of the progress of Percy's *Reliques*. The correspondence between Weston-under-Lizard and Easton Maudit was abruptly broken off.[61]

Percy also numbered Richard Farmer and Edward Blakeway among his correspondents at this time, although it is not clear when he began to exchange letters with them. The friendship with these two Cambridge dons was cemented during Percy's visit to the Pepysian Library. Farmer accommodated him in Emmanuel, and Blakeway had obtained permission for him to use the collection. Blakeway also presumably provided the six amanuenses Percy employed.

On Monday evening, 17 August 1761, Percy arrived in Cambridge to read and transcribe Pepys's collection of ballads in Magdalene College Library. In about 1654, Samuel Pepys (1633–1703) had borrowed a collection of broadside ballads from the antiquary John Selden, and began to enlarge it. On Pepys's death the whole

---

[59] Ibid. 22.   [60] Ibid. 23.

[61] Percy mentioned to Shenstone that he had affronted Williams, 'and the ferment in his Welsh blood is not yet allayed' (ibid., vii. 162). Fearful of losing Evans, he asked Shenstone to placate the Welshman.

collection ran to over 1,800 ballads and songs which were pasted into five folio volumes, or bound in Pepys's collection of 'Merriments' or chapbooks. Percy's researches concentrated on the five volumes of broadsides. The first volume contained the nucleus of Selden's collection (which Pepys had never returned) and consisted mainly of broadside ballads up to about 1640. The remaining four volumes covered the years 1660–1700. The most modern pieces, the white-letter broadsides, filled the final volume, while the first four volumes were almost entirely composed of the black-letter.[62]

Pepys's own arrangement across volumes was therefore broadly chronological, but he also divided the ballads thematically. The first volume consisted of ten chapters:

    I. Devotion & Morality
   II. History—True & Fabulous
  III. Tragædy
   IV. The Times
    V. Love Pleasant
   VI. Love Unfortunate
  VII. Marriage &c.
 VIII. Sea
   IX. Drinking
    X. Humour, Frollicks &c.
Small Promiscuous Supplement[63]

These headings were then more or less divided over the next three volumes: volume ii covering the first four subjects, volume iii the 'Love' ballads, and volume iv constituted a significantly 'Promiscuous' supplement to the 'Love' ballads, 'Marriage &c.', and 'Sea'. The final volume was, like the first, much broader in scope, covering 'Tragædy', 'State & Times', 'Love Unfortunate', 'Sea', and 'Various Subjects'. The arrangement of the Pepys ballads was to see Percy through the publication of the *Reliques*: it provided a compelling template, twisting together different historical strands and themes in a broad chronological weave.

While Pepys himself had had no ambitions to edit or publish these broadsides, his decision to organize the material does show that he conceived some overall shape for the collection, and

---

[62] See *Pepys Ballads* and Robert Latham (ed.), *Catalogue of the Pepys Library at Magdalene College, Cambridge,* 7 vols. (Cambridge, 1978–91).
[63] *Pepys Ballads*, i, p. i.

distinguished his own connoisseurship. For example, his emphasis on 'Sea' ballads reflected his position as Secretary to the Admiralty. Percy carefully recorded these features of Pepys's method, and his unpublished notes on the Pepysian Library are in Harvard. He compiled a cross-referenced index to the ballads by subject rather than by title (having counted 1,686 ballads he was not prepared to catalogue the complete holdings).[64] His notes employed Pepys's own headings in order to give a sense of the anatomy of the collection: Percy carefully noted, 'Contents of the Several Volumes under the following Heads of Assortment' and gathered all the page references to 'Devotion and Morality', 'History, true and fabulous', and so on. The arrangement was therefore vertical. The headings outlined groups rather than order; the precise (horizontal) arrangement of the Pepys broadsides did not matter to Percy—or indeed to Pepys. What did matter was the fact that they were collected under titles, with no apparent hierarchy.

Percy also composed brief descriptions of the contents of each volume. Again this is revealing because it shows where his interests lay:

Vol.1.

MSS. and Long Ballads ancient

Vol.II.III.IV

Common Ballads in Black Letter.

Vol.V.

Verse Ballads in the White Letter.*

*NB. Most of these are play Hous songs &c. with the Musical Notes: but not in copper plate.[65]

Percy's main concern was with the variegated composition of the first volume: it was a cocktail of manuscript and print, and possibly in consequence contained the oldest pieces. This emphasis on the composition of the first volume is also displayed in a deleted note on the same sheet: 'MSS Ballads. 4. & an ancient printed one.' Percy listed the four manuscript ballads on the first page of his own 'Contents' page. He was most excited by ballads which lay across the apparent divide of manuscript and printed culture. As will become increasingly evident, this enabled him to engage in both

---

[64] Houghton, bMS Eng. 893 (278), fo. 6^r.

[65] Houghton, bMS Eng. 893 (278), fo. 6^v.

the inventive editing he practised on sources such as the Folio MS, and the reverence for print he displayed in carefully collating the texts of *Old Ballads*. He was also attracted to the most insistently miscellaneous aspects of Pepys's collection, drawing a good deal from the final chapter of the first volume, 'Small Promiscuous Supplement upon most of the foregoing Subjects'. This too would provide a precedent for Percy's own semi-miscellaneous order.

The ballads of volumes ii, iii, and iv were grouped together by Percy in this list because they could be cross-referenced with the subject index. There is also an implication in Percy's grouping of these three volumes that all printed broadsides had relative authority. He had access to most printed pieces by means of his own broadside collection, *Old Ballads*, and other anthologies. The emphasis on playhouse songs is of more interest. Percy was certainly trawling Dodsley's edition of *Old Plays* and David Garrick's private collection of old plays at this time, but had also signed a contract with Jacob Tonson on 12 June 1761 to edit the works of George Villiers, second Duke of Buckingham.[66] His schemes overlapped: the Pepysian Library was not only of importance to the *Reliques*, but a potential source for his other projects. Furthermore, the description of this volume showed an awareness of the niceties of typography and medium as an index of textual fidelity.

Percy also transcribed Pepys's single comment on the provenance and range of the collection, written on the title-page of the first volume. His essentially accurate, if rushed, copy reads:

Title Page to Pepys' Collect, Vol. 1.
  My Collection of Ballads.
    Vol. 1.
Begun by M[r]. Selden, Improved by the addition of many pieces elder thereto in time <time>; and the whole continued to the year 1700. When the form, <till then the Form>, till then peculiar thereto, viz[t]. of the black Letter with Pictures seems (for Cheapness sake) wholly laid aside, for that of the White Letter without Pictures.

But on the back of the title-page he found a far rarer prize: a remark by Selden that sanctioned an antiquarian interest in ephemera.

[66] Davis (1989), 79.

Seldeniana. Title *Libells*

Though some make slight of Libells; yet you may see by them how the wind sits. As take a straw, and throw it up into the air: You shall see by that, which way the wind is;—which you shall not do by casting up a stone. More solid things do not shew the Complexion of the times, so well as Ballads and Libells.[67]

Percy reproduced Selden's comment as the epigraph to the second volume of the *Reliques*. Percy found more in Magdalene Library than ballads—he appropriated Pepys's own justification for indulging his antiquarian taste in popular culture.

Less than a fortnight in the Pepysian Library gave Percy at least three dozen texts for the *Reliques*.[68] Of Percy's Pepysian ballads, 135 direct transcripts by eight unknown amanuenses survive among the Houghton Percy Papers and British Library.[69] Percy might have been trying to emulate the bustle and industry of Johnson's dictionary workshop during his trip. Interestingly, Percy also took with him to Cambridge several transcripts and also his copy of *A Collection of Old Ballads*. He was able therefore to collate directly onto the page: hence the source notes prefacing the *Old Ballads* texts and the minute changes recorded—and most importantly the appearance of Farmer's hand in the volume (for 'Fair Rosamond' and 'Sweet William's Song'). Where an *Old Ballads* copy was used for collating several variant texts, Percy signed Pepys's variations 'P' or 'PL'. So Percy had many more Pepysian texts than simply the transcripts. Even if the *Old Ballads* pieces cross-referenced to the Pepysian collection were not collated, Percy was still able to get a good sense of what was included in the Pepysian Library, and thereby identify the ballad archive.[70] Only two of the actual transcripts are in Percy's own hand (both laid out in the early style, see above), but all the copies were annotated by him: some corrected, a few collated, and every one marked with Pepys's volume and page numbers and Percy's own indexing notes.[71]

[67] Houghton, bMS Eng. 893 (278), fo. 5ᵛ.   [68] Davis (1981), 78.

[69] Houghton, bMS Eng. 893 (19, 20, 27–163), BL, Add. MS 39547, fos. 43–193. According to Percy's journal, only six copyists were employed (BL, Add. MS 32336, fos. 29–31).

[70] Davis (1989), 87. James Francis Child, however, identified eight hands (autograph catalogue notes, Houghton, bMS Eng. 893 (27–123)).

[71] The two in Percy's hand are 'How the goddess Diana transformed Acteon into shape of a hart' and 'Lullaby' (Houghton, bMS Eng. 893 (46)–(47); Percy's titles).

The ways in which he arranged these transcripts disclose the unfolding structure of his own collection. Provenance was carefully recorded, detailing the location within the Pepys volumes of a certain ballad, any Pepys duplicates, and in a few cases subsequent versions discovered, such as in Thomas D'Urfey's popular, lewd, and lusty anthology *Pills to Purge Melancholy.* Percy then made a series of notes on the initial recto of each ballad. He usually grouped these clusters of numbers and letters in the top left corner, and nibs and inks show that each reference figure was written at a different time. They show Percy confronted with both aesthetic problems and the practical difficulties of negotiating his way around a large collection of manuscripts.

The first of these notes simply indicated whether the transcriber had been paid ('P^d.'), and predictably none survive which lack this endorsement. Marks of approbation ('+', '*', '++') or of disapprobation ('O', '* Rejected') followed, occasionally elucidated by related comments ('ancient', 'App^d.', 'Doubtful', 'Rejected'). Most ballads were also marked with two numbers in red and black, which was a transitional way of organizing the pieces (see below). Capital letters were derived from significant words in the title and written in red ink to enable the pieces to be arranged alphabetically for Percy's catalogue (for example 'Y' for 'The two Yorkshire lovers'). Nearly all ballads were also designated a subject heading: 'Trag. Hist.', 'Eng. Hist.', 'War', 'State', 'Sea', 'Com[ic]', 'Mirth', 'Past[oral]', 'Love', 'Mor[ality]' (later replaced by 'Relig'), or some combination. (Most unexpected among these headings is a small group of 'Magic' ballads about Faustus and the Lincolnshire witches.) This headline was usually written in red on the final verso but sometimes on the initial recto, and most notices of other copies were written in the same nib. Lastly, many were numbered for inclusion in early drafts of the *Reliques* (see below).

As already noted, the different headings employed by Percy were based on Pepys's own. Percy took extensive notes of the contents of Pepys's five volumes. He gave the 'Heads of Assortment' with minor variations. 'Tragedy' he glossed 'vizt. Murders, Executions Judgments of God. &c', 'The Times' became 'State and Times', 'Cuckoldry' was added to 'Marriage', 'Love Gallantry & Actions' explained the contents of the 'Sea' ballads, and 'good fellowship' joined with 'Drinking'. The other heads remained as Pepys gave them.[72]

---

[72] Houghton, bMS Eng. 893 (278), fos. 1–2.

Percy's arrangement of these ballads shows that he was thinking of three definite themes for his own collection. The vast majority of extant Pepys transcripts are concerned with history, love, and religion. Indeed, Percy collected many of the religious ballads in a folder he titled 'A Series of Religious Historical Ballads from Scripture'.[73] Likewise, several of the historical ballads helped to make up a thick manuscript book, 'A Series of Ballads on English History', which was arranged chronologically by subject matter.[74]

These arrangements may have had some influence on the eventual form of the *Reliques*. For example, Stephen Vartin analyses the structure of the *Reliques* from internal evidence only, and concludes that the first volume dealt with Percy–Douglas border conflicts and Shakespearean pieces; the second with historical and satirical ballads; and the third with metrical romances, legendary history, and love songs.[75] Vartin does not however consider Percy's methodological use of Pepys, which must qualify his account somewhat. Percy's arrangement of the Pepys material was inspired by Pepys himself, but only affected the subject matter in the *Reliques* in general ways. Percy soon abandoned thematic heads as a way of organizing material as diverse as historical works and love poetry, and took to more arcane arrangements. It is no surprise that the religious/moral group was entirely dropped, and minor groups such as the nautical or magical ballads had no influence.

The random order of the Pepysian Library has been stressed before the implications of the Pepysian methodology are examined. Despite Percy's attempt to impose headings, his collection was to remain in some degree disordered, mingled, and confused: in both Pepys's and Johnson's word, 'promiscuous', what might be termed 'associative' today.[76] Diversity of material is certainly a feature of such ballad collections—subjects, characters, and themes jostle for attention, as do fount, layout, and illustration. The miscellaneous nature of such collections was a feature necessarily carried into the *Reliques*.[77] It demonstrated the vivacity of the Gothic source against the simplicity of the oral. It is now time to examine Percy's 'Alphabet Collection' of broadsides to ascertain

---

[73] Houghton, bMS Eng. 893 (19).   [74] Houghton, bMS Eng. 893 (20A).
[75] See Vartin, 96–7.   [76] *Letters*, vii. 96.   [77] Noted by Vartin, 80.

how the Pepysian order affected his own resources, and how his taxonomy inevitably affected the primary drafts.

'THE GREATEST PRINTER OF BALLADS IN THE KINGDOM'[78]

About June 1761, Percy made the acquaintance of Cluer Dicey, a prosperous publisher of broadsides. Cluer was the son of the Northampton printer William Dicey, ran his father's Bow Church-yard presses, and promised Percy 'to romage into his Warehouse for every thing curious that it contains'. When on 19 July Percy wrote to Shenstone about 'the greatest printer of Ballads in the kingdom', he had already received 'above fourscore pieces . . . some of which I never saw before'.[79]

Cluer Dicey (b. 1713–19) had inherited the family chapbook and broadside business when his father William died in 1756. William Dicey had built his fortune on chapbooks, ballads, and quack medicine, cannily employing his balladmongers to hawk Dr Bateman's Pectoral Drops alongside their printed ware—literally pills to purge melancholy! Cluer Dicey (who along with his father's presses also inherited a valuable third-share in Dr Bateman's Pectoral Drops) seems to have enjoyed good business as well, later issuing a catalogue in association with Richard Marshall listing 150 chapbooks ('Small Histories') and a stagger-ing 3,000 ballads (1764; Marshall's son eventually succeeded to Dicey's empire). The Dicey publications are certainly among the most numerous of extant eighteenth-century broadsides and chap-books.[80] It was to Cluer Dicey's warehouse (from 1753 at 4 Aldermary Churchyard: 'Opposite the South Door of Bow-Church in Bow-Church-Yard') that James Boswell went in 1763 to buy his collection of chapbooks.[81]

Perhaps Boswell was slightly more at home there than Percy was. The very first thing that Percy said of Dicey to Shenstone was

---

[78] *Letters*, vii. 109.   [79] Ibid. 109.

[80] Victor E. Neuburg, 'The Diceys and the Chapbook Trade', *Library*, 5th ser. 24 (1969), 219–31. Sue Dipple, *Chapbooks: how They be collected by sondrie madde Persons, and something of their trewe Historie* (Society for the Study of Children's Books, 1996).

[81] 'Curious Productions' is now in the Houghton, 25276.44*. It is worth noting that none of Percy's thirty chapbooks has a Dicey or Bow Churchyard imprint, and so they may have been obtained elsewhere.

that he was an 'Acquaintance of a much lower stamp' than his
other collaborators, and in spite of receiving over three hundred
white-letter broadside ballads from Dicey's Printing Office, he
neglected to record his thanks to the man in the *Reliques*. Nevertheless, these broadside ballads, totalling 314 (including duplicates), are extremely revealing in the making of the *Reliques*. The
size of the broadside collection alone obliged Percy to develop
Pepys's taxonomy and refine his research methods, and some of
the Dicey broadsides supplied Percy with specific texts and went
into the *Reliques* almost untouched.[82]

Percy catalogued the ballads alphabetically and thematically,
and referred to his white-letter broadsides as the 'Alphabet Collection'.[83] This taxonomic principle was completely straightforward
and admirably practical. He took a copy of the 1754 Dicey
catalogue, *A Catalogue of Maps, Prints, Copy-Books, Drawing-
Books, &c. Histories, Old Ballads, Broad-Sheet and other Patters,
Garlands, &c.*, and had it interleaved. Twelve pages in the *Catalogue* (pp. 45–56) contained 'A Catalogue of Old Ballads: Printed
in a neater Manner, and with CUTS more truly adapted to each
Story, than elsewhere', and these 'Old Ballads' were listed more or
less alphabetically. Percy simply reordered a few and then
numbered the lot, listing any broadsides acquired that were not
listed in the 1754 catalogue on the interleaved pages. Either
Dicey's stock had increased, or Percy acquired a few from other
sources. He then added the leading letter and catalogue number to
each broadside sheet as appropriate, and kept them in alphabetical
and numerical order. Nearly every ballad in the *Catalogue* was
marked with a '+'—presumably meaning he had purchased
virtually all of Dicey's 'old Stock'—but the pieces in Percy's
Alphabet Collection bear a variety of imprints: William Dicey
(Cluer's father) at London or Northampton, a few to Robert
Dicey (Northampton) and W. & C. Dicey at St Mary Aldermary,
a handful to other printers (such as R. Powell or Sympson's in

---

[82] Percy's broadside ballad collection is now at the Houghton, *pEB75 P4128C
(1–321). The collection includes a few miscellaneous items which are not broadside
ballads, and there are three fugitive broadsides among the Percy Papers (*A Pleasant
Ballad of Tobias* (Houghton, bMS Eng. 893 (19K)), [*Three Carols*] (Houghton, bMS
Eng. 893 (19S)), and *The Merry Wedding: or O Brave Arthur a Bradley* (Houghton,
bMS Eng. 893 (25G)), no dates).

[83] The alphabetical arrangement generally persists at Houghton. The 'Alphabet
Collection' is mentioned in, for example, Houghton, bMS Eng. 893 (50).

Stone-Cutter's-Street, L. How in Petticoat-Lane, even John White in Newcastle), and inevitably several were printed anonymously. The vast majority however are Dicey pieces ('Printing-Office, Bow-Church Yard, London'), and Dicey presumably stocked and distributed the products of several presses.

What this means is that almost all Percy's broadside ballads—his archive—were purchased from Dicey, and that significantly Dicey also provided the means of organizing, cataloguing, and using the collection. It also suggests that the ballads missing from the Houghton collection are indeed the black-letter ballads (which for some reason had been removed to Northumberland House, where they were consumed in the fire of 1780).[84] Percy appears to have purchased 228 ballads from Dicey to which he added a further 59, making his working collection 287, from a list of 355 (all of which he numbered). In due course, he obtained another 27 (at least some of the Houghton broadsides post-date the *Reliques*). He had therefore established an archive of some 441 'Old Ballads' for the *Reliques*.

Percy used thematic headings to cross-reference the broadsides with other material, though these were much less frequently employed than in his other sources such as transcripts from the Pepysian Library or loose sheets from his disbound copy of *A Collection of Old Ballads*. As described in the last section, these headings were derived from the Pepysian Library. (There were some refinements: a handful of 'Misc' ballads were also noted as 'Robin Hood'.) Blakeway had described these heads to Percy in 1760, and Percy had communicated this information to Shenstone in November: 'the pieces were arranged under *ten* heads: viz. *Comic, Tragic, Historical* etc.'[85] Only thirty-nine of the Alphabet Collection broadsides were significantly annotated by Percy, and there has been no attempt until now to analyse his notes. The following account uses a specific example to demonstrate Percy's handling of these unusual sources.[86]

---

[84] *The Letters of Walter Scott*, ed. Herbert Grierson (1932), i. 108 n.; Bertram H. Davis, 'Thomas Percy, the Reynolds Portrait, and the Northumberland House Fire', *RES* 33 (1982), 23–33. Two survive at Houghton, *pEB75 P4128C (304) and (309).

[85] *Letters*, vii. 81.

[86] Save for the 1754 Dicey *Catalogue* in the Bodleian, no printed catalogue of the Percy Broadside Ballads exists, and Smith makes no more than a passing reference to them (255–6).

The first reference to specific Dicey broadsides is in a letter to Warton, dated by David Fairer to about late June 1761. Percy referred to two Shakespearean ballads, 'A Ballad on King Lear' and 'Titus Andronicus'. Editors M. G. Robinson and Leah Dennis, and Fairer too, note that Percy's source was probably the *Golden Garland*.[87] Among his Alphabet Collection, however, are *King Lear and his Three Daughters* and *The Lamentable and Tragical History of Titus Andronicus*.[88] It seems reasonable to assume that he was alert to the broadsides, having just obtained them from Dicey, and the transcripts taken from the *Golden Garland* do not feature either. It will become evident that the primary *Reliques* source, for *Titus Andronicus* at least, was not the *Golden Garland*.

The full title of this particular broadside is

The Lamentable and Tragical History of Titus Andronicus, with The Fall of his Sons in the Wars of the Goths, with the Manner of the Ravishment of his Daughter Lavinia, by the bloody Moor, taken by the Sword of Titus, in the War; with his Revenge upon their cruel and inhumane Act.

It was printed in Northampton by William Dicey about 1730.

Percy wrote his catalogue notes on the verso, 'T 14' (the alphabetic code derived from the *Catalogue*), 'Trag. Hist.', 'Trag. His' (thematic codes), and '5/3' (explained below). He collated the text with four other copies, and from the spacing of these notes it is possible to restore the chronology of annotation. Corrections from the *Golden Garland* were first added at Easton Maudit in red. The copy was then taken to the Pepysian Library and collated with two copies there, so there was no need for an amanuensis transcript of *Titus Andronicus Lament*.[89] These revisions were indicated in black ink with a 'p' for 'Pepys', although Percy noted that 'The Old spelling is not inserted here'. Lastly, when he returned he collated it with another copy in Ballard's Collection, signing each note 'Ball^d.' in black (February–March 1763).

Introducing the text of this ballad that was printed for the first state of the *Reliques*, Percy claimed, 'The following is given from a

---

[87] *Letters*, iii. 16; Fairer, 97; see also Percy's letter to Farmer which attributes Capell's chilliness to '*the inexpiable Crime of "forestalling him in the Ballad of Titus Andronicus"*' (*Letters*, ii. 87).   [88] Houghton, *pEB75 P4128C (133), (267).

[89] *Pepys Ballads, Titus Andronicus Complaint*, i. 86; *The Lamentable and Tragical History of Titus Andronicus*, ii. 184–5.

Copy in "The Golden Garland" . . . compared with three others, two of them in black letter in the Pepys Collection."[90] But his collational notes show a surprising faith in his Dicey broadside: he recognized that the eighteenth-century popular text was basically sound, and recovered earlier versions by recording them as marginal notes. So the Pepys and *Golden Garland* texts were marginalized in collation, but took authority for the text of the ballad in the *Reliques*. In other words, Percy deconstructed the text of the Dicey broadside ballad, making an authority of his marginal notes and reversing them for the text he printed. The working source was denied and dismantled. Cultural authority was vested in the black-letter typography of old books and ballads, rather than in the contemporary white-letter ephemera of a London printer. Just as Cluer Dicey was absent from Percy's acknowledgements for the *Reliques*, so the foundation of the popular broadside went unrecognized.

The following two stanzas appear towards the end of *The Lamentable and Tragical History of Titus Andronicus*, lines 101–8 as printed. The broadside reads:

> I feed their foolish Veins a little Space,
> Until my Friends did find a secret Place,
> When both her Sons unto a Post were bound
> And just Revenge, in cruel sort, was found.
>
> I cut their Throats, my Daughter held the Pan.
> Betwixt her Stumps wherein the Blood it ran;
> And then I ground their Bones to Powder small,
> And made a Paste for Pies straight therewithall.

Percy underlined several words in red, and filed their revisions in the margin—the use of red ink indicating that they were derived from the *Golden Garland*—and the stanzas were revised to read thus:

> I fed their foolish Veins a certain Space,
> Until my Friends and I did find a place
> Where both her Sons unto a Post were bound,
> where just Revenge, in cruel sort, was found.
>
> I cut their Throats, my Daughter held the Pan.
> Betwixt her Stumps wherein the Blood then ran;

[90] Houghton, *pEB75 P4128 765ra, iii. 204 (italics reversed).

> And then I ground their Bones to Powder small,
> And made a Paste for pyes streight therewithall.

All the revisions, with the exception of 'then', were ratified by the addition of a 'P' in black ink, indicating that they conformed to the Pepys versions. There were also three divergences between Pepys and the *Golden Garland*: 'certaine' for 'certain', 'Throates' for 'Throats', and 'in powder' for 'to Powder'. The first two are of interest because at the head of the notes Percy professed not to have recorded the 'Old spelling'. In addition, two changes ('fed' and 'where') also received the sanction of Ballard.

But despite the general agreement of antique versions over the popular modernizations, when Percy came to print these lines, he did so as follows:

> I fed their foolish veines a certaine space,
> Untill my friendes did find a secrett place,
> Where both her sonnes unto a post were bound,
> And just revenge in cruell sort was found.

> I cut their throates, my daughter held the pan
> Betwixt her stumpes, wherein the bloud it ran:
> And then I ground their bones to powder small,
> And made a paste for pyes streight therewithall.

The text is remarkable. It restores broadside readings, most notably line 102 ('secrett'), and uses the older texts simply to provide a precedent for dressing the whole thing up in fanciful archaism. The final 'e', as we saw in the last chapter, was a favourite, also 'y' for 'i' and inconsistently doubling consonants. The 'Old spelling' was derived from Percy's impression of the style of the *Golden Garland* and Pepys texts, the earliest of which actually reads:

> I fed their foolish veines a certaine space,
> Untill my friende and I did find a place,
> Where both her sons vnto a post were bound,
> Where iust reuenge in cruell sort was found.

> I cut their throates, my daughter held the pan,
> Betwixt her stumps, wherein the blood then ran,
> And then I ground their bones in powder small,
> And made a paste for pies straight therewithall.[91]

[91] See *Pepys Ballads*, ii. 185.

This example reveals how heavily Percy relied on less esoteric sources and his own instincts regarding the 'Old spelling' of his texts. The readings of old ballads were determined by reading new ballads, and in spite of what was later claimed in the *Reliques*, Percy's references were retrospective. The black-letter texts collated by Percy ultimately served merely as a guide to archaizing, and a mythology of sources. Percy's texts in the *Reliques* did not give a faithful account of antique literature. He edited the past in line with his Gothicism, adding a multitude of copious and redundant archaic ornament that served as a perpetual visual reminder that these were written texts rather than oral performances.

This reliance extended to sending the broadsides to other scholars for them to collate. *A Worthy Example of a Virtuous Wife* (retitled '*The Roman Charity*' by Percy) was given to Richard Farmer to correct from a copy in the Pepysian Library, possibly during Percy's visit in August 1761.[92] Farmer made twenty-three revisions. Shenstone had recommended the same piece from *A Collection of Old Ballads* (ii. 137–44, called there 'Wife suckling her Father') in his second 'Billet' ('++'), but Percy relied on his revised Alphabet copy.[93] In consequence, Percy was often editing a text several times removed from the supposed original. Percy sent *Old Ballads* to Shenstone, who annotated and returned the copy, later forwarding a list of his recommendations. Percy recognized a version of one ballad in his Alphabet Collection, and sent this copy to Farmer who collated it and returned it. Despite this application and diligence, and after being included in the 'First Draft', 'The Roman Charity' was subsequently rejected from the *Reliques*.

This movement of texts perfectly illustrates the corporate effort involved in the *Reliques*: Percy was as much the mastermind behind a gang of textual bibliographers as he was the editor of a parcel of old ballads. Manuscript letters enclosing references, collations, and transcripts were delivered frequently, and Percy's own experiments with self-projection in his correspondence were happening at a time when he was beginning to organize his manuscript sources into an order fit for the press. Indeed, the whole art

---

[92] Houghton, *pEB75 P4128C (297). Percy also sent transcripts for Farmer to correct against Pepysian versions: for example 'Sᵗ George and the dragon' (*Letters*, ii. 12).   [93] Percy's *Old Ballads*, ii. 137–44.

of letter-writing, as well as the mechanics of the mail and parcel services, facilitated Percy's research. It is unlikely that he could have engaged such a range of scholars in his campaigns without the Earl of Sussex's franking privileges, and the support of Dodsley's wagons in carrying and fetching books.

There are also external connections between *Old Ballads* and the 'Alphabet Collection'. Dianne Dugaw notes that many of Percy's *Reliques* have an even more complex provenance. As is suggested in the Diceys' specific marketing of 'Old Ballads', there was a 'ballad revival' at a popular as well as a sophisticated level.[94] In fact, provenance is often insoluble: ballads may derive variously from the Folio MS, the Alphabet Collection, the Pepysian Library, *Old Ballads*, borrowed anthologies such as the *Golden Garland*, or some combination of all five.[95] It would require an immense programme of parallel reading and analysis of manuscript notes to determine which texts Percy used, a project that would become maddeningly futile because of the interrelationships between the very texts: many of the Dicey broadsides were directly plagiarized from *Old Ballads*. Most striking are a series of ballads in Percy's Alphabet Collection which were printed with not only the *Old Ballads* illustrations, but the headnotes as well. Dugaw states that Dicey 'derived a good deal of his early ballad stock from the anonymous 1723 collection, whose contents he liberally filched—texts, headnotes, illustrations and all'.[96] Percy cannot have failed to notice this. He did not even bother to supply references to *A Collection of Old Ballads* on any of his broadsides. Yet his own anthology nevertheless met the popular demand. By

---

[94] Dugaw, 'Popular Marketing', 72.

[95] This is apparent even from simply reading the printed introductions in the *Reliques*.

[96] Dugaw, 'Popular Marketing', 75. In the 'Alphabet Collection' these are (Houghton, *pEB75 P4128C) *An Unhappy Memorable Song of the Hunting in Chevy-Chace* (47), *Coventry made Free by Godina* (59), *The Unfortunate Concubine* (88), *Faithful Friendship* (95), *Johnny Armstrong's Last Good-Night* (122), *The Woful Lamentation of Jane Shore* (123), *King John and the Abbot of Canterbury* (132), *King Alfred and the Shepherd* (134), *An Excellent Ballad of the Deposing of King Richard the Second* (138), *The Honour of a London 'Prentice* (152), *The Overthrow of Proud Holofernes* (191), *Robin Hood and Little John* (228), *Robin Hood's Rescuing Will. Stutely* (229), *The Bishop of Hereford's Entertainment by Robin Hood* (232), *The Pedigree, Education, and Marriage of Robin Hood, with Clorinda* (235), *A Warning-Piece to England* (291), and *A Song of the Wooing of Queen Catherine* (300). All Dicey broadsides printed at Northampton or London, no dates [*c*.1725–50].

Dugaw's calculation the *Reliques* contained over sixty ballads that were already circulating as Dicey broadsides.[97]

So the *Reliques* was in part a familiar and canonical collection, and became an influential source for the very ballad printers themselves. As John Brewer has argued, until the House of Lords ended perpetual copyright in 1774, 'the transmission of cultural heritage in its printed forms had been under the exclusive control of London's major booksellers'.[98] For popular ephemera like ballads, it more or less remained so after 1774 too. The *Reliques*, like *A Collection of Old Ballads*, disseminated texts back into the popular culture. The preface to the third volume of *Old Ballads* argued that the collection had a pedagogic aim, seeking to disseminate the salient facts of national history in reliable versions of memorable ballads: 'History, especially our own, has for many Years been too much neglected, and the generality of *English*-Men are such strangers to ancient Facts and the Customs of their Kingdom, that they are easily misled by any Sixpenny Pamphleteer;' a state neatly rectified, of course, when the Diceys plundered the work.[99] Although no comparable study has been made of the *Reliques*, it too was pillaged by later anthologists and chapbook printers. Richardson and Urquhart's supplement to Dodsley's *Collection*, *A Collection of the Most Esteemed Pieces of Poetry, that have appeared for Several Years* (1767; sometimes attributed to Moses Mendez, d. 1758), included seven pieces apparently taken from the *Reliques*.[100] By collating the texts, it is evident that all except one of these were based on *Reliques* versions.[101]

This Dodsley supplement was published in 1767, the year of the second edition of the *Reliques* and only two years after the first edition was first published. A more telling example of the influence of the *Reliques* is in *Poetry: Original and Selected*, a

---

[97] Dugaw, 'Popular Marketing', 83.

[98] Brewer, *Pleasures of the Imagination*, 477.

[99] *Old Ballads*, iii, pp. iii–iv, see also iii. 17.

[100] Robert Dodsley (ed.), *A Collection of Poems, by Several Hands* (1782 edn.), ed. Michael F. Suarez, SJ, 6 vols. (1997), i. 183.

[101] *A Collection of the Most Esteemed Pieces of Poetry, that have Appeared for Several Years*, ed. Moses Mendez [Richardson and Urquhart] (1767), 144–59: 'Bryan and Pereene', 'The Passionate Shepherd to his Love', 'My Mind to Me a Kingdom is', 'Cupid's Pastime', 'Winifreda', 'Admiral Hosier's Ghost', and 'The Shepherd's Resolution'; *Reliques*, i. 313–16, 199–201, 268–71, 293–6, 304–5, ii. 367–71, iii. 120–1. Only 'My Mind to Me a Kingdom is' had a separate source.

cheap Scottish anthology of poetry published in 1798. It bears out Percy's apologetic boast to his 'Cuz Will': 'M^r. Dodsley is printing two or three Vol^s. of Grubstreet Ware for me.'[102] Purchasers could buy these three volumes as an indexed set, singly for 2s. each, or in chapbook gatherings of eight pages, each independently titled, numbered, and paginated. The 'Correct copy of the celebrated ancient heroic ballad of Chevy-Chace', poem 51 in gathering XXI, volume iii, was printed verbatim from Percy's text of 'The More Modern Ballad of Chevy Chace'. It was evidently set up straight from the version in the *Reliques*, and, moreover, from the first edition of 1765 (i. 231–46).[103] The remarkable congruence of the respective 1765 and 1798 versions is demonstrated in, for example, stanza 12. The chapbook has:

> But if I thought he would not come,
>   No longer wold I stay.
> With that a brave younge gentleman
>   Thus to the earl did say;

Over thirty years earlier Percy had printed:

> But if I thought he would not come,
>   No longer wold I stay.
> With that, a brave younge gentleman
>   Thus to the earle did say;

The careful differentiation between 'would' and 'wold' (lines 1–2) is particularly revealing, making the omitted comma (line 3) almost irrelevant. There are odd variations in spelling and pronunciation conforming to different printers' conventions, such as 'earl' (line 4) here, but none in diction. What really clinches the chapbook's source, however, is the almost exact duplication of Percy's two footnotes, and the variation (ll. 109–24) in subsequent editions of the *Reliques* fixes the precise source of this, one of the most renowned and enduring English ballads ever written, as the first edition (or some reliable copy).[104] Another example is a series called *Ancient and Modern Songs* (among Francis Douce's volumes of 1820s chapbooks in the Bodleian Library, bound as *Irish Vulgaria*). This very cheaply printed songbook contains 'The

---

[102] Letter to William Cleiveland, 19 Nov. 1761, BL, Add. MS 32333, fo. 29^v.
[103] *Poetry: Original and Selected* (Glasgow, 1798), iii, preface.
[104] *Reliques* (1893), 958–60.

Friar of Orders Gray', the only piece in the *Reliques* which Percy admitted to composing himself.

In the tradition of *Old Ballads* then, the *Reliques* was to become a handy source book for ballad printers, fuelling the next forty years of popular taste. The movement between highbrow and lowbrow, volume and broadside, editor and printer, was highly conservative. The contemporary market dictated a great deal of the material in Percy's *Reliques*, and Percy reciprocated with authoritative versions. This was the inevitable result of privileging printed texts as sources for the *Reliques*: their very accessibility and uniformity drew attention to narrow textual variations across a widely disseminated field, rather than charting the evolution of texts within a circulating chirographic system. Percy was not attempting to restore an archetypal text, but realized that minute fluctuations could be exploited to legitimize his own interference, and ultimately establish an authenticity for his own versions for a generation more deeply impressed with typographic culture. Popular culture was made historically static, and ultimately nostalgic. It was restrained, and could be analysed by the antiquarian method of textual criticism—a specular gaze that focused fetishistically on tiny details. Popular culture was also enlisted in Percy's grand theory of cultural regeneration—the fundamentally English myth of Gothic origins. But popular culture was also now an invention of the present class of gentlemen and scholars who had appropriated the popular ballad.

'THE UMPIRAGE OF CHAOS'[105]

From the Folio MS, *Old Ballads*, books borrowed from correspondents, the Pepysian Library, the Dicey broadsides, Percy had read thousands of ballads, songs, and metrical romances, and obtained copies of many hundreds of them. Within four years he had assembled surely the largest private collection of 'Old Ballads' in the country. He had set the stage for his theory of ancient English minstrelsy in *Five Pieces of Runic Poetry*, and had secured a contract to print. Now he needed to organize it into a publishable form. It would prove an infernal task. Twice he tried to

---

[105] *Letters*, vii. 136: Shenstone's description of his attempts to order the *Reliques*.

organize his material before Dodsley commenced printing the *Reliques*, and attempted a third plan shortly after printing had begun. All of these arrangements were abandoned, and, as the next chapter shows, as printing dawned, Percy was obliged to arrange his work on the hoof as the press demanded copy and he continued his researches. The three arrangements that he made are therefore crucial records of his shifting conception of the *Reliques*, and of his increasingly desperate attempts to complete the collection. The prized Folio MS was at stake if he failed to deliver. Moreover, only the last of these early drafts has been discussed before; the earliest has not even been noticed.

We begin with a single folio sheet, listing in three headed columns a proposal for each volume of the *Reliques*.[106] Of the total 166 pieces in the 'First Draft', just half (84) were included in the first edition of the *Reliques*. Albert Friedman has analysed, and christened, this 'First Draft', constructing an index to enable scholars to recreate the text of this 'Pre-*Reliques*'. Interestingly, such an undertaking is anachronistic by necessity: for example, Friedman is frequently forced to refer to Child's *English and Scottish Popular Ballads*. Friedman also partially accounted for Percy's annotations to the manuscript. Many ballads were ticked off with a single diagonal stroke, a few were underlined, and one was struck through. In addition, Percy used a series of marks to highlight some pieces: '+', '++', '+++', and 'O'. Friedman explains that the diagonal strokes indicate pieces printed in the *Reliques* and the marks were Percy's system of grading.

For Friedman, the main interest of the 'First Draft' lies in its relationship to the *Reliques*—implicit even in his term, 'Pre-*Reliques*'. For example, the absence of almost every Scottish ballad Percy eventually published is noted, but interpreted as evidence of his zeal: 'Percy was holding back material for the multitude of future projects teeming in his brain.'[107] But, as I have shown in Chapter 3, the arrangement of the Scottish pieces was a perpetual headache for both Percy and Shenstone. It should not be inferred that their absence from this draft denotes a decision to save them wholesale for an additional supplement.

---

[106] Houghton, bMS Eng. 893 (278), fo. 16. See Friedman, 'First Draft', 1233–49. The Percy–Darby *Reliques* is at Houghton, *EC75 P4128 765ra; Rodney M. Baine, 'Percy's Own Copies of the *Reliques*', *HLB* 5 (1951), 246–51. See *Reliques* (1996), i. 69–78.   [107] Friedman, 'First Draft', 1245.

Friedman also emphasized that several pieces unique to the Folio MS were included in this draft but ultimately rejected, that the Shakespeare ballads go unmentioned, and that there were few 'refatimentoes'. All of these elements eventually received their rightful place to make the *Reliques* 'a richer, more glamorous, more varied body of poetry'.[108] Friedman's 'First Draft' is judged retrospectively as a necessary staging post on the highway that led towards the authoritative edition. He therefore assumes that the aim of the 'First Draft' was to delineate the *Reliques*.

Stephen Vartin gives a full description of the 'First Draft' in his thesis, on the grounds that he decodes the underlinings and super-script 'O', both of which were employed by Percy to query the suitability or placement of pieces. Vartin also comments on the rough chronological arrangement of the 'First Draft', and the preponderance of modern broadsides, most of which were even-tually dropped.[109] Yet in the main, Vartin relies heavily on Friedman. The following account of the 'First Draft' will question these orthodox interpretations of Percy's various annotations and provide a new reading of the manuscript, arguing that it was instead a working draft. The manuscript actually describes a process of thought rather than an envisaged publication.

Percy evidently had the 'First Draft' to hand when the first edition was finalized (November 1764) because he struck through each piece he had printed. The nib used reveals that this checking was all done at the same time and was not a gradual ticking off of printed pieces. With regard to the underlining and the editorial diacritic 'O', Vartin's argument seems valid: these are simply marks to indicate doubt. Initially Percy used the superscript 'O' but soon replaced this with the more immediate sign of under-lining. If one compares the Pepys transcripts or the Alphabet Collection, the 'O' was used there in just such a fashion. Less clear is Percy's use of 'marks of approbation', as Friedman calls them. Some ballads are marked with one of three different marks: '+', '++', '+++'. Friedman claims that these are based on 'Shenstone's Billets'—'the more crosses, the greater merit'—and Vartin follows Friedman entirely.[110] But there are problems with this interpretation: not every piece is graded, and the grades (if

---

[108] Friedman, 'First Draft', 1247.   [109] Vartin, 153–60.
[110] Friedman, 'First Draft', 1234 n.; Vartin, 159 n.

they are grades) bear no relation to the printing or selection of pieces. In fact, it appears that the marks actually correspond to volume number.

Out of forty-nine pieces in the draft of the first volume, thirteen are marked, all with what Friedman would call the lowest mark of approbation; '+'.[111] This does not explain why the first five of these were the first five to be printed, and why, more importantly, they were Percy's favourite ballads to send to correspondents. He would hardly send transcripts of third-rate ballads to new correspondents he was endeavouring to impress, and was equally unlikely to commence his anthology with them. It seems improbable then that these are grading marks.

The second volume makes most interesting use of these diacritics: of sixty-four pieces, thirty are marked '++', plus two each '+' and '+++'. These last four ballads are also exceptional in other ways. 'Lord Wigmore' (ii. 46) is marked '+', but also '(1', indicating, I believe, an intended shift to volume i. Likewise, 'Tis not Love thy Pulse's Beat' (ii. 48) also seems destined for the first volume by the same sign. Again, this is the case with 'The Complaint of Harpalus' (ii. 42): 'graded' '+++', but overwritten with the number '3' and so presumably moved to the third volume. Lastly, 'When this Old Cap was New' ('Time's Alteration', ii. 38) was both signified '+++' and the whole entry crossed out horizontally (as opposed to diagonally struck through), again suggesting it was to be repositioned rather than dropped completely. The marks '+', '++', '+++' are therefore revisions of volume number. Lastly, for the third volume itself, eighteen out of 51 are marked, each '+++'.

Having described the editorial decisions that Percy was recording on the 'First Draft', a chronology of this manuscript will now be proposed. The 'First Draft' is actually a record of several drafts. Friedman treats the manuscript as if it were a document recording a specific act of arrangement rather than as a series of accretions. It seems to me that the document emphasizes the ongoing process of revision in Percy's arrangement of his materials.

First, Percy listed 164 songs and ballads in three columns, marked 'Vol.1.', 'Vol.2.', and 'Vol.3', across a folio sheet. This

---

[111] Friedman is wrong to assign 'The Boy and the Mantle' '++'—an examination of the manuscript reveals it to be '+'.

basic list, the very first version of the 'Draft', is reproduced in Appendix IV. Admittedly, Friedman does print a useful version, but it is impossible to discern Percy's original layout (and consequently the status of his revisions) from Friedman's text. One should however go to Friedman for information of provenance and printing history.[112] This must be a fairly advanced draft itself because the fifteen or so more entries in the second volume compared with the other two show that Percy was conscious of the varying lengths of different pieces. He was planning a printed set of a certain size and format. Also, neither the two versions of 'The Boy and the Mantle' (i. 1 and i. 47, the Folio MS version and Shenstone's revisal, respectively) nor the two 'Chevy Chases' (iii. 2 and iii. 17, ancient and modern, respectively) are distinguished— Percy already had a strong mental picture of the placing of these pieces. The draft might be defined better as an aide-mémoire.

The precise sequence of events now is blurred, but it is a sequence nonetheless. The 'Draft' was revised in the following ways. Two pieces were added: the ribald 'Cock Lorrel' was inserted between the drinking song 'Old Simon the K.' and 'Distracted puritan', a mad song about Abeizer Coppe (ii. 52 and ii. 53), and 'Maudlin' was slipped in before the Folio MS song 'Come, Come, Come' (iii. 18). This gave a total of 166 pieces. Doubts were expressed initially concerning the first four pieces in volume ii, a connected series on Agincourt and the fifteenth century, marking these four 'O'.[113] 'Rosamond' (ii. 30) and 'Matthew Shore' (ii. 33) were also marked in this way. But Percy felt this method of highlighting was insufficiently clear, and these six were then underlined, as were fourteen others.[114] It is notable that all but one of these doubtful pieces occur in the second volume, to make it commensurate with the size of the other two. Possibly the large second volume was in fact deliberately overpopulated as Percy intended to cull it at his leisure. Percy

---

[112] Friedman, 'First Draft', 1235–44.

[113] 'Hymn at Agincourt' (ii. 1), 'The Siege of Harflet' (ii. 2), 'The battle of Agincourt' (ii. 3), 'The Erle River's Balet' (ii. 4).

[114] 'Fair Margarets Misfortune' (ii. 25), 'Cupid & Campaspe' (ii. 26), 'What bird so sings' (i. 28), 'Death's Final Conquest' (ii. 34), 'Boldness in Love' (ii. 40), 'The Complaint of Harpalus' (ii. 42), 'He that loves a rosie cheek' (ii. 44), 'Fine young folly' (ii. 45), 'Lord Wigmore' (ii. 46), 'Tis not Love thy pulses beat' (ii. 48), 'Alexander & Lodowic' (ii. 51), 'Repentance too late' (ii. 54), 'Cupid's Pastime' (ii. 58), 'Harpalus' (iii. 6).

also seems to be querying whole clusters of connected pieces: 'Boldness in Love', 'The Complaint of Harpalus', 'He that Loves a Rosie Cheek', 'Fine Young Folly', 'Lord Wigmore', and 'Tis not Love thy Pulses Beat' comprise a group of seventeenth-century lyrics spanning ii. 40–8. Some of these marks of doubt concerned in which volume pieces should appear. The first way of indicating this particular query was to strike through the pieces ('When this Old Cap was New', ii. 38), but as I have suggested, a more obvious form was found: 'The Complaint of Harpalus' (ii. 42), was noted '3'; 'Lord Wigmore' (ii. 46) and 'Tis not Love thy Pulses Beat' (ii. 48) were each marked '(1', and 'Harpalus' (iii. 6), was marked '2'.

Some time later, Percy reversed his use of the draft. Instead of noting deviations from the original order, he now only annotated to confirm it. This is when he employed the symbols '+', '++', and '+++' to affirm the volume of each piece. Status within a volume now required positive confirmation—it was not implied by the presence of a piece in the 'Draft'. The actual anatomy of the arrangement was revised (see Appendix V). Of these 69 pieces, 45 got into print, and most of those remaining exist in fair copy in the Houghton, many numbered for the press.[115] These marks were therefore used as a way of affirming a sense of order in a protean draft, and making decisions.

The final act of annotation appears to be a piece of anachronistic revision: corroborating which ballads and songs did achieve a place in the first edition, by crossing them diagonally—which is exactly how he indicated read and returned books in his notebook on book borrowing. However this reading assumes that the purpose of the 'First Draft' was only to provide a text for the *Reliques*. Percy did not cross out the pieces he had not printed, and the fact that the pieces that were printed required a positive indication of status within the 'First Draft' illustrates that the 'First Draft' remained a working repository for the pieces Percy

---

[115] 'Mark Anthony & his Eg^tian. Queen', 'A Brave warlike Song', 'Ballade of the Marygolde', 'Buckingham betrayed', 'Godina', 'Boldness in Love', 'Sir Rich^d. Whittington', 'To Lucasta from Prison', 'Rusticae Academiae Descriptio', 'Westcountry batchelor's complaint', 'Sir Hugh of the Grime', 'John o' th side', 'The Erle of Westmorland', 'Christopher White', 'Sir John Butler', 'Old Times past', 'Maudlin', 'The Hunting of the Gods', 'A Cauilere', 'O Wat where art thou', 'Lancashire song', 'Imitations of Chevy chase', 'When this old Cap was new', 'The Complaint of Harpalus'; see Friedman, 'First Draft', for more detail.

might publish at some later stage. Many of these unprinted pieces
were ready for a fourth volume of the *Reliques*.

Friedman dates the manuscript of the 'First Draft' to October–
November 1761. This is a compromise between September 1761
(because it includes Pepys ballads) and 22 December 1761, when
Percy wrote to Astle and mentioned that the *Reliques* would
feature ballads illustrating Shakespeare, none of which appear in
the 'First Draft'. The case is not so clear-cut, however, especially
on the question of Percy's Shakespeare researches. Percy actually
wrote to Astle, 'You must know I am collecting all the Songs and
Ballads quoted in Shakespear, and have already procured a good
many that will contribute to throw light upon his works.'[116] This
is not, as Friedman claims, a 'determination to include a series of
ballads associated with Shakespeare'.[117]

When the *Reliques* was published, the second book of the first
volume was titled 'Ballads that illustrate Shakespeare', but it seems
that this section was in fact a fairly late addition. As described in
the next chapter, the first sheets of the *Reliques* were printed as
early as January–February 1762. The printing commenced with
the third volume, followed by the second, completed by December
1763. It was only as the printing of the second volume drew to a
close, on 9 October, that Percy wrote to Farmer asking for help
with the Shakespearean pieces. It is strange that he makes no
reference to this little book of Shakespeareana earlier if, as
Friedman suggests, he had settled on it as early as December
1761. Farmer was his most energetic and erudite associate in
compiling and collating the Shakespeare ballads.

Indeed, Friedman's primary piece of evidence for dating the
'First Draft' no later than 1761 hinges on the letter Percy wrote
to Astle on 22 December 1761. But as we saw at the beginning of
this chapter, Percy's comments to correspondents should not be
taken at face value. In this published letter to Astle, Percy listed a
modest eight pieces quoted by Shakespeare, suggesting that he had
some project in mind, if only to enliven Johnson's edition.[118] On

---

[116] Harlowe, 26.   [117] Friedman, 'First Draft', 1234, 1246.
[118] These eight were printed in the *Reliques* as 'Sir Lancelot du Lake', 'A Song to the
Lute in Musicke', 'Corydon's Farewell to Phillis', 'The Aged Lover Renounceth Love',
'Willow, Willow, Willow', 'King Cophetua and the Beggar-Maid',—['The Friar of
Orders Gray'], 'The Passionate Shepherd to his Love'. Percy's transcripts of 'Songs
from Shakespeare' (Houghton, bMS Eng. 893 (186)) lists ten further pieces.

the other hand, this letter is printed with a postscript listing twenty-seven pieces, suggesting that Percy's Shakespearean ambitions were far more advanced. (The *Reliques* (1765) eventually contained seventeen, including Percy's own pastiche 'The Friar of Orders Gray'.) Yet although this postscript was printed by S. H. Harlowe as part of the letter to Astle, or at least an enclosure, the manuscript in the Folger Shakespeare Library shows it to be written in the unmistakable hand of Richard Farmer.[119] In fact, it probably originates from a lost letter to Percy of January–February 1764, perhaps as part of the 'Shakespearian Parcel' for which Percy thanked Farmer on 12 February—a crate of some thirty volumes.[120] Percy had only mentioned the Shakespearean project to Farmer on 9 October 1763, and in another problematic postscript, this time sent to Farmer, listed sixteen '*Songs and Ballads quoted by Shakespear*'.[121] It is unlikely that Percy could have reduced Farmer's original twenty-seven pieces to sixteen over the course of two years' research. Farmer's list must have been compiled much later. Percy's letter of 31 December 1763 reiterated his plan for the then third volume: 'My whole 2^d book is to relate to Shakespear's ballads, your own subject.'[122] It would seem that Percy did not commit himself to publishing Shakespeareana until he was sure he had enough pieces to fill a whole book, and it was therefore the pattern of printing that dictated where (and when) the pieces would appear, if at all.

So there is considerable doubt that the latest limit of the 'First Draft' is December 1761. Possibly Percy was collecting Shakespeare ballads at this time in an attempt to woo Johnson back to the *Reliques*. Perhaps it was work undertaken simply as a favour for Johnson's edition of Shakespeare, which did contain several such notes contributed by Percy.[123] In any case, it is likely that the 'First Draft' should be dated much later. The first two pieces to be printed were the Arthurian ballads from the Folio MS:

---

[119] Folger Shakespeare Library, Y c 1452 (26).

[120] *Letters*, ii. 63. Among the books Farmer had lent were Warburton's edition of Shakespeare, three volumes of Shakespeare quartos, and a further three unbound quartos (Bodl., MS Percy b 2, fo. 190^r). Farmer had started sending books shortly after Percy returned from his Pepysian Library trip (17 Nov. 1761), and parcels arrived regularly throughout 1762 and 1763 (Bodl., MS Percy b 2, fos. 97^r, 98^v, 101^v).

[121] *Letters*, ii. 54.   [122] Ibid. 57.

[123] Arthur Sherbo, *The Birth of Shakespeare Studies: Commentators from Rowe* (1709) *to Boswell–Malone* (1821) (East Lansing, Mich., 1986), 18–19.

'The Boy and the Mantle' and 'The Marriage of Sir Gawaine', which appear as i. 1 and i. 2 in the 'First Draft'. It is my contention that the 'First Draft' may have been to some degree a retrospective list. These two pieces were Percy's favourite standbys from the Folio MS: he had sent transcripts of them at least to Shenstone, Warton, and Evans, and they therefore ended up with the printer as well. Percy would introduce himself to his readers in the same way as he had won the support of his different collaborators: with ballad fables of the Matter of Britain.

Percy sent the first sheet (Sheet B) to Warton on 28 February 1762, but told Farmer around 10 May that they had not yet got to the fifth sheet of the then first volume.[124] It seems likely that Percy in fact compiled his 'First Draft' between these two dates. The first three sheets printed (B, C, and D) follow the order of the 'First Draft':

B 'The Boy and the Mantle';
   'The Marriage of Sir Gawaine'.
C 'The Marriage of Sir Gawaine';
   'King Ryence's Challenge';
   'King Arthur's Death';
   'The Legend of King Arthur'.
D 'The Legend of King Arthur';
   'A Dittie to Hey Down';
   'Glasgerion';
   'Old Sir Robin of Portingale'.

The order of the last two pieces of sheet D are reversed in the 'First Draft', and the fourth and fifth sheets (E and F) are substantially different. Friedman's 'First Draft' is consequently a list compiled by Percy during the printing of the second and third sheets in order to guide his researches over the next two years. The swift deviation of the 'First Draft' from the printed sheets does suggest that the early correspondence of drafting and printing was simply the result of writing the 'First Draft' after the first two sheets had already been printed. This is also backed up by the revision of the 'First Draft', the volume mark ('+'), which follows sheets B and C only. The dilatoriness of the printer was fortunate for Percy and permitted him to collect references and collations from his correspondents actually during the printing, working

---

[124] *Letters*, iii. 33; Fairer, 113; *Letters*, ii. 2.

only to a sequence of deadlines. Furthermore, as shown in Chapter 6, Percy's arrangement of the pieces for printing was extraordinarily chaotic, despite the map of the 'First Draft'.[125] Percy therefore worked on the 'First Draft' in the following way: printing began, sheets B and C completed, wrote 'First Draft', revised it, sheet D printed.

The excruciating complexities of Percy's working methods are well illustrated in unravelling the 'First Draft', but at least we have a manuscript. Percy's papers in fact divulge two other, much earlier, drafts. These arrangements have gone almost entirely unnoticed by scholars and are reconstructed here for the first time.[126] They consist of one or two sets of little numbers written in the upper margins of transcripts and broadsides. The two drafts of the *Reliques* described and reconstructed below exist only in traces, and not on documents repeatedly revised. They demonstrate that there were at least two stages in Percy's attempts to mould his collection into a manageable shape. First, he produced eleven numbered groups; some time later he attempted to produce a running sequence for three volumes, inspired by the earlier grouping.

The initial grouping is evident on transcripts marked usually with a red figure over a black one: 5/1 (2 pieces only), 5/2 (5), 5/3 (7), 5/4 (13), 6/1 (20), 6/2 (25), 6/3 (22), 6/4 (13), 6/5 (1), 6/6 (11), and 6/7 (3) (see Appendix VI). This constitutes Percy's earliest attempt to organize his transcripts and broadsides into an anthology. Percy seems to have taken Johnson's advice to arrange promiscuously very literally, as the pieces appear to be scattered quite indiscriminately under the eleven numerical headings, particularly in the thinly populated groups 5/1–4. What these numbers represent remains open to speculation, but may refer to materials distributed across two volumes, numbered v and vi. Percy's contract with James Dodsley was for two or three volumes, but why, if he first planned a two-volume *Reliques*, should he number the volumes v and vi rather than i and ii? It

---

[125] In any case, Percy was already organizing his material by the time he visited Cambridge: in conference with Shenstone or Johnson, in the 'Alphabet Collection', and in the thematic arrangement derived from Pepys's headings.

[126] Friedman, 'First Draft', remarks on one set of 'dockets' in passing, but is quite wrong to say that they approximate 'the order of the first draft' (1248–9).

may be that Percy was seized with a sudden enthusiasm to tie together his researches. He was already translating Mallet (*Northern Antiquities*, two volumes, including the *Edda*) and had disclosed to Evans his plans for *Specimens of the Ancient Poetry of Different Nations* (consisting of Chinese poetry, *Five Pieces of Runic Poetry*, and *The Song of Solomon*, and perhaps some other examples). This could fill a third volume. The fourth volume might have been the essay on 'The Ancient Metrical Romances' generously supplemented with the examples of metrical romances Percy was collecting (he entertained publishing a selection of these as well). Finally, these four volumes would be followed by two volumes of ancient English poetry, prefaced by the essays 'The Ancient English Minstrels', 'The Origin of the English Stage', and 'The Metre of Pierce Plowman's Visions'. Percy's six-volume magnum opus would therefore liberally chart Gothic literature from biblical times to the modern day with a profusion of illustrative examples: a hybrid between a cultural history and a literary anthology. It is characteristically overambitious of Percy, and no surprise that this plan was not subsequently pursued. But a speculation of this sort does demonstrate that Percy's works constitute a coherent argument.

The proposed arrangement for the two-volume *Reliques*, volumes v and vi of, for want of a better title, 'Gothic Antiquities', is listed in Appendix VI. On this model, volume v would have included three essays followed by four chapters of verse; volume vi would have seven chapters of verse. One hundred and twenty-two pieces are included, a few others have doubtless been lost. There is no attempt to order the pieces using the Pepysian heads, nor to offer disciplined thematic series. At first sight, the profusion and variety of the ballads under each volume and series number seems wildly Gothic in its freedom from the tyranny of order. There is little to tie the four chapters of volume v together, which appear entirely capricious (this is perhaps due to the relative scarcity of pieces assigned to this volume). Most are placed in volume vi, which does yield a discernible order: ancient historical ballads and hunting songs (6/1), historical narrative ballads (6/2), Renaissance verses (6/3), sequences of seventeenth-century love songs (6/4), the Rebellion (6/5), regional ballads (6/6), and the Restoration (6/7). It gives a broadly chronological survey by subject matter, littered with love songs to allow the weary reader some moments of respite from the implacable juggernaut of Gothic literature.

Percy's next task was to organize these eleven groups into a linear series. By this time he was expecting to produce a three-volume *Reliques*. Again, this draft is not a draft that appears on a single folio sheet, but a series of references on transcripts and broadsides. These disclose a linear form of arrangement, rather than the spatial groupings of theme and subject just described. It is an index. These notes, in a faded red ink, all appear to have been written at the same time, and designate the volume number and place within a sequence. For example, 'V.1.9.' written on the recto of 'See the Building', means that it should be the ninth piece in volume i. Of course, Shenstone had asked Percy on 1 October 1760 to transcribe the pieces to be included into a 'Large Paper-book', and perhaps Percy considered docketing a less laborious task than transcribing all the pieces for Shenstone.[127] There is no evidence, however, that Shenstone ever received the material in this form, and from what we are learning of Percy's working methods, there was never any possibility of finalizing a manuscript draft.

The list is incomplete, but there are eighty-three ballads listed, nearly every one of which appears in the two-volume draft. Most of the fifty-odd pieces in the two-volume draft not included in the next indexing stage were marked 'Rejected', and many of those that do go on to the manuscript draft were 'Approved'. The two stages of drafting were therefore intimately connected. Less than a dozen pieces that appeared in the index draft were not included in the two-volume draft, and some of these appeared anyway in alternative versions, and there were presumably further titles now lost that featured in both drafts. There is a small amount of duplication in the index, and the positions of several ballads were revised.[128] This might argue that this draft, like its predecessor, was not a one-off event designed to facilitate printing like the 'First Draft', but an ongoing process, subject to revision.

Any conclusions drawn from this incomplete source must be qualified, but in the case of the index draft, each volume is already implicitly conceived as three books (a structure made explicit in the preface of the *Reliques*, i, p. xii). Several linked sequences were taken straight from the two-volume draft, and the following 'movements' in the abstract are discernible:

---

[127] *Letters*, vii. 72.   [128] See Appendix VII.

Volume i:
Miscellaneous history (a mix of 5/3 and 5/4);
Hunting sequence (6/1);
Seventeenth-century and Restoration love songs (6/4 and 6/6).

Volume ii:
English history (6/2);
Historical narratives (6/1);
Miscellany of love songs and Scottish pieces.

Volume iii:
Renaissance verses (6/3);
Miscellaneous (5/3 and 5/4);
Miscellaneous Renaissance and seventeenth-century verses (6/3, 6/4, and 6/6).

In other words, the first volume was devoted to earlier social and cultural history, the second to English military history, and the third to the Renaissance and seventeenth century. Like the Pepysian collection, each volume had its own chronological identity, but also contributed towards a broader historical sweep. Indeed, Pepys provided both the chronologically diverse arrangement, and the idea of concluding the volumes with a 'Small Promiscuous Supplement upon most of the foregoing Subjects'. There are also definite connections with the later 'First Draft': the first volume of the index is shadowed fairly closely by the third volume of the 'Draft', as is the third with the first. The second volume of each is based on English history. The broad movement of each is similar, although the ballad-to-ballad order frequently varies.[129] A few features were carried into the later scripted 'Draft', such as the 'Hunting' sequence of i. 24–7 (*The Modern Ballad of Chevy Chase*, 'The Hunting of the Gods', 'A Cavilere', 'O Wat Where art Thou!'), which appeared in the 'First Draft' as iii. 17, 19–21, before being rejected.

In consequence, it is most useful to regard the index as an initial, systematic attempt to order the variety of materials into a narrative. In light of this, Friedman's comments on these 'dockets' is unfortunately simply wrong. The 'Hunting' sequence does not 'introduce the collection', but would have helped to make up the second book of volume i. Neither should the docketed index be

---

[129] For example, abstract, i. 40–9, compared with 'Draft', iii. 36 ff.

considered 'an unculled collection'.[130] The docketing implies a total of at least 176 pieces, barely larger than the 'First Draft' (which contained 166 pieces), and exactly the same size as the first edition of the printed *Reliques*.

Percy needed to organize his material along two axes. His initial arrangements had all been 'spatial' groupings: collections of material that shared themes or subjects, or had originated from the same source or provenance. But when he faced publishing, Percy had to recognize the linear, temporal relationship of the material, and opted for loose chronologies. One of the most interesting folders among the Harvard Percy Papers is a thick stitched manuscript book titled 'A Series of Ballads on English History', which gives the chronicle of English history in a series of ballads.[131] Percy evidently built up the book over some time and from his favourite sources: paper, inks, and layout vary enormously. Many of these manuscripts also show signs of having been disbound and sent to scholars for annotation or to printers as copy. Of course, *A Collection of Old Ballads* also provided a template for arranging the material in this way. But Percy rejected this straightforward historical order. History was not linear, but genealogical: lineages multiplied with each generation, and it was Percy's task as a literary antiquarian and prospective minstrel to trace the pedigree of English letters through its succession and establish the Gothic inheritance of the present. The two-volume draft, the index draft, and the 'First Draft' each represent reconceptualizations of Percy's material: gradually more sophisticated attempts to conceive the work as a genealogical pattern rather than as a maze of interconnected headings. Each plan does this by implying a series of cultural progressions in each book and volume.

Inevitably, Percy's schemes to order the material involved a ninety-degree shift: from an axis of the simultaneous, the synonymous, and the polyvalent, to one of the linear, the genealogical, and the narrative. The former, vertical axis was appropriate for collecting and sifting materials; the latter, horizontal axis was required for the activity of printing and the concept of the book, even a piecemeal anthology. In fact, the intertextuality of

---

[130] Friedman, 'First Draft', 1249.　　[131] Houghton, bMS Eng. 893 (20A).

the former is typical of chirographic culture, while the latter is typographic. Percy's very arrangements were commentaries on the media of his sources. But Percy was also obliged by his method to produce a printed anthology that actually challenged the ideology of print. Inescapable elements of the vertical axis remained present in the finished anthology, and the associative nature of the anthology was exacerbated by his working methods. He could not completely rid himself of the architecture of the manuscript, in letters and collations, on the production of his work: the mingling so apparent in the *Reliques* underlined the problems in determining the status of different sources and the anxieties of committing them to print.

The relationship between manuscript and print was fundamental to Percy's attitude to his methodology and to his drafts. He docketed his texts into groups and used these groups to compile an index draft. He began printing, wrote a draft, revised it, rewrote it, pillaged it for a later work, retained it as a curio. The retrospective justification of the 'First Draft' by printing emphasizes the problems of assigning authority in Percy's drafts. Henceforth the *Reliques* was to be created at the printing house. The next chapter describes how Percy carried his protean text far beyond the normal constraints of the press, to produce a book that was unfinished and confused.

6

Printing the *Reliques*

The *Reliques* engaged Percy in labyrinthine researches, which persistently framed his work within new and unexpected contexts: from the parlour of Humphrey Pitt to the garden of William Shenstone, from the dusty libraries of Cambridge to the dirty warehouses of Cluer Dicey, from the edges of the empire to an elegant vicarage in Northamptonshire, and from the dim and distant past to the modern taste. It now arrived at the print shop, where it initially lay, mingled and confused, among the distributed type of a compositor's frame. It took James Dodsley two and a half years to print the *Reliques*. During that time, Percy was driven. He vigorously corresponded with Farmer, Warton, and Evans; made the significant acquaintance of the Scottish antiquary David Dalrymple; and his relationship with Shenstone enjoyed a minor renaissance before the latter's untimely death (11 February 1763). Amazingly, he had five other works published in the same period: his Chinese novel *Hau Kiou Choaan* (17 November 1761), a collection of cautionary tales about widows, *The Matrons* (28 May 1762), *Miscellaneous Pieces relating to the Chinese* (13 December 1762), *Five Pieces of Runic Poetry* (2 April 1763), and a translation of *The Song of Solomon* which assigned each verse a speaker (13 June 1764). He pressed on with editions of Buckingham and Surrey, began writing his *Key to the New Testament* (1765), signed contracts with Jacob Tonson to edit the *Spectator* and *Guardian*, and negotiated with Andrew Millar and John Newbery to translate Paul-Henri Mallet's *Introduction à l'histoire de Dannemarc*. He was indefatigable. He visited Cambridge again and was frequently in London; entertained Grainger, who had briefly returned from the West Indies and needed help revising his *Sugar-Cane* (published 26 May 1764); and for eight weeks during the summer of 1764, Percy enjoyed the pleasure of Johnson's company at Easton Maudit. He still had his clerical duties at Easton Maudit and Wilby to attend to, and the insistent domestic responsibilities of a growing family: daughters Anne and Barbara were born in 1760 and 1761, respectively, and his son Henry in 1763. Somehow, amid all this tireless activity, he was still collating and transcribing for the *Reliques*, drafting and redrafting, and composing fair copy for the press—which in at least one case was executed, in a moment of spectacular bravado, with his left hand![1]

The extraordinary vitality of Percy's literary life is only outlined here.[2] But the many projects that engaged Percy require further elucidation: they overlapped. Indeed, it was almost by necessity that they should. The first part of this chapter will examine the intersection of these texts in the light of renewed advice from Shenstone regarding the printing of the *Reliques*, and the context of Percy's spiralling circle of correspondents. Following this, we will investigate what was Percy's last chance to order the *Reliques* in manuscript. The order in which the pieces were sent to the printer, and notes on the printer's copy highlight Percy's inevitable last-minute revisions and changes, dramatically demonstrating the anxieties experienced during the production of his cultural artefact. The last section describes extant proofs and revises, examining some surviving printer's copy, previously overlooked. This demonstrates the extent to which the printer, probably John Hughs, was responsible for the final work, and makes use of two association copies of the *Reliques*: two surviving volumes of a trial issue which belonged to Richard Farmer, later purchased by Francis Douce (the Farmer–Douce copy), and Percy's own working copy—a heavily annotated and supplemented three-volume trial issue which he eventually presented to his secretary Meredith Darby (the Percy–Darby copy).

Printing the *Reliques* was to prove long and painful. The presses rolled for two and a half years between February 1762 and November 1764—an unusually slow and therefore expensive operation that would have tied up type and filled valuable warehouse space with growing piles of printed sheets.[3] The mounting

---

[1] Noted on transcript of 'Henry and Rosamond' Houghton, bMS Eng. 893 (172), fo. 1ʳ: 'written while I was trying to learn to write with my left hand circ. 1762'.

[2] This fantastic productivity is meticulously reconstructed by Davis (1989), 82–113. Percy earned £207 10s. from Dodsley alone for these contracts (*Willis's Current Notes*, 91).

[3] The completed first volume (the third as published) arrived at Easton Maudit on 6 Sept. 1763, the third volume (first as published) on 6 Feb. 1764 (Bodl., MS Percy c 9, fo. 94ᵛ).

production costs made it all the more crucial that the book, unlike the rest of Percy's output, should be a success. The path could certainly be smoothed by an efficient and understanding printer, and, as described in John Smith's *Printer's Grammar* of 1755, printers expected a certain etiquette to be observed in their dealings over copy. On the art of composing type, Smith repeated Moxon's warning against dealing with a 'humorous Gentleman' if at all possible, 'for *then* a Compositor is obliged to conform to the fancy of his Author'. Smith continued,

By the Laws of Printing, indeed, a Compositor should abide by his Copy, and not vary from it . . . . But this good law is now looked upon as obsolete, and most Authors expect the Printer to spell, point, and digest their Copy, that it may be intelligible and significant to the Reader.[4]

Unfortunately, Percy's authorial habits were to prove 'humorous' to the most exasperating and capricious degree. Indeed, what follows is almost the anti-type of eighteenth-century book production. The printers had encountered such behaviour before, and wearily prepared themselves for the worst. On Errata, Smith had remarked that,

the subterfuges that are used by Writers upon this occasion, are commonly leveled at the Printer, to make him the author of all that is a miss [*sic*]; whereas they ought to ascribe it to themselves: for, were Gentlemen to send in their Copy fairly written, and well corrected and prepared for the Press, they would have no occasion to apprehend that their work would be neglected, were they to leave the whole management thereof to the Printer, especially when it is written in his native language. But bad Copy, not revised at all by the Author, is one obstacle; and altering and changing the matter after it has been composed, is another means that obstructs the correctness of a Work; not to mention the several accidents to which it is exposed before it has passed thro' the hands of a Pressman.[5]

While Percy certainly expected he would publish his anthology of ancient English poetry, printing would prove to be as fraught as any of the earlier stages, and it is remarkable that the book was not abandoned. Worse still, Percy indulged in procrastination, sycophancy, mendacity, and subterfuge in the course of printing, and his pages bear the stains of these sins. But there was perhaps more to this than pride. Printing forced Percy to press together his

---

[4] John Smith, *The Printer's Grammar* (1755), 199.   [5] Ibid. 222.

antiquarian researches into ancient English minstrelsy, the Goths, medieval romances and ballads, and so forth, to confront practical issues of taste: editing, book production, and, most importantly, poetry. He could now see the wisdom of Shenstone's advice in not becoming too owlish in mumbling over literary mice—and Shenstone had himself been 'a most notorious Procrastinator'.[6] But Shenstone was dead, and some of Percy's fury and intractability with his printer might have been the expression of a futile rage and frustration in losing his weak, good-humoured, and unsteady guide. In mourning, Percy's attitude to printing changed, and he allowed Hughs a surprising amount of leeway in regularizing the text of the *Reliques*. Henceforth, Percy took a motto of Shenstone's and pasted into his own working copy of the book: 'Beauty alone is the Object of Taste, eternal & immutable; Whoever aims to form a just Idea of it, should guard equally against the seduction of Antiquity & of Novelty.'[7] The owl was about to join with the nightingale.

'DO NOT LET YOUR VOLUMES BE TOO THICK'[8]

William Shenstone had, predictably, always been sensitive to book design. One of his earliest extant letters (6 February 1741, to Richard Jago) recounts an unintentionally hilarious anecdote in which one Ralph Freeman produced some printed broadsides during a party. Shenstone's attention was drawn to something other than the poetry: 'I (not finding at first they were of his own composition) read one over, and, finding it a dull piece of stuff, contented myself with observing that it was exceedingly well *printed*.' Freeman was, not surprisingly, discomposed by Shenstone's bibliographical *aperçu*: 'His jollity ceased.'[9]

A few years later this concern with format had reached preposterous levels, and seems to have been relished among his friends as a characteristic foible. Writing to Lady Luxborough on 1 June 1748, he offered the (self-mocking) observation:

---

[6] Letter to William Cleiveland, 17 Jan. 1774, BL, Add. MS 32333, fo. 77^r.
[7] Percy–Darby, iii, front pastedown.
[8] *Letters*, vii. 167: Shenstone's final advice.
[9] Williams, 18 (Shenstone's emphasis).

As to ye Castle of Indolence I find one Fault wth it already which is that it is printed in an odious *Quarto* & I never cou'd approve such *unbindable* Editions. At least, if it *may* be *bound*, it makes but an ordinary *Person of a Book*. I am always in Hopes y^t whenever an Author is either a tall or even a middle-siz'd man, he will never print a Book but in Folio, octavo, or duodecimo; & on the other Hand, when he is short & squab, I collect y^t his partiality to a Figure of y^t kind, will induce him, to my great discomfort, to publish in *Quarto*. But Mr. Thomson, who is certainly of y^e *middle* Size, must be self-convicted.[10]

Authors were responsible for far more than mere words in siring their works. The elegance of a book was a reflection of the taste (and evidently the physique) of its author, and might—as in the case of Freeman above—be its only saving grace.[11]

Mention has already been made of Shenstone's *Miscellany*, a private anthology of friends' verse which Shenstone transcribed into a manuscript book in imitation of a printed book. He also constructed little mock booklets of his own verses.[12] This is doubtless where Shenstone's enthusiasm for a manuscript copy of Percy's own anthology derives, 'I would have you transcribe what you think proper, in a Large Paper-book, and let me consider them *all together*, before they are sent away to Press.'[13] For Shenstone, this might have been enough: his own Folio MS, a curiosity (curiously 'Large' for Shenstone) to display on his bookshelf, a source from which to derive pastoral inscriptions for his arbours. Eventually, such a manuscript might find its place in print.[14] It was this assumption which set Percy and Shenstone at loggerheads again. Percy needed to publish (lest he forfeit the Folio MS), but was having great difficulty in doing so, and Shenstone's gently chiding advice for neatness rather missed the point. It has already been shown that Percy privileged printed sources over manuscript sources, but in printing the *Reliques*, Percy seems to have refused to accept that print fixed his own work with any authority. His enormous reluctance to accept the closure of print

---

[10] Ibid. 144–5.

[11] Walter Ong has drawn attention to anatomical metaphors used to describe the book, such as chapter (*caput*) and footnote: 'Texts assimilate utterance to the human body' (Walter J. Ong, SJ, *Orality and Literacy: The Technologizing of the Word* (1982), 100).

[12] Margaret M. Smith (ed.) *Index of English Literary Manuscripts*, iii. 3 (1992), 293–4.   [13] *Letters*, vii. 72.

[14] Ibid. 5, 138.

condemned the *Reliques* to a twilight of confused printing, in which the authority of print was gradually eclipsed, and subsequently condemned to a perpetual limbo of shifting editions, continuous manuscript revision, and ultimately canonical rejection by Child and by Hales and Furnivall.

During Percy's visit to the Leasowes in August/September 1760, he had been spurred on by the encouragement of Shenstone to visualize the precise impact that printing the ballads would have, but this was almost catastrophically premature advice. Shenstone's subsequent letters to Percy were filled with suggestions for presentation and typography, while Percy himself was wrestling with the profound difficulties of wrenching his vast collection into a publishable shape. Percy had perhaps originally imagined that the publication of the Folio MS and associated pieces would produce a lightly annotated edition: Johnson providing a modest page-long essay for every two ballads printed, and Edward Lye contributing a glossary.[15] But the first Runic fragment that Percy sent to reward Shenstone's hospitality was weighed down with notes, 'You will probably be disgusted to see it so incumbered with Notes; Yet some are unavoidable, as the Piece would be unintelligible without them'.[16] Shenstone took one look at it, and remarked philosophically, 'The absolute *Necessity* of Notes, will be the rock that you may chance to split upon.' He suggested that notes should be collected in a glossary or a preface.[17] Shenstone was more curt with Percy's offer to reduce other Runic fragments to footnotes in an antiquarian argument: 'I think not, by any Means.'[18]

In this letter (1 October 1760), Shenstone, presumably under the influence of Robert Dodsley, was surprisingly businesslike. He set down brisk guidelines for what was eventually to become *Runic Poetry*: glossary, prefaces, prose translations in paragraphs, no originals, no short pieces—most of which Percy continued to ignore. Shenstone also proposed typographic conventions for editing the Folio MS ballads:

As to alterations of a *word or two*, I do not esteem it a point of *Conscience* to *particularize them* on *this* occasion. Perhaps, where a whole *Line* or *More* is alter'd, it may be proper enough to give some Intimation of it. The *Italick* type may answer this purpose, if you do not

---

[15] *Letters*, vii. 9–10.   [16] Ibid. 70.   [17] Ibid. 74.
[18] Smith, 'Thomas Percy', 473.

employ it on other occasions. It will have the appearance of a modern *Toe* or *Finger*, which is *allowably* added to the best old Statues: And I think I should always let the Publick imagine, that these were owing to *Gaps*, rather than to *faulty Passages*.[19]

The poet would patch holes, occasionally indicating by editorial marks the most elegant repairs. Bibliographical codes (such as punctuation or typeface) thus allowed the poet to participate in the work of the literary antiquarian. Indeed, it was advisable to do so, and, in the case of '*faulty Passages*', good poetry superseded bad antiquity. But curiously, Shenstone describes here an image of classical connoisseurship and poetic refinement, not the Gothic taste, and offers it only the most delicate touches of improvement. Percy was still trying to assemble his relics. The body of the minstrels' work was undone and needed to be stitched or cemented together before the limbs were smoothed and the odd digit (or head) restored. The limbs of minstrelsy were more scattered, and more wanting, than classical remains, and if the *disjecta membra* of the past needed to be made up physiologically as well as cosmetically, it was precisely because the classical aesthetic had undone them.

Percy of course followed Shenstone's advice insofar as he high-lighted editorial changes, but he employed the notorious single quotation marks rather than an italic fount: 'Where any thing was altered that deserved particular notice, the passage is distin-guished by two inverted 'commas'.' He also indicated where he had taken further 'considerable liberties' with a poem by sealing it with the figure *⁎*, but for some reason he declined to define this symbol until the fourth edition (i, p. xii).[20] Percy's use of such figures had classical precedents. The practice had begun in anti-quity: Hellenistic scholars used for example the *obelus* or dash to indicate a spurious line in a manuscript. Percy's use of single quotation marks to signal his own revisions therefore carried a hint of classical refinement. Shenstone advocated refinement as a way of articulating aesthetic detail; for Percy, it served just as much to articulate the difference of the Gothic, gleaned from

---

[19] *Letters*, vii. 72–3.
[20] *Reliques* (1794), i, p. xvii n. In one case, 'Gentle Herdsman, Tell To Me', Percy did use italics to indicate his conjectural emendations (ii. 72 ff.).

his cultural backwaters. And as Susan Stewart notes, such articulation 'increasingly served the interests of class'.[21]

Percy was in two minds about the whole classical vision of Shenstone. It threatened to stultify his ballads, retired to the cosy realms of pastoral simplicity rather than declared the heralds of lost history. A letter from Percy, now lost (xxvi, *c.*October 1760), presumably queried these orders because Shenstone's next (10 November) reported that he had taken up the question of layout with Dodsley. He appreciated that Percy was raking up masses of historical detail, and also wanted to provide notes on textual variation, but reiterated his own ambitions for the ballads:

I have been mentioning your Quere to M[r] Dodsley, about the *argument* or *Introduction* to each ballad—I will say *more* in my *next* Letter—at present, I shall only intimate, that I would wish you to consult for *Simplicity* as much as *possible.*—*Some* old words, I presume (which it will be perhaps necessary to preserve) must be explained by modern ones—For these alone, I would reserve the *bottom* of each Page—The remaining Quere will be, whether the little Anecdotes that you insert by way of illustration, should be placed at the *beginning*, or the *end* of the ballad—If they are short, perhaps, they may not be amiss in Italicks, at the beginning. However should you begin each Ballad at the head of a Page, you will often have *room* for notes of a larger extent at the Close of the Foregoing—and perhaps you may want here to introduce a *particular* note, as well as a *general* Argument. In this Case (the bottom, as I said, being reserv'd for mere *verbal* explanations) I would throw both the general argument and particular notes together at the *Close*; for otherwise your text will be almost smothered by these incumbrances in every part.[22]

Shenstone urged that the ballads' simplicity should be the prime feature of printing, by making generous use of whitespace.[23] He astutely recognized that the contextual material should occupy the horizontal axis and definitions the vertical. In other words, the historical and intertextual anecdotes were to be read as part of the printed linear text, part of the argument, part of the history; verbal elucidations would be associative, interchangeable within the text. This polyvalence was analogous to the features of chirographic culture, affirming the source materials, like the

---

[21] Stewart, *On Longing*, 29.   [22] *Letters*, vii. 77–8.
[23] See Shenstone on Baskerville's fount, ibid. 134.

miscellaneous sheaves of ballads that littered Percy's library. It was another residue of Percy's research techniques.

Shenstone's concerns were, however, well justified. Having seen the mess of annotation and errata that was Percy's Chinese novel, *Hau Kiou Choaan*, Shenstone pleaded with Percy that the *Reliques* 'might be an elegant edition'.[24] His particular objections to *Hau Kiou Choaan* were stifled until 12 September 1761, when at last he broke out:

I think the Publick must esteem itself as much obliged to the *Editor*, as the editor has grounds to be offended at the *Printer*. Very numerous indeed are the errors that remain, over and above what appear in the tables of errata; and very sollicitous *indeed* does the Editor appear, least, by the omission of any *possible* Improvement, he should disoblige the Publick.[25]

But Percy was oblivious to argument, threat, and mockery alike.

For a few months these discussions between Shenstone and Percy about printing the *Reliques* actually revitalized their relationship, now conducted in a spirit approaching irritation and obstinacy, which Percy was later to regret. If Percy had dismissed Shenstone's taste for ballads as critically unsound, he grudgingly admitted his friend's ability to design a tasteful book. On 4 December 1761, in response to another lost letter of Percy's, Shenstone finally reiterated his advice on laying out the ballads:

As to your First Quere, it would have a very odd appearance, were you to leave such *large* Intervals, as you necessarily must *sometimes*, were you to assign a fresh Page to the beginning of every Ballad. The Notes (which, I think, you place at the Close of each), would *sometimes happen* to fill this vacancy; but, at *others*, to make a fresh One. Well-judged and elegant wooden tail-pieces (an ornament much wanting to every Press in Europe) would leave you at Liberty to pursue this scheme; but unless *your* Press affords you some that are *tolerable*, I would have you think no more about it.[26]

Percy tried another tactic. His reply was filled with diplomatic enthusiasm for Shenstone's delight in the simplicity of ballads, and his hopes to extract similar delight from a simple book:

You have taught me to dislike a crowded Title-page, and therefore must pardon me if I object to the second of yours. The plain Title in 3 Lines of

---

[24] Ibid. 105.   [25] Ibid. 114, see also 121.   [26] Ibid. 119–20.

Capitals: with either an ornamental sculpture or a good Motto, or both, etc. should be all I would have for my full Title: and for my half Title, the same only devoid of all ornament motto or date.[27]

Unsurprisingly, no work of Percy's ever had such a title-page.

It is in fact worth noting that the design of Percy's title-pages differed significantly from similar works which emerged from Tully's Head. Both *A Select Collection of Old Plays* (1744) and *A Collection of Poems* (1758) made striking use of black and red inks and employed very simple and clean Augustan lines, emphasized in *Old Plays* by a rectangular engraving and border. This was also the case with books of modern poetry, such as a 1766 edition of Warburton's *Works of Alexander Pope Esq.* Percy's title-pages were Gothic in their very profusion of typefaces and rambling lines. This disparity with other Dodsley publications, and Shenstone's query regarding the ornaments available to Percy, might indicate that the printing of the *Reliques* was not contracted to Dodsley's usual printer. At the very least, it distanced Percy's anthology from its companion volumes, although, ironically, Percy did set the format for antiquarian anthologies. Macpherson produced a pamphlet, followed by two handsome quartos, before settling down with the octavo popularized by Percy, and later editors such as David Dalrymple generally conformed. Even the format of Ritson's works was based on Percy's *Reliques*.[28]

Despite Percy's persistent disagreements with Shenstone, he was loath to lose the support of an influential ally. On 22 February 1762, he wrote to Shenstone with a final plea for advice on how to distribute the Scottish pieces: the printing of the *Reliques* had at last begun, and still Percy remained perversely keen to involve Shenstone in the production of the book. The situation now became almost farcical. Not yet having mastered the printers' terminology, Percy forwarded Shenstone his author's proofs as they arrived, desiring his friend to correct and return them promptly. Unfortunately, Percy referred to these sheets as 'revises' (review proofs pulled to show that corrections had been made), and so Shenstone believed that his friend was simply sending corrected proofs, enabling him to survey the complete work as it left the press. Shenstone kept the sheets in anticipation of the next

[27] See Shenstone on Baskerville's fount, *Letters*, vii. 130–1.
[28] Johnston, *Enchanted Ground*, 123.

batch for two months before Percy's patience broke. Shenstone was probably less 'Foolish' in misunderstanding Percy than he later pretended.[29] He was now reluctant to expend too much energy on a project from which he felt he had been dismissed and he feared the worst of Percy's antiquarian pretensions. One particularly grumpy letter remarked:

You will think it proper to insert something that comprizes the actions of this great Champion *Guy*, as well as those of King *Arthur*; and yet there is evidently not a single particle of poetical Merit in *either* of the Ballads. Once for all, it is extremely certain that an *Over* proportion of *this Kind* of *Ballast*, will sink your vessel to the Bottom of the Sea. Therefore be upon your guard . . . But I've perhaps harped upon this string too Long, and will leave these matters to your own decision.[30]

On 20 November he wrote a concerned letter to Robert Dodsley,

What you say of Percy's ballads is perfectly just & sensible—I have preached so long to the same purpose, that I am quite weary & will preach no more. I am willing to *hope* that this collection will *still* have merit to engage the Publick: but am less sanguine than I should have been, had he shortened his notes, admitted more improvements, and rejected all such ballads as had no Plea but their *Antiquity*.[31]

With laborious proofing and intractable disagreements it is no wonder that printing was so slow. Percy sent 'St. George and the Dragon' (sheet Q) with his letter of 5 October 1762 and entreated Shenstone's revision: 'I put the finishing hand to the inclosed but this morning: and beg the favour of you to give it a close revisal and return it (if you please) soon. Tho' a copy of it is to be sent to the press on thursday next, yet I will not let the Proof be worked off, 'till I have received your corrections.'[32] The author's proofs were taking on the character of the manuscript transcripts that had shuttled between Easton Maudit and the Leasowes a few years earlier. Transcribed into print by Hughs, the first proof was corrected, a new proof pulled, sent by Dodsley to Percy, corrected, sent to Shenstone, corrected, and returned to Dodsley via Percy. Revises were then pulled and launched on the same interminable journey. In another letter dating from October 1762, Percy

---

[29] *Letters*, vii. 159.   [30] Ibid. 150.
[31] Tierney, 466. For Robert Dodsley's own editorial practices, see A. T. Brissenden, 'Dodsley's Copy-Text for *The Revenger's Tragedy* in his *Select Collection*', *Library*, 19 (1964), 254–8.   [32] *Letters*, vii. 160–1.

reassured his friend, 'You have a right to command what sheets you please of our ballads', but printing progressed at an extremely leisurely rate.[33] Percy, for example, requested that Shenstone forward Elizabeth Cooper's *The Muses Library*. He had left it at the Leasowes when visiting again with his wife Anne in late September 1762, and needed to consult it for the second volume. Much remained to be done, though it was still unclear precisely what. Probably the last thing Shenstone did for Percy's *Reliques* was to read and mark up Percy's copy of Thomas Blacklock's *Collection of Original Poems*, which Percy sent at the end of 1762. Percy heeded Shenstone's advice as little as he had the 'Billets': Shenstone marked forty-seven Scottish pieces with his signs of approbation, Percy ignored the lot.[34]

The features of renewed collaboration with Shenstone—joint-revision, migration of proofs, continuous research—were also characteristic of Percy's correspondence with Thomas Warton and Richard Farmer. Percy sent the first sheet pulled (sheet B) to Warton on 28 February 1762, sheet C on 25 April, and by 2 November had sent sheet H. Again he solicited aid: 'I beg you will criticise the inclosed sheets with all freedom: and favour me with any corrections or Improvements that occur to you.'[35] Warton demanded more proofs and promised to return the sheets, but he did so, for example in the case of Percy's rendering of 'Valentine and Ursine' (sheet S), 'untouched'.[36] Percy was unappeased. The next year he sent Warton the next sheet (T), containing 'The Dragon of Wantley', and chided peevishly, 'I have long expected two favours from you, which you must excuse me, if I still persist in soliciting. These are the List of Ballads in the Ashmol. Collec-tion. and the Collation of the old Song on the victory of Agincourt . . . As the press waits for the latter may I hope to receive it soon?'[37] The *Reliques* had been under the press for well over a year, but Percy was still gathering materials.

Percy's first extant letter to Farmer (10 May 1762) apologized for not sending any proof sheets—he claimed that Shenstone had

---

[33] *Letters*, vii. 163.
[34] Ibid. 168–9; Blacklock, *Poems*, Queen's, Percy 499–500.
[35] *Letters*, iii. 35, see also 58; Fairer, 116, 135.
[36] *Letters*, iii. 60, 63, 65; Fairer, 137, 140, 142.
[37] *Letters*, iii. 90–1; Fairer, 160–1.

got them all. But by 9 October Farmer too was being put to work: 'do me the favour to collate the inclosed ballad St George and the dragon with the Copy preserved in the Pepys Collection and return it as soon as possible, for it is sent to the press.'[38] Farmer evidently enjoyed the work—a lost letter from about October 1762 demanded more participation, and elicited the following response from Percy:

You inquire, what's my humour in sending You the sheets, when it's too late to profit by your corrections? My intention was to amuse and entertain you, by shewing you the progress of the work: Tho' I own you see it to the greatest disadvantage in the blundering proofs. That distich in pag. 178 which you have so ingeniously supplied from conjecture, was not deficient in my MS Copy, tho' the stupid compositor dropt it in the proof.—I flatter myself whenever you come to see the sheets, as finally worked off: you will find all, or most of your objections precluded.[39]

Percy's utter disdain of the mechanicals at the press (the compositor, elsewhere the printer, and the engraver) is comparable to his high-handed treatment of Cluer Dicey.[40] The grocer's son was indulging in the aristocratic pretensions that would soon win him patronage and power with the Northumberlands, and also effectively limit his scholarly career to Northumbriana. But he was critically sensitive to the adulterations that might be introduced to his texts even as they rolled off the press. Having immersed himself in the tides of textual variation that had blurred his texts, Percy fixed (or rather fixated) on a concept of ideal copy in order to preserve his ballads, his account of ancient English minstrelsy, and his hierarchy of sources. The culmination of the book in print therefore required (indeed presupposed) that printing had an absolute fidelity. The *Reliques* had to exemplify its own supremacist medium.

With regard to Farmer, it transpired that Percy was keeping him in reserve for his book of Shakespearean ballads. Cleanth Brooks prints the first mention of this project as a postscript to letter xiv, a letter stuffed with proofs of ballads and Percy's 'Essay on the

---

[38] *Letters*, ii. 12.   [39] Ibid. 15.

[40] Percy's earliest experiences of publishing were characterized by such haughtiness. In 1757, James Grainger wrote to him with fine arrogance: 'Should we not damn these lying scoundrel printers?' (*Illustrations*, vii. 246, also 249).

Metre of Pierce Plowman's Visions'. Unfortunately, Farmer's replies to this and the subsequent Shakespearean letters have not yet come to light, although Percy's letters are filled with queries of sources and authorship, and thanks for cruces resolved. A great deal of foundation work was only undertaken at this late stage. If we accept Brooks's dating of the postscript to letter xiv, Farmer first heard of the plan to include a book of ballads illustrating Shakespeare shortly after 9 October 1763. Eleven weeks later, Percy roused himself to request Farmer's editions of Shakespeare to supplement his own first and second Folios and Zachary Grey's *Notes* (1754). Furthermore, this work was being done when Farmer had already received a trial version of the first volume of the *Reliques*, with the second just completed.[41]

Most interestingly, Percy sought Farmer's aid in revising his Shakespearean collage 'The Friar of Orders Gray'. This was a morbidly redemptive verse Percy had compiled out of 'innumerable little fragments of ancient ballads' quoted in Shakespeare's plays.

> His cheek was redder than the rose,
> The comeliest youth was he:—
> But he is dead and laid in his grave:
> Alas, and woe is me![42]

Percy asked Farmer to 'Propose whatever corrections or alterations you please, and return my copy as soon as possible. It is my only copy, and if miscarried or delayed beyond the call of the press I am undone.'[43] The printed proof of this original ballad, which harped on themes of loss and recovery, acquired the status of a unique manuscript. But inevitably things did go astray. Percy's network frequently broke down and work had to be repeated. Warton lost the musical notation of the Pepysian 'For the Victory at Agincourt' when he was supposed to be collating it with a copy in the Bodleian. As the music was to be reproduced at the end of the second volume, Farmer was dispatched to retranscribe it, and

---

[41] *Letters*, ii. 48; iii. 93. Percy's transcriptions of 'Songs from Shakespeare', Houghton, bMS Eng. 893 (186).

[42] *Reliques*, i. 225 (italics reversed), 228. Percy's 'Friar' was derived from Goldsmith's ballad 'Edwin and Angelina' (*Poems of Gray . . . Goldsmith*, 596–606), published in 1765, and dedicated to the Countess of Northumberland—presumably on Percy's advice.　　　　　　　　　　　　　　[43] *Letters*, ii. 64–5.

his copy was sent straight to the engraver. As Percy apparently knew nothing of music, Farmer also corrected the proof.[44]

Potentially far more damaging were the conflicts that invariably arose among his council of advisers. Farmer derided the series of 'Mad Songs', and Percy weakly complained, 'see how Doctors differ! they were particularly selected and recommended to me by poor Shenstone, whose opinions have now acquired a kind of prophetic authority with me.'[45] Percy was relinquishing his own authority not only to his collaborators but beyond the grave to Shenstone. The relentless enthusiasm of Percy and the seemingly endless tedium of the *Reliques* had been perhaps too much for Shenstone, who much preferred taking gentle rests in his garden. He died unexpectedly in February 1763. Percy's adoption of the role of Shenstone's avatar literally shifted authority onto a higher plane, and the Mad Songs stayed in.

To some degree, Farmer took over Shenstone's role as the perpetual foil to Percy's mix of ambition, procrastination, obstinacy, and faltering confidence. For example, in his letter of 5 April 1764, Percy revealed he had sent his essay 'On the Origin of the English Stage' to Farmer for correction. Percy had corrected the essay himself and had had a revise pulled. Farmer then annotated the revise copiously, and most of his corrections were assimilated. David Dalrymple was also needlessly sent a proof of this essay: Percy did not have time to make further changes and warned, 'it will be printed off, before this reaches you'.[46] Preface proofs were also sent to Farmer on 10 November: 'Read over my PREFACE with care, and send me any Remarks that occur, but don't deface the Proof, if you please.'[47] Percy needed every encouragement from Farmer before finally committing himself.

There were, as indicated above, new collaborators. Percy began corresponding with David Dalrymple on 10 November 1762, having secured an introduction by means of Jacob Tonson and the planned edition of Buckingham. Dalrymple was a lawyer, historian, theologian, literary scholar, and a Scot, who later produced his own anthology of popular balladry, the influential

---

[44] Ibid. 68–70.

[45] Ibid. 66. Percy is alluding to Pope's 'Epistle to Bathurst' (*Moral Essays*, III, l. 1, in *Poems of Pope*, iii. 2: *Epistles to Several Persons (Moral Essays)*, ed. F. W. Bateson (New Haven, 1951), 81). Shenstone's recommendation is in Billet 7 (*Letters*, vii. 191).

[46] *Letters*, iv. 72.   [47] Ibid., ii. 79.

Ancient Scotish Poems (1770). Percy pressed Dalrymple into service on the board of the *Reliques*, and included some twenty pieces sent by the Scotsman.[48] Yet until Percy began to entertain plans for a further volume of *Ancient English and Scotish Poems*, Dalrymple's advice was never sought as assiduously as that of the Oxbridge men.[49] Dalrymple was not sent any sheets of the *Reliques* until 12 February 1763, when he received sheets G and H of the then first volume—but his remarks to Percy already required the revision of 'Gil Morrice'. Percy remained well aware of the potential evolution of the text even at this stage.[50] Likewise, Dalrymple provided material for the preface to the spurious *Hardyknute* which Percy included in the appended 'Additions and Corrections' of volume ii.[51] Percy acted as he had done with Farmer, sending corrected proof of the glossary and preface for re-correction. Following Shenstone's sudden death, Percy now had to rely upon the collective advice of his antiquarian friends, and he grieved to Dalrymple that he felt the loss 'in every step of the work'.[52] But Percy had now adopted a clear hierarchy in his collaborative research: favouring the advice of Warton and Farmer, whose remarks were generally included in the textual apparatus; frequently sending Dalrymple material too late for his suggestions to be incorporated (they were gathered instead in supplementary notes); and concealing the entire publication from Evans.[53] It is no wonder he warned Dalrymple at the end of the year, 'When you receive a finished set, you will find innumerable alterations both in the Plan and selections.'[54]

As indicated in a letter to Farmer dated 19 June 1764, the *Reliques* was effectively completed by that date, but Percy could not abandon it without rallying his correspondents once more for further 'supplementary remarks from all my friends' as a sympotic coda to the last volume, and he arranged for Farmer to receive an advance copy for such a purpose.[55] But now other projects were queuing for attention. As early as April, Percy had circulated a form letter to his cohorts mustering them for the next campaign, his edition of the *Spectator* and *Guardian*, and he devoted considerable time during Johnson's stay in June 1764 to this project.

---

[48] Listed ibid., iv, p. xxi.   [49] Ibid., appendix 3, 169–73.   [50] Ibid. 32–3.
[51] Ibid. 45, 49.   [52] Ibid. 58, 84–5, 66, 64.   [53] Ibid. 80, 85.
[54] Ibid. 91.   [55] Ibid., ii. 75.

Evan Evans was treated instead to an account of another forth-coming Percy product, *Northern Antiquities*.[56]

Indeed, mention should be made of Percy's relationship with Evan Evans during the printing of the *Reliques*, because it intro-duces his other projects. The relationship with Evans was main-tained on a completely different footing from that of the other correspondents discussed. Percy confided solely to Evans his plans for *Specimens of the Ancient Poetry of Different Nations*, of which the Chinese poetry at the end of *Hau Kiou Choaan*, *Five Pieces of Runic Poetry*, and *The Song of Solomon* at one time comprised a part.[57] Another particular facet of Percy's scholarly association with Evans was the translation of Mallet. This was apparently greatly advanced by May 1765 and the first volume had been almost printed off, although the book did not leave the press for another five years.[58] This too was part of the ancient poetry project, and *Northern Antiquities* would include an appendix of Saxon translations, set alongside the *Edda*.[59] But conversely, Percy maintained a strict silence on the subject of ballads until 18 December 1764. Evans had certainly been sent revises by Percy, but revises of *Runic Poetry*, which was being printed between July 1762 and the following April, concurrent with the *Reliques*.[60] In fact, Percy did not seek Evans's aid with the *Reliques* until 20 March 1764, when he sent his essay 'On the Origin of the English Stage'. He requested the titles of any old metrical romances Evans had seen, for inclusion in another essay. Eventually, in December 1764 he confessed to the forthcoming *Reliques* with a great show of self-effacement:

I have for a long time (at odd hours of leisure) been concerned in printing a work, which as I never intended to own, I have been shy of mentioning to you and my other friends, tho' I have occasionally shown you small essays, that make parts of it. At length an occasion has happened that will require me to give my name to it, and therefore I venture to divulge it to you. It is, a Collection of ancient English Poems of the more popular kind, viz. Old Heroic Ballads, Songs, &c. Which, fearful lest the pub-lication should be thought slightly of by some of my graver brethren, I had determine[d] to publish without any name: but several of these old songs, being written to celebrate the ancient Earls of Northumberland,

---

[56] Ibid. 72–3; iii. 105; iv. 81–2; v. 83–6.   [57] Ibid. v. 30, 98.
[58] Ibid. 105–6.   [59] Ibid. 98.   [60] Ibid. 27, 40, 45, 46–7.

the Present Countess has taken the work under her protection, and respect to her renders it necessary for me to subjoin my name to the Dedication . . . Not intending to own it, I had unluckily not stipulated for a sufficient number of copies to give away, so that I am affraid it will not be in my power to make you a present of a set: which I hope you will excuse. Dodsley having bought the property, I have no claim to any copies of my own.[61]

He also rather shamefacedly sent Evans a parcel of proof-sheets, recommending only the essays, 'The rest will serve to light your Pipe, or hold your Tea-kettle.'[62] Percy was deliberately cultivating the image of a very different kind of scholar, and seems almost ashamed to have rescued the Folio MS from the flames. Rashly, for a man who would lose two libraries and two complete editions of unpublished books in fires, he proposed dispatching the *Reliques* to its source—not the archive, but the basket of kindling.[63] It is an oddly bathetic coda to Percy's correspondence describing the making of the *Reliques*, but does invite a survey of the other works he published during the period.

'—NOR YOUR NOTES TOO VERBOSE—'[64]

It has already been suggested that at various times Percy envisaged his works as a whole and may even have planned a magnum opus on Gothic antiquities. Many of Percy's works presented problems in printing, and some reveal his ongoing preoccupation with the production of texts. At the very least, his parallel projects had a considerable impact upon the printing of *Reliques*; in some cases, they replicated the problems of authority and media that inhabit the *Reliques*.

As early as his Chinese novel *Hau Kiou Choaan or the Pleasing History* (1761), Percy showed great interest in textual transmission and the inscription of sources, describing his manuscript in the preface, 'THE following translation was found in manuscript

---

[61] *Letters*, iv. 102–3. Percy had forgotten that he had already mentioned the work to Evans on 23 Nov. 1761 (ibid. 22).   [62] Ibid. 104.

[63] Percy's *Don Quixote* collection of Spanish romances and books cited by Cervantes was given to Louis Dutens. This library therefore escaped destruction in the Percy's Northumberland House fire, but was lost in the fire that destroyed Thomas Johnes's library in 1807 (ibid. ix. 251).   [64] Ibid. vii. 167.

. . . first written with a black-lead pencil, and afterwards more correctly over-written with ink.'[65] Percy's editorial explications were interpolated in the text, contained within brackets, and there was also, to Shenstone's dismay, an extraordinary variety of extra-textual material: a bibliography, additions and corrections, errata, a list of proverbs omitted, a list of proverbs corrected, parallels omitted, and even a handy index to his own notes. Dodsley regarded the performance with a jaded eye, and told Shenstone he would 'never own' Percy's Chinese novel.[66]

Similar preoccupations were evident in *The Matrons* (1762), which also sank without a trace. Percy claimed jauntily in his dedication that 'to compile it (short as it is) we have been obliged to ransack the mouldy volumes of Antiquity, and to take a voyage as far as China'.[67] He tried his hand at conjectural emendation in 'The Roman Matron', this time italicizing his editorial interpola-tion. *The Song of Solomon* (1764), on the other hand, followed the conventions being established in the *Reliques*: 'Such words in the Translation as are added to fill up ELLIPSES in the Original are included within inverted commas, *'thus'*.'[68]

There were also other, more practical difficulties. *Miscellaneous Pieces relating to the Chinese* (1762) suffered from Percy's over-hasty scholarship. He apologized in a supplement to the preface for overlooking Warburton's critical work in the field of alphabet development: 'It was not 'till the following sheets were printed off, that he was recommended to peruse the second volume of the DIVINE LEGATION.'[69] *Five Pieces of Runic Poetry* (1763) contained an apology too, this time for Percy's delay in printing: 'N.B. THIS LITTE [*sic*] TRACT WAS DRAWN UP FOR THE PRESS IN THE YEAR 1761: BUT THE PUBLICATION HAS BEEN DELAYED BY AN ACCIDENT.'[70] There is a hapless quality to these accidents and apologies, which is unfortu-nately a feature of the slipshod *Reliques* too. Whether Percy was scrambling to borrow and return scarce books, or simply being

---

[65] *Hau Kiou Choaan*, i, pp. ix–x, xxii (italics reversed).

[66] Tierney, 432. Tierney suggests that this refers to Percy's desire to keep the book a secret, but it seems more likely to be a reflection upon Percy's ghastly work. Dodsley had little enthusiasm for the book (see 437, 450, 453).

[67] *The Matrons* (1762), p. ii, see also 189–90, 225.

[68] *The Song of Solomon, newly translated from the Original Hebrew* (1764), p. x (italics reversed).

[69] *Miscellaneous Pieces relating to the Chinese*, i, p. A5ᵛ (italics reversed).

[70] *Runic Poetry*, p. A1ᵛ (italics reversed).

'stung in ye eye' a few days after clinching the *Reliques* deal, he seems perpetually discommoded by the discipline expected of the writer. And his awe in the face of the printed word frequently manifested itself as defensiveness. Percy's anxieties at letting go his manuscripts and revises were dramatic and disabling, and the *Reliques* can be read as one long apology for 'having bestowed any attention on a parcel of OLD BALLADS'. This is why he cultivated such a distinguished circle of correspondents and advisers, but it is also why Percy applied himself so diligently—and brilliantly—to justifying his interest in ballads with a wholesale reinvention of English literature.

The most important parallel publication was Percy's edition of Buckingham, in two octavo volumes: the first of plays and including Percy's own 'New Key to the Rehearsal', the second of poems and prose. M. G. Robinson dates the work from 28 May 1761, when it was first mentioned in a letter to Warton, and the contract with Tonson was signed two weeks later on 12 June.[71] Percy, as ever, worked quickly, involving Warton, Farmer, Dalrymple, and Tonson, as well as Edward Blakeway, Thomas Birch, Lord Royston, and his old friend Thomas Apperley. By October 1763 the printing of both volumes had almost been completed. Then, for some reason, the work foundered—and Tonson meanwhile died in 1767. The edition of Buckingham fell out of Percy's correspondence, and was forgotten for the next twenty years. Nichols took the sheets of Buckingham (and Surrey) from Tonson's warehouse, saving them from the fire that destroyed Percy's work on the *Spectator*, and made periodic—if unsuccessful—attempts to resurrect the project.

In his edition of Buckingham, Percy intended to record textual variation by means of new points. In the proof of the advertisement for the *The Chances*, a play by Beaumont and Fletcher, derived from Cervantes and adapted by Buckingham, Percy denoted Buckingham's variations by using the inverted commas he was (occasionally) employing to indicate his own interpolation and conjecture in the *Reliques*. The printed text runs:

---

[71] M. G. Robinson, 'The History of Percy's Edition of Buckingham', *Letters*, iii. 148–67. Unfortunately, Robinson compiled this essay without the advantage of materials now in Queen's and NRO.

The Duke will not always be found to have consulted harmony in his alteration of particular lines; tho' he has generally improved the sense. To enable the Reader to form a judgment of this we have distinguished <his> corrections by inserted commas (') and shall give some of the original readings at the end.[72]

Percy revised this, deleting 'his' and adding '∧⌈every⌉addition<s>, omission<s> <or> ⌈and⌉ <&> correction<s>'. An autograph note was also added, which read:

We have taken yet still greater liberties: We have sometimes ⌈brought⌉ <fetched> back the original reading where either thro' the inattention of the Duke, or the carelessness of his Printer, a less proper one had got into its place. Sometimes we have restored a word wanting to complete the harmony of the line: and have once or twice ventured on a conjectural emendation: All this will be found included in brackets {}.[73]

This advertisement was further refined, and a later printed revise reads:

N.B. In the foregoing play, we have included within inverted commas ('') such words as the Duke has either added of his own, or substituted instead of those of his Author: which last will be found in the following list, except when they were of an inconvenient length. To slighter altera-tions we have only prefixed a single comma ('): And have subjoined that, or a similar mark (') where any passage of the original is omitted.

We have taken yet still greater liberties; we have sometimes brought back the original reading, where either thro' the inattention of the Duke or the carelessness of his printer a less proper one had got into its place. Sometimes we have restored a word wanting to complete the harmony of the verse, and have once or twice ventured on a conjectural emendation. All these will be found included in brackets [].[74]

In a sense, Percy's textual criticism was within a tradition of dramatic editing. Michael Dobson indicates that playwrights such as Colley Cibber used italics to distinguish Shakespeare's lines from the hand of the modern, which was preceded by a single inverted comma (').[75] But one can see from the above passage that Percy was in fact obscuring his own role in the transmission of the

---

[72] NRO, E(S)1210, fo. 12ʳ (italics reversed).
[73] See for example, NRO, E(S)1224, i, fo. Q1ᵛ.
[74] NRO, E(S)1224, p. 226 (italics reversed).
[75] Michael Dobson, *The Making of the National Poet: Shakespeare, Adaptation, and Authorship, 1660–1769* (Oxford, 1992), 99–100.

text, abdicating his own editorial diacritics to Buckingham. Note too the prominent figure of the careless printer hanging over these passages like a nightmare. Percy's scholarship and research was becoming a nervous shuffling of proofs and revises. This is also evident in the endnote to 'Political Reflections on a Poem called Absolon and Achitophel', where the whole practice of correcting proofs becomes a characteristic feature of literary-antiquarianism:

** The preceding Poem is so intolerably dull and stupid, so deficient not only in poetical merit, but even in sense, and grammar, that after it had gone thro' the press, and had been only admitted among the DOUBTFUL or SPURIOUS PIECES, the Editor was inclined to cancel the sheet and throw it out, had it not been suggested to him that in such a collection as this, it might be of use to shew the spirit of the times wherein it was published, both as to the extent of party rage, and inferiority of taste, which could admit of such wretched bad writing. That the DUKE OF BUCKINGHAM could not have had the smallest share in its composition, a slight perusal will convince the most inattentive Reader.[76]

Of course, one is also reminded of Shenstone's warning not to admit pieces into the *Reliques* which had only antiquarian merit. But the Buckingham edition was another outlet for Percy's incorrigible habits.

Of particular interest among the remains of Percy's Buckingham researches is a little autograph booklet titled 'List of plays read with a view to compose a Key to Rehearsal, 1761' and constructed from verso scraps of draft letters. At least one is the fragment of a letter to Shenstone (published here for the first time). The renewed emphasis on the simplicity of the *Reliques* fits perfectly with the amplification of space in the Buckingham corrections: 'perhaps upon the whole it may be the safest & most profitable way to print <????> ∧ ⌈the book⌉ in it's original simplicity—But I leave the matter entirely to your own choice & determination.'[77] Buckingham and the *Reliques* intersected perfectly.

The forwardness of the Buckingham edition also shows Percy's sensitivity to the layout of the page. Again, Shenstone had emphasized the necessity of whitespace, and Percy did take this advice when correcting the Buckingham, marking it up in red: 'Leave handsome space between the Title and the first Line of Text . . .

---

[76] NRO, E(S)1215, p. 249 (italics reversed).   [77] NRO, E(S)1211, fo. 76ʳ.

Leave some space here ... Leave some space here.'[78] Percy's edition of Surrey (*Tottel's Miscellany*), for which he exchanged contracts with Tonson on 24 March 1763 (not sent to the press until 1766), also demonstrates a deep concern to balance the visual design of the printed page: 'I want to see how the Current title would look with this Addition ... Let me see how this Current Title w[d]. look. Let all the other Pages remain unaltered, till I have considered which to adopt ... Run such a small Ornam[t]. as this along. In Italicks of the same Size as the Title in Page {1} Sheet c.'[79]

The editions of Buckingham and Surrey both demonstrate the bad habits and intense attention to minute particularities Percy was cultivating during the chaotic and wholesale correction of sheets for the *Reliques*. The press was almost treated as an ephemeral medium: the proofs were merely suggestions, the revises guidelines, and sheets were frequently rejected and re-designed.[80] There was no immediate sense that the printed copy carried authority. But it was the issue of authority that became traumatic in the Buckingham edition, and eventually destroyed it. Percy indicated Buckingham's own revisions to his sources by means of such editorial diacritics as inverted commas, and so Percy had to find a different set of meta-marks to distinguish his own editorial voice. This seriously threatened to confuse the proofs. Percy was required to make his typographic intentions absolutely clear to the printer: 'Let the Preface be printed in Roman Types of the same size as the rest. Let no part be printed in Italics nor any capital Letters be retained except where I have expressly appointed them by this mark (=) serving only at the beginning of periods &c.'[81]

He further highlighted these instructions by writing them in red, picking out the '(=)' in black. Buckingham's authorial intention was pegged out with obtrusive hammers and nails, but Percy's editorial intervention became almost invisible. The synoptic text

---

[78] NRO, E(S)1211, fo. 13.

[79] Bodl., Don. d 8, 2, 4, 31; see also *Letters*, ii. 179 n. Cleanth Brooks gives an account of the work as an appendix to his edition of the Percy–Farmer correspondence.

[80] The first printing of 'A Ballad of Luther, the Pope, a Cardinal, and a Husband-man' was rejected because the text needed to be dropped down by $\frac{1}{2}$" to allow sufficient space for an engraving; this resulted in the loss of a footnote (sheets interleaved in Queen's, Percy 505). [81] NRO, E(S)1216, fo. 26[v].

at once demonstrated the consummate skill of the editor able to compile such a work, but also disguised the editorial decisions being made beneath the gradients of authorial activity. In the edition of Buckingham, Percy was 'loading the text with quotation marks, with quotation marks within quotation marks, with italics, with square brackets, with pictographic gestures . . .', and the edition was lost amid a confusion of framing devices. The frames collapsed into each other, the edition was never, and could never, be printed. As Derrida suggests in *The Truth in Painting*, the frame is initially disclosed as a lack in the work, as its limit. It is a boundary, and the discourse of aesthetics is structured on the limit between the work (*ergon*) and the frame or border (*parergon*). In other words, criticism begins where the work finishes, where it recognizes the frame. So the frame is both part of the work and beyond the work, or rather, 'A parergon comes against, beside, and in addition to the *ergon*, the work done. . . . Neither simply outside nor simply inside.'[82] The continual crossing and recrossing, plotting and replotting, of this border in Percy's editorial frames produced a Chinese-box effect, which in the case of Buckingham cursed the book never to be completed: the printer became addled between the notes he was supposed to print, and the messages sent by Percy to clarify the instructions. But the *Reliques* was completed and published, and was held together by a labyrinthine and arcane architecture of extra-textual passages and critical culs-de-sac (introductions, headnotes, footnotes, endnotes, digressions, essays, glossaries, addenda, errata). The book of ballads was animated by sublime complexity and certainly not characterized by pastoral simplicity.[83] It emphasized the existence of an English past that was aesthetically strange and exotic—and in doing so it inspired the tortuous passages of the Gothic novel.

The Buckingham and Surrey editions were neglected by Percy as a direct result of Tonson's death in 1767, but work continued intermittently for the next forty years. Percy's friend and adoptive kinsman John Nichols took charge of the sheets, and urged Percy to complete the editions, but he was elderly and worked agoniz-

---

[82] Derrida, *The Truth in Painting*, 2, 54.
[83] Derrida (ibid). notes too that '*Parergon* also means the exceptional, the strange, the extraordinary' (58).

ingly slowly. On 8 February 1808, Nichols's warehouse burnt to the ground and the sheets of both editions were consumed.

'AND TAKE GREAT CARE WHAT YOU ADMIT'[84]

The press is a constant reminder of linear time.[85] The last chapter described in detail how Percy used his abstract and 'First Draft' to introduce a linear order to his materials. As suggested there, this organization was in part imposed retrospectively, once printing was under way. The following section will show conclusively that Percy's plans to arrange the *Reliques* did not cease when printing commenced, but continued through copies, proofs, and revises. Printing merely exacerbated the problems of production.

Scattered throughout the Harvard Percy Papers are several fair transcripts which represent a new phase in ordering the *Reliques*. They are copies made for the press and often include messages to the printer, prefatory material, and textual notes. Percy headed these copies with heavy roman numerals, giving a revised order as they were sent to the press, as upper-case roman numerals were used to number each piece in the finished printed work. These numerals were therefore part of the copy (the frame), and illustrate that Percy's transcripts were now interfacing with the printed proofs. In the merging of modes of production the *Reliques* was born, and the order which was gradually yet inevitably being imposed by the press was determining the very presentation of his manuscripts.

This scheme for printing the *Reliques*, the 'Copy Draft', is reconstructed in Appendix VIII. Again, this sequence is incomplete, but it is important for demonstrating at least one further stage in arranging the pieces in manuscript. Reconstructing the order, however, is not simply a matter of following the roman numerals. Volume and book number are only mentioned in a few cases, and pieces were numbered for each individual book of the *Reliques* rather than by volume, as they had been for the abstract and 'First Draft'. The difficulty therefore is that a piece like 'The Parting' from *Prince d'Amour*, while clearly numbered 'XIV', may have been intended for any of three books in any of three

[84] *Letters*, vii. 167.   [85] Eisenstein, *The Printing Press*, i. 186–7.

volumes. Consequently, the positioning of each piece has been compared with early arrangements, the index, and the 'First Draft', as well as later versions, the printed proofs, and first edition. 'The Parting' was never published, but it did appear as 'V.1.49' in the abstract. It is included below in the third volume because the volume order was reversed for the 'First Draft', which is the arrangement which influenced the order of the work sent for proofs (the stage currently under discussion), before the volumes were again reversed just prior to publication.

From internal evidence too, it seems likely that 'The Parting' was at some stage destined for the third printed volume. An interesting feature of these drafts is their thematic arrangement. The previous chapters have examined Percy's attempts to structure his material, and his enthusiastic embrace of that word favoured by both Pepys and Johnson, 'promiscuous'. Yet Percy maintained his quest for the Holy Grail of order, and the arrangement described below in fact represents a much more coherent plan than that eventually achieved. As printing began, Percy was able to derive a clear series from his 'first draft', itself drawn up to facilitate the printing plan. Yet evidently this series was deemed a failure. It was revised, in some books beyond recognition, for the trial issue (the Farmer–Douce and Percy–Darby copies), and again before eventual publication. Several pieces were rejected from this copy draft too, including two fabulous magical narratives: 'The seven Champions of Christendome' and 'The Frier and the Boy' (about Roger Bacon and his curious brazen head).[86]

As Appendix VIII shows, however, this arrangement is startling. The penultimate arrangement of the *Reliques* includes Percy's Scotticized 'O Nancy' (i. 3. XIX). 'O Nancy' had first been published in Dodsley's *Collection* in 1758, and the copy listed here is headed with the following introductory comment: 'A copy of this song, divested of its Scotticisms, <was> is inserted in the VIth Vol. of Dodsley's Miscellany Poems. It is here printed as it was first written.'[87] It is indisputedly intended as printer's copy, and the verso is moreover docketed in pencil 'Copy of Old Ballads. Vol. 1. Book 3^d.' The likelihood that Percy intended 'O Nancy' for the *Reliques* is also supported by another auto-

---

[86] Parts of 'The seven Champions of Christendom' were cannibalized for 'St. George for England' (iii. 286–306).   [87] Houghton, bMS Eng. 893 (257B).

graph copy, sent by Percy to Shenstone and forwarded by him to
John Macgowan in December 1761. Shenstone had originally
supported publication of the 'Song' in Dodsley's *Collection*, and
now Percy requested him to 'add some Scotticisms', while
Shenstone requested Macgowan's opinion concerning the quality
of the imitation.[88] This would certainly be consistent with Percy's
practice in soliciting Shenstone's aid described in the first
chapter.[89] Even Percy's standby love song became a text for
corporate re-editing. But there is another major surprise in this
arrangement. It is not a pattern for two volumes, or even three: it
is a four-volume *Reliques*. As early as 1764, and with Shenstone
now a year in his grave, Percy was evidently considering materials
for a fourth volume.[90]

The most radical and far-reaching of Percy's changes was made
apparently on the spur of the moment when printing had almost
been completed. Percy had no dedicatee. Before discovering they
held such apparently divergent views on the book, Percy had
intended to dedicate the work to Shenstone; but now Shenstone
was dead, and even Percy must have realized that a posthumous
dedication would have been at best hypocritical, at worst an
insult. (Perhaps Robert Dodsley, one of Shenstone's executors
and now doubly suspicious of the *Reliques*, had also intimated
that Shenstone should not be figured too prominently in the
book.) So, after Shenstone's death early in 1763, Percy drafted a
dedication to a new Northumberland: 'To His | Excellency | The
Earl of Northumberland | Lord Lieutenant of Ireland | &c | these
Volumes | (whose humble aim is to preserve a few ancient pieces
written to celebrate the house of Percy: which we see revived in our
time with so much splendour) | are | most respectfully | presented
by | The Editor.'[91] This draft is an empty and formulaic affair
(confirming Percy's opinion that 'Dedication is a paultry kind of
writing') and in the trope of reluctant authorship Percy abdicates
his editorial authority to the 'authenticity' of social order.[92] But
it clearly shows that Percy had already noticed his collection

[88] Houghton, Autograph file (copy).
[89] G. L. Kittredge, 'Percy and his Nancy', in *Manly Anniversary Studies in Language
and Literature* (Chicago, 1923), 204–18.   [90] See *Reliques* (1996), i. 49–52.
[91] Bodl., MS Percy c 4, fo. 26. Grenville appointed Hugh Smithson Lord Lieutenant
in 1763, and he became Duke of Northumberland in 1766, having been Earl since
1750.   [92] *Letters*, vii. 102.

could be construed as a celebration of the Northumberlands. However, the Earl Hugh Smithson had married into the family. He was not of the old blood. Percy turned his attentions to his wife the Countess. In April 1764, Elizabeth Northumberland accepted Percy's belated invitation to receive the dedication of the *Reliques*.[93]

Her acceptance had two immediate implications for the book. First, Percy had to prepare the promised dedication. It is an episode that has achieved a certain notoriety, but it may be that the composition of the dedication to the Countess of Northumberland has eclipsed something more profound. The reassessment of Percy's dedication began in 1791, when James Boswell inadvertently disclosed that in fact Samuel Johnson had composed it, and in 1800 Percy finally admitted to Robert Anderson that it owed its 'finest strokes' to that illustrious writer.[94] But perhaps its significance in the Johnson canon is more than mere literary jobbing.

Before his summer spent at Percy's vicarage in 1764, Johnson was in great distress. He had become 'entirely averse to society' and was in a 'deplorable state, sighing, groaning, talking to himself, and restlessly walking from room to room'. He felt that 'A kind of strange oblivion has overspread me', was utterly morbid and viciously self-critical of his indolence and negligence.[95] He even purchased a lock and fetters to restrain himself in the event of the feared descent into madness. He was profoundly depressed, and Percy, gallantly and magnanimously, invited him to spend the summer in the country. At a single day's notice, Samuel Johnson, his blind confidante Anna Williams, and his servant Francis Barber arrived in Easton Maudit for an eight-week stay. Boswell attributes Johnson's recovery to the care of Mrs Thrale, administered the following year in London, but Percy's immediate generosity and hospitality may well have saved Johnson from the lock and fetters. Johnson idled in the garden, waited on Mrs Percy, played with the children, read romances, and held forth at Percy's modest dinner parties. He worked too, correcting his Shakespeare proofs to

---

[93] She wrote from Dublin on 10 Apr., and Percy received her acceptance on 29 Apr. 1764 (BL, Add. MS 32334, fo. 2).

[94] *Boswell's Life*, iv. 555–6; *Letters*, ix. 26; Allen T. Hazen, *Samuel Johnson's Prefaces and Dedications* (Yale, 1937), 158–68.

[95] *Boswell's Life*, i. 482–3. See Walter Jackson Bate, *Samuel Johnson* (1984), 372.

answer Percy's lexicographical queries for the *Reliques* glossary, and would certainly have cast an eye over Percy's work.

On 13 August 1764, Percy noted in his journal, 'Preparing dedication of old Ballads'.[96] Johnson was repaying the hospitality and concern of his friend with a dedication that would help to secure Percy's own future, and it is likely that Johnson made a more culturally resonant contribution. The dedication is particularly notable for its phrase 'reliques of antiquity' (i, pp. vi–vii). Percy habitually (and confusingly) referred to his work as *A Collection of Old Ballads* (or occasionally *A Collection of ancient Ballads*). It is not known from where he chose the word 'relique' but he used it in translating 'The Battle of Brunanburh' from the *Anglo-Saxon Chronicle*, c.1762–3, and on 31 December 1763 wrote to Evan Evans, 'I conceive a very favourable idea of the merit of your ancient bards: and should be sorry to have their precious relicks swallowed up and lost in the gulph of time.'[97] On 2 June 1764, Percy wrote to Dalrymple, 'I think to intitle my Book "Reliques of Ancient Poetry: Consisting of old heroic ballads, songs, and other compositions of our earlier poets; chiefly of the Lyric Kind".'[98] Percy was writing from London, discussing the implications of the dedication with Dodsley and arranging Johnson's visit to Easton Maudit (he arrived on 25 June); it was conceivably Johnson who proposed the word 'Reliques' at this moment.

Johnson had defined 'relick' in his *Dictionary* of 1755 as:

1. That which remains; that which is left after the loss or decay of the rest.
2. It is often taken for the body deserted by the soul.
3. That which is kept in memory of another, with a kind of religious veneration.

He gave ten examples, taken mainly from Shakespeare, Milton, and Dryden, and listed 'relique' as the French derivation— although it was the preferred spelling of Spenser and Milton. 'Relique' had connotations of the court and the church, chivalry

---

and valour, antiquarianism and history, life and death memorials, and fragments and ruins. But it also fittingly described the remnants of the body of English poetry deserted by the modern poet, retained in memory as a function of nostalgia, of noumenal import. Simply, the word focused the values and status of the ancient English minstrels. And it arose from a dedication, perfectly pitched to win patronage, that was offered in thanks by a writer who believed he had narrowly escaped madness, to the friend who had saved him.

Intriguingly, Percy was not content to leave the dedication as it had been drafted by Johnson. He offered it to Dalrymple on 23 October, 'which I beg the favour of you to examine and wherever you think requisite to correct and alter', and at the eleventh hour (10 November) Percy desired Farmer's opinion.[99] Apparently it was still to be taken up by Johnson and once more revised before being presented to the Countess on 22 November 1764: 'I have made no alteration in it yet', he told Farmer, 'because I shall reserve your remarks and those of many other friends, till I consult my oracle, JOHNSON.'[100]

It seems unlikely that Percy should treat a Johnsonian dedication so lightly, and in fact of all Percy's texts the dedication shows probably the least variation between the two versions extant. Although it was printed in its entirety twice, the text was certainly settled by the time Dalrymple received the sheet at the end of October. The earlier printing of the dedication differs from that issued in point of typography only: it is set in a small fount and names are not capitalized, which gives the whole piece a mean look.[101] So although there was time to reset the whole text in a prouder typeface, Percy managed to restrain himself from making further changes. Johnson presumably checked the piece again a few months later when Percy was in London for the launch. He spent the first two days of this visit, 13–14 November, with Johnson, and these dates concur with the message sent to Farmer on the tenth. It does seem appropriate that Johnson, who first proposed editing a selection from the Folio MS, should have put the seal on the printed *Reliques*, although Percy's enthusiasm for Johnson's contribution strangely never warmed: he frantically

---

[99] *Letters*, v. 88–9.   [100] Ibid., ii. 79.
[101] Reprinted in Carver, ii. 190–216.

instructed Farmer to send any revisions straight to Dodsley's shop.[102]

There was, however, a far more serious implication in dedicating the *Reliques* to the Countess. The ballads had almost been printed off by April, and although printing the supplementary essays, glossaries, and so forth had not yet commenced, the book was nine-tenths finished.[103] Several of the ballads in the third volume comprised a group honouring the ancient Percys: 'The Battle of Otterbourne', 'The Rising in the North', Skelton's elegy on Henry Percy, the fourth Earl, and of course two versions of 'Chevy-Chase',

> The Persé owt of Northombarlande,
>   And a vowe to God mayd he,
> That he wolde hunte in the mountayns
>   Off Chyviat within dayes thre,
> In the mauger of doughtè Dogles,
>   And all that ever with him be. (i. 4)

Now that the *Reliques* was dedicated to a Northumberland, Percy realized that the tales of Percys' renown required more prominence. He could not cancel and reprint whole volumes, but he could reverse the volume order, which would place 'Chevy-Chase' at the head of the opening series, and ensure that the first volume was characterized by Northumbriana. This would necessitate cancelling title-pages and any references to the original order which might make his revision look opportunistic (which it undoubtedly was). Moreover, now the work was dedicated to a lady, he also had to castrate anything indecorous from the anthology. As he described the situation to Dalrymple, 'After a lady had accepted of the Book I was obliged to cancel all the more indelicate pieces and substitute others more inoffensive.'[104]

There were, then, two distinct stages in cancellation.[105] Leaves had been occasionally cancelled during the first two and a half

---

[102] Davis (1989), 128; *Letters*, ii. 80.
[103] 'Completed the ballad & Preface of yᵉ rising in the North', 14 May 1764 (BL, Add. MS 32336, fo. 49ᵛ).   [104] *Letters*, iv. 91–2.
[105] The printing of the *Reliques* has been described by several bibliographers: nearly all the cancellanda of the 1st edn. are extant. See A. N. L. Munby, 'Cancels in Percy's "Reliques"', *TLS* (31 Oct. 1936), 892; Powell responded to Munby in *TLS* (7 Nov. 1936), 908; and David A. Randall, 'Percy's *Reliques* and its Cancel Leaves', *New Colophon*, 1 (1948), 404–7.

years of printing as the work gradually evolved and Percy wished to reconsider material; leaves were also cancelled in the final stages of printing to make it a fitting gift for the Countess of Northumberland. Using Farmer–Douce, Percy–Darby, and copies from Quaritch and Chicago, we have an almost complete picture of the cancellations in the *Reliques*.[106] A good example of the initial stage of cancellation is E5 (volume iii), the detailed introduction to 'King Estmere', which discussed the ancient English minstrels. This digression was made redundant by Percy's later (and crucial) decision to write an essay on the subject, just as the first version of the preface subsequently required rewriting. The best example of the latter case is the cancellation of U2.3.4.5.6.7 (volume ii). This was originally occupied by the ripe verse on eating and farting, 'Cock Lorrel's Treat', and the associated sequence of loose songs, 'The Moral uses of Tobacco' and 'Old Simon the King'. Percy thought he could replace 'Cock Lorrel's Treat' with the more decorous 'The Heir of Linne', but, finding that it was significantly longer than the original song, decided to drop the other two pieces as well to make room. Minor changes, such as B1, 3 ('The Boy and the Mantle'), were necessitated by the change in volume order. This piece originally commenced volume i and so was headed 'SERIES THE FIRST', which had to be revised to 'SERIES THE THIRD'. Predictably, when certain passages had to be rewritten as a direct result of the volume change, Percy usually took advantage of these opportunities to tinker further with the text. In 'The Boy and the Mantle', he also noticed that a further line needed refining. B3 was cancelled because of line 70. The cancellandum reads,

All above the buttoucke

the cancellans,

'Before all the rout"

Note that the editorial marks to indicate Percy's emendation were not properly matched. The number of compositorial errors introduced at this stage suggest that Percy may not have proof-read the cancellantia.[107]

---

[106] See Powell, 'Percy's Reliques', and Carver, *passim*. Note that P3 was cancelled twice; the first cancel is in this copy, the second cancel is in the 1st edn.

[107] See Carver, i. 10–116.

There is some irony in the cancellation of Y2, the last page of volume iii (as it was by then). This was the result of having to retitle the glossary 'VOLUME THE THIRD', but the recto of Y2 contained the concluding stanzas of Shenstone's version of 'The Boy and the Mantle'. The inclusion of Shenstone's 'The Boy and the Mantle', 'AS REVISED AND ALTERED BY A MODERN HAND', had enabled Percy to give a reasonably accurate text of the Folio MS version of the ballad at the beginning of the volume (the aforementioned sheet B). The latter version had been printed off at Shenstone's death, but now Percy could not resist meddling. At the outset of the volume he had already compromised the Folio MS text by rewriting an offensive line; he now omitted the final stanza of Shenstone's version at the end. Shenstone's influence was symbolically curtailed.[108]

The two stages of cancellation meant that altogether fifteen printed pieces were removed from the *Reliques* before it was presented to the Countess. In the main, these changes reflect Percy's attempts to remove the obscene, restore the chaste and moral, and refine the historical narratives of old English ballads (see Appendix IX). Percy was scrupulous. He cancelled 'Verses by K. James I.', only to restore an exact facsimile of the text: the verses preceded 'Cock Lorrel's Treat', and he thought it prudent to remove the conspicuous catchword 'COCK'. Even the only slightly risqué 'Jolly Beggar' was replaced with a medieval moral allegory, 'The Tower of Doctrine'. These changes queered his imaginary history. The last volume was now filled with ballads of legendary Britain, while the first charted medieval national history. But such was Percy's fortune—or genius—that very early on he had eschewed a strict chronology. The *Reliques* was woven from threads and thematic sequences that placed chronology second to tradition, and so the reversal tended to deepen the enigma of Gothic antiquities, rather than wrecking its integrity. In fact, the most telling consequence was to shift the status of the minstrels from an enchanted role of bardic fabling to the courtly position of cultural legislators—which was all to Percy's good.

Yet it is clear from other extant printed pages that, as indicated

---

[108] For details of 'Edom o' Gordon' cancels see Falconer and Carver. Carver establishes from the stations of 'Edom o' Gordon' that the decision to reverse the volume order was taken between 5 and 23 Apr. 1764 (i. 67–8).

above, Percy rewrote revises substantially. The most interesting additions to the Percy–Darby volume are the sheets and leaves inserted between the concluding poem, Shenstone's revised 'The Boy and the Mantle', and the glossary. Percy was careful to present these pages as a credible appendix to the volume. Judith Carver bases a lot of her research on these early texts: they demonstrate, for example, that the whole of the first sheet to be printed, sheet B ('The Boy and the Mantle' and half of 'The Marriage of Sir Gawaine'), was reset after Percy decided to rewrite the fragmentary 'Marriage' to create a finished ballad. This decision was, as Carver says, 'momentous', because it established almost at the outset of printing that the anthology would consist of polished verses rather than antiquarian detritus.[109] For his testimonial copy of the *Reliques* (Percy–Darby), Percy completed the original version of the 'Marriage' in manuscript, once again demonstrating that he could present accurate transcripts of Folio MS material. For example, Percy's manuscript transcription of lines 190–3 reads,

> Sir Kay kissed that lady bright
> Standing upon his feete;
> He swore, as he was a trew knight,
> The spice was never soe sweete[110]

The Folio MS reads,

> Sr Kay kissed that lady bright,
> standing vpon his ffeete;
> he swore, as he was trew knight,
> the spice was neuer soe sweete.[111]

Percy regularized 'u/v' and 'ff', and expanded the contraction 'S^r', but he retained the archaic orthography. He clarified line 192 by adding the indefinite article 'a'. The version that eventually appeared in the issued *Reliques*, however, was altered to such an extent that there is no comparable stanza or even a comparable episode—Kay never gets a chance to kiss the erstwhile 'lothlye ladye'.

The intrusive marks of editorial interpolation (") were, further-

---

[109] Carver, i. 44.   [110] Percy–Darby, i, interpolated 22.
[111] Hales and Furnivall, i. 118 (corrected).

more, almost entirely absent in Percy's first printing and transcription, and he even faithfully indicated lacunae:

When * * *
* * * * * * * * *

Nine or ten stanzas wanting.
* * * * * * * * *

The accuracy of this piece is actually fraught with more irony. Ritson's famous attack on Percy caused the original fragment to be added to the succeeding (fourth) edition of the *Reliques*. In other words, the scraps and cancellenda were retained in the Percy–Darby copy for over three decades before they were directly responsible for parts of the last lifetime edition. The layout in 1794 was very much as it had been originally designed, and the verse quoted above was printed with absolute accuracy:

Sr Kay kissed that lady bright,
standing vpon his ffeete
he swore as he was trew knight
the spice was neuer soe sweete[112]

The only changes Percy made were in lineation and punctuation.

There is a third thread in the 'Marriage' episode which underlines one of my persistent points. The Folio MS was only quoted to authenticate texts in extratextual introductions and footnotes. Its influence was little felt in the texts as they were actually printed. Printing was already under way before Percy decided to retire the Folio MS from the *Reliques*, and from that moment it was paraded more as a token reference than as an absolute textual authority. The preface too was rewritten. Originally it sandwiched a brisk discussion of the minstrels between the more usual prefatory material of sources and acknowledgements. The account of the minstrels in the preface was extracted and formed the meat of the longer essay.[113]

Finally, on what may be gleaned from the Percy–Darby copy. Percy recorded many marginal notes attributing minor revisions to Shenstone, Farmer, Warton, and Dalrymple. The corporate nature of the *Reliques* stands out in the working copy.[114] For example, a

---

[112] *Reliques* (1794), iii. 357.   [113] See Carver, i. 118–23.
[114] Farmer's notes: i. 28, 87, 147; Dalrymple's notes: i. 77, 93, 132, interpolated 107; all references ascribed to Warton in this volume were derived by Percy from the 2nd edn. of the *Observations* (1762).

revision by Shenstone to 'The King and the Miller of Mansfield', part the second, was noted for line 49, 'Tushe, sir John, quoth his wife, never here frett nor frowne'. Shenstone proposed, 'why sh^d. you fret or frown?'[115] Shenstone's revision, suitably archaicized by Percy, was incorporated (although it was not attributed) in the second and subsequent editions: 'Tushe, sir John, quoth his wife, why should you frett or frowne?'[116]

We have seen that Percy produced eclectic texts, miscellaneously compiled from the versions he had available to him, silently corrected, and frequently emended. But very few examples of final printer's copy have survived: a leaf of 'The King of Scots and Andrew Browne', and the copy of 'Adam Bell, Clym of the Clough, and William of Cloudesly'. Both of these were sent by Percy to the printer.[117] 'The King of Scots and Andrew Browne' is a piece of stray copy, consisting of lines 69–117 (end), and bears the scars of the printing house in the printer's note on pagination and its overall dirty and tattered state. It was perhaps retrieved by Percy during a visit to London. As part of sheets N–O of the second volume, this ballad would have been printed in late 1763 or early 1764. 'Adam Bell' (sheets K–L of volume i, printed as volume iii) would have been printed in 1764. This is a much cleaner copy, with very little to indicate that it was used for printing except two page numbers added in the same hand as 'Andrew Browne'. Each is signed with a different press-figure, indicating that two different printing teams (out of a probable total of five) were employed on these two pieces. These examples enable us to appreciate for the first time the influence that the printer, probably John Hughs, exercised upon the text of the *Reliques*.

John Hughs was 'for many years an eminent and worthy Printer; and ranked very high in his profession. From his press almost the whole of the valuable and numerous publications of the

---

[115] Percy–Darby, i. 187.   [116] *Reliques* (1767), iii. 187.

[117] 'The King of Scots and Andrew Browne' (Houghton, bMS Eng. 893 (150); ii. 204–9); 'Adam Bell, Clym of the Clough, and William of Cloudesly' (BL, Add. MS 39547, fos. 54–77, taken from Garrick's collection; i. 129–60). Probably the transcript of 'Cock Lorrel's Treat' (Houghton, bMS Eng. 893 (165)) was also returned from the press, as was a transcript of 'The dying shepherdess' (Houghton, bMS Eng. 893 (163)), both cancelled before the 1st edn. was issued. There is also a fragment of an early version of the introduction and first four lines of 'A Sonnet by the Earl of Rivers' (BL, Add. MS 32330, fo. 69; ii. 43–4).

Dodsleys were produced.'[118] He is generally held to have published the *Reliques*.[119] He was employed by the Dodsleys for most of their publications, and indeed had already printed Percy's rambling *Hau Kiou Choaan*. Dodsley took Percy to Hughs's shop on 23 May 1761, the day after the contract for the *Reliques* was finalized. Carver problematizes Percy's relationship with Hughs, noting that Percy referred to Hughs in his journal only this once and that his dealings with other printers like Allen, Reeves, and Rivington continued throughout the printing of the *Reliques*. She seems, however, reluctant to accept her own fairly conclusive evidence in identifying Hughs's ornaments in Percy's work. Percy's own silence on the subject of his printer, only ever ominously referred to as 'the printer' in correspondence, is certainly uncharacteristic, but Percy probably mediated all his dealings through Dodsley. Other doubts have been aired above: for example, Shenstone seems not to have been familiar with Percy's printer, and so more conclusive evidence is required.

Hughs (or whoever the printer was) employed five presses or teams (numbered 1–5) and conclusions on their work can be drawn from examining the *Reliques*. Hughs seems to have arranged pieces for the convenience of the press. 'Adam Bell', for example, fills two whole sheets—which dictated the length of introduction Percy was permitted, or required, to provide.

The printing of 'The King of Scots and Andrew Browne' (team 1) displays both the habits of the printer and Percy's assumptions regarding accidentals (capitalization, italicization, punctuation, spelling).[120] It has already been shown that Percy usually neglected to transcribe punctuation, either omitting it completely or sketching in his own diacritics. Was he therefore prepared to leave it to the discretion of printers' conventions, or did he insist upon it in copy or proof correction? Indeed, the copy-text of 'The King of Scots and Andrew Browne' differs from the printed text to an enormous degree. Percy seems to have been writing shorthand for the press. The very first lines of copy show his intentions clearly:

---

[118] *Anecdotes*, v. 35.
[119] Powell, 'Percy's Reliques', 117; Davis (1989), 77, 109–10.
[120] W. W. Greg, 'The Rationale of Copy-Text', in *Collected Papers*, ed. J. C. Maxwell (Oxford, 1966), 374–91.

> My moth^r. banished O extreame,
> Unhappy fate & bitter bayne:

which by the revise (N8, uncancelled) are

> My mother banished, O extreame!
> Unhappy fate and bitter bayne!

This example shows that Percy expected the printer to expand his contractions ('moth^r.', '&') and punctuate as he saw fit, but follow any archaic or unusual spellings ('extreame', 'bayne'). Further lines show that the printer was responsible for modernizing capitalization—'Treason' in manuscript became 'treason' in print. Percy's lineation was followed, but capitals were in fact reserved for proper nouns—in line 102, 'The Earle Mourton' became 'The earle Mourton'—or for words commencing lines, which was not always the case in Percy's transcript. His text was systematically regularized. The footnote on page 209 (O1^r) was recorded as a marginal note by Percy, and the printer followed his underlining by italicizing. Italics in the *Reliques* were only ever used to distinguish notes from text; nowhere did they appear as part of the text of a piece to underline proper nouns.

A very interesting revision occurs at the top of page 209 (O1^r), line 89. The copy follows the source,

> Whereat they me<a>nt to sell the king,

whereas the printed sheet shows editorial revision,

> 'Another time' to sell the king

presumably altered by Percy in proof.

Also noteworthy is a note deleted in transcript by Percy. This gives the author (W. Elderton), imprint, source (Antiquarian Society call number), and typeface ('B.L.' fancily inscribed by Percy in black-letter script). All of this information was included in the introduction printed for the *Reliques* version, but its presence at the end of this transcript suggests that Percy was using the very copy he had made in the library of the Antiquarian Society, rather than bothering to retranscribe it. No other transcript of 'The King of Scots and Andrew Browne' in Percy's hand is extant (which may explain why he went to some lengths to retrieve it) although an incomplete fragment does appear in the Folio MS (ii. 265–8). The copy sent to Hughs, then, was ostensibly an accurate copy, but it was significantly altered in the printing shop.

'Adam Bell' (printed by team 4) is a much neater amanuensis transcript from Garrick's collection of plays (volume K. X), collated with a copy from Pepys's *Vulgaria*, and corrected from a Copland text and the Folio MS. Percy's revisions are written over the amanuensis's text: he punctuates the unpunctuated draft, and lists textual variations in the margin. Percy notes that 'The Introduction shall be sent in a future Post', copies out the first stanza to indicate indentation, and asks for spacing between the three parts of the ballad. The printing is extremely faithful, the only apparent divergences being the expansion of contractions and abbreviations, such as the ampersand.

A few more examples of Percy's rapid, shorthand technique are worth quoting. It seems very likely that Percy was prepared to send his sole transcript of 'The King of Scots and Andrew Browne' to the printer. Later, he would tear pages from the Folio MS rather than be troubled with transcribing. (The most criminal example of this has resulted in the loss of 'King Estmere'.[121]) Harvard also has what appears to be copy for 'The Seven Champions of Christendome', which was proposed for the *Reliques*, but never printed.[122] Percy again cut corners: he simply tore the relevant pages out of *A Collection of Old Ballads* and lightly revised them. Of particular interest is the fair transcript and printed text of 'On Saint Thomas a Becket'. This transcript was destined for the printer: Percy added a pencil note to the recto, 'PS I shall send a short Introduction hereafter by the Post.'[123] It was consequently set with a modest space between title and text to allow the introduction to be inserted. A similar example is the fair transcript 'Robin Hood and Allen a Dale'.[124] This did have an introduction, but it was written on the verso of the final page, inverted, and was evidently extemporized. Although the ballad was not printed for the *Reliques*, Percy salvaged most of this introductory material for his 'Essay on the Ancient English Minstrels'. The introduction eventually superseded the ballad it had been written

---

[121] Hales and Furnivall, ii. 200 n.   [122] Houghton, bMS Eng. 893 (181).
[123] Houghton, bMS Eng. 893 (164), fo. 1[r].
[124] Houghton, bMS Eng. 893 (169).

to illustrate—a fine example of Percy's use of ballad sources in constructing his imaginative history of the minstrels.[125]

There are also extant proof-sheets for the *Reliques*. Again, these have not been fully discussed. As Carver rightly points out, the great majority of the sheets in Percy–Darby are not proofs—they bear press-figures—but there are nevertheless some proofs extant in this copy. Both Baine and Carver discuss the cancelled sheet B (volume i), important for the original fragmentary impression of 'The Marriage of Sir Gawaine' and the original running title, 'SELECT SONGS | AND BALLADS', soon revised to 'ANCIENT SONGS | AND BALLADS'. There is not, however, a complete dearth of proof-sheets. Two fragments of 'Corydon's Doleful Knell' survive, both in Percy–Darby, completely overlooked.[126] The text is given in full below, and Percy's corrections and the published text are described in each subsequent comment.

The opening fragment is pasted to the foot of Percy–Darby, ii. 298:

VI.

CORYDON's DOLEFUL KNELL.

This litttle [sic] *simple elegy is given (with some conjectural emendations, and the transposal of some stanzas) from a (corrupt) copy in "The golden garland of princely delights."*

The

Percy revised this in black ink to read,

This little simple elegy is given, with some correction from two copies, one of which is in "The golden garland of princely delights."

When published, the text followed the revisions exactly.

The catchword '*The*' indicates that this introduction ran onto the following page, and the appropriate paragraph is extant on the recto of a tiny fragment loosely inserted in Percy–Darby, ii. 292–3:

The burthen of the song, DING DONG, *&c. is at present appropriated to burlesque subjects, and therefore may excite only hideous ideas in a modern reader; but in the time of our poet it usually accompanied the most solemn strains of woe. For want of attending to this circumstance, that fine pathetic air in Shakespear's Tempest,*

---

[125] Houghton, bMS Eng. 893 (169), fo. 2^r: see *Reliques* (1996), iii. 364.
[126] Percy–Darby, ii. 296–7.

"Full fadom five his father lies, &c.

is thought to have an unuitable [sic] *close,*

> *"Sea-nymphs hourly ring his knell,*
> *"Harke I have them, ding dong bell."*
> {*"Burthen: ding dong."*}

Whereas the poet intended to conclude in a manner the most solemn and expressive of melancholy.

> *At ver. 21. the reader will remember that it is a custom in many parts of England, to carry a fine garland before the corpse of a young woman who dies unmarried: and that ver. 33, &c. alludes to the painted effigies of alabaster anciently erected upon tombs and monuments.*

Percy, in black ink, revised '*hideous*' to 'ludicrous' and replaced '*woe*' with 'grief'. He restored the second sentence to a continuous whole, began to revise '*that*' before leaving it 'stet', and added the missing 's' to '*unuitable*'. The Shakespeare quote was therefore made a single text more pleasing to the eye, and underwent further revision; it lost '*his*' for 'thy', the '*&c.*' concluding the first line was deleted, 'now' was added to follow '*Harke*', and '*have*' was changed to 'heare'. The whole of the last section was struck through in red ink with the comment added in the margin, 'very uneven'. The passage as published displays further revision, following the first corrected proof for only a few lines:

> *The burthen of the song,* DING DONG, *&c. is at present appropriated to burlesque subjects, and therefore may excite only ludicrous ideas in a modern reader; but in the time of our poet it usually accompanied the most solemn and mournful strains. Of this kind is that fine aerial Dirge in Shakespear's Tempest,*

The Shakespeare lines were quoted as corrected, with the addition of the five connecting lines (the only minor changes are that '*Ding*' was twice capitalized and a comma rather than a semicolon followed '*Burthen*'). Lastly, Percy contracted his original rambling comment,

> *I make no doubt but the poet intended to conclude this air in a manner the most solemn and expressive of melancholy.*

The verso of this scrap records a few lines of the original verse:

> For my fair Phillida
>> Our bridal bed was made: 10
> But 'stead of silkes so gay,
>> She in her shroud is laid.
>>> Ding, &c.
>
> Her corpse shall be attended
>> By maides in fair array,
> Till th'obsequies are ended,   15
>> And she is wrapt in clay.
>>> Ding, &c.
>
> Her herse it shall be carried
>> By youths, that do excell:
> When that she is buried
>> I thus will ring her knell.   20
>>> Ding, &c.

Percy, in black ink, changed line 12 to read, 'She now in shroud is laid.' and line 19, 'And when that she is buried', and changed the full stop at the end of line 20 to a comma. In the published edition, line 12 remained uncorrected but the other revisions were incorporated.

More than anything else, this shows the enormous and no doubt infuriating degree to which Percy was prepared to rewrite proofs. It also shows that the printer did not assimilate every change Percy demanded—hardly surprising considering they were so numerous. One of the most interesting features is Percy's editorial obfuscation. Although he originally admitted that the song was largely reworked, he subsequently played down his considerable revisions and only half-acknowledged his sources. The text of 'Corydon's Doleful Knell' which was published had moved a considerable distance from its sources.

At the end of the *Reliques*, after a modest two pages of errata, Percy apologized for the promiscuousness of the printed text: 'THE Editor's distance from the press has occasioned some mistakes and confusion in the Numbers of the several Poems, and in the References from one Volume to another' (iii. [349]). He also reminded the binder to reverse the volume order. His profound wish to be at the press as each sheet was printed off reflected not simply the anxiety of an over-solicitous author, but the ultimate vision of his role as midwife to the ancient English minstrels. He had rescued the Folio MS from the fire and transcribed its treasures. He had understood its dynamic as the tradition of English minstrelsy, and he had collected its ballads from libraries, books, and stalls. He had proposed a millennial genealogy of transmission in expectation of a national Gothic revival and he had seen it through the press. Thomas Percy had realized the English tradition in print.

7

Conclusion

On 15 September 1798, William and Dorothy Wordsworth and Samuel Taylor Coleridge, having seen *Lyrical Ballads* through the press, left for Germany. Almost the first thing they did on arriving at Hamburg was to buy a copy of Percy's *Reliques*. It is as if they had forgotten to take their own copy and could not bear to be without it. Interestingly, Coleridge later annotated this copy, picking out a line to complain of Percy's collaborative emendations. The introduction to 'Sir John Grehme and Barbara Allen' indicated that an *'ingenious Friend'* had provided some lines, and Coleridge is able to spot one of these interpolations: 'Damn the "ingenious Friend!"', he writes, 'he must have been a Scotchman or a Lawyer.' In fact, he was both: David Dalrymple, Lord Hailes.[1] After thirty years, the interpolations were showing some strain: like discoloured glue they had perhaps aged more noticeably than the antique lines from broadsides and the Folio MS. Shortly afterwards, Coleridge would attack such ingenious friends in the pernickety antiquarian annotator who glosses 'The Ancient Mariner' from the margin.

Still, thirty years was a stupendous run for a parcel of old ballads. Wordsworth's public praise of the *Reliques* is well known, as is the claim that *Lyrical Ballads* is indebted to Percy, and while the above episode does not quite prove that Wordsworth and Coleridge did consult the work before *Lyrical Ballads* was published, their eagerness not to be without a copy strongly suggests that they had indeed read and studied and used the

---

[1] This association copy is Houghton, *EC8 W8915 Zz794p, and bears the inscription 'Bought at Hamburgh by William and Dorothy Wordsworth 1798'; Coleridge's note is iii. 131 and signed 'S.T.C. Sept. 5. 1800.'; the Dalrymple attribution is in Percy–Darby (i. 132). There are two copies of the *Reliques* noted in Dorothy Wordsworth's 1829 catalogue of William's library. Percy's *Reliques* was lent to the young Wordsworth by his schoolmaster and mentor Thomas Bowman (T. W. Thompson, *Wordsworth's Hawkshead*, ed. Robert Woof (London, 1970), 344; see also Duncan Wu, *Wordsworth's Reading 1770–1799* (Cambridge, 1993), 110–11).

work. They were not blind to its deficiencies, but recognized—in fact, relied upon—its significance. As Landeg White has argued, 'Percy's acceptance into the pantheon marks the point at which Romanticism ceased to be popular and iconoclastic and became preoccupied with establishing its own canon.'[2]

Cynics might argue that as with Gerard Langbaine's *Lives of the Dramatick Poets*, it was precisely the faults in the *Reliques* that made it irresistible to many readers who shared an eagerness to annotate and improve Percy's edition.[3] But, with the exception of Ritson (who in any case savaged almost everyone), ballad scholars were inspired by Percy to emulate him, or to extend the canon on his principles. Thomas Evans not only based his *Old Ballads, Historical and Narrative* (1777–84) on Percy, but even dedicated his work to the Duke of Northumberland; whereas Walter Scott collected in explicit homage to the *Reliques*. And despite the extraordinary fascination exercised on readers by the content of the *Reliques*, readers could still find many of its ballads on stalls, especially after 1765.

Percy's *Reliques* was an attempt to define that most eighteenth century of aesthetic concepts: taste—and it is no coincidence that Percy's first thought after the *Reliques* was to edit the popular embodiment of polite taste, the *Spectator*. In the *Reliques*, the past is a realm of contemplation rather than an antiquarian stew. Percy's very citation of Sir Philip Sidney, 'I never heard the old song of Percie and Douglas, that I found not my heart moved more than with a trumpet,' emphasizes both the nostalgic peal of the 'old song', and the sentimental appeal to bodily sensations. But the ballads are extravagantly bloodthirsty, and the sentimental is nowhere else conveyed by scenes of mass murder, cannibalism, and duels with horrifying monsters. Such episodes, it seems, embody a more intimate nostalgia: for childhood. Johnson noted the childish taste for romances and legends, 'Babies do not want (said he) to hear about babies; they like to be told of giants and castles, and of somewhat which can stretch and stimulate their little minds,' and

---

[2] White, 'The Bishop's Move', 24.

[3] A. Watkin-Jones, 'Langbaine's *Account of the English Dramatick Poets* (1691)', *ES* 31 (1936), 75–85: 'Langbaine simply cried out to be corrected, in matters of bibliography and biography' (78). See Percy's interleaved copy of Langbaine (Bodl., Malone 129–32), and notes on Langbaine (Bodl., MS Percy e 5, fos. 14–15), also *Illustrations*, vii. 574, and *Letters*, iii. 133–7; Fairer, 249–60.

Coleridge declared, 'Give me the works which delighted my youth! Give me the *History of St George*, and the *Seven Champions of Christendom*, which at every leisure moment I used to hide myself in a corner to read.'[4] Scott, the most renowned and ardent reader of the *Reliques*, specifically situated his formative and abiding reading of the book during childhood:

I remember well the spot where I read these volumes for the first time. It was beneath a huge platanas-tree, in the ruins of what had been intended for an old fashioned arbour in the *garden* I have mentioned. The summer-day sped onward so fast, that notwithstanding the sharp appetite of thirteen, I forgot the hour of dinner, was sought for with anxiety, and was still found entranced in my intellectual banquet. To read and to remember was in this instance the same thing, and henceforth I over-whelmed my schoolfellows, and all who would hearken to me, with tragical recitations from the ballads of Bishop Percy. The first time, too, I could scrape a few shillings together, which were not common occurrences with me, I bought unto myself a copy of these beloved volumes; nor do I believe I ever read a book half so frequently, or with half the enthusiasm.

The *Reliques*, itself a book about the past, and a secret, solitary, and absorbing vice, comes to the 13-year-old Scott already a childhood memory, and so it articulates a moment at which identity is born. The nostalgia of the child for an earlier period of childhood is, literally, a re-membering—the recognition of itself as a subject—which here banishes society and sustenance for its own new-born integrity.[5]

This pleasure of childhood nostalgia, particularly of children's literature, was most emphatically realized by Boswell when he made his collection of chapbooks. On 10 July 1763, he noted,

some days ago I went to the old printing office in Bow Church-yard kept by Dicey, whose family have kept it fourscore years. There are ushered into the world of literature *Jack and the Giants*, *The Seven Wise Men of*

[4] *Johnsonian Miscellanies*, i. 156 (*Thraliana: The Diary of Mrs. Hester Lynch Thrale (Later Mrs. Piozzi) 1776–1809*, ed. Katharine C. Balderston (Oxford, 1951), i. 160); Earl Leslie Griggs, *Collected Letters of Samuel Taylor Coleridge* (Oxford, 1956), i. 347 (see also Griggs, *Collected Letters*, i. 354, and John Livingston Lowes, *The Road to Xanadu: A Study in the Ways of the Imagination* (1951), 16, 459–61). Wordsworth's *Prelude* (V. 343–8) also echoes these sentiments (*The Fourteen-Book Prelude*, ed. W. J. B. Owen (Ithaca, NY, 1985), 102–3).

[5] J. G. Lockhart, *Memoirs of the Life of Sir Walter Scott, Bart.* (Edinburgh, 1845), II, 30.

Gotham, and other story-books which in my dawning years amused me as much as *Rasselas* does now. I saw the whole scheme with a kind of pleasing romantic feeling to find myself really where all my old darlings were printed. I bought two dozen of the story-books and had them bound up with this title, *Curious Productions*.[6]

He inscribed the title-page of the volume in a comparable fit of romantic sensation:

I shall certainly some time or other write a little story-book in the style of these. It will not be a very easy task for me; it will require much nature and simplicity and a great acquaintance with the humours and traditions of the English common people. I shall be happy to succeed, for he who pleases children will be remembered with pleasure by men.[7]

Certainly Percy was 'remembered with pleasure by men', as too was Samuel Johnson, whose children's fairy tale 'The Fountains' was published in 1766. The *Reliques* was moreover immediately parodied by John Newbery in *Mother Goose's Melody, or Sonnets for the Cradle*, the first English collection of nursery rhymes, and Oliver Goldsmith added mock-antiquarian notes in Percy's style:

> A Dirge
> Little Betty Winckle she had a pig,
> It was a little pig not very big;
> When he was alive he liv'd in clover,
> But now he's dead and that's all over;
> Johnny Winckle he
> Sat down and cry'd,
> Betty Winckle she
> Laid down and dy'd;
> So there was an end of one, two, and three,
> Johnny Winckle he,
> Betty Winckle she,
> And Piggy Wiggie.

A Dirge is a song made for the dead; but whether this was made for Betty Winckle or her pig, is uncertain; no notice of it being taken by Camden, or any of the famous antiquarians. WALL'S System of Sense[8]

Almost a century later, Lewis Carroll's student scrapbook *Mischmasch* (compiled in 1855) recorded 'A Stanza Of Anglo-Saxon

---

[6] *Boswell's London Journal*, 299 n.   [7] Houghton, 25276.44*.
[8] Hugh Haughton (ed.), *The Chatto Book of Nonsense Poetry*, (1988), 156–7.

Poetry'. This 'curious fragment' was engraved in angular runes, and followed by a glossary, translation, and editorial note, concluding, 'This is an obscure, but yet deeply affecting, relic of ancient Poetry'.[9] A few years later this stanza reappeared in *Through the Looking Glass*, where it was given the title 'Jabberwocky'.

The contemplation of the past as an activity of nostalgic sentimentalism is therefore deeply embedded in memories of childhood, and Percy's *Reliques* provided a grave and pedagogic companion for the young reader. Percy's smooth refatimentoes inculcated correctness and taste into corrupt popular traditions, and attempted to reinvent popular song as the Matter of Britain—noble, strong, chaste, and true. The *Reliques* was also an attack on luxury: a repudiation of the Gallic Celticism implicit in the Jacobite mythology of *Ossian*. Percy's Gothic scalds and medieval bards may have been savage, but they were not barbarous cannibals or polygamists. Polite society was maintained as inherently civilized through its native poetic traditions. Ballads, with their cast of extraordinary everyday folk, democratized the ideology of polite aesthetics.

As I have argued, Percy achieved this national and aesthetic synthesis through the figure of the ancient English minstrel. Like the storyteller, the minstrel either comes from afar with exotic news and fables, or remains at home recounting local tales and traditions. For Walter Benjamin, who in 'The Storyteller' considered the material implications of storytelling, these two aspects of epic and myth coexist among the travelling journeyman and master craftsman. These two artisans 'combined the lore of faraway places, such as the much-traveled man brings home, with the lore of the past, as it best reveals itself to natives of a place'. Yet this romantic materialism of the fable, rooted in the socio-economic activity of a community, does not hold for Percy's minstrels. He was a man of libraries, books, correspondence, and print, his community was the republic of letters, dependent on the press, and so he utilized the technology of the age in the invention of the past. The *Reliques*, as we have seen, was almost novelistic: a profoundly literate and literary work, in which his minstrels were graphemes rather than singers. Benjamin comments, 'What

[9] Lewis Carroll, *The Rectory Umbrella and Mischmasch* (1932), 139–41.

distinguishes the novel from the story (and from the epic in the narrower sense) is its essential dependence on the book. The dissemination of the novel became possible only with the invention of printing.'[10] In fact, the very dissemination of canonical literature only became possible with the invention of printing, and among the forms canonized by their printed status were old English ballads.

The printed collection was, therefore, a way of making antiquarianism visionary, a way of feeling the 'magic hardiness' of the Gothic. As Horace Walpole put it, 'One must have taste to be sensible of the beauties of Grecian architecture; one only wants passions to feel Gothic.'[11] The Gothic vision was communicated not only in how the book looked, but in how passionately, movingly, sentimentally it read. Percy realized that he had literally hundreds of tales he could tell in the shape of ballads, but that the most exciting story he had was his own master narrative recounting the adventures of the minstrels through English history.

In one way, Percy's ancient English minstrels embodied a tradition directly opposed to the proud professionalism of Samuel Johnson (variously a jobbing hack, playwright, poet, lexicographer, editor, critic, biographer, and journalist). Percy courted patronage and prestige, and offered what was almost a *captatio benevolentia* for his collection. Just as the humility tropes of medieval works deferred beginnings, so Percy situated his text behind apologies: a dedication, preface, essays, and notes. But through these pretexts, Percy worked out a model of the poet that aspired to magnificence. The minstrels coexisted in an almost Augustan equation of arts and politics, of state patronage and eulogizing poet. They were central to the cultural and imaginative well-being of society, and guardians of its history and identity. But they were also wanderers, singers of epic songs, self-evidently men of genius, who eschewed social position for the company of the muses and the pleasures of the imagination. Percy suggested that poets need be neither Grub Street poetasters, nor leisured connoisseurs perpetually disdaining the press. The fact that these inglorious Miltons were not mute, merely anonymous, added to their romance and allure. Almost by accident, Percy's theory refuted the conception of the writer as a definable commodity producer, and challenged the next generation to reframe the minstrel and contemplate his mystique for a new century.

As argued in Chapter 3, Percy's nationalist ambitions were pitched against Macpherson's *Ossian*, and were encoded in the respective literate and non-literate sources of each. But although the *Reliques* and *Ossian* differed profoundly in the medium of sources, they shared startling similarities. For the collected *Ossian* of 1765, Blair collected the names and testimonies of some twenty-five expert witnesses to the authenticity of the work. In the same year Percy validated his own source in the same way.[12] Percy estimated his Folio MS to have been written 'about the middle of the last century', although it conveniently contained 'compositions of all times and dates'.[13] Likewise, in the final instance the manuscripts of *Ossian* did not claim to be ancient documents of Ossianic provenance, but later copies, taken down from the mouths of bards.[14] At one point, Blair ingeniously argued that *Ossian* could only be forged if the forgery had been committed in the distant past.[15] Such a forgery would be as good as authentic: certainly as good as Percy's Folio MS.[16] Finally, Percy kept his manuscript carefully hidden. It was only in the 1790s that, like Macpherson in the 1770s, Percy claimed that the Folio MS had recently been exhibited at a bookseller's.

Evidently there was a great deal of confusion about the status afforded to literary-antiquarian evidence, and sources see-sawed between notions of authenticity and forgery. The definition of authenticity was not intrinsic to one historical theorem (Celts or Goths), but derived from the relationship between different theorems. Indeed, like all the pivotal opposites discussed in this book (antiquarian/man of taste, owl/nightingale, and so forth), authenticity and forgery seem less to be absolute terms than mutually supporting concepts. The definition of each element is determined by the other. While the late introduction of Ossianic manuscripts confirmed that Macpherson's work was of question-able provenance, the consideration given to covert manuscripts

---

[12] *Ossian* (1765), ii. 452–60. [13] *Reliques*, i, p. ix.
[14] Ibid., p. xxii. [15] Blair, *Critical Dissertation*, 19.
[16] See also Sir John Sinclair, 'A Dissertation on the Authenticity of the Poems', in *The Poems of Ossian, in Original Gaelic, The Highland Society of London* (1807), i, p. xlii.

undermined the validity of Percy's own presentation of his Folio MS, and eventually enabled Ritson to accuse Percy of forging the *Reliques*.

The most central figure for English literary antiquarians was of course William Shakespeare, and reviews of Percy's *Reliques* focused on Percy's book of Shakespearean ballads and his Shakespearean pastiche 'The Friar of Orders Gray'.[17] There was a feeling that the ballads would have to measure up to Shakespeare in order to pass muster for the canon. Comparing Percy's work on the *Reliques* with the eighteenth-century canonization of the bard shows that Percy was developing the critical canons of Shakespeare editing into new and significant areas. It also suggests that Johnson, who was editing Shakespeare at this time, developed his edition alongside Percy's collation and compilation of the *Reliques*.

Johnson had published *Miscellaneous Observations* on *Macbeth* (1745) in response to Thomas Hanmer's illustrated gentleman's edition for Clarendon (1744), and in 1756, having completed his *Dictionary*, published proposals to edit Shakespeare. Johnson's edition marks a major break with the gladiatorial duels of the first half of the century (between Pope, Theobald, and Warburton). Johnson acknowledged his predecessors, and recognized that he was a part of an ongoing tradition in Shakespeare scholarship. In consequence, he included all the previous Tonson prefaces, and reprinted Rowe's 'Life' with various additions.

Johnson's acknowledgement and ensuing incorporation of his editorial predecessors was only part of his achievement in the 1765 edition. Johnson was the first to advance the textual authority of the first Folio. He allowed very few of his conjectures to intrude on the text, and advocated examining Shakespeare's sources, although he had little time for the onerous activity of collation (despite his claims). But perhaps Johnson's most significant contribution was his preface, reaffirming Shakespeare's position in English literature. This essay revolutionized English literary criticism. As G. F. Parker, and more recently Marcus Walsh, have shown, Johnson's preface to Shakespeare was not

[17] *Gentleman's Magazine*, 35 (1765), 179–83, 231.

conventional critical wisdom, but a radical reassessment of the nature and purpose of criticism and editing.[18] Johnson's propositions will be recognizable in their influence on the *Reliques*. He argued that Shakespeare mingled tones, irony, and plot to create an innovatory 'tragi-comedy', and mingled species and 'nature' to create character. This was the promiscuous spirit that was becoming characteristically English.

In the next half-century, Johnson's eight-volume work evolved into a twenty-one-volume variorum edition that was the brilliant culmination of eighteenth-century Shakespeare editing. Johnson nominated his own successor, George Steevens, who in turn passed the work on to Edmond Malone, Isaac Reed, and finally James Boswell the younger. Editions of Shakespeare became a compilation of notes by the current and previous editors, and the contributions of an expanding circle of scholars and connoisseurs: Farmer, Hawkins, Percy, Reynolds, Warton—all contributed to Steevens. The Steevens–Malone edition of Shakespeare, as Gary Taylor puts it, was 'shaped by the social character of an entire period'.[19]

The Johnson Shakespeare dynasty therefore established principles of incorporation, collaboration, and cooperation. These were also features of the making of the *Reliques*, and, as with Johnson's Shakespeare, contributed to its success. Johnson recognized that Shakespeare editing had become a history, and not a text, and promulgated a practical textual authority above the Pope/Theobald/Warburton controversy—even if he ultimately lacked the requisite resources to execute his plan. Shakespeare, of course, existed only in print—there was barely a signature surviving in his own hand—and this provided Percy with a preliminary rationale for the *Reliques*. But Percy's innovation was in cultivating his anonymous minstrels into a class, and shaping these poets on the printing press. Johnson too had demonstrated the necessity of establishing a critical framework explaining characteristic literary features, and making it a principle of greatness. In particular, mingled, confused promiscuity became a principle of the Gothic, and motivated Percy's activities.

---

[18] G. F. Parker, *Johnson's Shakespeare* (Oxford, 1989), 2–3; Marcus Walsh, *Shakespeare, Milton, and Eighteenth-Century Literary Editing* (Cambridge, 1997), 165–75.   [19] Taylor, 'The Renaissance', 128.

But there should be a caveat to this account of Johnson's Shakespearean effect on Percy's *Reliques*. Boswell has little information regarding Johnson's life over the years 1760–2, directly before they met: 'Johnson was now either very idle, or very busy with his Shakspeare.'[20] Perhaps he was already declining into the second of his nervous breakdowns, and, maybe not unconnected, was feverishly attempting to produce a comprehensive variorum of Shakespeare. I have already suggested that Johnson might have been rescued from his later mental despair by Percy. He frequently dined with Percy at this time, and so the editorial principles for Shakespeare and the *Reliques* may well have been hatched together. The texts, like their editors, might have soothed each other. In 1764, Johnson was 'afflicted with a very severe return of the hypochondriack disorder', and said, 'I would consent to have a limb amputated to recover my spirits.'[21] Instead, he spent that summer with Percy at Easton Maudit; to correct Shakespeare proofs, read Percy's romances, and enjoy his host's *Reliques of Ancient English Poetry.*

> That old and antique song we heard last night:
> Methought, it did relieve my passion much;
> More than light airs, and recollected terms,
> Of these most brisk and giddy-paced times.[22]

What this study has clarified, I hope, is that a microbibliographical examination of the making of Percy's *Reliques* demonstrates that the text was not the result of 'bad editing' (or even 'literary forgery'), but rather social and cultural processes, changing conceptions of authorship and composition, material interventions in correspondence and lent books, and a series of bibliographical accidents from the fireplace to the print shop. But as hinted at the outset, the story of the *Reliques* is also the story of the antiquary and the minstrel, the owl and the nightingale. For the Romantic generation, the nightingale became a powerful symbol of the empathetic and creative imagination, most prominently in Coleridge, Keats, and Clare, but also in dozens of periodical poems. Yet despite its descanting reinventions, the nightingale also remained the metamorphosis of Philomela. The nightingale's

---

[20] *Boswell's Life*, i. 353.   [21] Ibid. 483.
[22] *Twelfth Night*, II. iv. 3–6 (*Johnson–Steevens–Malone*, iv. 202–3).

song, the song of the minstrel, recalls Ovid's story: Philomela's
unwitting seduction of Tereus, and her dreadful fate. Her tongue
cut out, she could only communicate by weaving a tapestry to tell
of her rape, her mutilation, and her imprisonment. She was
rescued by her sister Procne, the wife of Tereus, and together
they plotted a sickening revenge, butchering Tereus' son and heir
Itys before cooking him, and serving him for dinner. In the subsequent revelation and flight, Procne becomes a swallow, Tereus a
hoopoe, and Philomela of course a nightingale. The chilling story
of Philomela's metamorphosis, effectively retold in dozens of
ballads, deepens and darkens the nightingale qualities of the
minstrel described at the beginning of this study. Like Philomela,
the minstrel tradition appears to have been (metaphorically)
raped, mutilated, and locked away from the mainstream; like
her a 'text' (the noun comes from the Latin verb *texere* 'to weave')
remains to tell the tale—a hideous tale of woe; like her, the oral
returns, chokes up the paternal tradition with visceral guilt, and
flies away, singing.[23] It is a song of crossing boundaries. The
nightingale, heralding the night's sleep, is the bird of 'sweet
lullaby' in *A Midsummer Night's Dream*, but crucially other
lullabies find the song, with its rather melancholy associations
of assault and cannibalism, very doleful.[24] It is a song that signals
the collapse of posterity (Tereus eats his own son), and moreover,
as a myth about futurity and generational conflict, signals the
collapse of classical inheritance and the old heritage. It is a song
that confuses sleep with oblivion and easeful death. Though the
song of the minstrel was, like Philomela, almost completely
silenced, it returned on the wings of a new Romantic theory of
cultural history and textual authority. It awoke, and sang in Percy's
Reliques.

[23] Ong derives 'text' from *texere* (*Orality*, 13); Barthes recalls the derivation *tissu*
(fabric) (Roland Barthes, *The Pleasure of the Text*, tr. Richard Miller (Oxford, 1990),
64).
[24] See Marina Warner, *No Go the Bogeyman: Scaring, Lulling, and Making Mock*
(1998), 224–37.

First Transcriptions

Seventy-two transcriptions made 1761–2. Houghton call number (bMS Eng. 893) and, where appropriate, Hales and Furnivall cross-references are given. Most of these transcriptions are extant only in the following manuscripts rather than in the *Reliques*—many were never printed. All titles and sources are Percy's own.

From the Folio MS:
  'The Enquiry', (14), ii. 35,
  'Now the Springe is come', (14), iii. 230,
  'Cresside was the fairest of Troye', (15), iii. 301,
  'Dido', (17), iii. 260,
  'Buckingham betrayed by Banister', (20A), fo. 96, ii. 253,
  'The Shepherd's Resolution', (155), iii. 386,
  'See the building', (155), iv. 1,
  'A Lover of late was I', (157), iii. 389,
  'When first I sawe thee', (157), ii. 48,
  'Holla, my Fancye, Holla!', (162A), ii. 30,
  'A Cavilere', (162B), iii. 366,
  'O Wat where art thou!', (162C), iv. 121,
  'The Hunting of the Gods', (162D), iii. 303,
  'Old Times past', (162E), iii. 119,
  'Mark Anthony & his Aegyptian Queen', (166A), ii. 119,
  'Old Simon the King', (166D), iv. 124,
  'Come, come, come', (166G), ii. 52.

From *The Golden Garland of princely Delights*, ed. Richard Johnson (1690), (278) fo. 15ᵛ:
  'A Gallant Song of the Garter of England', (20A), fo. 48,
  'A courtly new song of the princely wooing of the fair Maid of London by King Edward', (20A), fo. 89,
  'A lamentable song of Lady Elinour', (20A), fo. 122,
  'The Inconstancy of the World', (54),
  'The Lover's Lamentation for the death of fair Phillis', (146),
  'Corydon's doleful Knell', (152),
  'The Shepherd's Dialogue', (156),
  'Diana's Song', (180),

'Corydon's Resolution', (180),
'You pretty Wantons Warble', (180),
'The Weaver's shuttle', (180),
'Of the Inconvenience by Marriage', (180),
'The Shepherd's Pipe', (182).

From *Select Collection of Old Plays*, ed. Robert Dodsley (1744):
'Pithias' song' (i. 249), (184),
'Not the Phœnix' (x. 272), (189),
'The jovial beggar' (vi. 376), (190),
'Where did you borrow that last sigh' (x. 140), (192),
'The Courtier's deceit' (x. 290), (252).

From *Poems. By Thomas Carew* (1640), (182):
'The Primrose',
'Go thou gentle &c.',
'Ladies, fly from Love's smooth table',
'Good Councell to a young maid',
'Ingrateful beauty threatened',
'Come, Celia, fire thine eyes on mine',
'Boldnesse in love',
'A pastoral Dialogue',
'Sweetly breathing Vernal Air',
'Ask no more where Jove &c',
'The Hue & cry',
'The Mole',
'Love's Duel'.

From John Lyly, (185):
'Cupid indicated' (*Galathea*, iv. 2),
'Arme, Arme, &c' (*Sapho & Phao*, iii. 2),
'Apollo's Song' (*Midas*, iv. 1),
'Pans Song' (*Midas*, iv. 1),
'O Cupid, Monarch over kings' (*Mother Bombi*, iii. 2),
'Hymen, God of marriage-bed' (*the Shepherd's Holday*, v, ult. scene),
'The Watchmen's Song' (*Endimion*, iv. 2).

From *Small poems of diverse parts* by Aston Cockain (1658), (191B):
'I saw a proud Lass',
'Of Women'.

From *Select Poems of Edmund Prestwich* (1659):
'Gain in Loss', (193),
'A Remedy against Love', (194).

Also,

'A Dirge (from *The Woman-hater arraigned by women* (1620), iv. 2), (188),

'Ye deserts and dark cells' (from William Lower's *The Noble Ingratitude* (1661)), (198),

'Walking in a shady grove' (untraced), (199),

'The protestation' (from Roger Baron's *The Cyprian Academy* (1647)), (200).

From the Society of Antiquaries:

'A New Ballade of the Marigolde', (20A), fo. 139,

'A doleful ditty or sorrowful sonnet of the Lord Darnly', (20A), fo. 152.

From the Pepysian Library (the only transcriptions in Percy's hand):

'An Excellent most pleasant New Sonnet Showing how the Goddess Diana transformed Acteon into the shape of a Hart', (46),

'An excellent song called Lullaby', (47).

From the Cottonian Library:

'A Merye Ballet of the Hathorne Tre', (138),

'A life content exceedeth all', (167),

'A Ballet of the Judgement Day', (173).

From Ballard's Collection:

'An Invitation to Lubberland', (166F).

From a black-letter broadside:

'The bonny Scot', (176).

APPENDIX II

A Collection of Old Ballads

Vartin lists twenty-five pieces Percy derived from *A Collection of Old Ballads* as (Percy's titles):

'Sir Launcelot du Lake',
'King Leir and His Three Daughters',
'The More Modern Ballad of Chevy Chase',
'Gilderoy',
'The Gaberlunzie Man',
'Fair Rosamond and King Henry II',
'Queen Eleanor's Confession',
'The Beggar's Daughter of Bednall Green',
'Sir Andrew Barton's Death',
'The Spanish Lady's Love',
'Jane Shore' ('The Lament of Jane Shore'),
'King Cophetua and the Beggar Maid' ('Cupid's Revenge'),
'King John and the Abbot of Canterbury',
'The Baffled Knight',
'Lord Thomas and Fair Ellinor',
'The Lady Turned Serving Man',
'The Lady's Fall',
'The Wanton Wife of Bath',
'The Bride's Burial' (as this replaced 'The Wanton Wife of Bath', the total should in fact be twenty-four),
'The King of France's Daughter',
'Children in the Wood',
'The King and the Miller of Mansfield',
'St. George and the Dragon',
'The Dragon of Wantley',
'Margaret's Ghost' ('William and Margaret').[1]

A further twenty-one were included in Friedman's 'First Draft' (Percy's titles):

'The seven Champions',
'King Alfred & the Shepherd',

[1] Vartin, 92.

'The Scotsman outwitted' ('The Northern Ditty'),
'Alphonso & Gonsalo',
'The Roman Charity',
'The Battle of Agincourt',
'Buckingham betrayed',
'Rosamond' ('The Unfortunate Concubine'),
'Godina',
'When this old Cap was new' ('Time's Alteration'),
'Sir Richd Whittington',
'The beggar wench of Hull',
'The London Prentice',
'Johnny Armstrong',
'Maudlin',
'The Hunting of the Gods',
'Patient Grisell',
'Ballad on Tobacco',
'The revengeful Moor',
'Suffolk miracle',
'The Lawyer outwitted'.[2]

[2] Houghton, bMS Eng. 893 (278), fo. 16.

Robin Hood's Garland

Houghton 25276.44* (30).

Robin Hood's Garland: being a compleat History of all the Notable and Merry Exploits Perform'd by Him, and his Men, On divers Accounts and Occasions. To which is added the whole Life of bold Robin Hood, Earl of Huntington; Being a more particular Account of his Birth, &c than any hitherto Publish'd (n.p., 1749).

1. Robin Hood's *Parantage and Birth*.
2. Robin Hood's *Progress to* Nottingham.
3. Robin Hood *and the Pinner of* Wakefield.
4. Robin Hood *and the Bishop*.
5. Robin Hood *and the Butcher*.
6. Robin Hood *and the Tinker*.
7. Robin Hood *and the Tanner*.
8. Robin Hood *and* Allen a-Dale.
9. Robin Hood *and the Shepherd*.
10. Robin Hood *and the Frier*.
11. Robin Hood *Reviv'd*.
12. Robin Hood *and Queen* Catherine.
13. Robin Hood's *Chase*.
14. Robin Hood's *Golden Prize*.
15. Robin Hood *and* Will. Stutely.
16. Robin Hood's *Preferment*.
17. Robin Hood's *Delight*.
18. Robin Hood *and the Beggar*.
19. Robin Hood *and the Prince of* Arragon.
20. Robin Hood *and the Four Beggars*.
21. Robin Hood *and the Ranger*.
22. Robin Hood *and* Little John.
23. Robin Hood *and the Bishop of* Hereford.
24. Robin Hood *and the valliant Knight*.

'Robin Hood and the jolly Pinner of Wakefield': Percy notes Pepysian cross-references, text collated by Shenstone. 'Robin Hood and the Tanner': Percy notes Pepysian cross-reference. 'Robin Hood and Allen-a-Dale': Pepysian and *Old Ballads* cross-references, text collated by Shenstone.

APPENDIX IV

The 'First Draft'

Percy's own titles are given. Corrections to Friedman are marked with an asterisk.

Volume i:
1. 'The Boy and the Mantle',
2. 'The Marriage of sir Gawaine',
3. 'King Ryence's challenge',
4. 'King Arthur's death',
5. 'The Legend of K. Arthur',
6. 'A dittye to hey downe',
7. 'Old sir Robin of Portingale',
8. 'Glasgerion',
9. 'Young Andrew',
10. 'The wanton wife of Bath'*,
11. 'Little Musgrave',
12. 'The Flower of Servingmen',
13. 'Lady Isabella's Tragedy',
14. 'Lord Thomas & Fair Ellenor'*,
15. 'The Shepherds daughter',
16. 'The Legend of Sir Guy',
17. 'The Bailiff's daughter of Islington',
18. 'Amintas',
19. 'The Prince of England's courtship',
18. [sic] 'The seven Champions',
19. [sic] 'Sappho's song',
20. 'St. George and the King of Egypts daug^r.'*,
21. 'Mark Anthony & his Eg^tian. Queen'*,
22. 'A Brave warlike Song',
23. 'King Alfred & the Shepherd',
24. 'The Enquiry',
25. 'Ask no more where Jove bestows',
26. 'A Lover of late was I',
27. 'The Spanish Virgin',
28. 'The Scotsman outwitted',
29. 'Alphonso & Gonsalo',
30. 'Go thou gentle whispering wind',

31. 'The Roman Charity',
32. 'Dulcina',
33. 'The Baffled Knight or Lady's policy',
34. 'George Barnwell',
35. 'No more shall meads',
36. 'The Lady's Fall'*,
37. 'Good Counsel to a young maid',
38. 'S⁺. Geo. & the Draggon'*,
39. 'The Primrose',
40. 'Musedorus & Amadine',
41. 'The Fairies farewell'*,
42. 'You meaner beauties',
43. 'Thro' the cool shady woods',
44. 'Lord Henry & fair Catharine',
45. 'The Mole',
46. 'The Dragon of Wantley',
47. 'The Boy & the mantle'*.

Volume ii:

1. 'Hymn at Agincourt',
2. 'The Siege of Harflet',
3. 'The Battle of Agincourt',
4. 'The Erle Rivers's balet',
5. 'Little of John Nobody',
6. 'A lyfe content exceedeth all',
7. 'Ballade of the Marygolde',
8. 'Gentle Herdsman',
9. 'Sir Aldingar',
10. 'Fair Rosamond',
11. 'Queen Eleanor',
12. 'As ye came from the holy land',
13. 'Dialogue between Truth & Ignorance',
14. 'Jane Shore',
15. 'Buckingham betrayed',
16. 'The Beggar's daughter of Bednal Green',
17. 'Mary Aumbree',
18. 'The Winning of Cales',
19. 'The Spanish Lady's Love',
20. 'Sir Andrew Barton',
21. 'Earl Bodwell',
22. 'Lady Anne Bodwell's Lament',
23. 'Andrew Browne & th K. of Scots'*,
24. 'The complaint of Conscience',

25. 'Fair Margaret's Misfortune',
26. 'Cupid & Campaspe',
27. 'Godina',
28. 'What bird so sings',
29. 'My Mind to me a kingdom is',
30. 'Rosamond',
31. 'King John & the Abbot',
32. 'The Pedlar's Song',
33. 'Matthew Shore',
34. 'Death's final Conquest',
35. 'King Henry & the Millar',
36. 'Lord Willoughbie',
37. 'Victorious Men of earth no more',
38. 'When this old Cap was new',
39. 'The Wandring Jew',
40. 'Boldness in Love',
41. 'Sir Richd. Whittington'*,
42. 'The Complaint of Harpalus',
43. 'The London Prentice',
44. 'He that loves a rosie cheek',
45. 'Fine young folly',
46. 'Lord Wigmore',
47. 'Happy Life',
48. ''Tis not Love thy pulses beat'*,
49. 'The beggar wench of Hull',
50. 'The Lunatic Lover',
51. 'Alexander & Lodowic',
52. 'Old Simon the K.'*,
53. 'Distracted Puritan',
54. 'Repentance too late',
55. 'Sir John Suckling's Expedition',
56. 'Loyalty confined',
57. 'To Lucasta from Prison',
58. 'Cupid's Pastime',
59. 'When love with unconfined',
60. 'Rusticae Academiae Descriptio',
61. 'Rebellion hath given over House',
62. 'West-country batchelor's complaint',
63. 'Lilli-bullero'*,
64. 'Will. & Marg^t.'*.

Volume iii:

1. 'Otterborne',
2. 'Chevy Chace',
3. 'By west of late',
4. 'King Estmere',
5. 'Child Waters',
6. 'Harpalus',
7. 'Lord of Lorne',
8. 'Sir Hugh of the Grime',
9. 'John o' th side'*,
10. 'Johnny Armstrong',
11. 'Rising ith north'*,
12. 'Northumberlande betrayd'*,
13. 'The Erle of Westmorland',
14. 'Christopher White',
15. 'Sir John Butler',
16. 'Old Times past',
17. 'Chevy Chase',
18. 'Come, come, come',
19. 'The Hunting of the Gods',
20. 'A Cauilere',
21. 'O Wat where art thou',
22. 'Æneas wandring prince'*,
23. 'Edwd. 4th. & the Tanner'*,
24. 'Holla! my Fancy holla!'*,
25. 'Barbara Allen',
26. 'O yes, if any maid',
27. 'Patient Grisell',
28. 'Hue & cry after Cupid'*,
29. 'Constance of Cleveland',
30. 'Lancashire song',
31. 'Ballad on Tobacco',
32. 'Brides Burial',
33. 'Bateman's Ghost',
34. 'Children in the wood',
35. 'Willy & Cuddy',
36. 'The revengeful Moor',
37. 'Ingrateful Beaty threatned',
38. 'Constance & Anthony',
39. 'First shall the bee',
40. 'Suffolk miracle',
41. 'The old Courtier',
42. 'Over hills & high mountains',

43. 'Penelope',
44. 'Go ask the Poles',
45. 'The Lawyer outwitted',
46. 'The bonny Milkmaid',
47. 'There is one black & sullen hour',
48. 'A young man walked once alone',
49. 'Love in phantastic Triumph late',
    'Imitations of Chevy chase' (by Pope and Wharton)*.

The Revised 'First Draft'

All titles are Percy's own.

Volume i, '+':
1. 'The Boy and the Mantle',
2. 'The Marriage of sir Gawaine',
3. 'King Ryence's challenge',
4. 'King Arthur's death',
5. 'The Legend of K. Arthur',
16. 'The Legend of Sir Guy',
19. 'The Prince of England's courtship',
18. 'The seven Champions',
20. 'St. George and the King of Egypts daug^r.',
21. 'Mark Anthony & his Eg^{tian}. Queen',
22. 'A Brave warlike Song',
38. 'S^t. Geo. & the Draggon',
46. 'The Dragon of Wantley',
47. 'The Boy & the mantle',
ii. 46. 'Lord Wigmore',
ii. 48. ''Tis not Love thy pulses beat'.

Volume ii, '++':
7. 'Ballade of the Marygolde',
8. 'Gentle Herdsman',
10. 'Fair Rosamond',
11. 'Queen Eleanor',
12. 'As ye came from the holy land',
13. 'Dialogue between Truth & Ignorance',
14. 'Jane Shore',
15. 'Buckingham betrayed',
16. 'The Beggar's daughter of Bednal Green',
17. 'Mary Aumbree',
18. 'The Winning of Cales',
19. 'The Spanish Lady's Love',
20. 'Sir Andrew Barton',
21. 'Earl Bodwell',
22. 'Lady Anne Bodwell's Lament',

23. 'Andrew Browne & th K. of Scots',
24. 'The complaint of Conscience',
27. 'Godina',
35. 'King Henry & the Millar',
39. 'The Wandring Jew',
40. 'Boldness in Love',
41. 'Sir Rich^d. Whittington',
50. 'The Lunatic Lover',
52. 'Old Simon the K.',
53. 'Distracted Puritan',
55. 'Sir John Suckling's Expedition',
56. 'Loyalty confined',
57. 'To Lucasta from Prison',
59. 'When love with unconfined',
60. 'Rusticae Academiae Descriptio',
61. 'Rebellion hath given over House',
62. 'West-country batchelor's complaint',
63. 'Lilli-bullero'.

Volume iii, '+++':
    1. 'Otterborne',
    2. 'Chevy Chace',
    8. 'Sir Hugh of the Grime',
    9. 'John o' th side',
  10. 'Johnny Armstrong',
  11. 'Rising ith north',
  12. 'Northumberlande betrayd',
  13. 'The Erle of Westmorland',
  14. 'Christopher White',
  15. 'Sir John Butler',
  16. 'Old Times past',
  17. 'Chevy Chase',
  17b. 'Maudlin',
  19. 'The Hunting of the Gods',
  20. 'A Cauilere',
  21. 'O Wat where art thou',
  30. 'Lancashire song',
        'Imitations of Chevy chase',
ii. 38. 'When this old Cap was new',
ii. 42. 'The Complaint of Harpalus'.

Friedman is unable to identify ++ 60. 'Rusticae Academiae Descriptio'. This is probably Lord Somers's 'Rustica Academiæ Oxoniensis', transcribed by Percy into his copy of Anthony à Wood's *Athenae Oxoniensis* (London, 1721).[1]

[1] Queen's, Percy 727–8.

The Two-Volume *Reliques* Draft
('Gothic Antiquities')

The draft below, reconstructed from relevant manuscripts, is fairly complete; less than a dozen texts are missing, and some appear anyway in alternative versions. Of the manuscripts listed below, most of the fifty-odd pieces not included in the next stage are marked 'Rejected' by Percy, many of those that did go on to the manuscript draft are marked 'Approved'. Call number (usually Houghton, bMS Eng. 893) is given, followed by thematic heads. For ease of cross-referencing, the 'Index Draft' docketing (see Appendix VII) is also given, where appropriate, as volume and text number. I have made no attempt to order the ballads in each series.

5/1 (2):
    ii. 3. 'The Ballad of Little John Nobody', (27), 'Religion', 5/1,
'A Merye Ballet of the Hathorne Tre', (138), 'Mirth', 5/1.

5/2 (5):
    ii. 5. 'A New Ballade of the Marigolde', (20A), fo. 139, no head, 5/2,
    ii. 13. 'Buckingham betrayed by Banister', (20A), fo. 96, 'Eng. His.', 5/2,
    ii. 47. *The Beggar-Wench of Hull*, *pEB75 P4128C (17), 'Mirth', 5/2,
'Pithias's Song', (184), '<Mirth> Misc', 5/2,
'Sir Hugh of the Grime', (59), 'Trag Hist', 5/2.

5/3 (7):
    i. 12. 'Holla, my Fancye, Holla', (162A), 'Misc', 5/3,
    i. 20. *The Lamentable and Tragical History of Titus Andronicus*, *pEB75 P4128C (267), 'Trag. Hist.', 5/3,
    ii. 24. *Godina, Countess of Chester*, *pEB75 P4128C (59), 'Eng Hist.', 5/3,
    iii. 10. 'Old Times Past', (162E), 'Misc.', 5/3,
    iii. 14. *The Lady turned Serving Man*, *pEB75 P4128C (93), 'Love. His', 5/3,
    iii. 44. *the baffled Knight*, *pEB75 P4128C (10), 'Mirth', 5/3,
'Sir Andrew Barton', (48), 'Trag. Hist./Sea War', 5/3.

5/4 (13):
  i. 9. 'See the building', (155), no head, 5/4,
  i. 13. *Fair Margaret & Sweet William*, *pEB75 P4128C (90), 'Love His', 5/4,
  ii. 18. *Johnny Armstrong's Last Good-night*, *pEB75 P4128C (122), 'Scot.', 5/4,
  ii. 28. *the Beggar's Daughter of Bednall-green*, *pEB75 P4128C (6), no head, 5/4 (6/1 on verso),
  iii. 19. *Maudlin, The Merchant's Daughter of Bristol*, *pEB75 P4128C (174), 'Love His.', 5/4,
  iii. 20. 'The passionate shepherd to his love', (144), 'Past.', 5/4,
  iii. 22. 'Come, come, come', (166G), 'Misc', 5/4,
  'Cresside was the fairest of Troye', (15), 'Love', 5/4,
  'Dido', (17), 'Love', 5/4,
  'Cupid indicated', (185, fo. 1), 'Love', 5/4,
  'Arme, Arme, &c', (185, fo. 2), 'Misc', 5/4,
  'The Watchmen's Song &c', (185, fo. 5), 'Misc.', 5/4,
  'A pleasant Country Maying Song', (35), 'Past', 5/4.

6/1 (20):
  i. 24. *The modern ballad of Chevy Chase*, *pEB75 P4128C (47), 'War <Trag. His.>', 6/1,
  i. 26. 'A Cavilere', (162B), 'Misc', 6/1,
  i. 27. 'O Wat where art thou!', (162C), 'Misc', 6/1,
  i. 28. *Patient Grissel*, *pEB75 P4128C (214), (21) (1), 'Trag. His', 'Trag His', 6/1,
  i. 30. *The penyworth of wit*, *pEB75 P4128C (219), 'Trag. His.', 6/1,
  i. 31. 'How the goddess Diana transformed Acteon into the shape of a Hart', (46), 'Past', 6/1,
  ii. 26. *The Unfortunate Concubine: Or, Rosamond's overthrow*, *pEB75 P4128C (88), 'Eng Hist.', 6/1,
  ii. 27. *King John and the Abbot of Canterbury*, *pEB75 P4128C (132), 'Mirth', 6/1,
  ii. 28. *the Beggar's Daughter of Bednall-green*, *pEB75 P4128C (6), no head, 5/4 (6/1 on verso),
  ii. 29. 'The Pedlar's Song', (166C), 'Mirth', 6/1,
  ii. 30. 'Matthew Shores Lament', (20A), fo. 91, 'Eng. Hist.', 6/1,
  iii. 24. 'Phillis[s] complaint of Amyntas', (163), fo. 3, 'Love', 6/1,
  iii. 26. 'Mark Anthony and his Ægyptian Queen', (166A), 'Misc', 6/1,
  iii. 27. *King Alfred and the Shepherd*, *pEB75 P4128C (134), 'Mirth', 6/1,
  iii. 29. 'Leanders Love to Loyal Hero', (37), 'Love Hist.', 6/1,
  'Now the Spring is come', (14), no head, 6/1,

'The seven champions of Christendome', (18(I)), 'War', 6/1,
'Phillis's complaint at Amyntas', (163), 'Love', 6/1,
'Walking in a shady grove', (199), 'Love', 6/1,
'The Lancashire Song', (209), 'Mirth', 6/1.

6/2 (25):

i. 33. 'Constance of Cleveland', (45), 'Trag. Hist', 6/2,

i. 37. *Bateman that hangd himself for love*, *pEB75 P4128C (20), 'Trag. His.', 6/2,

i. 38. 'The Weavers Song', (121), 'Misc', 6/2,

i. 40. 'The Unkind Parents', (112), 'Love', 6/2,

ii. 33. *The London 'Prentice*, *pEB75 P4128C (152), 'War', 6/2,

ii. 35. 'King Edward the fourth and the Tanner of Tamworth', (58), 'Mirth', 6/2,

ii. 36. 'Old Simon the King', (166D), 'Mirth', 6/2,

ii. 40. *The Scotch Lover's Lamentation: Or, Gilderoy's Last Farewell*, *pEB75 P4128C (104), 'Scot', 6/2,

ii. 43. *The Judgement of God shewed upon me: John Faustus Doctor in Divinity*, British Library, Add. MS 39547, fos. 187–8, '<Magic.> Trag. Hist.', 6/2,

iii. 23. *The Seven Champions of Christendom*, *pEB75 P4128C (242), 'War', 6/2,

iii. 30. 'When this old cap was new', *pEB75 P4128C (197), 'Misc', 6/2,

iii. 33. 'The brave noble warriors', (30), 'War', 6/2,

iii. 39. *The Scotchman out-witted*, *pEB75 P4128C (188), 'Scot', 6/2,

iii. 40. *Alphonso and Ganselo*, *pEB75 P4128C (95), 'Trag. His.', 6/2,

'Since my old Hat was new', *pEB75 P4128C (196), no head, 6/2,

'The Roman Tragedy', *pEB75 P4128C (297), 'Trag. Hist.', 6/2,

'The Shepherd's Resolution', (155), 'Love', 6/2,

'The Shepherd's Dialogue', (156), 'Past.', 6/2,

'When first I saw thee', (157), 6/2,

'A Lover of late was I', (157), 6/2,

'The Praises of Tobacco', (166E), '<Love> Misc', 6/2,

'A Dirge', (188), 'Mor', 6/2,

'Where did you borrow that last sigh', (192), 'Love', 6/2,

'The Inconstancy of the World', (54), 'Mor', 6/2,

'Lord Wigamore and the Fair Maid of Dunsmore', (115), 'Love Hist', 6/2.

6/3 (22):

i. 4?. 'An admirable new northern song', (50), cropped, 6/3,

i. 42. 'Ingrateful beauty threatened', (182), no head, 6/3,

ii. 36. 'Boldnesse in love', (182), 'Love', 6/3,

ii. 37. 'The complaint of the shepheard Harpalus', (41), 'Pastoral', 6/3,
ii. 39. 'Sir R^d. Whittington'/'Whitington and his cat', Bodleian Library,
MS Eng. Misc. e 219, fos. 16–19, 'Misc', 6/3,
ii. 44. 'The Courtier's deceit', (252), 'Misc', 6/3,
ii. 49. 'The two faithfull friends', (29), 'Trag. Hist.', 6/3,
ii. 58. 'The Mole', (182), fo. 12, 'Love', 6/3,
iii. 28. 'The Enquiry', (14), no head, 6/3,
iii. 32. 'Ask no more where Jove &c', (182), fo. 10, 'Past', 6/3,
iii. 41. 'Go thou gentle &c', (41), 'Pastoral', 6/3,
iii. 48. 'Good Councell to a young maid', (182), fo. 4, 'Mor', 6/3,
iii. 49. 'Dead and alive', (95), 'Mirth', 6/3,
iii. 57. 'The wandering Prince and Princess', (78), cropped, 6/3,
'Sir R^d. Whittington' (from *Old Ballads*), Bodleian Library, MS Eng.
Misc. e 219, fos. 16–19, 'Misc', 6/3,
'A pastoral Dialogue', (182, fo. 8), 'Past', 6/3,
'Sweetly breathing vernal Air', (182, fo. 9), 'Past', 6/3,
'The Hue & cry', (182. fo. 11), 'Past', 6/3,
'Not the Phœnix in his death', (190), no head, 6/3,
'An Excellent song called Lullaby', (47), 'Scot', 6/3,
'The old Courtier and the New', (61), 'Com. Misc.', 6/3,
'Pyramus and Thisbee', (69), 'Love Hist.', 6/3.

6/4 (13):
i. 44. 'The protestation', (200), 'Past', 6/4,
i. 45. 'The Suffolk Miracle', (21), 'Trag. Hist', 6/4,
i. 47. 'The wandring maiden', (70), 'Past', 6/4,
i. 49. 'The Parting', (181), 'Love', 6/4,
i. 57. 'No, not yet', (77), 'Love.', 6/4,
i. 58. 'The Lover's Invitation', (91), 'Love.', 6/4,
ii. 46. 'To one professing love to all women', (195), 'Love', 6/4,
iii. 54. 'The pensive maid', (62), 'Love', 6/4,
Cupid's Courtesie (*pEB75 P4128C (42)), originally 'V.4.55', 'Love',
6/4,
'The Shepherd's Joy', (180, fo. 3), '<Misc> Past', 6/4,
'A Sing-Song on Clarinda's Wedding', (216), 'Misc', 6/4,
'Love without Luck, Or the Maidens Misfortune', (38), 'Love past', 6/4,
'The diseased Maiden Lover', (40), 'Past', 6/4.

6/5 (1):
'Rebellion given over House-keeping or A General Sale of Rebellious
Houshold Stuff', (56), 'State', 6/5.

6/6 (11):

i. 54. *The Lawyer outwitted*, *pEB75 P4128C (45), 'Love Hist.', 6/6,
i. 55. 'The Bonny Milk-Maid', (108), 'Past', 6/6 1/5,
i. 56. 'Beauties cruelty', (84), 'Love', 6/6,
iii. 53. 'Repentance too late', (85), 'Love', 6/6,
iii. 59. *Lord Henry and Fair Katherine*, *pEB75 P4128C (162), 'Love Hist.', 6/6,
The Berkshire Lady, *pEB75 P4128C (16), 'Love Hist', 6/6,
The Famous Ballad of Badsworth Hunt: Or, The Fox-Chace, *pEB75 P4128C (120), 'Misc.', 6/6,
'The West Country Batchelor's Complaint', (203), 'Scot', 6/6,
'Harry and Moll', (217), 'Mirth', 6/6,
'Time's Darling', (53), 'Mor', 6/6,
'Coy Jenny, And Constant Jemmy', (87), 'Love', 6/6.

6/7 (3):

ii. 59. 'Monmouth's Lamentation', (20A), fo. 168, '<Eng Hist.> State', 6/7,
The Old Man's Wish, *pEB75 P4128C (192), 'Misc', 6/7,
'The Fiddle', (21), 6/7.

The Index Draft

Percy's own titles are given, followed by call numbers (Houghton, bMS Eng. 893, unless indicated otherwise) and Percy's thematic heads, derived from Pepys. Note that bMS Eng. 893 (27–123) are the Pepys transcripts.

Volume i:
9. 'See the building', (155), no head,
12. 'Holla, my Fancye, Holla', (162A), 'Misc',
13. *Fair Margaret & Sweet William*, *pEB75 P4128C (90), 'Love His',
20. *The Lamentable and Tragical History of Titus Andronicus*, *pEB75 P4128C (267), 'Trag. Hist.',
24. *The modern ballad of Chevy Chase*, *pEB75 P4128C (47), 'War <Trag. His.>',
25. 'The Hunting of the Gods', (162D), 'Misc',
26. 'A Cavilere', (162B), 'Misc',
27. 'O Wat where art thou!', (162C), 'Misc',
28. *Patient Grissel*, *pEB75 P4128C (214), (21) (1), 'Trag. His', 'Trag His',[1]
30. *The penyworth of wit*, *pEB75 P4128C (219), 'Trag. His.',
31. 'How the goddess Diana transformed Acteon into the shape of a Hart', (46), 'Past',
33. 'Constance of Cleveland', (45), 'Trag. Hist',
37. *Bateman that hangd himself for love*, *pEB75 P4128C (20), 'Trag. His.',
38. 'The Weavers Song', (121), 'Misc',
4?. 'An admirable new northern song', (50), cropped,
40. 'The Unkind Parents', (112), 'Love',
41. *The bloodthirsty blackamoor*, *pEB75 P4128C (109), no head,
42. 'Ingrateful beauty threatened', (182), no head,
44. 'The protestation', (200), 'Past',
45. 'The Suffolk Miracle', (21), 'Trag. Hist',
47. 'The wandring maiden', (70), 'Past',
49. 'The Parting', (181), 'Love',

---

[1] There is also a copy of 'Patient Grizell' from *Old Ballads*, (21(1)), 'Trag His.', marked 'V.1.28'.

54. *The Lawyer outwitted*, *pEB75 P4128C (45), 'Love Hist.',
55. 'The Bonny Milk-Maid', (108), 'Past',
56. 'Beauties cruelty', (84), 'Love',
57. 'No, not yet', (77), 'Love.',
58. 'The Lover's Invitation', (91), 'Love.'

Volume ii:

2. 'Upon the battle of Agincourt', (12A), no head,
3. 'The Ballad of Little John Nobody', (27), 'Religion',
5. 'A New Ballade of the Marigolde', (20A), fo. 139, no head,
6. 'Locrine', (206), no head,
12. *The Lamentation of Jane Shore*, *pEB75 P4128C (123), 'Eng. His.',
13. 'Buckingham betrayed by Banister', (20A), fo. 96, 'Eng. His.',
14? 'Dazzled with heighth of place', (20A), fo. 98, no head,[2]
18. *Johnny Armstrong's Last Good-night*, *pEB75 P4128C (122), 'Scot.',
21. 'Sir Hugh of the Grime', (59), 'Trag. Hist',
24. *Godina, Countess of Chester*, *pEB75 P4128C (59), 'Eng Hist.',
26. *The Unfortunate Concubine: Or, Rosamond's overthrow*, *pEB75 P4128C (88), 'Eng Hist.',
27. *King John and the Abbot of Canterbury*, *pEB75 P4128C (132), 'Mirth',
28. *the Beggar's Daughter of Bednall-green*, *pEB75 P4128C (6), no head,
29. 'The Pedlar's Song', (166C), 'Mirth',
30. 'Matthew Shores Lament', (20A), fo. 91, 'Eng. Hist.',
33. *The London 'Prentice*, *pEB75 P4128C (152), 'War',
35. 'King Edward the fourth and the Tanner of Tamworth', (58), 'Mirth',
36. 'Old Simon the King', (166D), 'Mirth',
36. 'Boldnesse in love', (182), 'Love',
37. 'The complaint of the shepheard Harpalus', (41), 'Pastoral',
39. 'Sir R^d. Whittington'/'Whitington and his cat', Bodleian Library, MS Eng. Misc. e 219, fos. 16–19, 'Misc',
40. *The Scotch Lover's Lamentation: Or, Gilderoy's Last Farewell*, *pEB75 P4128C (104), 'Scot',
43. *The Judgement of God shewed upon me: John Faustus Doctor in*

---

[2] This song, from Sir Henry Wotton (*Reliquiae Wottonianae*), follows 'Buckingham betrayed by Banister' in 'A Series of Ballads on English History'; Percy has written at the top, 'I wish this poem could be rendered worthy [of] my Collection: I want some such little Ode to come in after a Ballad on the fall of the Duke of Bucks.' He adds, 'Try to improve this there is some glimmerings of Thought in it.'

Divinity, British Library, Add. MS 39547, fos. 187–8, '<Magic.>
Trag. Hist.',
44. 'The Courtier's deceit', (252), 'Misc',
46. 'To one professing love to all women', (195), 'Love',
47. *The Beggar-Wench of Hull*, *pEB75 P4128C (17), 'Mirth',
49. 'The two faithfull friends', (29), 'Trag. Hist.',
58. 'The Mole', (182), fo. 12, 'Love',
59. 'Monmouth's Lamentation', (20A), fo. 168, '<Eng Hist.> State'.

Volume iii:
10. 'Old Times Past', (162E), 'Misc.',
14. *The Lady turned Serving Man*, *pEB75 P4128C (93), 'Love. His',
19. *Maudlin, The Merchant's Daughter of Bristol*, *pEB75 P4128C
(174), 'Love His.',
20. 'The passionate shepherd to his love', (144), 'Past.',
22. 'Come, come, come', (166G), 'Misc',
23. *The Seven Champions of Christendom*, *pEB75 P4128C (242),
'War',
24. 'Phillis' complaint of Amyntas', (163), fo. 3, 'Love',
26. 'Mark Anthony and his Ægyptian Queen', (166A), 'Misc',
27. *King Alfred and the Shepherd*, *pEB75 P4128C (134), 'Mirth',
28. 'The Enquiry', (14), no head,
29. 'Leanders Love to Loyal Hero', (37), 'Love Hist.',
30. 'When this old cap was new', *pEB75 P4128C (197), 'Misc',
32. 'Ask no more where Jove &c', (182), fo. 10, 'Past',
33. 'The brave noble warriors', (30), 'War',
39. *The Scotchman out-witted*, *pEB75 P4128C (188), 'Scot',
40. *Alphonso and Ganselo*, *pEB75 P4128C (95), 'Trag. His.',
41. 'Go thou gentle &c', (41), 'Pastoral',
44. *the baffled Knight*, *pEB75 P4128C (10), 'Mirth',
45. 'Lord Wigmore and the Fair Maid of Dunsmore', (115), 'Love
Hist',
48. 'Good Councell to a young maid', (182), fo. 4, 'Mor',
49. 'Dead and alive', (95), 'Mirth',
49. *the Lady's Fall*, *pEB75 P4128C (151), 'Trag. Hist.',
53. 'Repentance too late', (85), 'Love',
54. 'The pensive maid', (62), 'Love',
57. 'The wandering Prince and Princess', (78), cropped,
58. 'Rebellion given over House-keeping', (56), 'State',
59. *Lord Henry and Fair Katherine*, *pEB75 P4128C (162), 'Love
Hist.'.

The list is incomplete, but a few ballads are allocated the same number, making a total of eighty-three positions recorded. Such duplication argues that the abstract was not a one-off event designed for the 'First Draft', but an ongoing process, subject to revision itself.[3] This makes the total number included sixty-two, and the positions of several ballads were revised.[4]

[3] 'V.2.36': 'Old Simon the King', and 'Boldnesse in love'; and 'V.3.49': 'Dead and alive', and *the Lady's Fall*.

[4] *The Beggar-Wench of Hull* ('V.2.47') was originally 'V.2.52'; 'The two faithfull friends' ('V.2.49') 'V.2.54'; 'The Mole' ('V.2.58') 'V.2.42'; 'Monmouth's Lamentation' ('V.2.59') 'V.2.63'; *Alphonso and Ganselo* ('V.3.40') 'V.3.35'; 'Go thou gentle &c', ('V.3.41') 'V.3.37'; 'The pensive maid' ('V.3.54') 'V.3.49'; and, most interestingly, *Cupid's Courtesie* (*pEB75 P4128C (42)) was originally 'V.4.55'.

The Copy Draft

The following scheme for printing the *Reliques*, the 'Copy Draft', is here reconstructed for the first time. Percy's own titles are given, followed by call number (usually Houghton, bMS Eng. 893) and remarks on copy. Parts of vol. iv were in preparation for *Ancient English and Scotish Poems*, 1774–80.

Volume i, Book 1?, Fabulous History?:
I. 'The seven Champions of Christendome', (181); revised sheets from *Old Ballads* (1st edn.).
IV. 'The Frier and the Boy', BL, Add. MS 39547, fos. 156–66, Pepysian transcript; number revised from 'V', and introduction claims that this is the third poem in the book.

Volume i, Book 2?, Popular Ballads of Love:
IX. 'The dying shepherdess', (163); printed as 'Amintas'.
XV. *the Famous Flower of Serving-Men*, *pEB75 P4128C (93), broadside.
XVII. 'Pretty pretty Poll', (165A), 'A translation from the French'.
XVIII. 'Margaret's Ghost', position inferred from note on 'Pretty pretty Poll'.
XIX. *True Love Requited: Or, The Bailiff's Daughter of Islington*, *pEB75 P4128C (9), broadside.
XX. 'A Lover of late was I', (157ᵛ).
XXV. 'The Devonshire Maiden', (21, 5), excised sheets from *Old Ballads*, number revised from 'XXIII'.

Volume i, Book 3?, Scots:
I. 'the Gaberlunzie Man', (139H); this and the following four from notes sent to Benjamin Hutchinson.
II. 'The Ew-bughts Marion', (139H).
III. 'Sweet William's ghost', (139H).
IV. 'Waly, waly, Love be bonny', (139H).
V. 'The auld gude man', (139H).
VII. 'Willie Stewart and John', (4B).
VIII. 'Younge Andrew's Disloyalty', (8D); also to feature in *Ancient English and Scotish Poems* (see below).

XI.   'The Lord of Lorne', (4C).

XIX. 'The fairest of the fair. In imitation of the Scottish manner', (257); Percy's 'O Nancy'.

Volume ii, Book ?, English History:

   V.   'On Saint Thomas a Becket', (164).

   VII. *King John and the Abbot of Canterbury,* *pEB75 P4128C (132), broadside.

   XII. 'Robin Hood and Allen a dale', (169).

Volume ii, Book ?:

   X.   'Return hameward, my heart, a Scottish Song', (168); see letter to Dalrymple (*Letters*, iv. 27 n.).

   XII. 'A life content exceedeth all', (167).

Volume iii, Book 1, Border History:

   XIII. 'The rising in the North', (20A), fo. 144; revised from 'XVIII' and 'XIV'.

   XIV.   [XV] 'Northumberlande betrayd by Douglas', (20A), fo. 147.

   XV.   'Sir Hugh of the Grime', (10), (59).

   XVI.   *Johnny Armstrong's Last Goodnight,* *pEB75 P4128C (122); broadside.

   XVII. 'Christopher White', (8A); also for the fourth volume.

   XX.   'The Earl of Westmoreland', (20A), fo. 151.

   XXI.   'King Edward the fourth and the Tanner of Tamworth', (58).

Volume iii, Book 2, Ballads Illustrating Shakespeare and Beaumont and Fletcher:

   I.   'Adam Bell, Clym of the Clough, and William of Cloudesly', BL, Add. MS 39547, fos. 68–77, Pepysian transcript.

   V.   'The ballad of Constant Susanna', (19H).

   IX.   'The Praises of Tobacco', (166E).

   XIII. 'The forresters Song', (186), fo. 1.

   XV.   'Ingratitude', (186), fo. 2.

   XIX. 'Duneame's Sonnet', (186), fo. 3.

Volume iii, Book 3, Popular Seventeenth-Century Songs:

   VI.   'The restlesse paynes of the Lover forsaken', (161).

   IX.   'Ask no more where Jove &c', (182), fo. 10.

   X.   'The Primrose', (182), fo. 1.

   XIV. 'The Parting', (181).

   XIX. 'Cupid indicated', (185), fo. 1; 'O yes, if any maid'.

Volume iv, Book 1, Longbow:
    I. 'Lollai, lollai, litil Child', (159).

Volume iv, Book 2, Union:
    VIII. 'Younge Andrew's Disloyalty', (8D); with a note in red, 'Dissertation on Wolves in *England*'.
    XIV. 'John o' the Side', (22B); this and the following two were to form a sequence in *Ancient English and Scotish Poems*, 1774–80.
    XV. 'Sir Hugh of the Grime', (10), (59).
    XVII. 'Christopher White', (8A).

The Cancelled Ballads

Volume i (before the reversal in order):
'On Saint Thomas a Becket' (iii. 23–5, probably to make way for the completed version of 'The Marriage of Sir Gawaine'),
'The Song-Birds' (iii. 92, to allow for a longer version of 'The Lady Turned Serving Man'),
'The Protestation' (iii. 245–6, to enable the end of 'The Baffled Knight' to be rewritten and the addition of 'Why So Pale'),
'Alphonso and Gonsalez' (iii. 247–54, replaced by 'The Spanish Virgin'),
'The Dying Shepherdess' (iii. 255–7, replaced by 'The Aspiring Shepherd' and 'Constant Penelope'),
'Allen and Mary' (iii. 371–2, originally concluding a much longer first volume).

Volume ii:
'Verses by K. James I.', 'Cock Lorrel's Treat', 'The Moral Uses of Tobacco', and 'Old Simon the King' (ii. 307–18, replaced by 'The Heir of Linne'; 'Verses by K. James I.' restored).

Volume iii:
'The Jolly Beggar' (i. 87–9, replaced by 'The Tower of Doctrine'),
'Edom o' Gordon' (i. 99–107, to remove Dalrymple's conclusion).

See *Reliques* (1996), iii. 365–403 for texts.

The Order of the First Edition (1765)

These titles are taken from the contents page of the *Reliques* and occasionally deviate from those given in the text.

Volume the First:
Dedication
Preface
Essay on the ancient Minstrels
Book the First
  1. The ancient Ballad of Chevy-chace
  2. The battle of Otterbourne
  3. The Jew's Daughter. A Scottish Ballad
  4. Sir Cauline
  5. Edward, Edward. A Scottish Ballad
  6. King Estmere
  7. Sir Patrick Spence. A Scottish Ballad
  8. Robin Hood and Guy of Gisborne
  9. The Tower of Doctrine
 10. The Child of Elle
 11. Edom o' Gordon. A Scottish Ballad
 12. An Elegy on Henry 4th earl of Northumberland

Book the Second (Containing Ballads that illustrate Shakespeare)
  Essay on the Origin of the English Stage
  1. Adam Bell Clym o' the Clough, and William of Cloudesly
  2. The aged Lover renounceth Love
  3. A Song to the lute in musicke
  4. King Cophetua and the Beggar-maid
  5. Take thy old cloak about thee
  6. Willow, Willow, Willow
  7. Sir Lancelot du Lake
  8. Corydon's Farewell to Phillis
       The Ballad of constant Susannah
  9. Gernutus, the Jew of Venice
 10. The Passionate Shepherd to his Love
       The Nymph's Reply
 11. Titus Andronicus's Complaint

12. Take those lips away
13. King Leir and his three daughters
14. Youth and Age
15. The Frolicksome Duke, or the Tinker's good Fortune
16. The Friar of Orders gray

Book the Third
1. The more modern Ballad of Chevy-chase
2. Death's final conquest
3. The Rising in the North
4. Northumberland betrayed by Douglas
5. My mind to me a kingdome is
6. The Patient Countess
7. You meaner beautyes
8. Dowsabell
9. The Farewell to Love
10. Ulysses and the Syren
11. Cupid's Pastime
12. The character of a happy life
13. Unfading Beauty
14. Gilderoy. A Scottish Ballad
15. Winifreda
16. Jemmy Dawson
17. The Witch of Wokey
18. Bryan and Pereene. A West India Ballad
19. Gentle River, Gentle River. Translated from the Spanish
20. Alcanazor and Zayda, a Moorish Tale
The Glossary
Additions to the Glossary, see at the End of Vol. 3.
Additional Notes and Corrections   ibid.

Volume the Second:
Book the First
1. Richard of Almaigne
2. On the Death of K. Edward I.
3. An original ballad by Chaucer
4. The Tournament of Tottenham
5. For the Victory at Agincourt
6. The Not-browne Mayd
7. A balet by the Earl Rivers
8. Cupid's Assault. By Lord Vaux
9. Sir Aldingar
10. On Thomas Lord Cromwell

8. Verses by King James I.
9. The Heir of Lynne
12. [*sic*] The old and young Courtier
13. Sir John Suckling's Campaigne
14. To Althea from Prison
15. The Downfall of Charing-Cross
16. Loyalty confined
17. Verses by King Charles I.
18. The Sale of Rebellious Houshold Stuff
19. Old Tom of Bedlam. Mad Song the first
20. The Distracted Puritan. Mad Song the second
21. The Lunatic Lover. Mad Song the third
22. The Lady distracted with Love. Mad Song the fourth
23. The Distracted Lover. Mad Song the fifth
24. The Frantic Lover. Mad Song the sixth
25. Lilli-burlero
26. The Braes of Yarrow. In imitation of the ancient Scottish Manner
27. Admiral Hosier's Ghost
The Glossary

Volume the Third:
Book the First
  Essay on the ancient Metrical Romances
    1. The Boy and the Mantle
    2. The Marriage of Sir Gawaine
    3. King Ryence's Challenge
    4. King Arthur's Death
    5. The Legend of King Arthur
    6. A dittye to Hey Downe
    7. Glasgerion
    8. Old Sir Robin of Portingale
    9. The Gaberlunzie man. A Scottish Song
    10. Child Waters
    11. Phillida and Corydon
    12. Little Musgrave and Lady Barnard
    13. The Ew-bughts Marrion. A Scottish Song
    14. The Knight and Shepherd's Daughter
    15. The Shepherd's Address to his Muse
    16. Lord Thomas and Fair Ellinor
    17. Cupid and Campaspe
    18. The Lady Turned Servingman
    20. [*sic*] Gil Morrice. A Scottish Ballad

Book the Second
    1. Legend of Sir Guy
    2. Guy and Amarant
    3. The Shepherd's Resolution
    4. Fair Margaret and Sweet William
    5. Barbara Allen's Cruelty
    6. Sweet William's Ghost. A Scottish Ballad
    7. Sir John Grehme and Barbara Allen. ditto
    8. The Bailiff's daughter of Islington
    9. The Willow Tree. A Pastoral Dialogue
    10. The Lady's fall
    11. Waly, waly, Love be bonny. A Scottish Song
    12. The wanton Wife of Bath
    13. The auld good man. A Scottish Song
    14. Lady Isabella's tragedy
    15. A Hue and cry after Cupid
    16. The King of France's Daughter
    17. The sweet neglect
    18. The Children in the Wood
    19. A Lover of late was I
    20. The King and the Miller of Mansfield
    21. Dulcina
    22. The Wandering Prince of Troy
    23. The Witches Song
    24. Robin Good-fellow
    25. The Fairy Queen
    26. The Fairies Farewell

Book the Third
    1. The Birth of St. George
    [2.] [*sic*] George Barnwell
    3. St. George and the Dragon
    4. The baffled Knight, or Lady's Policy
    5. Why so pale
    6. The Spanish Virgin, or Effects of Jealousy
    7. The Aspiring Shepherd
    8. Constant Penelope
    9. To Lucasta, on going to the Wars
    10. Valentine and Ursine
    11. The Dragon of Wantley
    12. St. George for England. The First part
    13. St. George for England. The Second part
    14. Lucy and Colin

15. Margaret's Ghost
16. The Boy and the Mantle. Revised, &c.
The Glossary
Additional Notes to Volume I.
Additional Notes to Volume II.
Additional Notes to Volume III.

Index

Only those ballads mentioned in the text are given, and titles have been standardized. The Appendices have been indexed only very lightly. Some ballads, such as those concerning Robin Hood, are listed under 'Robin Hood' rather than by title. Works are generally indexed by author only, and entries are given for footnote citations in lieu of a bibliography.